Latin America Confronts the United States

Asymmetry and Influence

Latin America Confronts the United States offers a new perspective on U.S.–Latin America relations. Drawing on research in six countries, the book examines how Latin American leaders are able to overcome power asymmetries to influence U.S. foreign policy. The book provides in-depth explorations of key moments in post–World War II inter-American relations – foreign economic policy before the Alliance for Progress, the negotiation of the Panama Canal Treaties, the expansion of trade through NAFTA, and the growth of counternarcotics in Plan Colombia. The new evidence challenges earlier, U.S.-centric explanations of these momentous events. Though differences in power were fundamental to each of these cases, relative weakness did not prevent Latin American leaders from aggressively pursuing their interests vis-à-vis the United States. Connecting with studies of foreign policy and international relations, the book examines how Latin American leaders achieved this influence – and why they sometimes failed.

Tom Long is Lecturer at the University of Reading (United Kingdom). He has been a visiting professor in International Relations at the Centro de Investigación y Docencia Económicas in Mexico City and previously taught at American University's School of International Service, where he completed his Ph.D. His research focuses on dynamics of asymmetry in international relations, particularly foreign policies of Latin American states vis-à-vis the United States. His work has been published in *International Security, Diplomatic History,* and *Latin American Research Review* and has won prizes from the International Studies Association's Diplomatic Studies Section and the Middle Atlantic Council of Latin American Studies.

"*Latin America Confronts the United States* is a landmark study that both helps us understand the dynamics of contemporary U.S.–Latin American relations and contributes significantly to the fields of comparative politics and international relations.

"Even though the phenomenon of Latin American countries challenging U.S. policies, behavior, and demands seems to be recent, Dr. Long's detailed, meticulously researched study demonstrates that the conventional wisdom about compliant Latin American states mischaracterized the nature of the asymmetrical relationships since at least the 1950s. *Latin America Confronts the United States* provides a complex, nuanced, and compelling analysis that demonstrates Latin Americans have long been agents of their own history, not mere puppets of the United States.

"Based on archival research in five Latin American countries and the United States, and in-depth elite interviews with key policy makers, the study systematically elaborates four cases in which Latin American leaders were able to resist U.S. pressure and even change U.S. perceptions of a problem, thus influencing the United States to adopt new policy goals.

"Dr. Long's clear articulation of the way this study departs from prior analyses of U.S.–Latin American relations and from prevailing conceptions about power and asymmetry in the international system enables *Latin America Confronts the United States* to serve as an instructive model of how an internationalist approach can deepen and change our understanding of global relations in a world characterized by asymmetry. Indeed, the United States has an asymmetrical relationship with most countries, because of its wealth and military capabilities. *Latin America Confronts the United States* thus offers important policy implications as well as theoretical insights."

– Philip Brenner, Professor of International Relations and Director of the
Graduate Program in U.S. Foreign Policy, American University

Latin America Confronts the United States

Asymmetry and Influence

TOM LONG
University of Reading

CAMBRIDGE
UNIVERSITY PRESS

CAMBRIDGE
UNIVERSITY PRESS

University Printing House, Cambridge CB2 8BS, United Kingdom

One Liberty Plaza, 20th Floor, New York, NY 10006, USA

477 Williamstown Road, Port Melbourne, VIC 3207, Australia

4843/24, 2nd Floor, Ansari Road, Daryaganj, Delhi - 110002, India

79 Anson Road, #06-04/06, Singapore 079906

Cambridge University Press is part of the University of Cambridge.

It furthers the University's mission by disseminating knowledge in the pursuit of education, learning and research at the highest international levels of excellence.

www.cambridge.org
Information on this title: www.cambridge.org/9781107547056

© Tom Long 2015

First published 2015
First paperback edition 2017

A catalogue record for this publication is available from the British Library

Library of Congress Cataloging in Publication data
Long, Tom (Thomas Stephen)
Latin America confronts the United States : asymmetry and influence / Tom Long.
  pages cm
ISBN 978-1-107-12124-9 (hardback)
1. Latin America – Foreign relations – United States.   2. United States – Foreign
relations – Latin America.   I. Title.
F1418.L664   2015
327.8073–dc23   2015023285

ISBN 978-1-107-12124-9 Hardback
ISBN 978-1-107-54705-6 Paperback

To Robert A. Pastor

1947–2014

*a mentor, intellectual inspiration, and an example of how to confront
adversity with determination and good humor*

Contents

Acknowledgments

During the research and writing of this book, I was surrounded by excellent teachers, caring mentors, brilliant colleagues, and dedicated friends. First among them was Robert A. Pastor. To my profound sadness, Dr. Pastor did not live to see the publication of this book, but he never doubted that I would complete and publish it. Dr. Pastor encouraged me to wrestle with big questions and important cases. Even – perhaps especially – as his illness progressed, he was extraordinarily generous with his time, energy, and encouragement. I learned an incalculable amount from Dr. Pastor about U.S. foreign policy and U.S.–Latin American relations. But that pales in comparison to what he taught those around him, by power of example, about courage in the face of challenges, dedication to meaningful work, and caring for colleagues, friends, and family. I am grateful to the Pastor family, Margy, Kip, and Tiffin, for their friendship during this time.

I am intellectually and personally indebted to many former professors and past and current colleagues, particularly Max Paul Friedman and Philip Brenner. Their work and teaching provided the inspiration for this project, and I was privileged to work closely with each of them. Many others have been a sounding board for ideas and provided comments on sections of the draft. Warm thanks to Boaz Atzili, who kindly checked on my progress every time we crossed paths and offered detailed feedback on earlier versions of this manuscript. I benefited from the wisdom and experience of Louis Goodman, particularly in thinking about how to frame the central questions of this book early in the process. Christopher Darnton helped organize several panels on which I presented portions of this book in its early stages; his feedback consistently challenged and encouraged me to improve the project. I learned a great deal about U.S.–Mexican relations from Christopher Wilson and Manuel Suárez-Mier. Mariano Bertucci read portions of the manuscript, which improved with his comments. Conversations with these and other scholars deepened my approach to

IR and U.S.–Latin American relations. Thanks to Leandro Morgenfeld, professor of History at Universidad de Buenos Aires, for his hospitality, friendship, and expertise. Portions of the book were presented at conferences of the International Studies Association, Latin American Studies Association, and Middle Atlantic Council of Latin American Studies, where I received helpful feedback. Many thanks to the team at Cambridge University Press, especially Lewis Bateman and Elda Granata, for their support of this project and their hard work to improve it. Thank you, too, to the anonymous reviewers for their thoughtful readings of the manuscripts.

I am grateful for the backing, financial and otherwise, that I have received while working on the research and writing of this book, which began as a doctoral dissertation. American University's School of International Service, under Deans Louis Goodman and James Goldgeier, supported me enormously. Steve Silvia and Sharon Weiner were of great help at the early and late stages of the project, respectively. My research assistant Max Bing-Grant assisted with the revision of the manuscript. Much of the research was funded by grants from the School and from the Office of the Vice Provost for Graduate Studies and Research. I am grateful to the Tinker Foundation, which provided funding to support my travel to Panama and Argentina. A fellowship at the AU Center for Latin American and Latino Studies allowed me to travel, research, and write. I appreciate the support of the Center's director, Eric Hershberg, whose knowledge and connections throughout the Western Hemisphere have few equals. Thanks to Ryan Briggs, Daniel Dye, Sebastian Bitar, Kate Reese, Jason Rancatore, Tazreena Sajjad, Andy Hardig, Josh Jones, Eddy Lucas, Kia Hall, Shoon Murray, David Bosco, Randy Persaud, Michael Schroeder, and many others at American University for comments, intellectual comradeship, and friendship. I completed the revisions of this book during a fruitful visiting professorship at the División de Estudios Internacionales at the Centro de Investigación y Docencia Económicas in Mexico City. The excellent colleagues at CIDE made the experience richer and more enjoyable, and I continue to benefit from their depth of knowledge about Mexico and the region.

The project took me to five countries and a dozen archives. My research was greatly assisted by able archivists and officials, and I would be remiss not to thank them. Particular thanks go to Mauricio Tovar and the staff at the Archivo General de la Nación in Bogotá; the staff at the Departamento Administrativo at the Presidencia de la República de Colombia, especially Carlos Vargas and John Erick Valencia; the staffs at the Panamanian Foreign Ministry and the Fundación Omar Torrijos; Lourdes Ida Nakamura and Nayeli Montero at the Secretaría de Economía in Mexico City; and the staffs at the Itamaraty archives in Brasilia and Rio. Many of the participants in the events studied here were generous with their time, conceding interviews and introducing me to other participants. Thank you.

I want to thank my family and friends for their patience and support. My wife, Marta Sainz Jauregui, graciously endured my long hours, absences from the country, and piles of books and papers. I wouldn't have gotten through this without her love and support. (In fact, I would not have been capable of undertaking this research had she not given me such good reason to improve my Spanish many years ago as an undergraduate abroad!) Finally, I owe an unending debt to my mother and father for their love and encouragement during this and previous stages of my education. It was their dedication to improving peoples' lives in Honduras that first sparked my interest in Latin America almost twenty years ago.

Asymmetry, Influence, and U.S.–Latin American Relations

Generations of realist scholars have cited Thucydides' maxim, "the strong do what they will, and the weak suffer what they must," as a founding principle of International Relations.[1] The well-worn phrase emphasizes the importance of power as a constraint on the leaders of relatively weak states. Scholars of U.S.–Latin American relations have likewise referred to the mighty Athenians' destruction of the Melians as a metaphor for hemispheric politics. At first blush, power seems to be a reasonable explanation for much of the history between the United States and Latin America, particularly for the predominantly small and weak nations that line the Caribbean. The evidence of power politics is so frequently cited that it will be familiar to most readers when distilled into evocative events and declarations: the Monroe Doctrine, the Roosevelt Corollary, the Platt Amendment, the coups of Guatemala 1954 and Chile 1973, the interventions at the Bay of Pigs, Santo Domingo, and Operation "Just Cause" of Panama.

Indeed, a focus on U.S. power defines the study of U.S.–Latin American relations. "Establishment" scholars argue the United States is on the whole a beneficial presence, while revisionist scholars argue that the northern colossus has harshly pursued its own narrow interests. Despite their differing conclusions, both schools have focused on U.S. power and decisions with comparatively little attention to the actions of Latin American leaders.[2] Perhaps this is with good reason. The United States economy is more than 2.5 times larger

---

[1] Following common usage, I use capitalized International Relations or IR to refer to the academic discipline and lowercase international relations to refer to relations between state (or nonstate) actors.

[2] Max Paul Friedman, "Retiring the Puppets, Bringing Latin America Back In: Recent Scholarship on United States–Latin American Relations," *Diplomatic History* 27, no. 5 (2003); Robert A. Pastor and Tom Long, "The Cold War and Its Aftermath in the Americas: The Search for a Synthetic Interpretation of U.S. Policy," *Latin American Research Review* 45, no. 3 (2010).

than the combined product of all of Latin America and the Caribbean. Even during a Latin American export boom, the United States exported about 60 percent more than the region as whole.[3] Though U.S. policymakers have occasionally decried a surge in Venezuelan military spending, the United States' armed forces outspend the rest of the hemisphere by a multiple of ten.[4] This asymmetry is hardly a new feature of U.S.–Latin American relations; estimates of GDP ranging back to the eve of World War I indicate that the gap was even larger then.[5] Furthermore, since the late nineteenth century the United States has deployed these awesome resources via numerous military interventions in countries that border the Caribbean.

In light of these disparities, there has been less attention to the foreign policies of Latin American countries. Given the United States' overwhelming capabilities and its history of interventions, the ability of Latin American leaders to influence U.S. policy would seem negligible. However, a puzzle emerges. Despite these advantages, the United States has often failed to determine outcomes or control the course of events in the region that it supposedly dominates. Diplomatic historians, exploring recently opened archives throughout the region, have unearthed evidence that points to weaknesses in the dominant theoretical approaches. A focus on the United States is insufficient for understanding U.S.–Latin American relations. Far from being "puppets," Latin American leaders have exhibited an independent streak – often challenging U.S. policies and creating space for autonomy. I extend this insight to ask how Latin American leaders define and pursue their priorities vis-à-vis the "colossus of the North."

Likewise, much of IR theory continues to accord little agency to small states. Recent work has argued that "vulnerabilities rather than opportunities are the most striking consequence of smallness," and that small states "lack real independence."[6] For decades, modified versions of realism were used explain the situations of smaller states, emphasizing systemic factors, an overwhelming need to focus on survival, and the constraints imposed by international

---

[3] According to the World Bank, Latin American and the Caribbean had a combined GDP of $5.646 trillion in 2011, compared to a U.S. GDP of $14.99 trillion. The United States exported $2.094 trillion, far exceeding Latin America and the Caribbean's total of $1.328. *World Bank DataBank*. Available online: http://databank.worldbank.org.

[4] According to the SIPRI database, the United States spent $689.6 billion on its military in 2011, compared with $67.6 billion for all of Latin American and the Caribbean (figures in constant 2010 U.S. dollars). SIPRI Military Expenditures Database. Available online: www.sipri.org/research/armaments/milex.

[5] Though much debated, the most widely cited estimates come from Angus Maddison, *The World Economy*, vols. 1–2 (Academic Foundation, 2007), pp. 361, 509.

[6] Anthony Payne and Þórhildur Hagalín, respectively, qtd. in Godfrey Baldacchino, "Thucydides or Kissinger? A Critical Review of Smaller State Diplomacy," in *The Diplomacies of Small States: Between Vulnerability and Resilience*, eds. Andrew F. Cooper and Timothy M. Shaw (New York: Palgrave Macmillan, 2009), pp. 21–22.

structures. Meanwhile, critical scholars applied insights from dependency theory to foreign relations, arguing that insecurity is the defining feature of the "third world" in international relations.[7] Both of these approaches offer narratives in which small states play little role. Even classic articles examining small-state influence excluded U.S.–Latin American relations on the assumption that U.S. relations with its Latin American and Caribbean neighbors are very different from those with Canada or small European states.[8]

This book contributes to IR literatures on asymmetrical relations between great powers and weaker states and on weaker-state agency to argue that Latin America has exercised more influence in U.S.–Latin American relations than is usually acknowledged. Latin American leaders have been able to achieve substantial degrees of autonomy. Furthermore, they have at times influenced U.S. policy. Instead of implicitly treating Latin American states as passive "takers" of U.S. policy, this book demonstrates that Latin American states actively shaped the dynamics of their asymmetrical relations. Latin American leaders were also policymakers. The United States' coercive capabilities were central to the structure of the relationships, but capabilities alone did not determine outcomes. Material asymmetry does not eliminate the possibility for influence by the weaker power.

This chapter turns briefly to scholarly treatments of U.S.–Latin American relations before arguing that we can better understand hemispheric relations by turning to work on the foreign policy power of small states and middle powers. This literature offers insights into U.S.–Latin American relations, but also has notable shortcomings. The conceptualizations of power and influence that are common to IR obscure the possibility of meaningful action from medium and small states like many of those that occupy Latin America. To really understand the relationship between U.S. and Latin American leaders, we must acknowledge the agency of both sides. This requires a broader conceptualization of power and a focus on actors and their strategies in asymmetrical contexts. That framework structures my empirical analyses of how Latin American leaders seek to influence U.S. foreign policy and whether they might succeed in doing so.

The Study of U.S.–Latin American Relations

Since World War II, a body of scholarship has grown around the study of U.S.–Latin American relations. This literature is thematically oriented, and not a subfield of any one discipline, which has created empirical richness, but has

---

[7] Mohammed Ayoob, "Inequality and Theorizing in International Relations: The Case for Subaltern Realism," *International Studies Review* 4, no. 3 (2003); Ozgur Cicek, "Review of a Perspective: Subaltern Realism," *The Review of International Affairs* 3, no. 3 (2004).

[8] Robert O. Keohane, "The Big Influence of Small Allies," *Foreign Policy*, no. 2 (1971).

limited theoretical conversation. Explicit theoretical frameworks remain relatively rare.[9] Despite the diversity, three general "schools" can be distinguished.

The first grouping, to borrow Russell Crandall's term, is the "establishment" school.[10] The school has three defining characteristics. First, its explanations of U.S. policy to Latin America center on the U.S. desire to exclude extraterritorial rivals from the hemisphere. Second, establishment authors argue that the United States is, on the whole, a beneficial presence. Third, the establishment school has focused on Latin American reactions to U.S. policy, but Latin American actions have not been a central object of study. These works see U.S. policy as imperfect but on the whole providing benefits for the region. Criticism is generally offered with the intention of drawing attention to or fixing a certain policy failure, as opposed to questioning the fundamental role of the United States in the hemisphere.[11]

Robert A. Pastor described the "security thesis" as the central tenet of this school.[12] The security thesis shares much with a realist vision of the world, as Gregory Weeks has noted.[13] First advanced by Samuel Flagg Bemis, this thesis argues that the overriding goal of U.S. policy in Latin America has been to prevent any extra-hemispheric power from establishing a base within the hemisphere from which it could threaten the continental United States. The Monroe Doctrine made this clear even before the United States had the power to enforce its proclamations. After watching foreign creditors shell the harbors of debtor nations, Theodore Roosevelt articulated more extensive conditions under which the United States would intervene – and intervene the United States did during the next three decades. The Good Neighbor Policy tried to accomplish these same goals through partnership. During the Cold War, Washington at times abandoned nonintervention to prevent the emergence of threats. The United States seemed drawn into the region by crises

---

[9] For articles that have made these points, see Gregory Weeks, "Recent Works on U.S.–Latin American Relations," *Latin American Research Review* 44, no. 1 (2009); Mariano Bertucci, "Scholarly Research on U.S.–Latin American Relations: Where Does the Field Stand?," *Latin American Politics and Society* 55, no. 4 (2013); Ana Margheritis, "Interamerican Relations in the Early Twenty-First Century," *Latin American Politics and Society* 52, no. 4 (2010); Jeanne A. K. Hey, "Three Building Blocks of a Theory of Latin American Foreign Policy," *Third World Quarterly* 18, no. 4 (1997).

[10] Russell Crandall, *The United States and Latin America after the Cold War* (Cambridge, New York: Cambridge University Press, 2008).

[11] This is the tone of quadrennial collections like Abraham F. Lowenthal, Theodore J. Piccone, and Laurence Whitehead, *The Obama Administration and the Americas: Agenda for Change* (Washington, D.C.: Brookings Institution Press, 2009).

[12] Robert A. Pastor, "Review: Explaining U.S. Policy toward the Caribbean Basin: Fixed and Emerging Images," *World Politics* 38, no. 3 (1986). See a slightly different formulation in G. Pope Atkins, *Latin America in the International Political System* (Boulder, Colo.: Westview Press, 1989), Chapter 5.

[13] Gregory Weeks, *U.S. and Latin American Relations* (New York: Pearson Longman, 2008).

in "an alternating cycle of fixation and inattention."[14] The Cuban Missile Crisis represented the ultimate nightmare of the security thesis – an existential threat ninety miles from U.S. shores.

The major tension in the establishment school reflects old debates about power and principle. Pastor argues that the United States has married the security thesis with an exceptional approach to world affairs – a "revolutionary vision."[15] Establishment authors argue that U.S.–Latin American relations have created mutual benefits in three categories: stability, economics and trade, and democracy. Interstate war has been infrequent in the Western Hemisphere. Since the War of the Pacific in 1879–1883, territorial conquest has been minor and rare. Peaceful settlement of disputes has been the norm, with the United States playing a direct role in the arbitration of numerous border conflicts. The region has been a leader in the creation of multilateral institutions, reflecting traditions of Bolivarianism and Pan-Americanism.[16] The promotion of democracy has been a central element of U.S. policy dating to Woodrow Wilson's emphasis on elections, though there is much debate about both the effectiveness and sincerity of the effort. According to Crandall, U.S. interventions have often helped spur democracy.[17] Perhaps a more frequent critique in recent years – and at intervals since World War II – is that the United States *should* be doing more good in Latin America in place of its current nonpolicy of "neglect."[18]

Both of these central establishment claims lead to a focus on U.S. actions at the expense of Latin American actors. In the security thesis, the key concern is the U.S. perception of threats. Latin America is present as a space from which dangerous attacks could occur, not as an actor. Threatening actors are primarily nonhemispheric challengers, taking advantage of Latin America's proximity to U.S. shores.[19] The second claim paints Latin Americans primarily as recipients

---

[14] Robert A. Pastor, *Exiting the Whirlpool: U.S. Foreign Policy toward Latin America and the Caribbean* (Boulder, Colo.: Westview Press, 2001), p. 18.

[15] Robert A. Pastor, "The United States: Divided by a Revolutionary Vision," in *A Century's Journey: How the Great Powers Shape the World*, ed. Robert A. Pastor (New York: Basic Books, 1999).

[16] Arie Marcelo Kacowicz, *The Impact of Norms in International Society: The Latin American Experience, 1881–2001* (Notre Dame, Ind.: University of Notre Dame Press, 2005), esp. Chapter 4; Louise L'Estrange Fawcett, "The Origins and Development of the Regional Idea in the Americas," in *Regionalism and Governance in the Americas: Continental Drift*, eds. Louise L'Estrange Fawcett and Mónica Serrano (New York: Palgrave Macmillan, 2005).

[17] Russell Crandall, *Gunboat Democracy: U.S. Interventions in the Dominican Republic, Grenada, and Panama* (Lanham, Md.: Rowman & Littlefield Publishers, 2006).

[18] For example, see Peter Hakim, "Is Washington Losing Latin America?," *Foreign Affairs* 85, no. 1 (2006); Laurence Whitehead, "A Project for the Americas," in *The Obama Administration and the Americas: Agenda for Change*, eds. Abraham F. Lowenthal, Theodore J. Piccone, and Laurence Whitehead (Washington, D.C.: Brookings Institution Press, 2009).

[19] This definition emerges from the Monroe Doctrine itself.

of benefits generated by U.S. power and principle. Latin Americans *react* to U.S. policies, but their actions are not the primary object of analysis.

A "revisionist synthesis" solidified during the 1980s and early 1990s.[20] This school goes well beyond the acknowledgment of imperfections or aberrations in U.S. policy to reject its fundamental precepts. This synthesis draws upon the work of scholars like Walter LaFeber, who saw a union of U.S. business and government interests in a quest to economically dominate Latin America. LaFeber argued that U.S. geography allowed it to be isolationist, but "internal developments, as interpreted by American policymakers," led the United States to imperial behaviors.[21] In another classic work, *The Open Veins of Latin America*, Uruguayan scholar Eduardo Galeano traced how the land and people of the continent have been exploited in the production of basic commodities.[22] The conclusions of these histories coincided in many respects with dependency theory, and these scholars have been variously termed "radical," the "neodependency antithesis," "counterconventional," and "anti-imperialist."[23] Mark Gilderhus' term "revisionist" recognizes that the scholarship grew as a response to a then-dominant establishment view. By the early 1990s, revisionists so dominated work on U.S.–Latin American relations that even thoroughly establishment works recognized revisionist contributions in demonstrating the gap between public rhetoric and private interests in U.S. policy to Latin America. U.S. complicity with human rights violations in the Southern Cone and massive bloodshed in Central America during the 1970s and 1980s gave this criticism powerful contemporary resonance.

From its economic origins, the school evolved to incorporate other critical perspectives. Revisionists probed the prejudices of U.S. policymakers, examined U.S. cultural and economic interventions, and argued that Latin America was a "workshop" for the global American empire.[24] Starting with *Beneath the United States*, Lars Schoultz has produced influential works that mine U.S.

[20] Mark T. Gilderhus, "An Emerging Synthesis? U.S.–Latin American Relations since the Second World War," *Diplomatic History* 16, no. 3 (1992), p. 432.

[21] Walter LaFeber, *The New Empire: an Interpretation of American Expansion, 1860–1898* (Ithaca, N.Y.: Cornell University Press, 1963), p. 2; Walter LaFeber, *Inevitable Revolutions: The United States in Central America* (New York: Norton, 1983).

[22] Eduardo Galeano, *Open Veins of Latin America: Five Centuries of the Pillage of a Continent* (New York: Monthly Review Press, 1973).

[23] Pastor, "Review: Explaining U.S. Policy toward the Caribbean Basin: Fixed and Emerging Images"; Crandall, *The United States and Latin America after the Cold War*; Abraham F. Lowenthal, "United States Policy toward Latin America: 'Liberal,' 'Radical,' and 'Bureaucratic' Perspectives," *Latin American Research Review* 8, no. 3 (1973).

[24] Martha L. Cottam, *Images and Intervention: U.S. Policies in Latin America* (Pittsburg: University of Pittsburg Press, 1994); Greg Grandin, *Empire's Workshop: Latin America, the United States, and the Rise of the New Imperialism* (New York: Metropolitan Books, 2006); Michael Grow, *U.S. Presidents and Latin American Interventions: Pursuing Regime Change in the Cold War* (Lawrence, Kan.: University Press of Kansas, 2008).

historical records to examine the impacts of U.S. policymakers' racial biases.[25] Schoultz's work on U.S. relations with Cuba illustrates how U.S. policymakers' beliefs in their own superiority and disregard for Cuban nationalism spanned decades, with deleterious effects.[26] The revisionist synthesis has expanded to reflect new currents including "gender theory, ethnohistory, cultural studies, and business history to reexamine and offer fresh insights into what was once the most conventional of topics," noted Thomas O'Brien.[27] The seminal volume *Close Encounters of Empire* compiled these diverse approaches to illustrate how the subject of U.S.–Latin American relations can be explored beyond the realm of government action.[28]

Despite the school's breadth, U.S. interventions have remained a central theme.[29] Greg Grandin has been the most visible recent scholar, starting with his scholarly work *The Last Colonial Massacre*, in which he argues that U.S. interventions in Guatemala and elsewhere were less about ending communism than about stamping out social democracy.[30] His popular polemic, *Empire's Workshop*, argued that George W. Bush's worldwide display of unilateralism was a natural outgrowth of long-standing U.S. policies in Latin America.[31]

Grandin's work points to an area of frequent division that is useful for illustrating the difference between the establishment and revisionist approaches: the use of "empire," "hegemon," and "colonial" to describe the United States and its policies. In their use of these terms, establishment and revisionist scholars seem to be talking past one another more than talking to one another. Rather than starting with a clear definition of what an empire is, much of this work starts with the proclamation of the United States as an empire, with little attention to previous usage of the term.[32] While the term "empire" might be a potent criticism of U.S. policies, it has less acknowledged, deleterious effects on our understanding of Latin America. The term treats U.S. relations with two

[25] Lars Schoultz, *Beneath the United States: A History of U.S. Policy toward Latin America* (Cambridge, Mass.: Harvard University Press, 1998).

[26] Lars Schoultz, *That Infernal Little Cuban Republic: The United States and the Cuban Revolution* (Chapel Hill: University of North Carolina Press, 2009).

[27] Thomas F. O'Brien, "Interventions, Conventional and Unconventional: Current Scholarship on Inter-American Relations," *Latin American Research Review* 44, no. 1 (2009).

[28] Gilbert M. Joseph, Catherine LeGrand, and Ricardo Donato Salvatore, eds., *Close Encounters of Empire: Writing the Cultural History of U.S.–Latin American Relations* (London: Duke University Press, 1998). Some of the chapters, including those by Piero Gleijeses on Cuban policy in Africa fit more closely with the internationalist turn described below.

[29] O'Brien, "Interventions, Conventional and Unconventional: Current Scholarship on Inter-American Relations."

[30] Greg Grandin, *The Last Colonial Massacre: Latin America in the Cold War* (Chicago: University of Chicago Press, 2004).

[31] Grandin, *Empire's Workshop: Latin America, the United States, and the Rise of the New Imperialism.*

[32] Alexander J. Motyl, "Is Everything Empire? Is Empire Everything?," *Comparative Politics* 38, no. 2 (2006).

dozen Latin American states as relatively homogenous. The history of relations with Nicaragua has little in common with relations with Brazil, as Carlos Gustavo Poggio Teixeira recently argued.[33] "Empire" presents an exaggerated and unvariegated notion of U.S. power, under which the United States should be successful in getting its way more often than not. Traditionally "empire" had been used to describe a relationship of near-total political control of peripheral territory by a central power; peripheral states have no autonomy in foreign policy and very constrained freedom to set domestic policy.[34] To call the United States an empire in Latin America risks denying Latin Americans' autonomy and agency.

Latin American Scholarship

While the relegation of Latin American actors to subordinate status could be the result of one-sided Northern scholars, the main currents of IR scholarship in Latin America have similarly denied a major autonomous role for Latin American states. Guided by the Economic Commission on Latin America and Brazil's Instituto Superior de Estudos Brasileiros, Latin American social scientists' internationally minded scholarship was heavily economic in focus. Dependency theory grew out of these scholar–policymakers' concerns about an unequal and worsening global distribution of production. These traditions inspired a focus on international structures and U.S. intervention. Foreign policy scholars who drew on dependency theory often treated Latin American leaders as U.S. lackeys who exploited their intermediate positions for personal gain. This critique was reinforced by a surge in authoritarianism during the late 1960s and 1970s.[35] These studies bred a concern with autonomy as a central concept in the study of Latin American IR – though autonomy has been discussed as a constant quest for enlightened elites rather than an (imperfect) reality.[36] In an influential critique, Carlos Escudé argued that the quest for

---

[33] Carlos Gustavo Poggio Teixeira, *Brazil, the United States, and the South American Subsystem: Regional Politics and the Absent Empire* (Lanham, Md.: Lexington Books, 2012).

[34] For a similar argument in greater depth, see Jack Donnelly, "Sovereign Inequalities and Hierarchy in Anarchy: American Power and International Society," *European Journal of International Relations* 12, no. 2 (2006).

[35] The preceding paragraph draws on Arlene Tickner, "El Pensamiento sobre las Relaciones Internacionales en América Latina," in *Relaciones Internacionales y Política Exterior de Colombia*, eds. Sandra Borda and Arlene B. Tickner (Bogotá: Universidad de los Andes, Facultad de Ciencias Sociales, Departamento de Ciencia Política-CESO, 2011); Arlene Tickner, "Latin American IR and the Primacy of *lo Práctico*," *International Studies Review* 10, no. 4 (2008).

[36] Sean W. Burges, *Brazilian Foreign Policy after the Cold War* (Gainesville: University Press of Florida, 2009); Roberto Russell and Juan Gabriel Tokatlian, "From Antagonistic Autonomy to Relational Autonomy: A Theoretical Reflection from the Southern Cone," *Latin American Politics and Society* 45, no. 1 (2003).

autonomy could undermine the quest for development, so leaders should ally themselves with the United States and derive benefits from the alliance.[37]

There has been much recent work on Brazilian foreign policy, in particular, which employs a more multinational perspective. Amado Luiz Cervo's *Historia da política exterior do Brasil* is perhaps the foundational survey of Brazilian foreign policy.[38] Cervo notes that North American theorists enjoy a privileged place in Brazilian IR.[39] Recently, Carlos Poggio Teixeira argued that IR studies of U.S.–Latin American relations have failed because scholars have treated the whole of Latin America as one subordinated system. Instead, South America and North/Central America need to be approached as distinct subsystems. In South America the United States has been an "absent empire" largely because of Brazil's presence as a status quo–seeking, middle power.[40] Luiz Alberto Moniz Bandeira employs impressive multinational archival research in exploring the shifting relations and allegiances between the United States, Argentina, and Brazil from the 1864 War of the Triple Alliance until the middle of the first decade of the 2000s.[41] In a rare, quantitative study of the foreign policy of a Latin American country, Octavio Amorim Neto attempted to weigh competing explanations for Brazil's foreign policy orientation, arguing that Brazilian policy has become more independent from the United States.[42]

IR scholars in Mexico and Colombia are shaping a less U.S.-centric body of work in countries with deeper U.S. involvement. Mario Ojeda's classic text presented Mexico as a "weak country" whose "relative independence" was limited by U.S. power and proximity. Within those conditions, however, Mexico took a stand that defended and advanced its interests where it could.[43] With the end of the Cold War and the country's greater integration with the United States and world market, Mexico's foreign policy shifted dramatically. It has prioritized expanding trade and investment and adopted less rigid

---

[37] Carlos Escudé, *Foreign Policy Theory in Menem's Argentina* (Gainesville, Fla: University Press of Florida, 1997).

[38] Amado Luiz Cervo and Clodoaldo Bueno, *História da Política Exterior do Brasil* (Brasília, DF: Editora UnB, 2011).

[39] Amado Luiz Cervo, "Política Exterior e Relações Internacionais do Brasil: Enfoque Paradigmático," *Revista Brasileira de Política Internacional* 46, no. 3 (2003).

[40] Teixeira, *Brazil, the United States, and the South American Subsystem*. For a different view, see Sean W. Burges, "Mistaking Brazil For a Middle Power," *Journal of Iberian and Latin American Research* 19, no. 2 (2013).

[41] Moniz Bandeira, *Brasil, Argentina e Estados Unidos: Conflito e Integração na América do Sul: da Tríplice Aliança ao Mercosul* (Rio de Janeiro: Civilização Brasileira, 2010).

[42] His dependent variable looks at how often Brazil votes with the United States in the UN General Assembly. Octavio Amorim Neto, *De Dutra a Lula: a Condução e os Determinantes da Política Externa Brasileira* (Rio de Janeiro, Brazil: Elsevier: Campus, 2012).

[43] Mario Ojeda. *Alcances y Límites de la Política Exterior de México* (Mexico City: Colegio de México, 1976). See also, Blanca Torres, "Estrategias y tácticas mexicanas en la conducción de sus relaciones con Estados Unidos (1945–1970)," *Foro Internacional* 50, no. 3–4 (2010), pp. 661–688.

interpretations of sovereignty and nonintervention. Pragmatism and bilateral cooperation guide Mexico's foreign policy and have often led it away from high-profiled diplomatic stands.[44] In addition, there has been great interest in Mexican IR regarding how international changes have affected Mexico's democratization, liberalization, and foreign policy.[45] Colombian scholars have understandably focused on the international dimensions of their country's decades-long civil conflict.[46] This has led to interest in the relationship between the domestic and international spheres in U.S.–Latin American relations and its effects on questions like military bases.[47] As in work on Brazil, new scholarship from these two countries often reflects an appreciation for both constraints on and possibilities for independent foreign policies.

An Internationalist Approach

Authors in both the establishment school and revisionist synthesis concentrate on U.S. power and its effects on the region, though with very different emphases and interpretations. This led Max Paul Friedman to note that despite the diverse approaches in the literature, there was also one-sidedness: "Mononational research tends to produce mononational explanations and to ignore the role of players from countries other than those whose words are examined."[48] The previous literature on U.S.–Latin American relations had largely ignored Latin American actors for empirical and theoretical reasons. For one part, archival materials were scarce or difficult to obtain. Even when those sources were available they were often ignored because of a "theoretical model in which the United States was the actor and Latin America the dependent, defenseless object."[49]

In 2003, Friedman could point to several historians whose work demonstrated the value of multinational research.[50] This trend has grown into an

---

[44] Guadalupe González González, "Las Estrategias de Política Exterior de México en la Era de la Globalización," *Foro Internacional* 41, no. 4, (2001), pp. 619–669.

[45] For example, see Soledad Loaeza, "La Política de Acomodo de México a la Superpotencia. Dos Episodios de Cambio de Régimen: 1944–1948 y 1989–1994," *Foro Internacional* 50, no. 3–4 (2010), pp. 627–660.

[46] See the contributions to Sandra Borda and Arlene B. Tickner, eds., *Relaciones Internacionales y Política Exterior de Colombia* (Bogotá, Colombia: Universidad de los Andes, Facultad de Ciencias Sociales, Departamento de Ciencia Política-CESO, 2011); Alejandro Gaviria Uribe and Mejía Londoño, eds., *Políticas Antidroga en Colombia: Éxitos, Fracasos y Extravíos* (Bogotá, Colombia: Universidad de los Andes, 2011), pp. 205–234.

[47] Sebastian E. Bitar, *US Military Bases, Quasi-Bases, and Domestic Politics* (New York: Palgrave MacMillan, 2015).

[48] Friedman, "Retiring the Puppets, Bringing Latin America Back In: Recent Scholarship on United States–Latin American Relations," p. 625.

[49] Pastor and Long, "The Cold War and Its Aftermath in the Americas: The Search for a Synthetic Interpretation of U.S. Policy," p. 263.

[50] Kyle Longley, *The Sparrow and the Hawk: Costa Rica and the United States during the Rise of José Figueres* (Tuscaloosa: University of Alabama Press, 1997); Paul Coe Clark, *The United States and Somoza, 1933–1956: A Revisionist Look* (Westport, Conn.: Praeger, 1992).

"internationalist approach" to the study of U.S.–Latin American relations, which argues that both the United States and Latin Americans should be treated as actors – though this does not imply that their actions carry equal causal weight. Historians began exploring newly opened archives after the Cold War to elucidate the Latin American side of key events. Studies of the Cuban missile crisis, following Graham Allison's *Essence of Decision*, had long focused on the United States and Soviet Union. More recent studies have recognized Cuba as a protagonist whose actions had much to do with the crisis' final outcome.[51] In his exploration of the causes of continued rivalry versus successful rapprochement, Christopher Darnton demonstrates that the primary actors were Latin Americans – presidents, bureaucrats, and generals – with the United States playing only a bit part. Often, the colossus was preoccupied with events outside the hemisphere; at other times, the United States favored peacemaking among its Cold War allies but had little influence.[52] In a reevaluation of U.S.–Bolivian relations, James F. Siekmeier uses a "synthetic perspective" to demonstrate how Bolivia not only reacted to U.S. policy but actively sought to moderate Washington's response to its revolution. Centrists in the revolution then used U.S. assistance to promote their interests at the expense of leftists in their own party. Bolivians ceased to be passive recipients of U.S. policy; in fact, they turned it to their advantage.[53] Piero Gleijeses' research in Havana unearthed how Fidel Castro acted on his own accord, not at the behest of Moscow, in much of Cuba's revolutionary foreign policy.[54] Richard Feinberg has argued that often Latin American leaders pushed the United States on trade policy, not vice-versa.[55]

The internationalist approach has been slower to make its way into the general histories that serve as frequent teaching tools and more often propose general, theoretical perspectives. Hal Brands has made the most extensive effort to date to "reconstruct the history of Latin America's Cold War in a way that is both multinational and multilayered." Brands rejects both "triumphalist assessments" and narratives "dominated by Right repression and U.S. complicity." U.S. involvement was one piece of overlapping global and local conflicts.

---

[51] Though access to Cuban archives is still limited, researchers have accessed some materials, employed Soviet archives, and conducted conferences and interviews to explore the crisis in Cuba. For example, see Michael Dobbs, *One Minute to Midnight: Kennedy, Khrushchev, and Castro on the Brink of Nuclear War* (New York: Alfred A. Knopf, 2008); James G. Blight and Philip Brenner, *Sad and Luminous Days: Cuba's Struggle with the Superpowers after the Missile Crisis* (Lanham, Md.: Rowman & Littlefield Publishers, 2002).

[52] Christopher Darnton, *Rivalry and Alliance Politics in Cold War Latin America* (Baltimore, Md.: The Johns Hopkins University Press, 2014).

[53] James F. Siekmeier, *The Bolivian Revolution and the United States, 1952 to the Present* (University Park, Pa.: Pennsylvania State University Press, 2011).

[54] Piero Gleijeses, "The View from Havana: Lessons from Cuba's African Journey, 1959–1976," in *In from the Cold: Latin America's New Encounter with the Cold War*, eds. Gilbert M. Joseph and Daniela Spenser (Durham: Duke University Press, 2008).

[55] Richard E. Feinberg, "Regionalism and Domestic Politics: US–Latin American Trade Policy in the Bush Era," *Latin American Politics and Society* 44, no. 4 (2002).

While Brands shifts the focus to the central role of Latin American elites, he tends to treat their conflictive relations with the left as balanced – assigning blame equally, when in terms of people killed and disappeared, right-wing, state-sponsored violence was by far the larger of the two evils.[56] The book's multiarchival research, while impressive, privileges breadth over depth.

Recent scholarship in Latin America and the United States increasingly examines Latin American foreign policy, but primarily explores how Latin Americans maneuver around the immutable realities of U.S. power. The internationalist approach presents an opportunity both for building IR theory and for furthering a fruitful conversation between a broader range of IR scholars and diplomatic historians. There is little work that asks whether Latin American leaders can influence U.S. policies. In general, when IR scholars have tried to explain U.S.–Latin American relations, they have turned to IR's dominant theory, realism.[57] Realism's focus on great powers, defined in terms of material capabilities, reinforces the marginalized treatment of Latin American states. However, influence need not be a one-way street, even under conditions of substantial asymmetry in material resources.

Dynamics of Asymmetry

It is not controversial or novel to claim that asymmetry is the defining characteristic of U.S.–Latin American relations. But what can the study of U.S.–Latin American relations – often treated as somehow "outside" the domain of mainstream IR theories – tell us about asymmetry more broadly? Hemispheric relations should be a fertile ground for exploring structures of power and the limits and possibilities for influence. A close examination questions both realist and dependency-inspired arguments about the way in which material asymmetries of power structure hemispheric relations. If the United States is vastly more powerful than any single country or possible coalition in Latin America, why have its policies so often struggled there? Why is U.S. influence in the hemisphere, in the view of many analysts, in an inexorable decline when its economic and military dominance remain unassailable? Furthermore, as this book's case studies seek to demonstrate, how is it that Latin American leaders have retained not just an important degree of domestic and foreign

---

[56] Hal Brands, *Latin America's Cold War* (Cambridge, Mass.: Harvard University Press, 2010). For reviews, see W.M. Schmidli, "Tracking the Cold War in Latin America," *Reviews in American History* 40, no. 2 (2012). Daniel Sargent et al., "Online Roundtable: Hal Brands' Latin America's Cold War Hal Brands, Latin America's Cold War," *Journal of American Studies* 46, no. 01 (2012). For another look at how global, regional, and local conflicts overlapped, see Aaron Coy Moulton, "Building Their Own Cold War in Their Own Backyard: The Transnational, International Conflicts in the Greater Caribbean Basin, 1944–1954," *Cold War History* 15, no. 2 (2015).

[57] Weeks, *U.S. and Latin American Relations.*

autonomy, but managed at times to change the policies of U.S. decision-makers and restructure their countries' relationships with the superpower?

Perhaps the most relevant contemporary discussion about the dynamics of asymmetry in has been about hierarchical relationships within an anarchical world order. In *Hierarchy in International Relations*, David Lake offers an account based on relational power, instead of purely coercive capabilities. While the assumption that anarchy is the ordering condition for international politics has defined much of IR theory in the United States,[58] Lake argues that world politics is, and has long been, characterized by relationships of both hierarchy and anarchy, with the former garnering little attention.[59] Lake describes hierarchy as a social contract that confers rights and benefits between ruler and ruled. The weaker state cedes aspects of its sovereignty in security and/or economic policy in exchange for protection, the provision of order, and other benefits. Subordination is the outcome of a negotiated process between senior and junior partners and leaves both parties better off. Lake's framework encompasses the context of asymmetry that characterizes U.S.–Latin American relations without painting weaker states as inherent victims. Subordination offers advantages to the weaker states – or more to the point, to the rulers of the weaker state.[60] Lake sees Brazil in the 1950s as part of a U.S. sphere of influence; Panama in his view was an informal empire. Both countries recognized the authority of the United States over at least some aspects of policy. However, Lake's concept of hierarchy and his treatment of Latin America differ from the study of asymmetry and influence advanced here. Lake's framework denies the ability of subordinated states to influence dominant state policy, beyond negotiating the bounds and benefits of the hierarchical relationship.

This study focuses on asymmetry instead of hierarchy. Asymmetry is a practical, if not a principled, requirement for establishing hierarchy in international relations. Unlike hierarchy, however, asymmetry does not necessarily imply legitimacy, which combines authority and coercive capabilities, in Lake's terms. As Jack Donnelly wrote, "The relationship between authority and capabilities, however, is actually a contingent empirical matter."[61] Because the question

---

[58] "English School" scholars such as Hedley Bull, and more recently Andrew Hurrell, have questioned the meaning of that assumption, as have constructivists including Alexander Wendt. See Hedley Bull, *The Anarchical Society: A Study of Order in World Politics* (New York: Columbia University Press, 1977); Andrew Hurrell, *On Global Order: Power, Values, and the Constitution of International Society* (Oxford, New York: Oxford University Press, 2007); Alexander Wendt, *Social Theory of International Politics* (New York: Cambridge University Press, 1999).

[59] It must be noted, as Lake does briefly, that Latin American dependency theorists certainly described a type of hierarchical relations, presaged on economics but extending into political authority. Dependency theory exercised a tremendous influence on diplomatic histories of U.S.–Latin American relations, which rarely assumed formal–legal equality of states.

[60] Lake acknowledges this division, but as an analytical choice treats the state as a coherent unit.

[61] Donnelly, "Sovereign Inequalities and Hierarchy in Anarchy," p. 142.

here is whether and how the weaker states of Latin America can influence the preponderant United States, the legitimacy of the United States to issue commands and expect compliance is not the central issue – and the notion would likely be rejected by many leaders. Instead of trying to establish the authority of larger states as Lake does, the study explores asymmetrical relationships from the position of states that relatively lack the military and economic resources associated with power and coercion. Whereas the authors on whom I draw have written about "small states" or "weak powers," I refer to "weaker states" to emphasize the relational and relative nature of power – but not to strip them of the possibility of influence.

A frequent mistake in the study of U.S.–Latin American relations has been to conflate different concepts of power – to assume that the possession of resources almost always allows the United States to determine outcomes. Dahl criticized this as the "lump-of-power fallacy."[62] When power is understood as resources, as in the "elements of national power" approach, there is no question that the United States dominates. However, convenient and measurable indicators of power, such as GDP, military expenditure, and commercial might, rarely convert directly into control over outcomes. Resource power is mistaken for relational power. Analysts are primarily interested in forms of relational power that depart from Dahl's classic formulation: "A has power over B to the extent he can get B to do something that B would not otherwise do."[63] Resources may be bases for the exercise of relational power, but they do not guarantee success. Less frequently noted, but relevant to U.S.–Latin American relations, is that the ability to resist another actor's exertions also demonstrates relational power. Increasingly, internationalist authors have emphasized the myriad ways Latin American leaders have resisted U.S. pressures, or even turned them to their own ends.

In the half century since Dahl's seminal article, the expansive literature on power in the social sciences has emphasized that power and influence work in subtle ways. The "faces of power" debate drew attention to the importance of controlling agendas and subtly shaping interests, even when concrete decisions and actions are difficult or impossible to observe.[64] Power is reflected in structures that affect how decisions are made.[65] Throughout these debates, the focus was largely on exploring additional ways in which the power of those with resources extended beyond observable confrontations. More recently, both liberal and constructivist approaches to power and influence have stressed

---

[62] Robert A. Dahl, *Modern Political Analysis* (Englewood Cliffs, N.J.: Prentice Hall, 1976).

[63] Robert A. Dahl, "The Concept of Power," *Behavioral Science 2*, no. 3 (1957), pp. 202–203.

[64] Peter Bachrach and Morton S. Baratz, "Two Faces of Power," *American Political Science Review* 56, no. 04 (1962); Steven Lukes, *Power: A Radical View* (London: Macmillan, 1974).

[65] Susan Strange, "The Persistent Myth of Lost Hegemony," *International Organization* 41, no. 04 (1987).

the possibilities for less materially oriented forms of power and influence.[66] This more expansive approach to power does not deny that material resources matter, but it indicates the possibility of influence by actors who lack them. Differences in material capabilities certainly matter, but they are not the only thing that matters.

Understanding asymmetrical relations requires a reevaluation of the traditional perspective that "equate[s] 'smallness' with a lack of power."[67] Scholars working on "small states," have increasingly done this, moving away from the effects of the international system to instead examine foreign policy strategies. Alan Chong and Matthias Maass argue that "The challenge lies in identifying the often particular and unconventional sources of small states' foreign policy power."[68] Jacqueline Braveboy-Wagner notes that, traditionally, small states have been studied "from the perspective of dependence or vulnerability, not power." In her state-centric approach, even a state as small as Trinidad and Tobago can be seen as an actor in its own right.

> A weak power approach ... aims to show that there are indeed some small states that may be not only resilient enough to deal with global economic pressures but also proactive enough to locate spaces in the international system where they might be able to successfully promote their interests. This does not mean that they are not vulnerable in many respects (as are all states to some degree or another) but that they are capable of employing strategies, both foreign and domestic, which allow them to overcome many of these handicaps.[69]

This can apply to Latin American states in their relations with the United States. Asymmetries in material resources affect the formulation of national interests and the execution of foreign policy in both great powers and weaker states. In situations characterized by asymmetry, who can influence and how? The question is twofold. First, where can we identify the influence of material asymmetries on U.S.–Latin American relations? Though often implicit, this first question has long been central to the study of U.S.–Latin American relations. This book seeks to explore a second question through four case studies. Within this context of asymmetry, what are the possibilities for influence

---

[66] Joseph S. Nye, *Soft Power: The Means to Success in World Politics* (New York: Public Affairs, 2004); Stefano Guzzini, "The Concept of Power: A Constructivist Analysis," *Millennium: Journal of International Studies* 33, no. 3 (2005); Michael Barnett and Raymond Duvall, "Power in International Politics," *International Organization* 59, no. 01 (2005).

[67] Christopher S. Browning, "Small, Smart and Salient? Rethinking Identity in the Small States Literature," *Cambridge Review of International Affairs* 19, no. 4 (2006).

[68] Alan Chong and Matthias Maass, "Introduction: The Foreign Policy Power of Small States," *Cambridge Review of International Affairs* 23, no. 3 (2010).

[69] Jacqueline Braveboy-Wagner, "Opportunities and Limitations of the Exercise of Foreign Policy Power by a Very Small State: The Case of Trinidad and Tobago," *Cambridge Review of International Affairs* 23, no. 3 (2010).

by the weaker party? How do weaker states overcome the handicaps imposed by asymmetry? Though they are relatively deficient in the resources highlighted in the elements-of-national-power approach, weaker states draw on other sources of power.

Regarding the first question, the effects of asymmetry are deep and have affected the histories of Latin American states, domestically and internationally. In ways that are perhaps impossible to separate out causally, past power disparities with the United States have shaped the political institutions that exist in Latin America to the current day, with these effects almost certainly most pronounced in Mexico, Central America, and the Caribbean. As dependency theory argued, asymmetry framed the economies of Latin America, orienting their exports to the United States and Europe, and spurred economic policies geared toward overcoming that legacy. More directly related to this study, an asymmetrical context shapes the formulation of interests and objectives, the choice of foreign policy strategies, and the nature of interactions. To say that asymmetry in material capabilities shapes interests is not the same as saying that it determines them. However, interests are defined with reference to asymmetry, particularly where the United States is directly concerned. How could it be otherwise? Just because interests are conditioned does not mean that they should treated as irrelevant or exogenously defined (on this point, dependency scholars might well disagree). Even the preferences of the powerful are affected by situations partly beyond their control, as Marx's famous dictum that "men make their own history" but under circumstances not of their choosing recognizes. Different countries respond to the context of asymmetry, and even direct U.S. pressures, in different ways. If we are to take seriously the foreign policies of Latin American states, we must start with an examination of how interests are defined, what objectives are set, and how those objectives are pursued.

Material asymmetry provides a structure that shapes U.S.–Latin American relations. However, this book demonstrates that it does not eliminate the possibility for Latin American autonomy and influence. Autonomy is understood as the ability to make decisions that are not determined by external pressures. The concept of autonomy, or the quest for it, has been important in scholarship on recent Brazilian foreign policy.[70] After the structural confines of the Cold War, Latin American autonomy today seems prevalent, exemplified through regional organizations that exclude the United States and in the diversified economic relationships of the Southern Cone. During the Cold War, I will argue, autonomy still existed, even if at times there were harder limits on relations with the Soviet bloc. Influence is "defined as the

---

[70] Tullo Vigevani and Gabriel Cepaluni, "A Política Externa de Lula da Silva: a Estratégia da Autonomia Pela Diversificação," *Contexto Internacional* 29, no. 2 (2007); Russell and Tokatlian, "From Antagonistic Autonomy to Relational Autonomy: A Theoretical Reflection from the Southern Cone."

ability of an actor to bring outcomes close to his or her preferred position."[71] This does not necessarily imply that the starting point is open conflict, or that its means are coercive.

Influence within asymmetry takes three main forms. These will often seek to change a dominant power's policies, though at times they may also seek to maintain a beneficial status quo. The first group of actions might be understood as restraint-seeking. These actions seek to alter the behaviors of the larger power in ways that restrict the potential for unilateral actions. Regardless of the professed intentions of a great power, weaker states are likely to fear unilateral, seemingly arbitrary actions. An implication of asymmetry is that actions that seem minor from the perspective of a very large state can have very big effects on smaller powers. Through the use of territorial denial, strategic noncooperation, institutions, and forms of "soft balancing," weaker states will seek to tie down their local Gulliver. For example, faced with the possibility of unilateral trade restrictions based on new U.S. legislation, Mexico attempted to enmesh the United States institutions and dispute-resolution mechanisms.

A second, often related, type of action will be autonomy-enhancing, aimed at increasing a state's room for maneuver. These strategies could be oriented at increasing either domestic or international autonomy. Relatively weaker states might seek to enhance their own capabilities or reduce foreign influence in their domestic politics. Though it also had international implications, a key driver for Panama's effort to abolish the Canal Zone was to increase its domestic autonomy. Panamanian leaders sought to decrease the political, military, and economic weight of the United States inside the country; at the same time, they hoped to enhance their own state's capabilities through enhanced revenues from the canal. Internationally, relatively weaker states in asymmetrical relations are likely to champion expansive versions of sovereignty, bristle at impositions, and try to reshape the international environment in ways that question a "might makes right" ethos of world politics. This has been a clear trait of Latin American international jurisprudence since the late 1800s, but it has also been coupled to diplomatic actions aimed both changing U.S. behaviors in ways that create restraint and enhance Latin American autonomy.[72]

A third type of action will be gains-seeking. These actions attempt to influence the more powerful state's behavior in ways that improve the condition of the smaller state vis-à-vis third parties. Again, gains-seeking can have domestic and international components, depending on whether the third party is a domestic or foreign rival. Internationally, weaker states have often tried to

---

[71] Lisa L. Martin, *Democratic Commitments: Legislatures and International Cooperation* (Princeton University Press, 2000), p. 9.

[72] Max Paul Friedman and Tom Long, "Soft Balancing in the Americas: Latin American Opposition to U.S. Intervention, 1898–1936," *International Security* 40, no. 1 (2015).

involve more powerful states in regional and subregional balances of power. Though it is not covered in the cases studied here, a traditional aspect of Brazilian foreign policy before the late 1950s tried to use close ties with the United States to keep an upper hand in rivalries with Argentina and Chile. David Lake's discussion of hierarchy in international relations focuses particularly on the domestic aspect of gains-seeking, through which the leaders of weaker states "submit" to a greater power in exchange for support in cementing their rule. In the case of the Colombian conflict, Arlene Tickner referred to this dynamic as "intervention by invitation." I contend, contra Lake, that engaging in gains-seeking behavior does not imply submission to the larger power, in the sense of considering its orders as legitimate commands. Instead, I see gains-seeking as a way in which smaller states adjust to material asymmetries, compensating for their own relative deficiencies by basing power on a relationship with a larger state. This may have the longer-term objective of improving the smaller state's overall position – in fact reducing its dependency and ameliorating (to an extent) the effects of asymmetry. For example, in the case of Operation Pan-America, Brazil's gains-seeking actions regarding the United States and the region had the ultimate goal of establishing Brazil's position as a major regional power that would be better able to participate as an equal in the Western alliance.

Each of these categories is profoundly influenced by the context of asymmetry; however, while asymmetry creates the context for both interests and the strategies used to pursue them, it does not remove agency, or the potential to influence, from the relatively weaker state. The above categories help us understand attempts to influence – to change U.S. policy in ways that bring it closer to the Latin American leaders' preferences – and how these are intimately related to asymmetry. They do not tell us the likelihood of success. This will depend on myriad factors, including the international environment, conditions in the United States, the degree of resolve in the smaller state, and strategic decisions by the weaker state about how goals are pursued. This last point is addressed in greater depth in the conclusions, which seek to examine what forms of relational power weaker states can exercise in asymmetrical relations.

Foreign Policy under Asymmetry

I advance an approach to U.S.–Latin American relations that examines the interactions of different countries through a focus on how decision-makers define and pursue their states' national interests. This does not imply that a state's leaders necessarily represent the "true" interests of their people – a concept that requires the analyst to presume he or she knows those interests. This study focuses on the conceptualizations, strategies, and negotiations of political decision-makers who represent states with significantly different levels of material resources. I use the following five analytical stages to structure the book's case studies and guide its inquiry into these processes.

1. Problem understanding
2. Foreign policy goals
3. Foreign policy strategies
4. Actions and responses (i.e., dyadic interactions)
5. Outcomes

The stages offer a simplified version not solely of one side of the policy-making process, but of interactions between policymakers. In an ideal process, the stages would progress in a linear fashion: a problem must be understood before goals can be articulated; goals must be articulated before strategies to achieve them can be crafted; strategies are needed to guide actions that elicit responses; actions result in outcomes. In practice, I expect more fluidity. Events can introduce new information, which affects how policymakers understand the problem they face. Responses from other actors could lead to expanded or curtailed goals, and so on. That fluidity also points to the importance of process in each stage – the process of defining goals and choosing strategies, for example – that I explore in the case narratives.

The first step focuses attention on how a problem is defined and understood by Latin American and U.S. leaders. Problem definition is not a purely rational matter, and precedes cost–benefit calculations.[73] Going beyond a single-country focus, we need to examine the interaction between Latin American and U.S. understandings. Influence is particularly likely when problems are not clearly defined, for example, when issues appear on the political agenda for the first time.[74] A second type of uncertainty involves a breakdown in the "policy paradigm" that had been applied to a problem. Moments of crisis might signal that a policy has failed, allowing for shifts in the understanding of a problem.[75] If U.S. conceptions are malleable or divided, this offers an opportunity for Latin American leaders to influence U.S. policymakers' decisions by shaping the definition of the problem itself.[76]

---

[73] Alex Mintz, "Applied Decision Analysis: Utilizing Poliheuristic Theory to Explain and Predict Foreign Policy and National Security Decisions," *International Studies Perspectives* 6, no. 1 (2005).

[74] David Patrick Houghton, "Reinvigorating the Study of Foreign Policy Decision Making: Toward a Constructivist Approach," *Foreign Policy Analysis* 3, no. 1 (2007); Yuen Foong Khong, *Analogies at War: Korea, Munich, Dien Bien Phu, and the Vietnam Decisions of 1965* (Princeton, N.J.: Princeton University Press, 1992); Alex Mintz and Steven B. Redd, "Framing Effects in International Relations," *Synthese* 135, no. 2 (2003).

[75] J. Gustavsson, "How Should We Study Foreign Policy Change?," *Cooperation and Conflict* 34, no. 1 (1999); David A. Welch, *Painful Choices: A Theory of Foreign Policy Change* (Princeton, N.J.: Princeton University Press, 2005); David Skidmore, "Explaining State Responses to International Change: The Structural Sources of Foreign Policy Rigidity and Change," in *Foreign Policy Restructuring*, eds. Jerel A. Rosati, Joe. D. Hagan, and Martin W. Sampson III (Columbia, S.C.: University of South Carolina Press, 1994).

[76] Very similar concepts to the idea of problem definition have been referred to by others as "framing" or "common knowledge." Framing also has a connotation of positioning a policy in political posturing, so I avoid it here. The "common knowledge" literature is more closely tied to negotiations.

The second step in understanding the successes and failures of Latin American foreign policy toward the United States is to establish the goals leaders are pursuing. The realist assumption that interests are defined in terms of power is poorly suited to Latin America because incremental increases in material capabilities are unlikely to guarantee security vis-à-vis a superpower. Instead, the definition of interests is best treated as an empirical question, meaning we need to examine how policymakers understand the problems they face. These understandings will often combine domestic political situations with international factors – with the role of United States a major factor. Asymmetry plays an obvious role: the obstacles may be greater and the opportunities fewer for the leader of a weaker state. Leaders will anticipate the constraints they face, which could limit the ambition of their goals. They are likely to push cautiously against those constraints.

Moving from goals and strategies to actions and responses, it is important to assess the initial U.S. response to the initiative or demand presented by Latin American leaders. This response, in addition to asymmetry, will condition the options available to Latin American leaders, who will have to choose which strategy or combination of strategies to pursue with the United States. In the cases studied, an initial negative response from Washington did not necessarily dissuade Latin Americans from their goals, but it did push them to alter their approaches. Latin American leaders at times changed the initial U.S. response, which leads to a focus in the case studies on how Latin American leaders achieved this unexpected influence. Going beyond the initial response, the study of interaction explores how leaders understand problems, generate solutions, and attempt to persuade one another.

Strategies and action-and-responses are likely to be iterative. U.S. responses will lead to changes in Latin American strategies as leaders continue to pursue goals in changing circumstances. The dynamics of interaction could lead Latin American leaders to internationalize an issue instead of working through bilateral channels, seek to change the international agenda, or try to redefine their goals in language that is more salient in Washington or elsewhere. An initial positive response from U.S. leaders does not mean that Latin Americans quickly obtained all they requested, but it did tend to keep Latin American demands in bilateral channels. Within those channels, Latin American leaders still faced the challenge of negotiating within an asymmetrical relationship, which was often exacerbated by having to consider the U.S. executive and legislative branches as almost entirely different negotiating partners.[77]

Finally, I offer an assessment of the effectiveness of Latin American actions in the cases studied. This assessment seeks to weigh the influences above, ascertain the effectiveness of Latin American actions, and discern the conditions under

---

[77] Though it was not a primary focus of the study, there was general support in several cases for Peter B. Evans, Harold Karan Jacobson, and Robert D. Putnam, eds., *Double-Edged Diplomacy: International Bargaining and Domestic Politics* (Berkeley: University of California Press, 1993).

which those actions mattered. The United States might also want to change its own policy for a variety of reasons – policy failure, personnel change, changing priorities, or Congressional or public pressure. Careful process-tracing is needed to separate and weigh sometimes intertwined, competing explanations. In some cases, past U.S. policy might be seen as no longer serving U.S. interests. It is important to assess how those interests were redefined, and whether it is the influence of Latin American leaders or other, exogenous factors that explain that change. In these cases, if Latin American leaders have a hand in defining the new interests or providing policy options for the pursuit of those interests, it can be said their actions had influence.

Methods and Case Selection

This book uses with-in case and cross-case analysis to examine how Latin American leaders define and pursue their interests and goals vis-à-vis the United States. The with-in case analysis applies my central research questions in four theoretically focused, historical cases. George and Bennett argue for process-tracing to build these narratives, understand causal mechanisms and causal effects, and avoid equifinality, in which multiple hypotheses are consistent with a given outcome. Process-tracing requires gathering a large body of data from different sources to minimize the likelihood of reflecting just one interpretation of events. The collection of this data is focused on specific events, processes, and key (as opposed to representative) actors.[78] The cross-case comparison in the concluding chapter employs George and Bennett's "structured, focused comparison."[79]

U.S.–Latin American relations provide an apt set of cases to study the influence in asymmetric relations, precisely because Latin American agency has been treated as so unlikely. Latin America can be seen in methodological terms as a source of "hard cases" to prove the possibility of weaker-state agency in asymmetry. Jack Levy colorfully refers to this logic as the "'Sinatra inference' – if I can make it there, I can make it anywhere."[80] That logic suggests cases from U.S.–Latin American relations could be useful for theory building on the dynamics of asymmetry more generally. Within Latin America, the Caribbean Basin should provide harder cases still, given that proximity and heightened U.S. interest led to more frequent interventions and exertions of U.S. power. In short, if Latin American leaders provide examples of active, effective foreign

---

[78] Alexander L. George and Andrew Bennett, *Case Studies and Theory Development in the Social Sciences* (Cambridge, Mass.: MIT Press, 2005); Gerardo L. Munck, "Tools for Qualitative Research," in *Rethinking Social Inquiry*, eds. Henry E. Brady and David Collier (Lanham, Md.: Rowman & Littlefield, 2004).

[79] George and Bennett, *Case Studies and Theory Development in the Social Sciences*, Chapter 3, p. 76.

[80] Jack S. Levy, "Qualitative Methods and Cross-Method Dialogue in Political Science," *Comparative Political Studies* 40, no. 2 (2007), p. 209.

policy by weaker states, it is a clear illustration that that asymmetry should not
be seen solely through the lens of the powerful.

The four cases were selected because each focused on an issue with great resonance throughout Latin America at that moment. The cases all take place during the post–World War II era, during which the United States was the world's
leading power. During this period, U.S. attention shifted to the region mostly
on a sporadic basis during moments of crisis, as the country expended much
of its energy dealing with distant issues.[81] This provides an important contrast
with an earlier era in which Mexico, Central America, the Caribbean, and to
a lesser extent the northern coast of South America were more consistent U.S.
foreign policy concerns. The cases were selected to maximize variation; they
cover a swath of Latin American geography, countries of different sizes, and
diverse issues. The differences between the countries and time periods involved
are large, important, and intentional. There are major power differentials, the
foreign policy bureaucracies are not comparable, and the cases include democratic and nondemocratic countries. Without this variation, the study's scope
would be limited to explaining Latin American agency in a narrower geographical or thematic context. However, there are commonalities in the processes
present within the cases. Crucially, in each of these cases the Latin American
leaders were the demandeurs. Most of the literature on U.S.–Latin American relations presents the United States as making demands of Latin Americans, who
have few options apart from compliance. This perspective has even dominated
previous interpretations of these same cases. Latin American demands did not
lead to uniform trajectories. A key variation between the cases regards how the
United States initially responded. The cases studied include two in which the
United States was initially favorable to Latin American initiatives and two in
which the United States opposed or withheld support. The initial U.S. position
did not determine the eventual outcome of the case, as much of the literature
would lead us to believe, though it did condition the strategies pursued by Latin
American leaders.

The book deals with leaders and countries that seek to influence U.S. policies within relationships characterized by general cooperation, eschewing the
most conflictual relationships such as that between the United States and
post-revolutionary Cuba. These relationships have drawn a disproportionate
amount of attention from both scholars and U.S. policymakers, but in many
ways they are outliers. The question of whether and how leaders like Fidel Castro could influence U.S. foreign policy is a valid one. However, there is reason to
expect different processes of influence. Coercion is likely to be emphasized and
consultation rare.[82] The choice of cases, which does not include those in which

---

[81] Pastor, *Exiting the Whirlpool.*

[82] Though even in this conflictual relationship, there have long been secret consultations on areas
   of possible cooperation. William M. LeoGrande and Peter Kornbluh, *Back Channel to Cuba:
   The Hidden History of Negotiations between Washington and Havana* (UNC Press Books,
   2014).

there is opposition not just to a particular U.S. policy but at a more fundamental level, is a choice of scope. By focusing on the dynamics of broadly cooperative relationships, I explore the options available to those Latin American leaders. In most cases the costs of openly challenging the United States (during the Cold War) or the broader international system it shaped and continues to lead (after the Cold War) will usually outweigh the benefits; the options for most leaders exist within a broad spectrum of cooperation. However, this does not imply compliance. Leaders are not puppets simply because they do not seek to over-turn the international order. There is a large and meaningful middle ground in which Latin American leaders can pursue their own priorities. Latin American leaders sometimes gained acquiescence or even considerable assistance from the United States for their own goals. Even during the Cold War, the threat of "changing sides" would not seem to offer much leverage. The costs of taking this route would be quite high, and more so for a country geographically close to the United States – and U.S. leaders knew it. The option of allying with a foreign power has diminished since the end of the Cold War, though as the increasing Chinese presence in the region shows, today's world offers greater possibilities for diversifying diplomatic and economic ties. At the same time, the pressure to ally with the United States on most issues has fallen dramatically, though pressure remains on issues like the U.S.-led war on drugs.

I conducted archival work in Argentina, Brazil, Colombia, Mexico, Panama, and the United States. This multinational work reflects a choice to go beyond "mononational explanations."[83] Because the cases span a range of time and countries, the locations of the documents and the conditions of the archives varied considerably. I worked in formal archival settings for the earlier cases. For more recent cases, I often worked directly in government agencies that produced and stored the documents. For cases on the Panama Canal, NAFTA, and Plan Colombia, I also conducted elite interviews, including with former cabinet secretaries, ambassadors, and presidents, and worked insights from these into my case narratives. Where possible, I used documents in the interviews. Finally, I supplemented official documents with press accounts, memoirs, and scholarly work.

Plan for the Book

The principal focus of this book is to extend the insights of the internationalist approach to Latin American relations with the United States through an interactive, multinational approach. My guiding query throughout is: how do Latin American leaders define and pursue their priorities vis-à-vis the United States and to what effect? To answer that, I will pay particular attention to their foreign policy goals and strategies. The next four chapters apply this approach while employing multinational research to cases that range from the

---

[83] Friedman, "Retiring the Puppets, Bringing Latin America Back In: Recent Scholarship on United States–Latin American Relations."

mid 1950s to the early 2000s. Chapter 2 examines Operação Pan-Americana (OPA), a Brazilian-led foreign policy initiative in the late 1950s that sought to make development a hemispheric priority in order to strengthen the Western bloc. OPA was a forebear to John F. Kennedy's Alliance for Progress. Chapter 3 takes a long view of Panamanian efforts to shift U.S. policy regarding the Panama Canal. Astute Panamanian diplomacy helped redefine the issue and place it on the U.S. agenda years before the crucial participation of Jimmy Carter. Chapter 4 applies a new lens to the Mexican decision to seek a free-trade agreement with the United States in the early 1990s. Mexican leaders recalculated economic and foreign policy interests with dramatic effects for U.S.–Mexican relations. Chapter 5 looks at the initiation of Plan Colombia, a bilateral program that has funneled billions of dollars in counternarcotics funding to the Colombian government. The Colombian government actively sought U.S. assistance, in large part to secure its weak domestic position. In the concluding chapter, I return to these questions in comparative perspective. This allows me to assess the types of strategies employed by Latin American leaders, showing how they attempted to influence U.S. policies, when they succeeded, and when they failed. Finally, I synthesize the book's contributions to the study of U.S.–Latin American relations and IR theory on weaker states in asymmetrical relations.

2

Operação Pan-Americana

Fighting Poverty and Fighting Communism

Brazilian President Juscelino Kubitschek's first two meetings with Dwight D. Eisenhower had been cordial, but in the end, disappointing. The two men first met over breakfast in Key West, Fla., shortly before Kubitschek's inauguration. Six months later they talked privately at a meeting of American heads of state in Panama City. Both times, Kubitschek pressed the American president to attack poverty in Latin America, which he believed was a crucial, though largely ignored, problem.[1] Eisenhower's responses echoed what Latin American leaders had been hearing from their U.S. counterparts since the end of the Second World War. The United States was a global power with global responsibilities. Latin America would have to wait, but that need not hinder Latin American economic development. The region would do better by attracting private investment instead of looking for government handouts.

Publicly, Kubitschek mostly praised U.S. leadership. Privately, he was frustrated. He had threatened to skip the Panama meeting if the United States did not jumpstart several long-stalled development projects. In Kubitschek's mind, his ability to obtain development aid would play a major role in both his political fate and in the survival of Brazil's fragile democracy.[2] Kubitschek

---

[1] Juscelino Kubitschek, *Meu Caminho para Brasilia: A Escalada Politica*, vol. 2 (Rio de Janeiro: Bloch Editores, 1976), pp. 459–465.

[2] Developmentalism was the central tenet of Kubitschek's presidency. See Juscelino Kubitschek, *Meu Caminho para Brasília: Cinqüenta Anos em Cinco*, vol. 3 (Rio de Janeiro: Bloch Editores, 1978). For summaries in the U.S. and Brazilian literature, see Robert J. Alexander, *Juscelino Kubitschek and the Development of Brazil* (Athens, Ohio: Ohio University Center for International Studies, 1991); Licurgo Costa, *Uma Nova Política para as Américas: Doutrina Kubitschek e Opa* (São Paulo: Livraria Martins, 1960); Thomas E. Skidmore, *Politics in Brazil, 1930–1964: An Experiment in Democracy* (New York: Oxford University Press, 2007), Chapter 5; Gustavo Biscaia da Lacerda, "Panamericanismo entre a Segurança e o Desenvolvimento: O Operação

warned Eisenhower that the desperation of poor masses in Brazil and else-where in Latin America created a ripe recruiting atmosphere for local com-munist parties. However, inside the Eisenhower administration, the vision of the communist threat in Latin America had little to do with a revolution of disenfranchised masses. Brothers Secretary of State John Foster Dulles and CIA chief Allen Dulles were concerned largely with "subversives" who could infil-trate and undermine governments.[3] Kubitschek's warnings about poverty and endogenous unrest found little reception in the U.S. government from 1956 through early 1958.

On May 13, 1958, an opportunity arose that allowed Kubitschek to reframe his calls for economic aid, while also reiterating his commitment to the Western alliance. During a visit to Caracas, Vice President Richard Nixon's motorcade was attacked by an angry crowd, throwing into doubt the Eisen-hower administration's belief that the region was generally safe from com-munism. Though Nixon did not visit Brazil on that trip, Kubitschek and his aides recognized an opportunity.[4] Upon his return, Nixon, too, suggested a broader change in policy, saying "we must be dedicated to raising the stan-dard of living of the masses."[5] Though the anti-Nixon demonstrations had more to do with U.S. association with the recently ousted Venezuelan dictator than with communism,[6] Kubitschek recast his previous proposals to address U.S. fears.

Kubitschek partnered with other leaders in the region. To ensure Brazil's rivalry with Argentina did not undermine the project, he sought to include President Arturo Frondizi. Later, he approached Colombian President Alberto Lleras Camargo, considered a preeminent Latin American statesman. Like Kubitschek, both men presided over transitional democracies. "Operation Pan-America," an initiative to build a consensus to combat underdevelopment as part of a hemispheric approach to communism, was a plan for foreign relations

---

Panamericana e a Aliança para o Progresso" (M.A., Universidade Federal do Paraná, 2004), pp. 86–91.

[3] Stephen G. Rabe, *Eisenhower and Latin America: The Foreign Policy of Anticommunism* (Chapel Hill, N.C.: University of North Carolina Press, 1988), pp. 96–99, *passim*.

[4] Nixon had visited Brazil for Kubitschek's inauguration two years earlier. Kubitschek recounts his reaction in his memoirs, written in the 1970s. His discussion of OPA and the United States generally is more cynical than his pronouncements at that time. Kubitschek, *Meu Caminho para Brasília: Cinqüenta Anos em Cinco*, pp. 209–216. For another participant's account, which shows a more hopeful Kubitschek, see Autran Dourado, *Gaiola Aberta: Tempos de JK e Schmidt* (Rio de Janeiro: Rocco, 2000). Unfortunately, the initial meetings were informal; if documents were created, they do not appear to have been saved in the records of Itamaraty, the Memorial JK, or the National Archives.

[5] "Minutes of the Cabinet meeting," May 16, 1958, *FRUS, 1958–1960*, vol. 5, p. 238.

[6] Tad Szulc, "U.S. flies troops to Caribbean as mobs attack Nixon in Caracas," *New York Times*, May 14, 1958, p. 1; Szulc, "Venezuela: Anti-U.S. case history," *New York Times*, May 18, 1958, p. E14; Szulc, "Beneath the boiling-up," *New York Times*, May 25, 1958, p. SM19.

with the United States, and to confront the three leaders' domestic challenges. Its proposals were extraordinarily ambitious – an international echo of Kubitschek's campaign pledge to bring "fifty years of progress in five." Brazilian diplomats struggled to overcome opposition from the United States and discord among their fellow Latin Americans. Despite these challenges, Kubitschek and his allies achieved several long-desired policy changes from the fiscally conservative Eisenhower administration and built a foundation for OPA's better-known successor, the Alliance for Progress.

Background

As the United States shifted to a war footing in the 1940s, the payoff of President Franklin Roosevelt's "good neighbor" policy became clear. Latin America, with the exception of Argentina, stood with the Allies and supported the United States. Brazil and Mexico participated in military action, while other Latin American countries offered economic and political support, supplying oil and commodities to the Allied war machine at controlled prices. The United States responded with $263 million in lend–lease aid, some economic assistance, and increased lending.[7] As the war drew to a close, Latin American expectations coalesced around the idea that the United States owed economic assistance in return.[8] Instead, commodity prices fell while capital goods grew pricy, exhausting dollar surpluses that Latin America had accumulated during the war.

The region slipped to the second tier of U.S. concerns. The Truman and Eisenhower administrations assumed the area would remain part of its political, economic, and ideological bloc. While there was general consensus between U.S. and many Latin American policymakers on political and ideological aspects of the Cold War, this was less true in economic policy. U.S. foreign economic policies centered on liberalized trade and openness to private investment, leading the Truman and Eisenhower administrations to see Brazil's nationalist, state-led development schemes as problematic.[9] For their part, Brazilian policymakers expected greater assistance from Washington in return for support in the Second World War and because of an "unwritten alliance" that Brazilian

---

7 Peter H. Smith, *Talons of the Eagle: Dynamics of U.S.–Latin American Relations* (New York: Oxford University Press, 2000), p. 79; Stanley E. Hilton, "The United States, Brazil, and the Cold War, 1945–1960: End of the Special Relationship," *Journal of American History* 68, no. 3 (1981), pp. 600–601; W. Michael Weis, "The Twilight of Pan-Americanism: The Alliance for Progress, Neo-Colonialism, and Non-Alignment in Brazil, 1961–1964," *The International History Review* 23, no. 2 (2001).

8 Pastor, *Exiting the Whirlpool*, p. 206.

9 Alexandra de Mello e Silvia, "A Política Externa do JK: Operação Pan-Americana" (Fundação Getulio Vargas, 1992), pp. 6–7.

elites had considereded a founding foreign policy tenet dating to the godfather
of Brazilian diplomacy, the Baron of Rio Branco.[10]
As the United States committed to the reconstruction of Europe, Latin American hopes for aid grew even as the likelihood of it fell. As he departed for
the 1947 Rio Conference on hemispheric security, Ecuador's Foreign Minister Vicente Trujillo called for a conference "to draw up a sort of Marshall
Plan for Latin America."[11] Requests for an economic conference punctuated
the Rio summit, and the United States appeared amenable to holding one
the following year.[12] At the conference's close, President Truman emphasized the United States' global role and declared that the Americas' prosperity would rely on the private sector, not a new Marshall Plan.[13] That
year, the Organization of American States (OAS) Secretary General Lleras
Camargo urged an "extraordinary experiment of cooperation." Summarizing
the state of inter-American relations, he noted: "In politics, we have achieved
splendid results. In economics, we have not."[14] Disappointment would continue. At the 1948 Ninth International Conference of American States in
Bogotá,[15] Latin American delegates again called for a "Marshall Plan for Latin
America" and for a specific bank for Latin American development, reviving
a failed plan from before the war.[16] Truman responded with a request to

[10] For a summary of works on Brazilian foreign policy, see Amorim Neto, *De Dutra a Lula*. See
also Cervo, "Política Exterior e Relações Internacionais do Brasil"; Mônica Hirst and Andrew
Hurrell, *The United States and Brazil: A Long Road of Unmet Expectations* (New York:
Routledge, 2005); Maria Regina Soares De Lima and Mônica Hirst, "Brazil as an Intermediate
State and Regional Power: Action, Choice and Responsibilities," *International Affairs* 82,
no. 1 (2006).

[11] "A 'Marshall Plan' gains as a Rio topic," *New York Times*, April 13, 1947, p. 20.

[12] "The Chairman of the United States Delegation (Marshall) to the Acting Secretary of State,"
August 22, 1947, *FRUS, 1947*, vol. 8, pp. 53–54. The Associated Press, "Argentine urges
economic parley of all Americas," *New York Times*, August 15, 1947; C.P. Trussell, "Aid
later pledged," *New York Times*, August 14, 1947. Also see Stephen G. Rabe, "The Elusive
Conference: United States Economic Relations with Latin America, 1945–1952," *Diplomatic
History* 2, no. 3 (1978).

[13] Harry S. Truman, "Address before Rio de Janeiro Inter-American Conference for the Maintenance of Continental Peace and Security," September, 2, 1947, The American Presidency
Project. Available online: www.presidency.ucsb.edu/ws/?pid=12749.

[14] "Discurso de Alberto Lleras ante el Economic Club de Detroit," November 3, 1947. Carpeta.
28, documento 433, BLAA. Available online: www.lablaa.org/blaavirtual/exhibiciones/lleras/
pdf/carpeta-28/documento-433.pdf, p. 5. Translation by author.

[15] The conference was marred by the murder of a prominent Colombian politician and the out-
break of *La Violencia*, highlighting the region's explosive social situation. Stephen J. Randall,
Colombia and the United States: Hegemony and Interdependence (Athens, Ga.: University
of Georgia Press, 1992), Chapter 7; "The Ambassador in Colombia (Beaulac) to the Acting
Secretary of State," April 9, 1948, *FRUS, 1948*, vol. 9, p. 39.

[16] Peruvian Foreign Minister Armando Revoredo called for unified hemispheric defense against
communism and "for [a] Marshall Plan of [Latin America] including [an Inter-American] bank
to offer credits to [the American Republics]." "The Ambassador in Colombia (Beaulac) to the
Acting Secretary of State," Bogotá, April 7, 1948. *FRUS, 1948*, vol. 9, pp. 33–34.

Congress to increase funding for the Export-Import Bank "for the financing of economic development in the other American Republics" and with a modest expansion of Point IV technical assistance.[17]

Latin America was peripheral to Truman and his successor. As a candidate, Dwight Eisenhower criticized the previous administration for "neglect" of Latin America, but once in office he failed to launch major initiatives and instead curtailed Export-Import Bank lending.[18] A pro-business fiscal conservative, Eisenhower slowed funding for small development projects in Brazil and elsewhere.[19] Brazilians were irked by Washington's frequent admonitions to improve conditions for private capital and investment (particularly in the state-owned oil monopoly) in order to increase economic growth.[20]

Only when the Eisenhower administration needed to bargain for Latin American acquiescence to U.S. policies against Guatemala did the United States finally agree to Latin American calls for a conference dedicated to economic development. In 1954, Secretary of State John Foster Dulles was forced to trade for votes to back a resolution implicitly condemning Guatemala. In return, he promised to reinstate lending from the Export-Import Bank and to make good on a decade-old promise for an economic conference.[21] Even then, the Caracas resolution gave the sought-after condemnation of communism a focus on non-intervention and social factors.[22] The economic conference was finally held at Quitandinha near Rio de Janeiro in November 1954. The Economic Commission on Latin America's Raúl Prebisch offered a bold vision of state intervention and international assistance of "a minimum of 1000 million dollars annually, and for a period of not less than ten years."[23] The recommendations reflected Latin American desires, but U.S. positions at Quitandinha were less than Latin Americans had hoped for.[24] The conference set the tone on economics during Brazil's transition to democracy during 1955–1956.

---

[17] Harry S. Truman, "Special message to Congress on economic aid to Latin America," April 8, 1948, The American Presidency Project. Available online: www.presidency.ucsb.edu/ws/?pid=13148.

[18] Rabe, *Eisenhower and Latin America*, pp. 29, 66.

[19] Jerome I. Levinson and Juan de Onís, *The Alliance That Lost Its Way: A Critical Report on the Alliance for Progress* (Chicago, Ill.: Quadrangle Books, 1970), p. 38. For an extensive history of these delays, see Rabe, "The Elusive Conference."

[20] Hilton, "The United States, Brazil, and the Cold War, 1945–1960," pp. 603–605.

[21] Rabe, *Eisenhower and Latin America*, pp. 67–70.

[22] For a reevaluation of the conference, see Max Paul Friedman, "Fracas in Caracas: Latin American Diplomatic Resistance to United States Intervention in Guatemala in 1954," *Diplomacy & Statecraft* 21, no. 4 (2010).

[23] United Nations Economic Commission for Latin America, ed. *International Cooperation in a Latin American Development Policy* (New York: United Nations, September 1954), p. 129.

[24] Rabe, *Eisenhower and Latin America*, p. 76. The only major exception to this policy in Latin America came in Bolivia, where the Eisenhower administration spent heavily in support of moderate democratic forces.

Goals and Contexts: Kubitschek, Lleras Camargo, and Frondizi

The late 1950s saw the emergence of fragile democracies from military rule in Argentina, Brazil, Colombia, El Salvador, Peru, and Venezuela. These new democratic leaders faced immense and immediate challenges. Balance-of-payments crises loomed and military establishments lurked barely offstage. Despite common problems, these leaders also dealt with domestic peculiarities that conditioned their relations with the United States and (later) their approaches to Operation Pan-America. While Brazilian president Juscelino Kubitschek was the originator and primary champion for OPA, he was not alone. His strongest ally would become Colombian President Alberto Lleras Camargo, with the Argentine Arturo Frondizi playing an important role in the Operation's first stage. Though the case centers on Kubitschek, Brazilian foreign policy, and U.S.–Brazil relations, it also draws on Argentine and Colombian records to illustrate the roles, at times central, played by those leaders.

Kubitschek's Fifty Years in Five

Juscelino Kubitschek, a physician, emerged onto the national political scene as the center-left governor of the interior state of Minas Gerais. He built a reputation for completing high-profile public works with architectural flair. Inside the Partido Social Democrático (PSD), Kubitschek was a moderate. The PSD's founder, populist President Getúlio Vargas, was the defining figure in Brazilian politics from 1930 until he committed suicide in the bedroom of the presidential Palacio Catete in 1954. Even in death, Vargas remained a polarizing figure, and conservative elites distrusted the PSD. Unlike Vargas, who had concentrated the power of the Estado Novo in his own hands, Kubitschek was committed to democratic institutions. Democratic moderation made him more palatable to Brazil's military, which gradually transferred authority to civilian institutions. Kubitschek, referred to in Brazil as JK or "Juscelino," launched his candidacy under the term of appointed president João Café Filho.[25]

Despite years of strong growth, Brazil's economy was frequently on the edge of crisis. Vargas, Café Filho, and the military power brokers pursued a fairly consistent policy of state-led industrialization. The state compensated for limited domestic investment with deficit spending and, at times, by printing money. Inflation was a chronic problem. Brazil remained heavily dependent on a few commodities, primarily coffee, to earn the foreign exchange needed for its industrial projects. Complicating the situation, Brazil's state-owned energy

---

[25] The classic work on the period is Skidmore, *Politics in Brazil, 1930–1964*. The best English-language work specifically on Kubitschek, though it includes chapters on broader history and economic conditions, remains Alexander, *Juscelino Kubitschek and the Development of Brazil*; see also Maram Sheldon, "Juscelino Kubitschek and the Politics of Exuberance, 1956–1961," *Luso-Brazilian Review* 27, no. 1 (1990). In Portuguese, see the president's memoirs. Juscelino Kubitschek, *Meu Caminho para Brasília*, 3 vols. (Rio de Janeiro: Bloch Editores, 1974).

companies produced little oil or coal. The more Brazil industrialized, the more energy it imported, with oil often accounting for half its imports. When coffee prices slipped, the country faced drastic balance-of-payments deficits that forced it to turn to international financial institutions, foreign banks, and the U.S. government.

Despite these problems, Kubitschek set expansive development goals in his *plano de metas*. Hoping for U.S. backing, he offered to share the *plano* with the U.S. ambassador shortly before the election.[26] Influenced by the import substitution philosophy of the newly created Instituto Superior de Estudos Brasileiros, the *plano* set thirty goals for the Brazilian economy in order to cure balance-of-payments shortfalls with increased Brazilian manufacturing.[27] Though Brazil made impressive leaps in infrastructure and industry, shortfalls worsened due to debt service and energy imports. Inflation pushed up the cost of basic products like beans and rice, threatening to spark popular unrest. Kubitschek saw deficits and inflation as the cost of rapid industrialization, referring to inflation as the population's sacrifice for a developed future.[28]

Kubitschek's primary concerns were domestic and his foreign policy was also oriented to spur "fifty years of progress in five." Kubitschek saw Brazil as a natural ally of the United States, united in defense of "Western Christian civilization," as he often said. Traditional Brazilian grand strategy had prioritized a close relationship with the United States to help balance Argentina and give Brazil a freer hand with its neighbors.[29] Though the superpower competition of the 1950s structured Kubitschek's choices even further, he was more directly concerned about conservative elements of the Brazilian military, which warily eyed him and his vice president João Goulart as Vargas' heirs. Kubitschek survived reactionary coup plots and uprisings that first tried to block his inauguration and then attempted to overthrow him. Kubitschek was not personally disposed toward deep relations with the Soviet Union, which the military was unlikely to have permitted in any case. This did not translate into unqualified support for the United States, either. Kubitschek felt the country had been shortchanged by the Eurocentric Marshall Plan. A March 1955 U.S. intelligence estimate noted this common sentiment: "Brazilians feel that U.S. economic and financial assistance to Brazil has not been commensurate with Brazil's past services and present strategic importance to the United States, or with Brazil's value to the United States as a moderating influence in

---

[26] "Telegram from the ambassador in Brazil (Dunn) to the Department of State," October 15, 1955, *FRUS, 1955–1957, American Republics*, vol. 7, p. 678.

[27] The construction of the new capital city was later added as a thirty-first goal. Suely Braga da Silva, "50 anos em 5: O plano de metas," FGV: CPDOC. Available online: http://cpdoc.fgv.br/producao/dossies/JK/artigos/Economia/PlanodeMetas.

[28] Alexander, *Juscelino Kubitschek and the Development of Brazil*, Chapter 9.

[29] A recent analysis of Brazilian foreign policy argues that the relationship was based on Brazil's position as a status quo power in South America, to which the United States could in a sense delegate responsibility. Teixeira, *Brazil, the United States, and the South American Subsystem*.

Latin America and in UN affairs."[30] Kubitschek believed that external aid was necessary for development and that Brazil deserved it.

Lleras Camargo: A Statesman Seeks Stability

Alberto Lleras Camargo assumed the presidency in late 1958 as an experienced politician and statesman. He had been a key Latin American voice regarding the formation of the United Nations, where he advocated an independent regional body for the Western Hemisphere. After serving as the appointed, transitional president of Colombia from 1945 to 1946, Lleras Camargo was elected secretary general of the new Organization of American States. He later returned to Colombia to become president under a newly established, democratic regime. Lleras Camargo had a reputation as a moderate democrat and staunch anticommunist who could mobilize support in Latin America and with key figures in the United States, including the Rockefeller family, with whom he corresponded for decades.[31]

Lleras Camargo's Liberal Party government emerged from the solution to the party-fueled *La Violencia*, which had ravaged Colombia for a decade. In 1953, the military tried to end the upheaval by establishing a dictatorship under Gustavo Rojas Pinilla. To end military rule, the dominant parties agreed to a limited democracy with guaranteed representation for Liberals and Conservatives. This pact gave Lleras Camargo the widest latitude of the three leaders. Lleras Camargo was trusted by all sides and internationally respected. He was also one of the foremost proponents of inter-American cooperation, institutions, and understanding.[32]

Frondizi: Oil, Austerity, and the Generals

Unlike the United States and Brazil, U.S.–Argentine relations were traditionally prickly. The countries' exports competed in foreign markets, especially before World War I, and their diplomats battled for hemispheric leadership.[33] The tensions were reinforced by Argentina's belated and begrudging support in World War II. After his inauguration in May 1958, President Arturo Frondizi sought to change that history and build friendly relations with the world's

---

[30] U.S. National Intelligence estimate on Brazil, *FRUS 1955–1957, American Republics*, vol. 2, pp. 660–661.

[31] For example, see John D. Rockefeller III to Alberto Lleras. BLAA, Collección Alberto Lleras Camargo, caja X, carpeta 66, mss. 821–902/1; Exteriores to BrDel21, "Operação Pan-America. Declarações do Senhor Nelson Rockefeller," telegram exp. 8819, November 21, 1958, folder 82.286, Arquivo Histórico de Itamaraty, Brasilia (AHIB). Alberto Lleras to Nelson Rockefeller, telegram, March 15, 1945, Fondo Albert Lleras Camargo, BLAA.

[32] For general information on Lleras, see the excellent website and digital archives maintained by Colombia's principal library. "Alberto Lleras Camargo: Un estadista para la Colombia del siglo XX," Bilbioteca Luis Angel Arango. Available online: www.banrepcultural.org/blaavirtual/exhibiciones/lleras.

[33] Leandro Morgenfeld, *Vecinos en Conflicto: Argentina y los Estados Unidos en Conferencias Panamericanas* (Buenos Aires: Ediciones Continente, 2010).

top power. Vice President Nixon was sent to Frondizi's inauguration to recognize the Argentine's friendly overtures, before continuing to the eventful stop in Caracas. Like Kubitschek, Frondizi was elected president of a fragile, transitional democracy. Unlike Kubitschek, whose populist predecessor had committed suicide, Frondizi had to deal with the living specter of Juan Perón, whose followers remained a major force. Bans on *peronista* parties led to massive demonstrations, strikes, and occasional riots. Where U.S. economic policies frustrated Brazilians, U.S.–Argentina ties were improving from the Perón years. The United States authorized significant loans, transferred military equipment, and supported Argentine membership in the World Bank and IMF.

Before OPA, Kubitschek Tries to Jumpstart Pan-American Cooperation

The Eisenhower administration sought to keep Kubitschek's pre-inaugural visit informal. In January 1956, Kubitschek met the U.S. president over breakfast in Florida. Kubitschek made a favorable impression and quieted lingering concerns that he might be sympathetic to Brazilian communists.[34] According to the president's brother Milton Eisenhower, Kubitschek advocated a massive, U.S.-backed development campaign as early as this 1956 breakfast.[35] In his memoirs, Kubitschek recalled that President Eisenhower asked him about "communist infiltration" in Brazil, and he responded that the real problem was low living standards that should be met with a "long program of reforms." The only topic that really drew Eisenhower's interest was Brazilian state petroleum monopoly, which did not allow the foreign investment the U.S. president wished to promote.[36] Kubitschek then flew to Washington for meetings with U.S. officials and at the OAS.[37] Kubitschek hoped to gain support for his *plano de metas*; instead, the Eisenhower administration gave him old U.S. and IMF plans to address Brazil's situation – plans for austerity, not investment. U.S. leaders assured Kubitschek that capital would flow to Brazil if he improved conditions for foreign investors. Meanwhile, Secretary of State Dulles and others warned of the threat from communist agents.[38] With the U.S. government unreceptive, Kubitschek "planted the seed" of his development ideas with Latin American

---

34 "Memorandum of conversation between the President and Secretary of State," January 5, 1956, *FRUS, 1955–1957*, vol. 6, p. 685.

35 "[Kubitschek] talked of a program to be called 'Operation Pan-America,' which was the formation of a massive development fund with the United States putting up the bulk of the capital." Milton Stover Eisenhower, *The Wine Is Bitter: The United States and Latin America* (Garden City, N.Y.: Doubleday, 1963), p. 202.

36 Kubitschek, *Meu Caminho para Brasilia: A Escalada Politica*, pp. 460–463.

37 "Editorial note," *FRUS, 1955–1957*, vol. 6, p. 684.

38 Henry Holland, in particular, favored pressing the austerity approach on the Brazilian president-elect. "Memorandum of discussion at the 264th meeting of the National Security Council," November 3, 1955, FRUS, 1955–1957, American Republics, vol. 7, pp. 682–684; "Memorandum of a conversation: President-elect Kubitschek's talks with the Secretary of State," January 6, 1956, *FRUS, 1955–1957*, vol. 7.

ambassadors.[39] At Kubitschek's inauguration on February 2, 1956, his ministers presented the *plano de metas* and a request for $1.2 billion in assistance to the administration's emissary, Vice President Nixon. Nixon expressed little interest, announcing only a $35 million loan to expand steel production.[40]

Given the Eisenhower administration's coolness to Brazilian requests and its concerns about communism, connecting them was a natural step for Kubitschek and his ministers. During a late April 1956 visit, Vice President Goulart told U.S. Assistant Secretary of State for Inter-American Affairs Henry Holland "that people who are hungry and poor are receptive to communist propaganda and that the best way to fight communism is to raise living standards." Holland replied "that this was quite true but that there was another front on which we must be vigilant, that where we combat the clandestine espionage and subversive organization of communism."[41] Repeatedly, when Brazilian officials tried to link development to popular unrest and communism, they were rebuffed by U.S. officials who believed the threat was Soviet scheming. In June, Holland eyed Soviet commercial overtures in South America and recommended extending aid to Brazil and Argentina, even though "judged on purely banking and economic considerations, we would be justified in declining to extend that assistance." Holland added, "The sure and certain result would be acceptance of Soviet aid with the implications indicated."[42] Even then, the push for more assistance for Latin America failed in the face of opposition from Treasury Secretary George Humphrey. Humphrey favored low taxes, balanced budgets, and free markets as a means to economic growth at home and abroad, and he argued fervently for these policies in the National Security Council (NSC), with little concern for fostering democracies. Like John Foster Dulles, Humphrey was one of few cabinet members with a close relationship with the president.[43] The Dulles' fears of communism trumped Humphrey's concerns about spending in Asia and Europe, where allies received hundreds of millions in loans and grants, as a frustrated Kubitschek noted to U.S. Ambassador James Dunn.[44] In Latin American policy, however, economic conservatism reigned.

Kubitschek's frustration led him to consider boycotting the first major Pan-American conference of his presidency in July 1956. Eventually the U.S.

---

[39] Kubitschek, *Meu Caminho para Brasilia: A Escalada Politica*, p. 462.

[40] "Editorial note," *FRUS 1955–1957*, vol. 6, p. 692. Kubitschek, *Meu Caminho para Brasília: Cinqüenta Anos em Cinco*, pp. 17–18.

[41] "Memorandum of a conversation: Communism in Brazil," April 30, 1956, *FRUS, 1955–1957*, vol. 7, p. 700.

[42] "Memorandum from the assistant secretary of state for inter-American affairs (Holland) to the deputy director of the Office of South American Affairs (Belton)," June 7, 1956, *FRUS, 1955–1957, American Republics*, vol. 7, pp. 703–704.

[43] Stephen E. Ambrose, *Eisenhower: Soldier and President* (New York: Simon & Schuster, 1990), p. 290.

[44] "Telegram from the ambassador in Brazil (Dunn) to the Department of State," July 3, 1956, *FRUS, 1955–1957, American Republics*, vol. 7, pp. 703–704, 710–711.

administration met his condition and restarted funding for long-stalled projects approved by the Mixed Brazil–U.S. Commission. Once in Panama, Kubitschek outlined development problems and argued that U.S. aid was needed to protect against the communist threat to Latin America. Eisenhower was polite but uncompromising. The administration's long-standing economic policy for the region was restated in September in NSC 5613/1, which advocated "the development by private initiative of sturdy, self-reliant economies in Latin America which do not require continuing grant assistance from the United States."[45] In Latin America, only Bolivia had received significant grant assistance. The hemisphere received a tiny portion of overall U.S economic aid.

Kubitschek hoped to gain leverage when the U.S. Department of Defense renewed requests for military facilities in northern Brazil. The U.S. military had prized Brazilian bases for defending the Southern Atlantic during World War II. Brazil's geography made it valuable in the Cold War, as well. Defense wanted to construct a guided-missile station on the Brazilian island of Fernando de Noronha and a naval refueling station in the state of Pernambuco. Brazil approved the latter in a December 17, 1956 agreement that promised $100 million in equipment for the Brazilian military, along with clauses granting Brazilian military personnel the right to monitor operations. Kubitschek stressed – and likely exaggerated – the political risks he was taking in granting U.S. basing leases, and noted that economic cooperation should match military cooperation.[46] The blatant efforts by the Brazilians to link military and economic agreements annoyed Americans, leading U.S. Ambassador Ellis O. Briggs to note that Kubitschek was withholding the Fernando de Noronha station "for bargaining purposes."[47] Kubitschek exhausted much of his leverage placating his armed forces with military equipment. The president's key ally in the military was defense minister General Henrique Teixeira Lott, whose backing had helped end several small military revolts in 1955–1957. The military's support did not come cheap. In addition to equipment transfers and purchases, sizeable military pay increases worsened deficits and inflation.[48]

As U.S. and Latin American diplomats prepared for an economic conference in Buenos Aires, divisions on both sides became apparent. While the Eisenhower administration continued its emphasis on private investment, Congressional Democrats criticized the president for inattention to Latin America and coziness with dictators. The criticisms bubbled over in the confirmation hearings for Roy Rubottom, who was nominated to replace Holland as assistant secretary.[49] In Latin America, the conference sparked optimistic proclamations, but little real hope. Venezuelan president-elect Rómulo Betancourt

---

45 NSC 5613/1, qtd. in Rabe, *Eisenhower and Latin America*, p. 92.
46 Ellis O. Briggs, December 18, 1956, *FRUS, 1955–1957*, vol. 7, p. 730.
47 Briggs, January 9, 1957, *FRUS, 1955–1957*, vol. 7, p. 736.
48 National Intelligence Estimate on Brazil, January 7, 1957, *FRUS, 1955–1957*, vol. 7, p. 738.
49 Rabe, *Eisenhower and Latin America*, pp. 100–101.

predicted "platitudes," and not "concrete, dynamic agreements." He blamed the "demonstrated inability of the Latin American governments to agree on the same minimum, common plan to present to and argue for with the United States representatives."[50] Diplomats from Brazil, Colombia, and Uruguay tried to shape a shared agenda that advocated an inter-American development bank, steps towards a Latin American common market, and a payments union.[51] The United States argued that existing financial institutions were adequate and that an inter-American bank would be redundant with the IMF and International Bank for Reconstruction and Development.[52] As Betancourt forewarned, the conference produced few tangible results.

After the Sputnik launch on October 4, 1957, U.S. Ambassador Briggs worried that the poorly educated masses in Brazil would be drawn in by Soviet accomplishments. Ambassador Briggs cabled that "Our assumption that Latin America is a safe rear area might well be re-examined." Briggs worried the Soviets would step in where Eisenhower would not and encouraged "substantial additional Government credit."[53] The ambassador's warnings did not resonate among Eisenhower's closest advisors. CIA Director Allen Dulles downplayed the risk of communism in Latin America in Congressional testimony in February 1958.[54] At the same time, an increasingly desperate Brazil requested $100 million in standby credit from the Export-Import Bank. Increased global coffee production, particularly from Africa, caused projected prices to plummet for 1958. U.S. officials gave Brazilians lectures about fiscal responsibility and explained that the bank's rules did not contemplate standby credit. The Federal Reserve would not make the loans unless Brazil pledged gold collateral, of which it had little. U.S. officials sent Brazilians a list of all the loans Brazil had received from the United States – prompting a frustrated response that frequent debt payments were reminder enough.

Kubitschek and his ministers believed that Brazil's size, political importance, and long-standing cooperation with the United States merited special consideration. Kubitschek warned that he would have to consider Soviet trade offers for

50 Rómulo Betancourt, "Discurso del ex-presidente Rómulo Betancourt de Venezuela en la comida en su honor, Carnegie International Center, New York," January 12, 1957, *The Papers of Rómulo Betancourt, Toma XXXIV – XXXV (1957–1960)*, microfilm, roll no. 19, p. 7. Translation by author.

51 MREC, caja 12, orden 112, transferencia 7. Gabinete del Ministro, memorandos, 1957–1958, June 25, 1957, p. 38; MREC, caja 12, orden 112, transferencia 7. Gabinete del Ministro, memorandos, 1957–1958, August 2, 1957, p. 46.

52 "Memorandum from the Assistant Secretary of State for Inter-American Affairs (Rubottom) to Deputy Undersecretary for Economic Affairs (Dillon)," May 29, 1957, *FRUS, 1955–1957*, vol. 6, pp. 509–510.

53 "Despatch from the Ambassador in Brazil (Briggs) to the Department of State," December 31, 1957, *FRUS, 1955–1957*, vol. 7, p. 773.

54 Rabe, *Eisenhower and Latin America*, p. 92.

Brazil's coffee surplus. The State Department restated its opposition to further loans, while "deploring [the] obvious tactic."[55] John Foster Dulles hoped that if the Brazilians were convinced no U.S. "bailout" was forthcoming, they would "be forced to deal seriously with IMF as [their] only alternative."[56] In April, Brazil recalled its ambassador in Washington, Ernani Amaral do Peixoto, for consultations about Soviet–Brazilian relations.

Relations hit a low point in May 1958. Kubitschek's goals required changes to U.S. policy, which the Eisenhower administration had opposed for over two years. The two sides had very different understandings of development and communism in Latin America. For Kubitschek, there was a link that should make development a natural U.S. priority. U.S. officials, including Holland, Humphrey, the Dulleses, and the president did not share the concern. Communism – to the extent it was a problem in the hemisphere – should be dealt with through security measures. Kubitschek felt Brazil merited assistance based on political criteria. Countries in Europe and Asia received loans and grants because they were considered politically important. Though the U.S. ambassador and a few officials favored a more flexible and generous approach, they did not carry the day. Kubitschek interpreted the loan rejections as a denial of Brazil's importance to the West. However, he was constrained internationally and domestically from seriously pursuing Soviet help. Frustration and disappointment reigned when Nixon departed for Frondizi's inauguration – a trip intended to counter criticisms that Eisenhower neglected Latin America and favored dictators. Nixon planned stops in Uruguay, Peru, and Venezuela, bypassing Brazil.

Nixon in Caracas and the Birth of Operation Pan-America

Nixon first met furious demonstrators at Peru's University of San Marcos. The vice president's bodyguards warned of assassination rumors floating around Caracas.[57] As his motorcade moved from the Venezuelan capital's airport to a downtown monument, some 4,000 people blocked the road, attacking the car with "heavy sticks" and "melon-sized rocks." The crowd smashed the car's windows and, in Nixon's words, covered him "with glass and something

55 Given low coffee consumption in the Soviet Union at the time, this seems to have been in part wishful thinking from Brazilian coffee officials. Briggs, "Telegram from Embassy in Brazil to the Department of State," February 25, 1958, *FRUS, 1958–1960*, vol. 5, p. 660; Ernani do Amaral Peixoto, "Relações Estados Unidos de América-América Latina," March 10, 1958, letter, est. 51, pr. 3, no. 19, Washington, despachos, 1956–1958, AAHI-Rio.

56 John Foster Dulles, "Telegram from the Department of State to the Embassy in Brazil," March 29, 1958, *FRUS, 1958–1960*, vol. 5, pp. 669–670.

57 The Associated Press, "Nixon's bodyguards given report of possible attempt to kill him," *The Washington Post*, May 14, 1958, p. A2.

that was not rain."[58] Some protestors seemed intent on dragging Nixon from the car, but the driver forced the damaged sedan through the crowd and out of harm's way. Shortly afterward, Nixon blamed communist organizers, though most of the crowd was composed of citizens angry about U.S. complicity with the recently deposed Venezuelan dictator, Marcos Pérez Jiménez, who had recently established luxurious exile in Miami. Nixon noted: "Communists were able to gain great support from students… What we are seeing is a terrible legacy of the dictatorship."[59] In addition to granting the deposed dictator a visa, the Eisenhower administration had decorated him with the Legion of Merit in 1954, provided military assistance, and encouraged oil investments. Shortly before Nixon's visit, the United States cut Venezuela's oil quota; though the decision was driven by pressure from domestic producers, from Caracas it seemed like punishment.[60] The immediate analysis of the U.S. embassy in Caracas averred that "Undoubtedly the attack on the Vice President was organized by the Communists."[61] Eisenhower put the military on alert to carry the vice president to safety if needed.[62]

Upon his return, Nixon suggested a broader change in policy, saying "we must be dedicated to raising the standard of living of the masses."[63] This echoed the claims Kubitschek and Goulart had made since 1956. However, Nixon's view of democracy and development did not entirely coincide with Kubitschek's. On May 22, Nixon warned the NSC that Latin American democratization brought with it immense risks, empowering leaders and publics who were unwilling to attack communist influence. For countries "lacking in political maturity," leaders were likely to be "very naïve about the nature and threat of communism." Nixon emphasized: "The threat of Communism in Latin America was greater today than ever before in history."[64] After Nixon's trip, the Eisenhower administration dedicated more high-level attention to Latin America than it had for years. In a report, top administration officials recognized: "Many Latin American leaders continue to feel the area is being

[58] Szulc, "U.S. flies troops to Caribbean as mobs attack Nixon in Caracas," *New York Times*, May 14, 1958, pp. 1, 9. For an official report, see "Memorandum of a telephone conversation," May 15, 1958, *FRUS, 1958–1960*, vol. 5, pp. 226–227.

[59] Richard Nixon qtd. in Szulc, "U.S. flies troops to Caribbean as mobs attack Nixon in Caracas," *New York Times*, May 14, 1958, p. 9.

[60] Rabe, *Eisenhower and Latin America*, pp. 36, 39, 94. On Pérez's foreign policy approach to building support with Eisenhower, see C.A. Murgueitio Manrique, "Los Gobiernos Militares de Marcos Pérez Jiménez y Gustavo Rojas Pinilla: Nacionalismo, Anticomunismo y sus Relaciones con los Estados Unidos (1953–1957)," *Historia y Espacio*, no. 25 (2014), pp. 39–97.

[61] "Memorandum of a telephone conversation," May 15, 1958, *FRUS, 1958–1960*, vol. 5, pp. 226–227.

[62] Tad Szulc, "U.S. flies troops to Caribbean as mobs attack Nixon in Caracas," *New York Times*, May 14, 1958, p. 1.

[63] "Minutes of the Cabinet meeting," May 16, 1958, *FRUS, 1958–1960*, vol. 5, p. 238.

[64] "Memorandum of discussion at the 366th meeting of the National Security Council," May 22, 1958, *FRUS, 1958–1960*, vol. 5, pp. 239–243.

neglected or taken for granted by the United States" and that their share of U.S. aid was "disproportionately small."[65] Policy appeared open to revision in a way that it previously had not been.

By all indications, Kubitschek was nearly as surprised by the attack on Nixon as were members of the Eisenhower administration.[66] The Brazilian president was initially unsure how to respond and planned on sending a letter expressing his outrage at the attacks and expressing wishes for Nixon's well-being. Augusto Frederico Schmidt, a poet who was Kubitschek's confidante, advisor, and preferred speech writer, had grander visions. He reportedly told the president: "The moment has arrived to affirm yourself as a great statesman." Kubitschek should express a desire to "recompose continental unity, which has taken a hard blow." Though the letter should not say so, Schmidt believed the moment had arrived for the Latin American Marshall Plan.[67] Schmidt's idea met skepticism from influential finance minister José María Alkmin, who also saw the attack as an opportunity, but did not want to squander it on pie-in-the-sky plans. Instead, Alkmin argued that Brazil should address coffee prices, the recent denial of loans, and stagnant negotiations with the IMF. Schmidt appealed to the president's grandiosity.

The Americans are going to be so frightened when they get this letter that they will send high officials to Brazil to figure out what is going on. Then we can more easily address our tough immediate problems. We need to think big, Alkmin. We are not just making Brazilian policy, and even less *Mineira* policy [both came from the state of Minas Gerais]. We must be statesmen.[68]

Kubitschek decided that Brazil must do more than pursue short-term priorities. Following Schmidt's counsel, the president resuscitated his plans of Pan-Americanism for economic development, largely cast aside after the Panama Conference of July 1956. He was conscious of the need to act quickly to take advantage of "the bonfire of indignation in Washington's political circles."[69]

The first letter to Eisenhower was drafted in Kubitschek's inner circle, leaving aside the normally central foreign affairs ministry, Itamaraty, and minister

---

[65] "Report from the Operations Coordinating Board to the National Security Council," May 21, 1958, *FRUS, 1958–1960*, vol. 5, p. 5.

[66] In his memoirs, Kubitschek writes that "the attacks were not a surprise for me," because he had been observing the loss of U.S. prestige. However, the memoir's account of OPA's creation is fragmentary and contains multiple inaccuracies about Nixon's trip.

[67] Unfortunately, no official record of this meeting was found in the archives of the Memorial JK or Itamaraty. While agencies of the Brazilian government produced significant records, the same does not seem to be true of Kubitschek's closest advisers. The most complete account comes from the memoir of a participant, written much later. Dourado, *Gaiola Aberta*, pp. 75–76.

[68] Ibid., p. 80.

[69] Kubitschek, *Meu Caminho para Brasília: Cinqüenta Anos em Cinco*, p. 212.

Macedo Soares.[70] The slight provoked Soares' resignation days later.[71] Kubitschek showed the draft letter to U.S. Ambassador Briggs, who wrote that a "rebuff or even chilly initial response could have serious consequences at this juncture."[72] The letter to Eisenhower, dated May 28, 1958, expressed "solidarity" with Nixon, while noting that "the ideal of Pan-American unity has suffered serious impairment." Kubitschek added that "something must be done" to "correct the false impression that we are not behaving in a fraternal way in the Americas."[73] The initial letter did not offer concrete projects or mention "Operation Pan-America." Those proposals, and the name, evolved over several months. Though it is difficult to establish, it appears the name was chosen several days after the letter to Eisenhower, which centrally refers to "Pan-American unity," "Pan-American ideals," and "the right path in regard to Pan-Americanism." The name intentionally avoided emphasizing Brazil; instead it implied actions by and on behalf of all Americans.[74]

On June 10, Assistant Secretary Rubottom personally delivered Eisenhower's response to Rio de Janeiro. Like Kubitschek's initial missive, the reply was cordial but vague. The U.S. president called for bilateral consultations about Pan-American solidarity – specifically about how to implement the 1954 Declaration of Solidarity of the Tenth Inter-American Conference. That declaration arose as part of U.S. efforts to delegitimize the government of Jacobo Arbenz in Guatemala months before a CIA-backed overthrow. Reaffirming that declaration was not what Kubitschek was hoping for. However, Eisenhower's letter also suggested that Secretary Dulles visit Brazil in the near future. Though excited by the prospect of Dulles' visit, Kubitschek told Rubottom that "he had the feeling that the Secretary rarely if ever became interested in Latin American affairs."[75] Downplaying bilateral U.S.–Brazilian problems, Kubitschek focused on matters of hemispheric and global concern. The Brazilian physician-turned-president diagnosed the attack on Nixon as a symptom of frustration with low living standards and unmet expectations. Kubitschek described to Rubottom the central tenet of what soon became Operation Pan-America: that underdevelopment created communism, and that hemispheric cooperation for

[70] Dourado, *Gaiola Aberta*. Briggs, "Telegram from Embassy in Brazil to the Department of State," May 23, 1958, *FRUS, 1958–1960*, vol. 5, pp. 677–679.

[71] Kubitschek, *Meu Caminho para Brasília: Cinqüenta Anos em Cinco*, p. 212.

[72] Briggs, "Telegram from Embassy in Brazil to the Department of State," May 23, 1958, *FRUS, 1958–1960*, vol. 5, p. 678.

[73] The original two letters were published in the *Public Papers*, and are available at "Exchange of letters between the President and President Kubitschek of Brazil," June 10, 1958, in Woolley and Peters, eds., The American Presidency Project. Available online: www.presidency.ucsb.edu/ws/?pid=11089.

[74] I could not find in the archives of Itamaraty, memoirs, or in the secondary literature an account of the genesis of the name Operação Pan-Americana.

[75] Roy Rubottom, "Draft of a memorandum of a conversation, President Kubitschek's residence," June 10, 1958, *FRUS, 1958–1960*, vol. 5, pp. 679–683.

development was needed to win the Cold War in Latin America.[76] Kubitschek said: "Communists are opposed to the economic development of any under-developed country. They recognize that they cannot achieve their sinister design if economic development is carried out." Rubottom was still unconvinced and blamed agitators. The diplomat's intransigence encouraged Kubitschek to seek the support of the Brazilian public and Latin American diplomatic corps.[77]

Adding Details to the Brazilian Proposal

The outlines of Kubitschek's *Operação Pan-Americana* became clearer in a June 20, 1958 speech to Latin American diplomats. First, Kubitschek insisted that Latin Americans had not been sufficiently consulted in world affairs, given that global conflict constituted a threat to the whole hemisphere. Second, OPA could not be a Brazilian or bilateral initiative; it would succeed only if it superseded rivalries between American nations. Third, Brazil's proposal was inherently linked to the Cold War. Kubitschek said his letter to Eisenhower was "a cry of alert against the Cold War that already has presented its first symptoms in this continent." Kubitschek did not doubt that Latin America should stand with the United States in the Cold War. He praised the Marshall Plan, but turned his focus: "There the emphasis was placed on *reconstruction*, without equal interest being given to the very serious problem of the *development* of countries with rudimentary economies." Fundamentally, OPA would address underdevelopment within the framework of the Cold War. Fighting underdevelopment meant eradicating human suffering and creating the conditions under which people could prosper. Despite that grand design, Kubitschek's initial concrete programs amplified existing ideas instead of offering dramatic departures. The speech mentioned four programs, all in line with his *plano de metas*: pioneer investments, technical assistance, commodity price stabilization, and expansion of credit from international financial institutions. Addressing underdevelopment was strategic, preventative medicine against "antidemocratic" forces. Kubitschek closed his speech, saying, "The union of the Americas is more than an ideal, it is imperative for our survival."[78]

The clearest summary of OPA came in an *aide-memoire* circulated in early August 1958 to all the American republics. It employed much of Kubitschek's original phrasing, calling OPA a long-term "reorientation of hemispheric policy." OPA was both political and economic, intended to buttress Latin America's place in the Western alliance through rapid economic development.

---

[76] Biscaia da Lacerda, "Panamericanismo entre a Segurança e o Desenvolvimiento," pp. 147–153.

[77] For Kubitschek's recollections of the meeting with Rubottom and his thoughts on Eisenhower's response, see *Meu Caminho para Brasília: Cinqüenta Anos em Cinco*, pp. 217–222.

[78] All quotes in the preceding paragraph are from Kubitschek, speech to diplomatic representatives of the American Republics in Brazil, June 20, 1958, *Operação Pan-Americana Documentario*, vol. 1, Sala de Pesquisa, Memorial JK, Brasilia, pp. 31–37. Italics in original.

It should be multilateral and "pan-American" and serve to promote democracy in addition to development. The *aide-memoire* laid out seven "basic objectives":

1. reaffirmation of the principles of hemispheric solidarity;
2. definition of underdevelopment as a pan-American problem;
3. adaptation of inter-American organs and agencies, if necessary, to the requirements of fighting underdevelopment;
4. pioneering investments in economically backward areas of the Continent;
5. technical assistance aimed at improved productivity;
6. measures to stabilize the prices of basic commodities;
7. actualization and amplification of the resources on international financial institutions.[79]

In later versions – to reflect Argentine input and incorporate the U.S. perspective – points would be added on private investment and initiative. Reflecting sovereignty concerns, it was added that each country should be responsible for reforms to promote development.[80] With the outlines of the project becoming clearer, Brazil continued seeking Latin American backing.

Brazil Seeks Latin American Support

Even before Eisenhower responded to Kubitschek's first letter, Brazilian diplomats began contacting Latin American colleagues to build support. Where the letter to Eisenhower hinted that the crux of the Pan-American response should be to attack underdevelopment, in talks with Latin Americans, Brazilians were more direct. After Rubottom's visit, Kubitschek sensed that Eisenhower had not yet drawn the desired conclusions from the Nixon incident, and he intensified his search for Latin American unity.[81] Kubitschek's speech to Latin American diplomats was a call to action, and a signal to the Eisenhower administration that he sought something much broader than a restatement of anticommunist declarations from 1954. It also set a high bar for success, requiring substantial unity from Latin America, a policy shift from the Eisenhower administration, and a large commitment from the U.S. Congress – though Congress played little role in Brazilian strategizing.

Kubitschek personally pursed the cooperation of Colombian President Alberto Lleras Camargo, whose reputation as a statesman made him a key supporter. Kubitschek wrote his counterpart: "We have to respond to the Cold

---

[79] "Aide-memoire," archived on October 20, 1958, revised draft, folder 82.279, AHIB.

[80] For a later modification, see "Aide-memoire," August 9, 1959, Council of the Organization of American States, Special Committee to Study the Formulation of New Measures for Economic Cooperation, *Volume L Report and Documents, First Meeting, Washington, D.C., November 17-December 12, 1958* (Washington, D.C.: 1959), pp. 29–31. Available online: www.fordham.edu/halsall/mod/1958panamerica.html.

[81] Kubitschek, *Meu Caminho para Brasília: Cinqüenta Anos em Cinco*, p. 227.

War, which has already invaded the hemisphere, with the harmonious development of our economies to alleviate the sufferings, until now patiently borne, of millions of persons on this continent."[82] Lleras Camargo responded warmly, noting that while at the OAS, he was frustrated Brazil did not more actively lead. He argued that Latin American poverty could become a "grave danger" for the West in the Cold War, and he pledged Colombian support.[83] The two leaders also agreed to immediately pursue the creation of an inter-American bank for economic development.[84]

In the weeks after Kubitschek's speech, he garnered enthusiastic support from Latin America. Argentine President Frondizi announced his backing, which was notable due to the historic rivalry between the two countries. Days later, Frondizi wrote his own letter to Eisenhower citing economic "disequilibrium" as a cause of problems and offering Argentine support for a review of international economic policies.[85] After consultations with Peru, Ecuador, Colombia, and Panama, Venezuela announced support for OPA. Privately, the Venezuelan foreign minister wrote to the Brazilians: "The political cooperation of the American republics is well known ... But the same is not true of economic and cultural cooperation, and that fact dangerously weakens our system of continental organization." The leaders of Bolivia, Chile, Ecuador, Panama, Paraguay, Peru, Uruguay, and, jointly, Central America made statements of support.[86] Brazil sought unity "with the goal of avoiding possible differences of opinion that would be exploited by the Americans to reduce the reach and size of the Brazilian initiative."[87]

While these leaders offered broad support, two points of disagreement arose. First, many leaders preferred a foreign ministers' meeting instead of a presidential summit. Brazil quickly accommodated this by saying – despite earlier indications – that a ministers' meeting would be necessary as preparation for the heads of states' gathering. Second, there was a worry, including from Venezuela's Betancourt, that OPA would marginalize the OAS. Kubitschek

[82] "Carta del Presidente Kubitschek al Presidente Lleras," August 4, 1958, *Memorias de Relaciones Exteriores de Colombia*, 1959, p. 332.

[83] "Carta del Presidente Lleras al Presidente Kubitschek," August 20, 1958, *MdeRE Colombia*, 1959, pp. 333–335; Lleras Camargo to Kubitschek, August 20, 1958, letter, folder 960.3 Confidenciais asuntos gerais, AHIB.

[84] Jorge Olintho de Oliveira, "Criação de un instituto de fomento regional," September 1, 1958, tele. exp. 6787, folder 960.3 Confidenciais asuntos gerais, 1958, AHIB.

[85] Mario Gibson Barboza to Exteriores, "Carta do presidente Frondizi ao Presidente Eisenhower," July 1, 1958, tele. rec. 5963, folder 82.281, AHIB.

[86] René de Sola, "Posición de Venezuela ante la Operación Panamericana," July 11, 1958, memorandum, folder 960.3, Pan-Americanismo, 1958–1960, AHIB; Oscar Pires do Rio to Negrão de Lima, "Posicão da Venezuela na Operação Panamericana," July 12, 1958, letter, folder 960.3, Pan-Americanismo, 1958–1960, AHIB.

[87] Fernando Lobo, "Operação Pan-Americana," August 1, 1958, tele. rec. 7712, folder 960.3, Pan-Americanismo, delegações, AHIB.

tried to assuage these concerns, saying: "Brazil will not leave aside the mechanisms of the Organization of American States in realizing the objectives of the Operation."[88] However, Kubitschek feared that moving OPA under the OAS would transfer influence to the Washington-based bureaucracy and diplomatic corps.

To gain support, Itamaraty sought Latin American input in assembling an agenda for the meeting with Dulles.[89] The only major holdout was Mexico, which slowed Brazilian initiatives at various moments. In part, Mexican reticence seemed to be based on its rivalry with Brazil over leadership of Spanish-speaking America. More directly, Mexican diplomats argued that OPA's economic assistance would invite greater U.S. scrutiny and intrusion into domestic affairs, serving as a justification for U.S. intervention in Latin American economies and politics. Mexico did, in fact, have some reason for concern. U.S. economic assistance in Europe had come with conditions regarding market access for U.S. goods and investments, even inserting the United States into labor relations – an area that the ruling Partido Revolucionario Institucional closely guarded. With the goal of countering U.S. interventionism, Mexico at times sided with the United States in opposition to Brazil's proposals. Mexico highlighted the failed attempts to gain U.S. economic cooperation, including a year before in Buenos Aires, to paint the Brazilian initiative as futile.[90]

In the United States, criticism of Eisenhower's Latin America policy grew. After the Nixon trip, the Senate announced a review of U.S.–Latin American policy called the Draper Committee. Democrats on the Senate Foreign Relations Committee criticized Eisenhower for being insufficiently supportive of democracy and development.[91] The president sent Secretary Dulles to Brazil to demonstrate to Kubitschek "continuing interest in the constructive proposals you have recently made,"[92] but also to address Congressional criticism.

Brazilian officials fully expected that Dulles would be more interested in discussing communism than economics, so they strategized about how to best fit OPA into the East–West struggle. Officials at Itamaraty wrote: "The

[88] Exteriores to Brazilian Embassy in Buenos Aires, "Operação Pan-Americana," July 24, 1958, tele. exp. 5937, folder 82.281, AHIB; Exteriores to Brazilian Embassy in Lima, "Operação Pan-Americana, July 24, 1958, tel. exp. 5940, folder 82.285, AHIB; Manuel Prado (president of Peru) and Kubitschek, public exchange of letters, July 24, 1958, folder 82.285, AHIB; Exteriores to Brazilian Embassy in Bogotá, "Operação Pan-Americana," July 14, 1958, tele. exp. 5102, folder 960.3 Confidenciais asuntos gerais, AHIB.

[89] Exteriores to Brazilian diplomatic missions in Latin America, "Visita do Senhor Foster Dulles ao Brasil. Operação Pan-Americana," July 29, 1958, tele. exp. 5554, folder 960.3 Confidenciais asuntos gerais, AHIB.

[90] Mexican Foreign Ministry to Negrão de Lima, memorandum, September 1, 1958, folder 82.285, AHIB.

[91] W. Michael Weis, *Cold Warriors & Coups D'etat: Brazilian-American Relations, 1945–1964* (Albuquerque: University of New Mexico, 1993), pp. 114–115.

[92] Eisenhower to Kubitschek, letter, August 2, 1958, folder 82.285, AHIB.

attenuation of the purely military aspects and the growing emphasis on economic aspects of the conflict indicates an opportunity to raise the argument that the fight against underdevelopment in Latin America constitutes a global strategy for the West."[93] When Dulles arrived to Rio de Janeiro on August 4, he largely frustrated Brazilian expectations. Dulles deferred economic questions while arguing that U.S. history showed private initiative to be the best way to develop an economy.[94] The secretary wanted another anticommunist treaty. He was more interested in security and police reforms than in discussing poverty and unrest. Kubitschek saw Dulles as almost incapable of understanding or compromise.[95] The two men traveled to the enormous construction site that was Brasilia to craft the joint declaration. At Kubitschek's strong insistence, it noted the importance of Pan-Americanism and the need for economic development, though without specific initiatives. Kubitschek succeeded in keeping references to enhanced police cooperation out of the text.[96]

Foreign Ministers' Meeting

Foreign ministers from throughout the hemisphere gathered for an informal meeting in Washington in September 1958, scheduled to coincide with the annual meeting of the United Nations General Assembly. The idea came from Mexico as an alternative to a formal conference, and by accepting it, Itamaraty hoped to gain Mexican backing.[97] Brazil indicated to Latin American diplomats that it wanted a stand-alone, multilateral mechanism to coordinate hemispheric development efforts. Mexico demurred, and then attacked the Brazilian initiative in meetings with other diplomats.[98] The new Brazilian minister, Francisco Negrão de Lima, wrote Kubitschek on September 15:

Though we have the broad support of the majority, we are meeting stiff resistance from Mexico and the United States of America, which want to trust in the mechanisms of the Organization of American States. We are studying a way to reconcile our points of view, and at our suggestion, the Colombian delegation is convening a meeting of a Latin America group to deal with specifics of the Operation. With the goal of avoiding the impression that we want to undermine the OAS, we will be forced to move a little in the direction of the Mexican and U.S. points of view.[99]

---

93 Exteriores to Brazilian Mission at the UN, "Operação Pan-Americana," July 30, 1958, tele. exp. 6036, folder 960.3, Pan-Americanismo, delegações, AHIB.

94 "Memorandum of a conversation, Brazilian foreign office," August 5, 1958, *FRUS, 1958–1960*, vol. 5, pp. 692–695.

95 Kubitschek, *Meu Caminho para Brasília: Cinqüenta Anos em Cinco*, pp. 227–229.

96 Kubitschek and Dulles, "Joint Communique on Pan-American matters," August 6, 1958, memorandum, folder 82.280-B, AHIB.

97 "Memorandum," July 29, 1958, folder 82.280-B, AHIB.

98 Fernando Lobo, "Operação Pan-Americana," September 11, 1958, tele. rec. 7153, folder 960.3, Pan-Americanismo, delegações, AHIB.

99 Negrão de Lima to Kubitschek, "Operação Pan-Americana," September 18, 1958, tele. rec. 7377, folder 960.3, Pan Americanismo, delegações, AHIB.

Kubitschek pushed back against the compromise, seeing Mexico as a threat to
OPA. On the eve of the conference, he urged Negrão de Lima to "do everything
possible so that OPA produces something more concrete than a proliferation
of anodyne meetings and the flowering of a crop of innocuous declarations of
continental solidarity." Kubitschek's letter continued:

I do not think it necessary to remind you that the meeting in Washington will be a
culminating moment for OPA. The victory of the Mexican thesis would relegate OPA to
be merely a formula for revising Pan-Americanism, and it would be the final blow against
the de facto leadership we have exercised since the beginning of the Operation. . . . I urge
your Excellency to promote an understanding with the U.S. delegation that demonstrates
that the only hope for the creation of a powerful alliance of the states of this continent is
to avoid the stagnation of our initiative as mere revisionism under the OAS framework,
where it would certainly be fragmented and lost in bureaucracy.[100]

Despite Mexico's reservations, several Eisenhower administration officials
argued that the United States needed to address some of Brazil's concerns,
which were echoed by most Latin American leaders. In the days before the
meeting, the United States released word that it would unveil initiatives on
commodity prices and for a hemispheric bank. Newspaper headlines in the
region called the decision a "fundamental change" or declared with relief that
"the United States finally accepts the creation of an inter-American bank for
economic growth."[101] The administration also gave its blessing to the pursuit of regional common markets. However, what many in Latin America
read as the first of many changes in U.S. policy was seen by segments of the
Eisenhower administration as a way to remove the wind from Operation Pan-
America's sails. Inside the State Department, there was often disagreement
between Undersecretary of State for Economic Affairs C. Douglas Dillon, who
argued for a "positive approach," and Assistant Secretary of State for Economic Affairs Thomas Mann, who wanted to relax some economic policies
but saw Operation Pan-America as a Brazilian money grab.[102] Mann was a
lawyer and career Foreign Service officer who had grown up speaking Spanish
and English in Laredo, Texas, and was posted in Uruguay and Venezuela early
in his career. Dillon, the scion of a banking family, came into the government
with a background in Wall Street finance. He had been a prominent donor to
the Eisenhower campaign and Eisenhower appointed him as ambassador to
France in 1953. Shortly after Nixon's visit and continuing into the conference,

[100] Kubitschek to Negrão de Lima, "Operação Pan-Americana," September 20, 1958, tele. exp.
     7218, folder 960.3, Pan-Americanismo, delegações, AHIB.
[101] "Cambio fundamental de la política de E. Unidos ante América Latina," La Plata, September
     25, 1958; "Estados Unidos aceptó finalmente la creación de un banco interamericano para el
     fomento económico," La Mañana, September 27, 1958.
[102] Disputes between Dillon and Mann on economic policy pre-dated the Nixon attack and are
     clear in a review of economic policy that took place in March and April 1958, during which
     Mann largely got the upper hand.

Dillon's argument gained the upper hand. Dillon announced at an OAS meeting on August 12 that the United States had dropped its objections to the creation of an inter-American bank, though details remained sketchy.[103] Representing the State Department in an August 26 meeting with new Treasury Secretary Robert B. Anderson, Dillon argued that the bank "should be as flexible as possible" in granting "control to the Latin Americans."[104] As the face of this new attitude, Dillon won great respect from Latin American representatives. Lleras Camargo thanked Eisenhower for the recent changes in position, which would help Colombian development.[105] The Colombian congratulated Kubitschek for the "radical modification" of the U.S. position, calling it the "first symptoms of the improved state of American relations." Latin American countries must take advantage of the moment to gain "a realistic appreciation of our common needs and the dangers that affect our social, political, and economic stability," Lleras wrote.[106] While Brazil seemed to have won on these points, it had ceded on seemingly smaller ones, particularly bringing OPA under the OAS. Kubitschek's close ally Lleras Camargo supported moving the process to the organization he had once headed. With the rest of the news at the meeting looking so favorable, Brazilian diplomats accepted despite Kubitschek's reservations.

However, widespread changes were not assured. In a speech shortly after the conference, Rubottom said that Latin America should not expect broader changes from the United States. Brazilian diplomats saw Rubottom's statement as a "grave vitiation of the spirit of our movement," and the Brazilian press attacked the comments.[107] Inside the administration, a number of influential voices were even more critical of Brazil. When U.S. Ambassador Briggs consulted with Eisenhower, he noted the positive effects of responding promptly and at a high level to Brazilian entreaties, but cautioned "we should not under estimate the attractiveness to Brazil and other Latin American countries of Kubitschek's thesis that under-development is the root of all evil."[108] Thomas

---

[103] In the Buenos Aires Conference in 1957, the Eisenhower administration had not gone beyond accepting the study of such an institution – though there had been advocates for the bank inside the U.S. government dating to the failure to create such a bank during the Second World War. Likewise, Dillon advocated U.S. involvement in a new coffee pact as early as March 31, 1958, but had gotten limited support. *FRUS, 1958–1960*, vol. 5, microfilm supplement.

[104] "Minutes of the 269th meeting of the national advisory council on international monetary and financial problems," August 26, 1958, *FRUS, 1958–1960*, vol. 5, microfilm supplement.

[105] Lleras Camargo to Eisenhower, 1958, letter, folder 82.279, AHIB.

[106] "Alberto Lleras to Juscelino Kubitschek," Fondo Presidente de la República, Despacho Señor Presidente, September 13, 1958, trans. 6, caja 109, carpeta 30, pp. 10–12.

[107] Cyro de Freitas Valle, "Operação Pan-American. Discurso de Rubottom," October 12, 1958, tele. rec. 7960, folder 960.3, Pan-Americanismo, delegações, AHIB; see also "Advertencia de Rubottom com endereço errado: O risco é tambêm para os EE.UU.," Última Hora, October 13, 1958, folder 82.280-B, AHIB.

[108] Briggs, October 30, 1958, *FRUS, 1958–1960*, vol. 5, p. 706.

Mann wrote in January 1959 that "Brazil is attempting through Operation Pan-America to obtain the assurance of large-scale continuing financial assistance from the United States Government," which was "neither willing nor able to undertake a commitment of the sort which Brazil appears to have in mind." Mann argued that Dillon should lower expectations.[109]

The inter-American bank also had the strong support of Milton Eisenhower, based on his consultations with Latin Americans during a July 1958 trip to Central America.[110] Milton Eisenhower's report after that trip helped speed the departure from orthodox free-market policies to a greater acceptance of government involvement in Latin American economies. He recommended commodity stabilization and an expansion of credit to Central America. His initial report of August 1, 1958 did not include a recommendation on a development bank.[111] Later that month, Milton Eisenhower strongly supported the institution's creation. Several years later, Milton Eisenhower wrote that the bank's creation was "the most important recommendation [he] made in the field of credit." The president's brother emphasized that his support responded "to a request the Latin-Americans had been making for two decades."[112] Milton Eisenhower provided a more sympathetic ear for center-left Latin American leaders than did Humphrey or Dulles, picking up on Latin American suggestions and supporting moderate proposals he thought would encourage stability, democracy, and improved governance.

In addition to Mann's skepticism, there was bureaucratic opposition to the creation of a new development bank from the Export-Import Bank, the International Cooperation Administration, and parts of Treasury. Treasury Secretary Humphrey had opposed the bank for years, but he resigned in May 1957. His replacement, Robert Anderson, was more flexible and supported the president's decision on the bank. Bureaucratic resistance remained even after President Eisenhower's decision, with federal agencies and international organizations seeking to limit the bank's size and lending scope. Representatives of the International Bank for Reconstruction and Development, the Federal Reserve, and the International Cooperation Administration (ICA) all insisted on a slow planning process focused on preventing overlap with existing institutions. Months after Eisenhower had approved the project, the ICA's deputy director D.A. Fitzgerald wrote that the inter-American bank "seems to have

---

[109] Mann to Dillon, "Brazil and Operation Pan-America," January 26, 1959, *FRUS, 1958–1960*, vol. 5, pp. 708–710.

[110] "Minutes of the 269th meeting of the national advisory council on international monetary and financial problems," August 26, 1958.

[111] For documents on the planning of the trip, along with a summary, see *FRUS, 1958–1960*, vol. 5, pp. 249–266; the original report to the president is available in Milton Eisenhower, "Dr. Eisenhower reports to President on Central American trip," *Department of State Bulletin*, August 25, 1958, p. 309.

[112] Eisenhower, *The Wine Is Bitter*, pp. 229–230.

limited value."[113] Rubottom noted in a letter to Milton Eisenhower that "working level officials" at Treasury opposed moving ahead with the plans for the bank. Despite his earlier remarks, Rubottom argued that the United States needed to listen to Latin American views and "had much to gain by taking a positive approach."[114] With the State Department generally taking positions closer to Latin Americans' demands and other agencies adopting more conservative stances, implementation of the bank slowed to a crawl.

In South America, Itamaraty worked to keep OPA on its neighbors' agendas after the ministerial. In mid October, Brazil circulated an *aide-memoire* that sought to more clearly enunciate the spirit and objectives of the initiative. The memorandum noted that the "expansiveness of this fight against underdevelopment" would depend largely on the United States; therefore, it was incumbent upon Latin American leaders to persuade the U.S. government.[115] Itamaraty circulated a rough proposal for a regional economic organization with preferential tariffs and eventually a common market.[116] Through personal diplomacy, Kubitschek continually reached out to the region's presidents.[117] Despite these efforts, in the last months of 1958, the proposals from Kubitschek's letters and from September's meeting dropped from the presidential level. Kubitschek saw the foreign ministers' gathering as preparation for a meeting of heads of state, but the move to the OAS created a different path. The daily business of OPA became the concern of Latin American countries' ambassadors to the OAS and to Washington. Many Latin American countries favored this because it allowed them to use existing diplomatic resources where they had the largest staff. The ministers agreed to create a "Committee of 21," formed by the twenty Latin American countries and the United States.

Committee of 21

The Committee of 21 held several rounds of meetings, with the first session running from November 17 through December 12, 1958. It started optimistically, given the desire of major Latin American countries, except Mexico, to take advantage of the new U.S. disposition. Dillon's speech during the meetings'

---

[113] Fitzgerald, "Proposed inter-American development banking institution," December 23, 1958, *FRUS, 1958–1960*, vol. 5, microfilm supplement, ETA-15.

[114] Rubottom to Milton Eisenhower, November 19, 1958, *FRUS, 1958–1960*, vol. 5, microfilm supplement, ETA-15.

[115] "Aide-memoire," archived on October 20, 1958, draft, folder 82.279, AHIB.

[116] "Declaracao conjunta sobre preferencia regional inter-latinoamericana," Fondo MRE, Embajada de Colombia en Brasil, October, 27, 1958, trans. 8, caja 106, carpeta 104, pp. 22–24.

[117] Negrão de Lima to Raul P. Barrenechea, letter, October 22, 1958, folder 82.286, AHIB; Kubitschek to Frondizi, "Operação Pan-Americana. Apoio da Argentina," November 5, 1958, tel. exp. 10.138, folder 82.281, AHIB; Frondizi to Kubitschek, November 7, 1958, letter, folder 82.281, AHIB.

first week drew praise.[118] Brazilian delegate and early OPA advocate Augusto Frederico Schmidt seized upon positive words from Rubottom and Mann: "After the words of the U.S. representatives this morning in the private session of the Committee of 21, I do not hesitate to say that we can consider ourselves victorious in the political battle for OPA."[119] A few days later, Schmidt noted: "I heard Mann's confession that Latin America had been treated unjustly in the loans from international organizations, and that the moment had arrived to repair those injustices. I think this statement opens possibilities for all the countries to negotiate new loans. We should not miss this opportunity."[120]

Schmidt's optimism was not well founded. Though Dillon had first mentioned the policy change three months before, the administration still lacked concrete positions on the bank; Treasury insisted that Dillon should not discuss it during the meetings, which he saw as impracticable and politically unwise. Dillon favored meeting Latin American demands for loan flexibility as "absolutely necessary to meet both the urgent economic problems in Latin America and the political problem created by their increased expectations of U.S. assistance."[121] In practice, "flexibility" meant the bank would make "soft" loans repayable in local currency. Dillon's rationale was political, driven in part by the Brazilian delegation. He consistently argued for a greater initial U.S. contribution in total dollars and percentage of funds, but Treasury dithered and President Eisenhower did not weigh in on the interagency dispute.[122] The U.S. inability to enunciate a position on the bank helped exhaust the goodwill gained with the announcement in August.

Another reason for the slow progress was structural. Generally, delegations were headed below the ministerial level; few carried substantial political clout. Brazil appointed OPA's original advocate, Augusto Frederico Schmidt, to head its delegation. Schmidt was elegant and close to his president, but he made a poor diplomat, putting too much stock in public declarations while seeming oblivious to political machinations. His lack of experience showed. At one point, "Schmidt affirmed, in a threatening tone to the United States, that Brazil and other Latin American countries could intensify their relations with the

---

[118] "Discurso pronunciado por el ministro de relaciones exteriores, Doctor Julio César Turbay Ayala, en la Universidad de Medellín," November 24, 1958, *Memoria de Relaciones Exteriores, junio de 1958 a julio de 1959* (Bogotá: Imprenta Nacional, 1959), p. 16.

[119] Schmidt, "OPA. Comitê dos 21. Discursos dos representates dos Estados Unidos da America do Equador e do Mexico," November 21, 1958, tele. rec. 9159, folder 960.3, Pan-Americanismo, delegações, AHIB.

[120] Schmidt, "OPA. Comitê dos 21," November 24, 1958, tele. rec. 9186, folder 960.3, Pan-Americanismo, delegações, AHIB.

[121] Rubottom, "Inter-American development institution," November 24, 1958, *FRUS, 1958–1960*, vol. 5, microfilm supplement, ETA-11.

[122] "Minutes of the 273rd meeting of the national advisory council on international monetary and financial problems," November 25, 1958, *FRUS, 1958–1960*, vol. 5, microfilm supplement, ETA-12.

Soviet bloc if they did not receive substantial U.S. assistance in their fight against underdevelopment."[123] This forced the Brazilian foreign minister to gently repudiate his delegate's statements and reiterate Brazil's backing for the United States. The transparent tactic annoyed the U.S. delegation early in the process while crucial decisions on the size and scope of aid were still being made in the administration.

For Brazil, the *raison d'etre* of the Committee of 21 was to work out agreements that presidents could complete and sign. Schmidt noted that there had been general consensus on "questions of more or less – more capital, more technical assistance, more trade, less inflation, less underdevelopment, etc., etc." However, whenever Brazil tried to attach metrics to the goals, the consensus evaporated,[124] with Mexico at times opposing openly and the United States stalling. Given the lack of progress, Kubitschek solicited support from Colombian colleagues. Relations between Colombia and Brazil, at times strained over coffee sales, had been strengthened by an agreement on production levels. Colombian Foreign Minister Julio César Turbay Ayala spoke effusively:

President Lleras has lent decisive support to the initiative of the Brazilian President Juscelino Kubitschek, which aims to obtain from the United States sufficient cooperation to support Latin America in the crucial stage of overcoming its economic backwardness. Recognizing Brazil as the father of the healthy initiative of reframing to the United States the difficulties Latin America faces, Colombia decided to support Operation Pan-America. . . . Today, solidarity between Colombia and Brazil are stronger than ever because the two countries, under the direction of Presidents Lleras and Kubitschek, coincide in their proposals and ideals for continental prosperity.[125]

Turbay Ayala's description of OPA as "re-framing"[126] Latin American problems is an apt one. The problems were not new; many of the solutions were not new either. The value of Operation Pan-America was that it put these problems in a new framework that gave them added urgency. Argentines reiterated their support, even proposing that stronger Latin American economies like Brazil and Argentina offer "mutual aid" to Paraguay and Bolivia.[127]

As the first round came to a close, Brazilian diplomats had largely succeeded in maintaining Latin American unity, but were not able to do much to overcome U.S. indecision. On the bank in particular, the five members of the technical subcommittee (representatives of the United States, Brazil, Ecuador, Cuba,

---

[123] Negrão de Lima, "Operação Pan-Americana," telegram, November 27, 1958, folder 82.286, AHIB.

[124] Augusto Frederico Schmidt, speech in the OAS, November 25, 1958, folder 82.286, AHIB.

[125] Turbay Ayala, "Discurso pronunciado por el ministro de relaciones exteriors," November 24, 1958, *Memoria de Relaciones Exteriores, junio de 1958 a julio de 1959*, pp. 13–25.

[126] In the original Spanish, "replantear."

[127] Paulo Nogera Bautista, "Memorandum," November 28, 1958, folder 82.286, AHIB; Nogera Bautista, "Proposta argentina de criação de uma Comissão Regional de Assistência Econômica ao Paraguai e a Bolívia," November 29, 1958, folder 82.286, AHIB.

and Chile) produced a draft that restated the desire to create a bank, called on all American states to participate, and said the bank would provide technical assistance.[128] After a month of work, it did not address central questions of size, governance, or lending rules. Between rounds, Brazilians tried to advance proposals despite U.S. inaction, circulating a draft treaty for a Latin American common market and continuing coffee talks.[129]

Over the Washington winter, Brazil gained several useful allies in the U.S. Congress, where Democrats had been critical of administration policy on Latin America. After the unsatisfactory close of the first "Committee of 21" round, Senators Michael Mansfield and John F. Kennedy latched onto the Brazilian initiative as a counterweight to Eisenhower's policies. Though Brazil lacked a Congressional lobbying effort, Brazilians, including Kubitschek personally, sought to reinforce these ties with messages to supportive Congressmen.[130] Kennedy's remarks in a December 15, 1958 speech in Puerto Rico were warmly received in Brazil. Kennedy was already seen as a presidential contender and was granted extra sympathy as a Democrat – one Brazilian editorial called him "the new Roosevelt" – and a Catholic.[131] Brazilian diplomats in Washington surmised: "We can be optimistic about the possibility that the new Congress will attend to a petition from the Executive for the creation of a special fund for the planned inter-American financial institution."[132]

The Twin Shocks of 1959

By the time delegates reconvened the Committee of 21 in Buenos Aires in April, inter-American relations looked quite different. Most remarkably, earlier Eisenhower ally Fulgencio Batista had fled Havana before the triumph of Fidel Castro's revolution. The old regime's sudden collapse, and the anxiety

---

[128] "Propuesta de la comisión especial para estudiar la formulación de nuevas medidas de cooperación económica," December 8, 1958, folder Consejo de la OEA, AGNC, Presidencia, Despacho Señor Presidente, trans. 6, caja 187–188, carpeta 23, pp. 211–214.

[129] "Projeto de tratado de zona de livre comercio," December 31, 1958, memorandum, est. 14, pr. 1, no. 8, Bogotá, Telegramas, 1956–1959, AAHI-Rio, pp. 1–8; "Sanz de Santamaría to Alberto Lleras," December 15, 1958, Fondo Presidente de la República, Despacho Señor Presidente, trans. 6, caja 109, carpeta 30, pp. 30–35.

[130] Though the Draper Committee's review of Eisenhower's policy in Latin America drew Congress' attention to the region, I found no indication that the Brazilian government sought to directly influence or lobby the U.S. Congress on its behalf. Senate Foreign Relations Committee member Homer E. Capehart traveled to the region in 1959, but Congressional delegations do not appear to be a major factor. Milton Eisenhower's missions received more attention. Homer E. Capehart, news release, est. 14, pr. 1, no. 8, Bogotá, Telegramas, 1956–1959, AAHI-Rio; Schmidt, "Operação Pan-Americana," December 17, 1958, tele. rec. 9783, folder 960.3, Pan-Americanismo, delegações, AHIB; Kubitschek, "Operação Pan-Americana. Discurso do Senador John Kennedy," November 18, 1959, tel. exp. 9318, folder 82.298, AHIB.

[131] "O apoio de Kennedy, valioso para a OPA," December 18, 1958, *Diario Carioca*.

[132] Brazilian Embassy in Washington to Exteriores, "Declaraões do Senador Mansfield sobre a Operação Pan-Americana," December 22, 1958, letter, folder 82.282, AHIB.

about Castro, threw a spotlight on the administration's policies and heightened criticism from Congress. Also, in early 1959 Brazil once again neared an untenable balance-of-payments deficit. During the second half of 1958, Kubitschek had tried to divorce OPA from Brazilian appeals for assistance. The crisis forced Kubitschek to seek U.S. support for emergency relief, not just the longer-term, multilateral OPA. Kubitschek personally inquired about obtaining $300 million in new loans in late January.[133] Later that year, the CIA warned that Brazil would likely default on $2.2 billion in debt without outside assistance.[134] The two shocks created urgency for both Americans and Brazilians, but it was not clear whether the new priorities aligned.

In mid January 1959, the Eisenhower administration finally presented its position on the design for the bank, proposing an $850 million capitalization, of which about $400 million would come from the United States. Brazil had pressed for at least $2 billion from the United States, and $5 billion total. The administration's plan required Latin America's initial contributions to be considerable and mostly in dollars or gold, while limiting "soft" loans. Latin American leaders publicly criticized the proposal.[135] The administration sounded out Latin American views and got the impression that while there was some division regarding soft loans, there was a unanimous desire to increase the "callable capital" of the bank. State Department economic officer Alexander M. Rosenson reported that "the Latins seemed to have their hearts set very strongly on this matter, and refused to take 'no' for an answer." If the bank's initial capital was limited, they wanted the institution created in a way that would allow it to grow. Representatives from Argentina, Colombia, Chile, and El Salvador told Rosenson that Brazil was a "special problem in the current negotiations."[136] Several countries worried that Brazilian inflexibility could undermine the long-standing goal of setting up the bank. The issue threatened the unity of Brazil's coalition, a top Brazilian diplomat noted:

In a long conversation today, the Argentine ambassador told me that if Brazil takes an intransigent position in the matter of capital for the Bank, it will be entirely isolated, as the totality of Latin America wants the institution to be created as soon as possible with the hope that as it develops it will receive supplements of adequate capital.[137]

133 "Telegram from the Embassy in Brazil to the Department of State," February 3, 1959, *FRUS, 1958–1960*, vol. 5, pp. 711–712.

134 "The financial crisis in Brazil," National Intelligence Estimate, CIA, July 21, 1959. Available online: www.foia.cia.gov.

135 Ben F. Meyer, "Decepciona a Latino America el proyecto para el banco de fomento," *United Press International*, January 14, 1959, folder 82.283, AHIB.

136 Rosenson, "Inter-American bank," January 30, 1959; and Rosenson, "Inter-American bank issues," February 4, 1959, in *FRUS, 1958–1960*, vol. 5, microfilm supplement, ETA-17 and ETA-18.

137 Sergio Corrêa da Costa, "OPA. Instituição financeira interamericana," January 20, 1959, tele. rec. 480, folder 960.3, Pan-Americanismo, delegações, AHIB.

Kubitschek did not want OPA to end with the bank and wanted to make sure the focus remained on underdevelopment broadly. Brazil continued to press for concrete development metrics, starting with GDP per capita, with goals and timelines to show that OPA's collaborative effort was superior to Soviet economic plans. The Brazilians wanted a per-capita-income target of $470, to be achieved over a ten-year period. The U.S. team rejected the proposal. After a meeting with Mann, Rubottom, Randall, and Ambassador Briggs, Brazilian Ambassador Amaral Peixoto wrote: "They [the U.S. team] said they agreed fully with the Brazilian government's objective . . . but they disagreed not only with the practical value of fixing goals with a period of two decades to overcome underdevelopment, but also with the political advantages of comparing the economic growth with that of the principal communist countries."[138] Brazil claimed the United States was making ambitious promises, but refusing to agree to specifics.[139] Writing to Dillon, Mann denounced the Brazilian position as self-interested and out of line with the rest of Latin America.[140] At the same time, the State Department faced a transition. Illness forced John Foster Dulles to reduce his duties in early 1959, before resigning in April after six years as secretary. Dulles was replaced by Undersecretary Christian Herter.

While rhetorical support for Operation Pan-America continued, Brazil was losing allies. In part responding to pressures from the military, Frondizi adopted a more business-friendly approach. He opened Argentina's oil industry to foreign investment – drawing a sharp distinction with Brazil on a matter that had attracted U.S. attention. In a February visit to the United States, Frondizi at times seemed closer to the old Eisenhower line about reliance on private capital than to Kubitschek's state-led developmentalism.[141] Frondizi took a moderate stance, trying to take some cover in Argentina's role as host of the next round for the Committee of 21, to seek conciliation between the U.S. and Brazilian positions. In early March, the U.S. administration expanded its proposal to $1 billion in initial capital, to grow to $1.5 billion. The arrival of Fidel Castro and the Cuban delegation shook the conference. The Cubans insisted that the United States should establish a $30 billion fund dedicated to hemispheric development. Castro said: "What we need, we can only obtain from the United

---

138 Amaral Peixoto, "OPA. Posição dos Estados Unidos na cooperação financeira," January 18, 1959, tel. rec. 461, folder 960.3, Confidencial, Pan-Americanismo, Operacão Pan-Americana, delegações, AHIB.

139 João Carlos Muniz, "Operação Pan-American," February 10, 1959, tele. rec. 1061, folder 960.3, Pan-Americanismo, delegações, AHIB.

140 "Memorandum from the Assistant Secretary of State (Mann) to the Under Secretary of State (Dillon)," January 26, 1959, *FRUS, 1958–1960*, vol. 5, p. 709.

141 The Brazilian ambassador believed the "change in orientation" was driven by Argentina's own balance-of-payments crisis. Ernani do Amaral Peixoto to Negrão de Lima, "Visita do presidente Frondizi aos Estados Unidos da América," January 27, 1959, letter, folder 82.283, AHIB.

States." Brazil's chief, Schmidt, showered Castro with praise.[142] Uncertainty about the new Cuban regime, and the addition of a boisterous voice calling for even greater amounts of aid compounded the administration's desire to demonstrate concern for Latin America. Many Latin American delegations wanted the bank to begin operations as soon as possible, so when Brazil threatened to delay talks to pressure the Eisenhower administration, it was increasingly isolated. Shortly before the conference, Argentina's foreign ministry termed the Brazilian position "unrealistic" and largely accepted the U.S. proposal for the bank.[143] The Eisenhower administration wanted an initialed text by late March or early April, hoping for a Congressional appropriation for the next fiscal year. The prospect of a faster start to bank-funded projects outweighed specific concessions for many governments. With OPA's momentum fading, Brazil retreated. All twenty-one OAS members signed the bank's Articles of Agreement on April 8.[144] Remaining differences, including the location of headquarters, were sorted out over the course of May, and all OAS members passed the statutes passed on May 27.[145]

After agreement was reached on the bank, Mann pressed Brazilian delegates to close the Committee of 21, but from a Brazilian point of view, the real goals of OPA had scarcely been addressed.[146] Kubitschek knew that members of the Eisenhower administration believed OPA was about little more than Brazil's own economic problems. In late March, he had told the U.S. ambassador that "over and above these considerations . . . is Operation Pan-America and demand of underdeveloped people for better life. Our Communist enemies are eagerly waiting for the moment to get into the act."[147] When Mann stopped in Rio on May 11, Kubitschek tried to dispel "any impression Mann might have that Brazilians' OPA policy was intended [to] isolate US" or to address Brazil's own, short-term fiscal problem. The Eisenhower administration pressed

---

[142] "Castro asks for 30 billion in U.S. aid for Latins," *Washington Post*, May 3, 1959, p. A6.

[143] Bolitreau Fragoso, "OPA. Instituição financiera interamericana," March 7, 1959, tele. exp. 1692; and Luiz de Almeda, "Posição argentina no reunião dos 21 em Buenos Aires," March 24, 1959, tele. exp. 2522, folder 960.3, Confidenciais asuntos gerais, AHIB.

[144] "Editorial note," *FRUS, 1958–1960*, vol. 5, microfilm supplement, ETA-24.

[145] Venezuela strongly pushed to locate the institution in Caracas. The Eisenhower administration insisted only a Washington-based bank would win Congressional approval. Brazil, though sympathetic to Betancourt's wishes, did not fight much on his behalf after being at odds with Venezuela on other aspects of the bank. Exteriores to Brazilian Embassy in Caracas, "Instituicão financeira Interamericana," May 6, 1959, tel. rec. 5910, folder 960.3, Confidencial, Pan-Americanismo, Operacão Pan-Americana, delegações, AHIB; Herter to Eisenhower, "Suggested reply to President Betancourt," April 8, 1959, *FRUS, 1958–1960*, vol. 5, microfilm supplement, ETA-23.

[146] Christian Herter, "Circular telegram to posts in American republics," March 7, 1959, *FRUS, 1958–1960*, vol. 5, microfilm supplement, ETA-21; Sergio Correa da Costa, "Operação Pan-American. Continuadade do Comitê dos 21," April 13, 1959, confidential letter, folder 960.3 Pan-Americanismo-Delegações, AHIB.

[147] Briggs, "Telegram from the Embassy in Brazil to the Department of State," March 27, 1959, *FRUS, 1958–1960*, vol. 5, pp. 715–716.

Brazil to take austerity measures, some of which could increase the price of basic goods. Kubitschek warned Mann that overdoing austerity would lead to protests and "do irreparable harm to U.S.–Brazil relations" during the coming 1960 presidential election.[148]

Brazilians were concerned that without the Committee of 21, OPA would dissipate. They again called for a permanent organism for OPA.[149] After the conclusion of the second meeting, Itamaraty instructed its delegation at the OAS to make sure countries followed through on the ratification and implementation of thirty-five resolutions that had been passed during the Committee of 21 meetings. The Brazilians wanted a "support group" formed within the OAS to work on the subjects of the resolutions and craft more specific projects. They pressed a new "special fund" for the "broader implementation of Operation Pan-America."[150]

Despite what Kubitschek had told Mann, Brazil's immediate problems overwhelmed the president's focus on OPA. Kubitschek reiterated that he could not implement the IMF's reforms plans without provoking riots. On the evening of June 8, Kubitschek told the U.S. chargé in Brazil Woodie Wallner that Washington needed to understand that in the minds of Brazilians, there was no difference between the IMF and the U.S. government, and that the United States would be blamed for the IMF's refusal to extend new credit. Brazil needed a $300 million loan, so Kubitschek would have to implement the reforms, the U.S. chargé wrote, adding: "Obviously he [Kubitschek] would not wish to make a public break with the fund and the U.S."[151] Speaking at a political rally the next day, Kubitschek announced that he was doing just that – halting negotiations with the IMF because the organization's demands would impede Brazilian development. Kubitschek's appeal to sovereignty garnered the desired response, and the president enjoyed a burst of nationalist support. He also warned – having first reassured the military – that ties with the Soviets would be explored to finance Brazilian development.[152]

Kubitschek feared domestic upheaval and challenges to the precarious democratic system. Furthermore, the IMF demands impinged on how Kubitschek saw sovereignty and autonomy in the Brazilian context. To meet the conditions, Brazil would have needed to scale back or cancel sprawling development projects, including the construction of Brasilia. Biographer Robert J. Alexander wrote:

---

[148] Woodie Wallner, "Telegram from the Embassy in Brazil to the Department of State," May 11, 1959, *FRUS, 1958–1960*, vol. 5, pp. 721–722.

[149] Sérgio Corrêa da Costa, "Operação Pan-American. Continuadade do Comitê dos 21," April 13, 1959, confidential letter, folder 960.3 Pan-Americanismo-Delegações, AHIB.

[150] Sérgio Corrêa da Costa, "Operação Pan-Americana. Programa de ação para a OEA," May 25, 1959, memorandum, folder 82.298, AHIB.

[151] Wallner, "Telegram from the Embassy in Brazil to the Department of State," June 9, 1959, *FRUS, 1958–1960*, vol. 5, pp. 723–725.

[152] "Virada na política econômica," June 10, 1959, *Jornal do Brasil*, p. 1.

President Kubitschek gave clear indication that he did not believe that because the Latin American countries needed outside financial and technical assistance to help their economic development that these countries, and Brazil in particular, should allow the donor institutions to determine national development policy. That was the nub of the issue between the Kubitschek administration and the [IMF] in 1959–1960.[153]

The decision surprised the embassy and the administration, which quickly backtracked and agreed to discuss rescheduling Brazil's debt, though it still did not offer new money.[154] A U.S. intelligence estimate noted that Kubitschek was betting that U.S. interests in Brazil would push the administration to accommodation; in the short term, the Brazilian president let the United States take the blame for economic problems.[155]

In mid 1959, Kubitschek had a second opportunity to grab Eisenhower's attention. Relations between the United States and the new Cuban government were increasingly tense. At the same time, a crisis was brewing between Dominican autocrat Rafael Trujillo, Castro, and democratic leaders, especially Rómulo Betancourt of Venezuela. Castro and Trujillo exemplified two threatening ends of the spectrum, revolution from the left and repression from the right.[156] The growing crisis allowed Frondizi and Kubitschek to unite around democracy after their relation had cooled during the Buenos Aires meeting. The two governments consulted in the run up to the mid August ministerial consultation in Chile, trying to figure out how to strengthen democratic governments and isolate both Castro and Trujillo. The Argentines hesitated to back another push for aid, opposing putting development questions on the agenda to avoid "interminable debates that lead to nothing in practice."[157] The Caribbean crisis dominated the Santiago meeting, and the final declarations gave only the slightest nod to economic matters while emphasizing democracy, human rights, and principles of nonintervention.[158] Concerns were growing about Castro's sympathies, but Brazil was not immediately able to capitalize on them to generate the unity it did after the Nixon fracas.

Whereas 1958 had ended with hope, 1959 was a frustrating year for Brazilian aspirations as Kubitschek could not build on his initial accomplishments.

---

[153] Alexander, *Juscelino Kubitschek and the Development of Brazil*, pp. 296–297.

[154] Wallner, "Telegram from the embassy in Brazil to the Department of State," June 13, 1959, *FRUS, 1958–1960*, vol. 5, pp. 727–729.

[155] "Special National Intelligence estimate: The financial crisis in Brazil," July 21, 1959, *FRUS, 1958–1960*, vol. 5, pp. 733–739.

[156] Regarding the growing tension between the United States and both Caribbean leaders, see Rabe, *Eisenhower and Latin America*, Chapter 9.

[157] Boulitreau Fragoso, "V reunião de consulta," August 6, 1959, tel. rec. 5891, est. 14, pr. 2, no. 9, Buenos Aires, telegramas recibidas 1959, AAHI-Rio.

[158] OAS, "Quinta reunión de consulta de ministros de relaciones exteriores: Acta final," August 12–18, 1959, Santiago, Chile. Available online: www.oas.org/consejo/sp/rc/Actas/Acta%205 .pdf.

Brazilian goals remained largely unchanged and centered on the use of Pan-Americanism to secure external assistance for Latin America, which Kubitschek believed would help preserve democracy and strengthen the West. However, Brazilian attention was consumed, particularly since June, by Brazil's balance-of-payments crisis and the inability to come to agreement with the IMF. It was difficult for Brazil to advance a comprehensive, long-range plan for the economic development of the continent with its own economy on a precipice. Diplomatically, Brazilians struggled to preserve Latin American unity, persuade the United States, or take advantage of the opportunity presented by the Caribbean crisis. Over the course of the year, Douglas Dillon's position lost ground to that of Thomas Mann, who argued the easier case of continuing current policies and limiting fiscal demands. During this period, the administration essentially delayed major action. In December, the recently appointed U.S. Ambassador to Brazil John Moors Cabot[159] reflected on his first months and found U.S. policy lacking. The United States exaggerated Brazilian fecklessness and underestimated Kubitschek's achievements, Cabot argued. U.S. policy failed to adequately recognize Brazil's importance, and was not helping meet longer-term U.S. interests. Cabot reported:

The cold shoulder we have given the Brazilians in their economic plight has had its inevitable repercussions on the political orientation of the Brazilian Government. One symptom of this is the trade mission which is now in Soviet Russia. . . . I think we must anticipate a rough going over at the Quito Conference with the Brazilians, who have so often in inter-American conferences acted as moderators, now taking the leadership in turning the heat on us . . .

They yearn to be considered a great power, and they feel we have treated them on a par with Honduras. Even 25 years ago we consulted with them first on practically all inter-American and on many world problems – are they less important to us now?

Cabot went on to assess how the U.S. attitude had changed, saying the United States was "refer[ing] blandly" to the Inter-American Development Bank whenever OPA was mentioned. At the same time, the administration was willing to "foot the budget deficits" for non–Latin American nations. It should not be surprised at a lack of gratitude for U.S. loans that charged near-market interest rates with the Export-Import Bank acting like "lush banking operation" instead of an "instrument of national policy."[160]

<hr>

[159] For a fascinating, critical look at Cabot's role, see Stephen M. Streeter, "Campaigning against Latin American Nationalism: U.S. Ambassador John Moors Cabot in Brazil, 1959–1961," *The Americas* 51, no. 2 (1994).

[160] "Letter from the Ambassador in Brazil (Cabot) to the Assistant Secretary of State for Inter-American Affairs (Rubottom)," December 4, 1959, *FRUS, 1958–1960*, vol. 5, pp. 744–745.

New Year, New Fears

In early 1960, the Eisenhower administration again increased its attention to Latin America, especially Brazil. On December 30, 1959, Dillon mentioned the possibility of an Eisenhower visit to Brasilia to recognize the new capital. Eisenhower's tour had much to do with Cuba, as the administration and Castro engaged in escalating rounds of tit-for-tat. After Castro made public accusations against the U.S. ambassador in Havana Philip Bonsal, Bonsal was recalled to Washington. Brazil sensed an opportunity, not just for OPA but to expand its sugar exports at Cuba's expense.[161] Mexico's President López Mateos made a state visit to Brazil in January, intimating that he would lower Mexican opposition to OPA.[162] While Mexican leadership was publicly supportive of Castro, in private, it was very concerned and eager to advance moderate approaches, which seemed to contribute to its new attitude.[163] At the same time, Brazil's economic picture was a bit rosier: higher-than-expected coffee prices in the second half of 1959 had improved the balance of payments, and the IMF offered a smaller line of credit.

Kubitschek believed that Eisenhower would be much more sympathetic to the aims of Operation Pan-America if he had more direct knowledge of Latin America. When the U.S. president announced in early 1960 that he would visit South America, staying in Brazil from February 23–26, Kubitschek hoped to showcase what Brazil had accomplished.[164] Brazilian objectives during the visit were both political and economic. On the economic front Brazil called for a common pledge in the joint declaration to "eradicate underdevelopment" through international cooperation.[165] In world politics, the Brazilian president and ministers pressed for greater consultation in international affairs. Itamaraty pursued "methods to improve the political contacts between Washington and the other capitals of the continent." Excluding Latin America from

---

[161] This happened in July 1960. By that time, Brazilians had been trying to quietly position themselves for six months. Moreira Salles, "Situação política mundial. Relações Estados Unidos-Cuba," January 26, 1960, tele. rec. 727, vol. Washington, Telegramas Rec-Exp., 1960, AHIB.

[162] Sanz de Santamaría to Ministerio de Relaciones Exteriores, "Visita del Presidente López Mateos," Embajada de Colombia en Brasil, AGNC, January 26, 1960, trans. 8, caja 107, carpeta 115, ff. 60; Jorge Oliviera Maia, "Operação Pan-Americana. Reunião dos 21," February 17, 1960, tele. rec. 1605, folder 960.3, Confidencial, Pan-Americanismo, Operacão Pan-Americana, delegações, AHIB.

[163] Renata Keller, "A Foreign Policy for Domestic Consumption: Mexico's Lukewarm Defense of Castro, 1959–1969," *Latin American Research Review* 47, no. 2 (2012).

[164] Dillon first mentioned the visit to Brazilian Ambassador Moreira Salles on December 30, 1959.

[165] Exteriores to Brazilian Embassy in Washington, "Visita do Presidente Eisenhower ao Brasil," February 15, 1960, tele. exp. 1272, vol. Washington, Telegramas Rec-Exp., 1960, AHIB. The final declaration adopted many of these points in slightly softer language: "Joint statement of the President and President Kubitschek of Brazil," February 23, 1960, The American Presidency Project. Available online: www.presidency.ucsb.edu/ws/?pid=12105.

consultations could open a new divide in world affairs, Itamaraty argued: "The Brazilian government wants to call to the U.S. government's attention the danger that a worldwide North–South antagonism could occur, just as acute as the West–East antagonism that divides the world along the so-called Iron Curtain."[166] Foreign Minister Horácio Lafer and Schmidt made similar points to Secretary Herter, who noted that "[Schmidt] told me that a greater awareness of Brazil and a better understanding of her desire to be considered a great power entitled to consultation on world problems was of paramount importance and that economic problems would take care of themselves."[167]

Meanwhile, Kubitschek showed Eisenhower around the construction of Brasilia. The American seemed genuinely impressed at how much had been built in two years. Kubitschek hoped the new city's grandiosity would counter assumptions that Brazilian spending had disappeared into a pit of waste and corruption. During their conversations, the Brazilian president felt Eisenhower was "not sufficiently informed" about OPA, and that Eisenhower's general support had not been translated into action by the State Department. In the short term, the visit helped, as the Brazilian government restarted more favorable talks with the IMF, despite not having met earlier conditions. Kubitschek hoped the visit would pay dividends for OPA during the next Committee of 21 meetings.[168]

Eisenhower's visit to Brazil was followed on April 4, 1960 by Alberto Lleras Camargo's trip to Washington. The Colombian president pressed the goals of OPA with renewed vigor, to the delight of the Brazilians. With Kubitschek's term coming to an end, Lleras Camargo was taking the mantle. The Colombian president had extensive meetings with Eisenhower and Herter, met with the financial leaders in Washington and New York, and gave well-publicized addresses before the U.S. Congress,[169] at the OAS, before the National Press Club, and alongside Milton Eisenhower, president of Johns Hopkins University.[170] During the visit, Lleras Camargo obtained economic assistance, including for land reform, which he discussed with President Eisenhower. Cuba cast a shadow over the visit, but Lleras Camargo used it to his

---

[166] Brazilian foreign ministry to Brazilian cabinet, "Aide-memoire," February 23, 1960, folder 82.287-B, AHIB.

[167] Christian Herter, "Memorandum of a conversation between Secretary of State Herter and President Kubitschek's adviser (Schmidt)," February 25, 1960, *FRUS, 1958–1960*, vol. 5, pp. 766–768.

[168] Kubitschek, *Meu Caminho para Brasília: Cinqüenta Anos em Cinco*, pp. 327–329. Rubottom, "The Brazilian foreign minister's call on the President," *FRUS, 1958–1960*, vol. 5, pp. 769–770.

[169] I could find no record or press mention of official meetings between Lleras and Congressional leaders during which he might have pressed the case for OPA. However, Lleras did meet with Congressional leaders, including Senator William Fulbright, during official dinners.

[170] The *New York Times* printed eighteen articles about Lleras' ten-day trip, including several on the front page.

benefit.[171] On April 6, Lleras Camargo addressed the U.S. Congress, where he made both political and economic arguments for supporting Latin American democracy and development. Mentioning Operation Pan-America, the Colombian argued the massive loans would be repaid, but that the U.S. interest in the proposal was "fundamentally, a political act that cannot be judged by banking standards." After describing the desperate conditions of many Latin Americans, he asked Congress "to help these people exit from the final stage of underdevelopment, before their backwardness is converted into . . . an historic disaster."[172] *O Estado de São Paulo* editorialized that "it would have been difficult for Latin America to find at this moment a better spokesman before the North American government and people than the Colombian President Alberto Lleras Camargo."[173]

Lleras Camargo was even more dramatic at Johns Hopkins, where his views coincided with those of Milton Eisenhower. Helping Latin America would be like the Marshall Plan, Lleras Camargo insisted, but easier and most likely profitable. "It would consist of giving them [Latin Americans] a push out of a transitory impasse that if prolonged could shift its destiny toward anarchy and chaos." While Colombia had once accepted that it should trade primary goods for manufactures, views had shifted, the president argued. Several decades earlier, Latin Americans decided to use tariff protection to industrialize and increase living standards. Lleras Camargo told the audience at the university: "The movement against underdevelopment became the revolutionary force most accepted by the greater part of humanity. . . . In Latin America, rarely has there been a feeling so unanimous, so strong, so universally shared." The expanding population was growing impatient with the slow rate of progress, and "each of its acts of desperation will more greatly resemble communism."[174]

During the preparations for a meeting of the special committee on economic cooperation at Bogotá in September, Brazilians felt they had regained their footing. Lleras Camargo's visit demonstrated that they could get a little help. Kubitschek and Eisenhower renewed their correspondence. Eisenhower offered kind words about the visit and said the new capital had greatly impressed

[171] See "Proposed program for assistance to Colombia's agrarian reform program," March 25, 1960; "Secretary's call on President Lleras Camargo of Colombia," April 6, 1960; "Call on the President by President Lleras Camargo," April 6, 1960, in *FRUS, 1958–1960*, vol. 5, microfilm supplement, docs. CO-25, CO-27, CO-29.

[172] Lleras Camargo, "Discurso del Presidente de Colombia ante el Congreso de los Estados Unidos," April 6, 1960, carpeta 37, documento 547, BLAA. Also see, "Colombian urges rise in aid," *New York Times*, April 7, 1960, p. 1.

[173] A Spanish-language translation of the article was included in a cable from the Colombian consulate in Sao Paulo to the Colombian Ministry of Foreign Affairs. "Visita Pdte. Lleras a EE.UU.," AGN, Bogotá, fondo Ministro Relaciones Exteriores, organismos internacionales, transferencia 3, caja 1, carpeta 288, folios 49–51.

[174] Lleras Camargo, "Discurso Pronunciado por el Presidente de Colombia en la Universidad de Johns Hopkins, Baltimore," April 8, 1960, carpeta 38, documento 549. BLAA. Translation by author.

him. Most intriguingly, Eisenhower hinted at a policy change that could fulfill Kubitschek's aspirations:

I have now concluded that, notwithstanding our past efforts, we all need to exert additional strength in our common program to meet the challenge of this new decade during which our peoples are determined to progress to a new high plane of dynamic living, socially, economically, politically, and spiritually. I wanted you to know that I will be announcing within the next few days something of the plans of the United States toward participating more effectively toward our hemisphere objectives. I hope to request authority of the Congress which will be coming back into session early next month to move ahead with this program.[175]

Eisenhower's spokesman told the *Washington Post* that the plan had been in preparation for months.[176] Rumors circulated among Latin American delegations at the OAS about a forthcoming "Eisenhower Plan" for Latin America. It was clear that the impetus was to isolate Cuba, with the U.S. intimation coming alongside the suspension of Cuba's sugar quota. Brazil's Ambassador to the OAS Fernando Lobo noted that the moment for OPA seemed to have arrived:

The news that the United States is preparing an economic assistance plan for Latin America, in the mould of the Marshall Plan, is having a great impact amongst the representatives to the OAS. It will be presented at the meeting of 21 in Bogotá with the goal of countering the offensive of Soviet economic propaganda in the continent. In that regard, it appears Cuba will be excluded. Congratulations to your Excellency for the news, which will represent the crowning achievement of OPA. The text of the plan still has not been revealed.[177]

The enthusiasm was short lived. Just a day after Lobo had sent congratulations to the president, details leaked to the delegates and to the *Washington Post*. The president gave a press conference from his vacation in Newport, R.I., citing Kubitschek's "joint hemispheric concept known as Operation Pan-America," and speaking about stability, democracy, and development in language reminiscent of the Brazilian's. Answering questions from reporters, however, it became clear the "Eisenhower Plan" would be no Marshall Plan and that private investment was still considered primary.[178] As the outlines of the plan became clearer, Brazilians were angered that Eisenhower talked of Operation Pan-America, but in their opinion disregarded its core principles and concrete proposals. Lobo cabled back his disappointment.[179] The Brazilian chargé in Washington argued

175 Eisenhower to Kubitschek, July 9, 1960, letter, *FRUS, 1958–1960*, vol. 5, pp. 777–778.
176 "Ike, Herter to discuss Cuba crisis, aid plan," *Washington Post*, July 8, 1960, p. A1.
177 Fernando Lobo, "OPA. Reunião dos 21, Bogotá," July 11, 1960, tele. rec. 5991, folder 960.3, Pan-Americanismo, delegações, AHIB.
178 The statement and conversation with reporters was printed in "Ike's Latin America statement," *Washington Post*, July 12, 1960, p. A7.
179 Fernando Lobo to Horacio Lafer, "Questão Estados Unidos da América–Cuba," July 12, 1960, memorandum, folder 82.287-B, AHIB.

the plan was a short-term response to tensions in the Caribbean and a crass attempt to buy support: "[B]oth the local press and diplomatic channels see the American initiative as an attempt to favorably influence the attitude of Latin Americans at the moment that they could be key in the UN and the OAS for the approval of recommendations about the situation in the Caribbean."[180] While withholding judgment until seeing the final plan, Kubitschek said he did not consider "palliative measures" to be sufficient.[181] When word spread that the planned fund was for $500 million,[182] Brazil wanted to dissociate the plan from OPA. Though historian Stephen Rabe considers the July announcement "a turning point in inter-American relations,"[183] Brazilian leaders at the time did not agree.

On July 19, Kubitschek penned a reply to Eisenhower. The Brazilian's frustration came through under a surface of diplomatic niceties. The letter stated that Brazil was not satisfied having achieved the IDB and did not want OPA be substituted with a small U.S. aid program.

Permit me to reaffirm to Your Excellency what already has been said concerning Operation Pan America: It is not a question of an appeal to generosity, but of reason.... The fight which all of us must undertake together for the common ideals of the Americas will be valid only if we combat the causes of unrest and discontent, without seeking merely to correct and diminish their effects and consequences. We ought, therefore, to have the courage to draw the conclusions which reality presents to us. The truth is that, despite all previous efforts, not enough has been done and an adequate rate of development for the Latin American peoples has not been achieved. To wish to attribute the present unrest of these peoples to mere propaganda or agitation by extra-continental agents would be to ignore the fact that poverty and frustration of economically stagnant peoples have a much greater capability for agitation. The problem therefore consists in giving a new dimension to the work to be accomplished...

What appears to me to have been missing thus far, if Your Excellency will permit me to say it, is a truly constructive policy and the attribution of greater importance to this part of America.... To relegate to an inferior level almost 200 million men, whose rate of growth is the highest in all the world and whose integration in defense of the democracies is the surest road and inclination, is to commit an error.

The offer of a new policy of strengthening the American regional family is what I have understood Your Excellency to be announcing in your noble letter.... Your Excellency has resolved to sponsor a new, fecund and vigorous action, creative of wealth. As I have

---

[180] Bernardes, "Programa de assistência econômica à América Latina. Declarações do Presidente Eisenhower," July 12, 1960, tele. rec. 6119, vol. Washington, Telegramas Rec-Exp., 1960, AHIB.

[181] "JK responde a Ike: 'Meros palliatives não resolvem problemas do continente," July 13, 1960, *Última Hora*, Rio de Janeiro, p. 6; "Kubitschek hits Ike's Latin plan," *Washington Post*, July 14, 1960, p. A1.

[182] Murrey Marder, "Latin American aid program faces 'hard vs. soft' contest," *Washington Post*, July 16, 1960, p. A2.

[183] Rabe, *Eisenhower and Latin America*, p. 142.

already had occasion to state, it is not a plan of donations that I believe appropriate or even possible at this moment, but concrete and unpostponable measures of reciprocal interest to the country of Your Excellency and the other American nations and a more active collaboration in our development, through a new policy of public financing, in which would be observed other criteria than that of mere immediate economic profitability.[184]

Kubitschek closed by noting that great expectations produced by Eisenhower's visit had led to disappointing results. In a second message, relayed in a conversation between the Brazilian ambassador and Secretary Herter on July 28, Kubitschek asked Eisenhower to adjust his proposal so that it fit within the lines of OPA. Under the Eisenhower Plan, the United States would make direct, bilateral loans, eschewing the Pan-American multilateralism of OPA and erasing Brazilian leadership. Herter insisted the plan fit within OPA, though he also tried to decouple communism from development assistance.[185] The Eisenhower administration wanted Brazilian backing for anticommunist and anti-Castro declarations, but was wary about having Kubitschek connect those with his aid requests.[186] Mann criticized Schmidt for trying to take advantage of the darkening U.S.–Cuba relations to press Brazilian priorities, which included "massive" assistance under OPA, making the proposed fund multilateral, new PL-480 grants, and balance-of-payments help, if needed later. "Schmidt reportedly believes that Castro in Cuba and a little communism in Brazil are desirable from the standpoint of Brazil's bargaining with the U.S.," Mann wrote the secretary.[187] At the end of the month, Mann replaced Rubottom as Assistant Secretary of State for Inter-American Affairs, placing him at the center of U.S.–Brazilian relations.[188]

Brazil's delegation considered opposing what they saw as a stingy fund in Bogotá. The Brazilians made their disaffection known before the meeting, referring to the proposal as an emergency plan that failed to address longer-term issues.[189] When a draft of the U.S. proposal circulated in late August 1960, the Brazilians intensified their criticisms. "It is oriented to the symptoms of under-development instead of attacking the causes," the Brazilian foreign ministry

[184] Kubitschek to Eisenhower, July 19, 1960, letter, *FRUS, 1958–1960*, vol. 5, pp. 778–779; "Latin plan too timid, Kubitschek tells Ike," *Washington Post*, July 24, 1960, p. A7.

[185] Walther Moreira Salles, "OPA. Plano Eisenhower," July 28, 1960, tele. rec. 6828, vol. Washington, Telegramas Rec-Exp., 1960, AHIB; Alvaro Texeira Soares, "OPA. Plano de ajuda de Eisenhower," July 28, 1960, tel. rec. 8056, folder 82.287-B, AHIB.

[186] Horacio Lafer, "VI reunião de consulta. Posição do Brasil," August 13, 1960, tele. rec. 7515, vol. Washington, Telegramas Rec-Exp., 1960, AHIB.

[187] "Memorandum from the Assistant Secretary of State for Inter-American Affairs (Rubottom) to the Secretary of State," August 11, 1960, *FRUS, 1958–1960*, vol. 5, pp. 782–784.

[188] Mann was already an assistant secretary, but for economic affairs.

[189] Exteriores to Brazilian Embassy in Washington, "III Reunião do Comité dos 21," August 20, 1960, tele. exp. 7643, vol. Washington, Telegramas Rec-Exp., 1960, AHIB.

complained.[190] A Brazilian delegate, who would later serve as ambassador in Washington, said, "[T]here was a lot of dissatisfaction in Brazil with the rather cool reception given by Washington, under the Republican administration, to Operation Pan America. Brazil considered bringing things to a head and revealing an open split at Bogotá."[191] Instead Brazil decided to cooperate, hoping to take advantage of the warmer tone initiated in Eisenhower's visit and the dramatic Cuban situation to press for greater policy changes – even if they had to wait for a new U.S. administration. The decision to hold back and continue a cooperative approach owed more to communications between Colombia and Brazil, and the desire to maintain that cooperative relationship, than to U.S. pressure. Under Lleras Camargo's counsel, Kubitschek and Schmidt decided the Eisenhower Plan should be separated from OPA, rather than rejected entirely.[192] In Itamaraty's instructions to the Brazilian delegates, the ministry noted that because of the approaching election, Republicans could not "admit the failings of their Latin America policies." A Democratic administration might be more favorable to Brazilian initiatives. Until then, Brazilian delegates should thank the U.S. administration for its new initiative and its long-standing friendship before proceeding to attack the Eisenhower Plan for its divergences from OPA.[193]

The meetings in Bogotá, officially held under the nearly moribund Committee of 21, ran from September 5–11, 1960.[194] Undersecretary Dillon led the U.S. delegation and sought to ameliorate Brazilian frustrations. The economic conference was permeated by U.S.–Cuban hostility. The administration was sensitive to Latin American criticism, which Democrats echoed in campaign attacks. In the October 21, 1960, presidential debate, Kennedy attacked Nixon on both Castro and economic assistance: "You yourself said, Mr. Vice President, a month ago, that if we had provided the kind of economic aid five years ago that we are now providing we might never have had Castro. Why didn't we?"[195] Though Eisenhower did not budge on the central issues, Dillon and Mann made smaller changes to please Brazil. After the conference's

[190] Exteriores to Brazilian Embassy in Washington, "Projecto de resolução. Programa interamericana," August 30, 1960, tele. exp. 7980, vol. Washington, Telegramas Rec-Exp., 1960, AHIB.

[191] Roberto de Oliveira Campos, recorded interview by John E. Reilly, May 29–30, 1964, John F. Kennedy Library Oral History Program, p. 6.

[192] This came through in a meeting between Schmidt and Lleras Camargo before the Bogotá meetings began. Schmidt, "OPA. Comitê dos Vinte-Um. Audiência com o Presidente Lleras Camargo," September 4, 1960, tel. rec. 8218, folder 82.287-B, AHIB. See also, Kubitschek's letter to Lleras. Kubitschek to Lleras Camargo, September 1, 1960, BLAA, Colección Alberto Lleras Camargo, caja X, carpeta 65, mss. 821–876/1–4.

[193] Fernando Ramos, "Instruções para a delegação brasileira à III sessão da comissão," August 31, 1960, tele. rec. 8249, folder 960.3, Pan-Americanismo, delegações, AHIB.

[194] For a brief account, see Rabe, *Eisenhower and Latin America*, pp. 141–145.

[195] John F. Kennedy, qtd. in "Presidential debate in New York," October 21, 1960, The American Presidency Project. Available online: www.presidency.ucsb.edu/ws/?pid=29403.

opening session, Schmidt and a host of Brazilian diplomats met the U.S. team, including Dillon and Mann. Schmidt argued that the Eisenhower Plan appeared to "substitute" Brazilian development proposals. Schmidt wrote: "Douglas Dillon clarified his thinking, affirming that the Eisenhower Plan was just an additional initiative in the effort for economic development in Latin America." Dillon agreed past U.S. economic aid to Latin America had been insufficient. He hoped Brazilian delegates would work with the U.S. team to integrate OPA into Eisenhower's proposal.[196]

During an extended meeting with Schmidt and Argentine delegates, Dillon incorporated references to OPA into the Eisenhower Plan, which was renamed the Social Progress Trust Fund.[197] Schmidt wrote Kubitschek: "It was a great Brazilian victory to get the Americans to recognize that up to now their aid to Latin America has been insufficient."[198] The final declaration of the Act of Bogotá stressed Kubitschek's and Lleras Camargo's priorities: democratic institutions, cooperation for economic development and social progress, support for land reform, and more. All of this was to happen "within the framework of Operation Pan America."[199] What superficially appeared a Brazilian victory did not in practice fulfill Brazilian goals. The Social Progress Trust Fund would be U.S.-controlled, not multilateral, and there was no clear path forward for OPA. Closing the meeting, the Cuban delegation "violently" attacked the United States and the "merely palliative" nature of its aid to Latin America.[200] Though Schmidt downplayed that criticism, it echoed the very words Kubitschek had used to describe Eisenhower's original proposal.

The Act of Bogotá and the inauguration of the Inter-American Development Bank in December were Pan-American swan songs for Kubitschek and Eisenhower. However, they were not quite the tunes either wanted to sing. A few weeks later, on October 3, Jânio Quadros was elected the next president of Brazil, besting Kubitschek's designated candidate and casting uncertainty on whether Brazil would continue to lead OPA, which Kubitschek believed was far from complete. Quadros evinced little interest in OPA and far less desire than Kubitschek or previous Brazilian presidents to center his foreign policy around

---

[196] Frederico Schmidt, "OPA. Comitê dos 21 Bogotá," September 5, 1960, tele. rec. 8249, folder 960.3, Pan-Americanismo, delegações, AHIB.

[197] Schmidt, "OPA. Comitê dos 21 Bogotá. Plano de desenvolvimento econômico," September 7, 1960, tel. rec. 8312, folder 82.287-A, AHIB.

[198] Schmidt, "OPA. Comitê dos 21 em Bogotá Comissão de Financiamento." September 10, 1960, tel. rec. 8452, folder 82.287-A, AHIB. For the Brazilian account of the conference, see Schmidt, "OPA. Comitê dos 21. Inauguração da Conferência em Bogotá," September 6, 1960, tel. rec. 8311, folder 82.287-A; Schmidt, "OPA. Comitê dos 21 Bogotá. Discuros dos delegados do Paragui, Bolivia, Venezuela, Argentina e Peru," September 8, 1960, tel. rec. 8322, folder AHIB.

[199] "Act of Bogota," September 13, 1960, The Avalon Project (Yale Law School). Available online: http://avalon.law.yale.edu/20th_century/intam08.asp.

[200] Schmidt, "OPA. Ata de Bogotá. Ataque do delegado cubana," February 13, 1960, tel. rec. 8576, folder 82.288, AHIB.

an "unwritten alliance" with the United States.[201] From the Brazilian perspective, the United States was not keeping its end of the bargain. One month later, Nixon's loss to Kennedy set the stage for a transition in U.S. policy. During the dual transitions, Quadros brushed aside attempts from both Itamaraty and the State Department for coordination, even backing out on a meeting with President-elect Kennedy.[202] For Eisenhower, Bogotá was the last major hemispheric gathering before the U.S. election, in which Latin America had become a major issue. Eisenhower pushed for quick Congressional ratification of his Social Progress Trust Fund, which received a $500 million appropriation with strong Democratic support on September 8, 1960. It was a sweeter note compared with much of hemispheric relations during Eisenhower's tenure, but it did not rise above the cacophony of Kennedy's attacks over Cuba.

Kennedy's election set the stage for a dramatic departure in U.S.–Latin American economic relations. The climate for U.S.–Brazilian cooperation was less auspicious. The dispute with the IMF and U.S. officials over Brazil's balance of payments had eroded much goodwill. Though his fiscal policies were more conservative than Kubitschek's, Quadros stressed his intention to forge an independent foreign policy and disturbed U.S. officials with favorable public assessments of Fidel Castro. Weis writes: "By the time Kennedy and Jânio Quadros assumed office, mistrust permeated high levels of both governments." Quadros reestablished relations with the Soviet Union in 1961. Though Kennedy's Alliance for Progress cited OPA as inspiration, Quadros did not burnish Kubitschek's initiative. Rather, it was left to fade. Kubitschek and Lleras Camargo were invited to be special advisors to the Alliance, with the idea of giving Latin America a voice and linking the Kennedy policy to OPA. Both grew frustrated with a program they saw as political, U.S.-controlled, and ineffective.[203] After less than a year in the presidency, Quadros abruptly resigned. He was replaced by João Goulart, whom many in the United States saw as a communist sympathizer. Through the Alliance, the United States sought to control and then undermine Goulart, concludes Jeffrey Taffet. After Kennedy's death, Goulart was overthrown in a 1964 coup, which was welcomed by the Lyndon B. Johnson administration.[204] Six years after Kubitschek

[201] Weis, *Cold Warriors & Coups D'etat*, pp. 137–139.
[202] Carlos Alfredo Bernardes, "Economia e finanças," October 16, 1960, tele. rec. 10756, vol. Washington, Telegramas Rec-Exp., 1960, AHIB; Exteriores to Brazilian Embassy in Washington, "Encontro de presidentes eleitos do Brasil e dos Estados Unidos," November 24, 1960, tele. exp. 11026, vol. Washington, Telegramas Rec-Exp., 1960, AHIB. Carlos Alfredo Bernardes, "Noticiário Telegráfico do *New York Times* sobre a viagem do presidente eleito Janio Quadros," November 22, 1960, tele. rec. 10971, vol. Washington, Telegramas Rec-Exp., 1960, AHIB; "The forthcoming Quadros administration," December 13, 1960, *FRUS*, 1958–1960, vol. 5, pp. 795–796.
[203] Alberto Lleras Camargo, "The Alliance for Progress: Aims, Distortions, Obstacles," *Foreign Affairs* 42, no. 1 (1963).
[204] For summaries of the Kennedy–Quadros relationship, see Weis, *Cold Warriors & Coups D'etat*, Chapter 6; Stephen G. Rabe, *The Most Dangerous Area in the World: John F. Kennedy*

proposed a new era of U.S.–Brazilian cooperation, relations between the two countries hit an historic low.

The Operation and the Alliance

Kubitschek's efforts pushed the Eisenhower administration to take halting steps in U.S.–Latin American economic relations. However, there is also a larger question – to which close Kennedy advisors gave differing answers – about how much credit Operation Pan-America deserves for sparking the Alliance for Progress. Though a thorough review of Kennedy's Latin American policies is beyond the scope of this chapter, it is useful to consider how Kubitschek might have inspired or failed to inspire a later policy change. Political scientist Christopher Darnton has explored potential linkages between the Operation and the Alliance. He concludes: "Latin American diplomacy, particularly on the part of Brazil, was far more consequential for the origins of the Alliance for Progress, and more broadly for the inter-American agenda, than is generally acknowledged."[205] My own research concurs with Darnton's. The principal ideas of the Alliance were contained in Operation Pan-America, and the hemispheric consensus upon which the Alliance relied was built by the diplomacy of Kubitschek and Lleras Camargo through the OAS and the Act of Bogotá. Influential figures on the U.S. side of the Alliance for Progress had personal experience with OPA, including Douglas Dillon, who became Kennedy's secretary of Treasury, Assistant Secretary of State for Inter-American Affairs Edwin Martin, and Thomas Mann. Kennedy himself had endorsed OPA's central proposals in his December 1958 speech in San Juan, Puerto Rico, even before the victory of the Cuban Revolution. In March 1961, Lincoln Gordon highlighted both OPA and long-standing requests for a "Latin American Marshall Plan" in a report to advisor Richard Goodwin.[206] The Alliance was explicitly under the framework of the Act of Bogotá, itself an outgrowth of Kubitschek's proposals and diplomacy.

Policies like the Alliance for Progress emerge from a complex process, and there are rarely straight lines of causation. On its own, OPA was not a sufficient cause for the Alliance for Progress. However, Kubitschek's proposals were relevant during the transition from Eisenhower to Kennedy because of their consonance with modernization theory and Kennedy's attention to Latin America because of the Cuban Revolution. Kubitschek and his partners had

Confronts Communist Revolution in Latin America (Chapel Hill, N.C.: University of North Carolina Press, 1999), pp. 63–68; Jeffrey F. Taffet, *Foreign Aid as Foreign Policy: The Alliance for Progress in Latin America* (New York: Routledge, 2007), Chapter 5.

[205] Christopher Darnton, "Asymmetry and Agenda-Setting in US–Latin American Relations: Rethinking the Origins of the Alliance for Progress," *Journal of Cold War Studies* 14, no. 4 (2012).

[206] Lincoln Gordon, "Draft memorandum from the consultant to the task force on Latin America to the President's special counsel (Goodwin)," March 6, 1961, *FRUS, 1961–1963*, vol. 12, doc. 5.

prepared the diplomatic ground by building support for OPA, which was supplanted by a U.S. policy that seemed to adopt similar goals and promised billions of dollars in funding. As such, not only did OPA and the ensuing Act of Bogotá offer concrete proposals for hemispheric policy and highlight the security–development nexus to sympathetic U.S. policymakers, it lowered the diplomatic costs of implementing a new policy.

Conclusions

OPA is usually mentioned as a curious forebear of the Alliance for Progress, whether as a parent or a distant, awkward uncle. The U.S.-focused literature on the Alliance for Progress has examined the Alliance as a response to the Cuban Revolution and as an outgrowth of modernization theory. The argument about whether there was continuity or change between the Eisenhower and the Kennedy administrations has largely failed to note that one of the important reasons for the continuities was that Latin American leaders were more organized in presenting their demands. Intermingling of Latin American and U.S. ideas preceded the Alliance. The Alliance mirrored OPA in both the broad outlines of its stated purpose and in many of its details because the path from idea to policy was one of frequent interaction between U.S. and Latin American leaders.

As a foreign policy initiated by Brazilian President Juscelino Kubitschek and supported to differing degrees by other Latin American leaders, Operation Pan-America was a partial success. OPA emerged as a response to a crisis – the attack on Nixon in Caracas in May 1958 – but it carefully addressed Kubitschek's priorities, foreign and domestic, while tapping into long-standing Latin American demands. Though most of Operation Pan-America's goals were not new, OPA represented a strategic innovation regarding how to pursue those goals: closer hemispheric cooperation on political, security, and especially economic issues; the creation of multilateral mechanisms to tackle underdevelopment; a greater voice for Latin America in world affairs; and the growth of democratic governance in Latin America.

Much of the impetus for Kubitschek's goals was domestic, though concerns about Brazil's role in the hemisphere also mattered. He had to manage an economy on the brink of fiscal default, soaring inflation, and a military that was not always content with civilian authority. Internationally, the Cold War proved both a constraint and a bargaining chip. It limited economic relations with the Soviet Union, though this was unlikely for reasons that had little to do with Washington. Kubitschek was personally committed to democracy and what he saw as the defense of Western, Christian civilization. Furthermore, any serious move closer to the Soviet Union would have provoked a harsh reaction from economic elites and the Brazilian military (as it eventually did). Kubitschek sought to secure democratic institutions through prosperity while also establishing Brazil as a South American power. To understand the goals of

OPA, both the international and the domestic sources of Kubitschek's policies must be considered.

In the United States, the most important actors on a day-to-day basis were Undersecretary Douglas Dillon, Assistant Secretaries Roy Rubottom and Thomas Mann, and high-level officials in the Treasury Department and Export-Import Bank. Eisenhower and Secretary Dulles were sporadically involved, and Nixon's relevance faded after his visit. The U.S. Congress played an important role, sometimes serving as an intermediary through which Latin American concerns were turned into Democratic political criticisms; Eisenhower and Nixon were more sensitive and attentive to the latter as the November 1960 presidential elections neared. The Eisenhower administration's goals in Latin America were driven by security, politics, and economics, in that order. First, the administration abhorred instability in the hemisphere. Between the Guatemalan coup of 1954 and May 1958, the administration considered Latin America a safe zone in the Cold War. Kubitschek's initial proposals in 1956 received no serious consideration. The attack on Nixon and, later, the Cuban Revolution overturned that view. Second, the administration was concerned about the domestic political effects of problems in Latin America, which grew increasingly salient during the late 1950s. Third, the Eisenhower administration promoted economic growth in Latin America, but without large U.S. fiscal commitments. Philosophically, many in the administration believed free enterprise was a better long-term economic strategy, and that aid would not spur growth. The administration also wanted to limit U.S. outlays. It was not puritanical in avoiding commitments to guarantee security or political support, as its approach in other regions and Bolivia showed; however, Eisenhower was skeptical aid was needed in Latin America. The administration wanted to maintain Latin American stability and support, preferably on the cheap.

While Kubitschek's goals were not heavily influenced by his perception of U.S. policy, his strategy was almost entirely designed to take advantage of what he believed were the United States' main concerns. Operation Pan-America connected his developmental goals with the Cold War, though Kubitschek had reason to worry more about the Brazilian military than about communists as a threat to Brazil's weak democracy. By drawing a line between underdevelopment, instability, and communism, Kubitschek hoped to raise the profile of underdevelopment in Latin America and define it in a way that made it a U.S. national security interest. Economic asymmetry was important, as Kubitschek believed that Brazil needed foreign capital and technology to achieve the progress of "fifty years in five." The United States seemed the only viable source. That said, Brazil and its Latin American allies had considerable leeway in domestic economic policies, even when the United States wanted a policy change. Brazil refused repeated requests from Eisenhower himself as well as others in the administration to open its petroleum monopoly to foreign investment. The nature of OPA was quite different. At their core, Kubitschek's and Lleras Camargo's arguments were requests that the U.S. government give large sums of money to Latin American countries without guaranteed benefits. On that issue, Latin American leaders had little natural leverage. Their strategies were essentially designed to redefine the issue and to increase their bargaining power.

In the final accounting, did OPA influence U.S. interests, goals, and strategies, or are U.S. domestic politics more salient? Clearly, Kubitschek's OPA was not the only influence on the Eisenhower administration's foreign economic policy. Kubitschek realized that the primary U.S. interest was to maintain stability in Latin America and preserve its allegiance in the Cold War. With the Marshall Plan as a frequent metaphor, Kubitschek overestimated Eisenhower's willingness to spend heavily in pursuit of that goal. The administration's fiscal conservatism, embodied by Treasury Secretary George Humphrey, constrained spending. The Republican Party in Congress supported this position. After the May 1958 attack on Nixon, domestic political pressure on Eisenhower increased in the form of the Draper Committee's review of policy to Latin America. While some Democrats in Congress had already been critical of what they saw as Eisenhower's friendliness with dictators, congressmen including minority Senate whip Michael Mansfield and John F. Kennedy directly noted the Brazilian plan as early as late 1958.[207] In doing so, they expanded their criticism from the issue of democracy to economic policy.

Even without OPA, a reevaluation of U.S. policy to Latin America was likely in the latter half of 1958 and through 1959 because of the anti-Nixon Caracas demonstrations and the Cuban Revolution. In that case, what did Kubitschek accomplish? First, OPA channeled U.S. concerns. Though Caracas and Cuba drew attention, they did not have any innate connection to economic policy. A development bank was not an obvious response to rowdy demonstrators; in fact, John Foster Dulles first insisted on improved police cooperation. Kubitschek made the argument that not only was instability linked to underdevelopment, but also that both were linked to the global Cold War. Second, OPA helped create a common agenda for Latin American leaders. By September 1958, their insistence on a development bank became too strong to ignore, even though Brazil ultimately failed to maintain consensus on the details. Officials in the State Department, led by Dillon, referred to the near-unanimous Latin American calls to insist on the bank, trumping the concerns of fiscally conservative officials in other agencies. Kubitschek's OPA led directly to the creation of the Committee of 21, which allowed for frequent Latin American pressure on economic matters. OPA kept the underdevelopment–instability–communism argument on the U.S.–Latin American agenda so that others could pick it up

---

[207] Brazilian Embassy in Washington to Exteriores, "Declaraões do Senador Mansfield sobre a Operação Pan-Americana," December 22, 1958, letter, folder 82.282, AHIB; Press clipping, Kennedy, December 18, 1958, folder 82.279, AHIB.

in response to different events, including the Cuban Revolution and Kennedy's election.[208]

Kubitschek took advantage of the attack on Nixon in Caracas to shift the Latin American and U.S. agendas in the direction desired. For Kubitschek, this was a success in agenda-setting. Without a similar crisis, the president had failed to affect the U.S. or hemispheric agendas during both his pre-inaugural visit to the United States and in the Panama Conference in 1956. Following the Nixon trip in May 1958, Kubitschek got high-level U.S. attention, exchanging letters with Eisenhower, and receiving visits from Rubottom and then Dulles. Initially, the U.S. response remained focused on communist instigation and security measures. The Brazilian argument won followers in the Eisenhower administration and across Latin America. Eventually, these arguments would be accepted by the Eisenhower administration, at least instrumentally, in the Act of Bogotá on September 13, 1960.

Brazilian diplomacy was able to unite much of Latin America around general principles in June–August 1958, with the important exception of Mexico. The interpretation Kubitschek offered of instability in Latin America was neither exclusively his nor entirely novel. However, his deployment of it was astute. OPA's most visible successes came quickly, with the U.S. change to back the creation of the IDB and greater acceptance of common markets and commodity agreements. There was also an increase in external assistance to Brazil. Brazilian leaders thought in late 1958 that these changes augured even greater shifts. It would prove more difficult. Kubitschek employed a strategy of internationalization, but he struggled in 1959–1960 to maintain Latin American unity around a project that required deep multilateral cooperation and institution-building. After the agreement on the bank, many countries felt the main mission had been accomplished and were not eager to continue pressuring the United States.

During 1959, Brazil lost control of the agenda. Its initiatives stagnated in the slow bureaucracy of the OAS, a danger Kubitschek had warned his foreign minister to avoid. In the Committee of 21, Schmidt and other diplomats struggled to build a Latin American position that would have given Brazil a stronger negotiating position vis-à-vis the United States. Otherwise sympathetic partners felt Brazil's goals were unrealistic. Domestic constraints became more severe, and Brazilian energy was consumed trying to gain U.S. or IMF emergency loans. This fueled perceptions, clearly held by Thomas Mann, that OPA was less about hemispheric solidarity and development than about the Brazilian economy. In terms of Brazil's goals, it seemed like a lost year. However, as the year reached its end, a few reasons for optimism arose. In large part, these had to do with U.S. domestic politics, along with worsening U.S.–Cuban relations. Democrats in Congress and in the election sharpened their attacks on

---

[208] Darnton, "Asymmetry and Agenda-Setting in US–Latin American Relations."

the Eisenhower administration's Latin America policy, particularly regarding development and democracy.

After patching up ties with Mexico and Argentina and reinforcing warm relations with Colombia, Kubitschek was in a better position to press OPA when the tensions in the Caribbean reached crisis proportions. These efforts increased the pressure on Eisenhower to respond to Castro with more than just security-based solutions, as he had in Guatemala in 1954. The eventual product was the "Eisenhower Plan" and the Social Progress Trust Fund. It was far short of the "Marshall Plan for Latin America" for which Kubitschek had fought, but by that time his term had nearly expired. The ideas advanced under Operation Pan-America were left to other leaders, in the United States and Latin America.

3

Completing the Nation

*Omar Torrijos and the Long Quest
for the Panama Canal*

Se puede jugar con la cadena, ¡pero no con el mono!

You can play with the chain, but not with the monkey!
                    One of Omar Torrijos' oft-repeated aphorisms

Panamanians had waited for this moment for nearly as long as there had been
Panamanians. Omar Torrijos, a military man dressed in a civilian suit, sat next
to the president of the United States in the ornate hall of the Pan-American
Union in Washington, D.C. The general led a country of two million people,
one of the world's smallest in physical size and population. President Jimmy
Carter was the chief executive of a superpower with economic and military
strength that dwarfed the rest of the hemisphere. The signing ceremony was a
victory for both. However, there is little question the Panamanian victory was
larger. Panamanians had fought for decades against what they considered the
unjust treaty of 1903. It was Panamanians who spoke with desperate passion
about the incompleteness of their nation, of partial and wounded sovereignty,
and of humiliation borne of daily experience. The treaties in front of Carter
and Torrijos would transfer control of the canal from the United States to
Panama. They carried great political risks. Panama represented the main foreign
policy fight of Carter's first year. The treaties included major reversals of U.S.
positions from just a few years prior, including some that had been tightly
held over decades of negotiation. To many Americans, the canal was U.S. built
and owned and of great strategic and symbolic importance. For Torrijos, the
treaties had become his *raison d'être* over nine years in power.

   At the front of the Hall of the Americas sat a collection of Latin American leaders – many of whom held deep grudges against one another. Eighteen heads of state of the Western Hemisphere bore witness to the signing

ceremony.[1] The Chilean General Augusto Pinochet, despised by democrats like Venezuela's Carlos Andrés Pérez, watched as Torrijos achieved, with the stroke of a pen, the principal foreign policy goal in Panama's history. Many of these leaders had championed Panama's cause, chastising the United States for its inflexibility and issuing clarion calls for justice. A host of leaders from outside the hemisphere had also lent support. It was part of the political genius of Omar Torrijos, who had seized power in a military coup and ruled without electoral consent, that he was loved by leading democrats in his region. He astutely managed contradictions, drawing support internally and internationally by trumpeting his nationalism and demanding justice. "Carlos Andrés Pérez said that the man he most admired in Latin American politics was Omar Torrijos," said treaty negotiator Adolfo Ahumada decades later. "And now [Hugo] Chávez says the same thing!"[2] Torrijos was able to oppose the United States while working with it. He was able to befriend Fidel Castro, sending wealthy businessmen as his emissaries.

This case offers a window into the actions of one of the smallest Latin American states as it pursued a goal that was widely embraced across Panamanian society during several decades. It is a case where we would expect little possibility for weaker-state influence. Many in the United States viewed the canal as a central interest for security, prosperity, and national pride. The case offers exceptional lessons on the strategies of weaker-state leaders as they try to alter U.S. policies.

Much of what has been written about the Torrijos–Carter Treaties[3] has focused on President Carter – his political calculations and the backlash engendered among the "new right" in the United States.[4] Broader histories of the Panama Canal have usually treated the treaties as an epilogue.[5] The case has also been important to the study of inter-branch relations and "two-level

---

[1] Jimmy Carter, *Keeping Faith: Memoirs of a President* (New York: Bantam Books, 1982), p. 161; Omar Jaén Suárez, *Las Negociaciones de los Tratados Torrijos–Carter: 1970–1979* (Panamá: Autoridad del Canal de Panamá, 2005), pp. 634–638.

[2] Adolfo Ahumada, interview with the author, September 27, 2011, Panama City, Panama. Translation from Spanish.

[3] Here I use the name common in Panama. In the United States, Carter's name is usually first. The same is true of the Tack–Kissinger/Kissinger–Tack agreements, discussed below.

[4] Adam Clymer, *Drawing the Line at the Big Ditch: The Panama Canal Treaties and the Rise of the Right* (Lawrence, Kan.: University Press of Kansas, 2008); J. Michael Hogan, *The Panama Canal in American Politics: Domestic Advocacy and the Evolution of Policy* (Carbondale, Ill.: Southern Illinois University Press, 1986).

[5] See, for example, John Major, *Prize Possession: The United States and the Panama Canal, 1903–1979* (New York: Cambridge University Press, 1993); Julie Greene, *The Canal Builders: Making America's Empire at the Panama Canal* (New York: Penguin Press, 2009). Because negotiations were ongoing when it was published, it is outside the focus of the classic work David G. McCullough, *The Path between the Seas: The Creation of the Panama Canal, 1870–1914* (New York: Simon & Schuster, 1977).

games" in international negotiations.[6] Though Alan McPherson studied the 1964 flag riots and ensuing Robles–Johnson Treaties, thorough primary sources on later periods of negotiations are only recently available.[7] Until recently, the most comprehensive work on the negotiations was a memoir by William J. Jorden, who was on the National Security Council (NSC) during the Nixon and Ford administrations and then became Carter's ambassador to Panama.[8] While Jorden's account has much to offer, it is told through his eyes. Panamanian historian Omar Jaén Suárez, himself a minor player in the talks, has written a meticulously researched account built on U.S. and Panamanian sources, but his work is scarcely available outside Panama.[9]

This chapter employs underutilized sources in Panama and the United States to argue that our understanding of the Panama Canal negotiations has underplayed a significant part of the story – Panama. If we are to understand how the canal came to be on Carter's agenda, and how the issue was interpreted when he came to office, we need to understand the Panamanian government's years of struggle. Robert Pastor, both a participant in and a student of the treaty negotiations, wrote: "Panama implemented a very sophisticated strategy to achieve a nearly impossible mission . . . Panama's success can be understood only if one abandon's the region's stereotypes of the United States."[10] It is a story of frictions, frustrations, and failures – but finally of common ground.

Background

History cast a long shadow over the negotiations of the Panama Canal treaties. The Panamanians' key claims and appeal for justice were based on their interpretation of how the Republic of Panama was born and the canal created. From the time of colonization, Panama's unique geography has been its greatest asset, as well as a curse that attracted frequent meddling. The Spanish shipped silver from Potosí across the isthmus to the Iberian Peninsula. As Spain declined, Great Britain and the emergent United States jousted for dominance in the northernmost province of New Granada, later Colombia. U.S. continental

---

[6] Robert D. Putnam, "Diplomacy and Domestic Politics: The Logic of Two-Level Games," *International Organization* 42, no. 3 (1988); Robert A. Pastor, "The United States and Central America: Interlocking Debates," in *Double-Edged Diplomacy: International Bargaining and Domestic Politics*, eds. Peter B. Evans, Harold Karan Jacobson, and Robert D. Putnam (Berkeley, Calif.: University of California Press, 1993); George D. Moffett, *The Limits of Victory: The Ratification of the Panama Canal Treaties* (Ithaca, N.Y.: Cornell University Press, 1985).

[7] Alan McPherson, "Courts of World Opinion: Trying the Panama Flag Riots of 1964," *Diplomatic History* 28, no. 1 (2004), pp. 83–112.

[8] William J. Jorden, *Panama Odyssey* (Austin, Tex.: University of Texas Press, 1984).

[9] Omar Jaén Suárez, *Las Negociaciones sobre el Canal de Panamá: 1964–1970* (Bogotá: Grupo Editorial Norma, 2002); Jaén Suárez, *Las Negociaciones de los Tratados Torrijos–Carter: 1970–1979*.

[10] Pastor, *Exiting the Whirlpool*, p. 13.

expansion fed the desire for more rapid transit between the coasts, especially with the explosion of migration that followed the California gold rush in 1848. In 1850, construction began on a trans-isthmian railroad, which led to an influx of labor. U.S. attention spurred frequent small interventions to ensure the train's continued operation. These "police actions" often followed riots, which Washington saw Bogotá's government as incapable of preventing. That same year, the United States and Great Britain concluded the Clayton–Bulwer Treaty, in which the two powers agreed to build a canal only in cooperation under a joint protectorate – leaving out Colombia and Nicaragua, the states whose territory was in question.[11]

Though dreams of a canal stretched back to Spanish colonizers, the first serious attempt began in 1876. After the successful construction of the Suez Canal, French businessman Ferdinand de Lesseps gained approval from the Colombian government to connect the Atlantic and Pacific Oceans. To some in the United States, the concession seemed to portend a new French colony and violate the Monroe Doctrine. The French company was overwhelmed by tropical disease, intense rains and landslides, and difficult terrain that ruined the plans for a sea-level canal. De Lesseps' effort went bust. A new French company took over the concession but added little work to the excavation done during the previous decade.[12]

U.S. expansionists' desire for a canal, fueled by a renewed narrative of "Manifest Destiny," grew during the 1898 war with Spain. During the war, the battleship *Oregon* famously had to journey around Cape Horn to reach Cuba, nearly missing the war. The United States, having largely elbowed Britain out of Central America with the abrogation of the Clayton–Bulwer Treaty, weighed the possibility of taking over the French route or beginning anew in Nicaragua. When the French company dropped its price to $40 million, President Theodore Roosevelt gained Congressional approval to acquire the concession. Weakened by a recent civil war, Colombian diplomats agreed to the Hay–Herrán Treaty, which granted the United States a hundred-year lease in exchange for a $10 million payment and a $250,000 annuity. The Colombian senate rejected the pact, insistent upon greater compensation. Angered by what he saw as perfidious Colombians, Roosevelt pondered exploiting separatist tensions.

The United States did not invent the Panamanian independence movement, which had been active nearly since South America's independence. Colombia had at times needed U.S. help to control revolts, nearly twenty since the 1850s.

---

[11] "The Clayton–Bulwer Treaty," The Avalon Project (Yale Law School). Available online: http://avalon.law.yale.edu/19th_century/br1850.asp.

[12] This summary draws on John Major, *Prize Possession: The United States and the Panama Canal, 1903–1979* (New York: Cambridge University Press, 1993), pp. 1–33; McCullough, *The Path between the Seas*; Michael L. Conniff, *Panama and the United States: The Forced Alliance* (Athens, Ga.: University of Georgia Press, 2001).

In 1903, Panamanian elites made it known they were willing to make a deal on the canal. Philippe Bunau-Varilla, a French representative of the failed canal company, acted as a spokesman in Washington for Panamanian separatists – though his true loyalty was to the company. Bunau-Varilla interpreted a meeting with Roosevelt to mean Panamanian independence enjoyed U.S. support, or at least acquiescence. Roosevelt would not guarantee U.S. backing, but his furor toward the Colombian government was clear. The U.S. government expected another uprising.[13] After the meeting, the U.S. Navy dispatched ships to the Panamanian coast. The U.S.-controlled railway refused to transport Colombian reinforcements to Panama City. On November 3, secessionists arrested the representatives of Bogotá. The Colombian detachment soon departed Colón, and the United States recognized an independent Panama on November 6.[14] Negotiating with the French representative of a new Central American republic, the United States obtained within two weeks a treaty considerably more favorable to the United States than the deal rejected by the Colombian senate. Under the implicit threat that Washington would withdraw its protection, Panama ratified a pact that gave the United States a ten-mile-wide zone through the middle of the country, in perpetuity.[15]

Panama began to contest the Hay–Bunau-Varilla Treaty almost immediately, asking for revisions due to how, and by whom, it was negotiated. The effects of asymmetry could not be clearer. Reference to the U.S. guarantee of Panama's independence was enough to close the possibility of revisions.[16] Over the decades, the complaints only grew. During the decade-long construction, Panama criticized the treatment of local workers, who were paid much less, if they were hired at all. The U.S.-government-run construction authority instituted complex pay and work divisions based on race and nationality, none of which favored the natives of the land where the great ditch was being dug.[17] President Belisario Porras called the treaty "inadequate" in 1916, and made unsuccessful attempts to renegotiate it. The first successful revision took place in 1936 under the auspices of Franklin Roosevelt's Good Neighbor policy, removing the broad legal right of the United States to intervene in Panama under a clause similar to the Cuban Platt Amendment. The revision did not change the status of the Canal Zone, where the Second World War provoked

[13] Notes of the meeting survive through a rather tendentious route. For an explanation of the source, as well as the text of the surviving memorandum, see Thomas Schoonover, "Max Farrand's Memorandum on the U.S. Role in the Panamanian Revolution of 1903," *Diplomatic History* 12, no. 4 (1988).

[14] Major, *Prize Possession*, pp. 34–42.

[15] The revolt is treated in great depth in *FRUS, 1903*, pp. 231–243. Jaén Suárez, *Las Negociaciones sobre el Canal de Panamá*, p. 27.

[16] For the original treaty, see "Convention between the United States and the Republic of Panama for the Construction of a Ship Canal," *FRUS, 1904*, pp. 543–552.

[17] For a critical history of exceptional detail on living and working in the zone during the construction of the canal, see Greene, *The Canal Builders*

an immense U.S. military build-up, representing a highpoint for the canal's strategic value.

In 1953, Panama agitated for further revisions, including an end to perpetuity, recognition of full Panamanian sovereignty, and a $5 million annuity.[18] The 1955 Eisenhower–Remón Treaty increased the annual payment to Panama to nearly $2 million. It officially eliminated the gold and silver payroll system and adjusted some labor and taxation policies; in practice, discrimination continued. Both the 1936 and 1955 treaties reflected marginal adjustments to the 1903 treaty. Resentment at the very basis of the 1903 treaty – the existence of the Canal Zone as a state within a state – continued to build. As decolonization and third-world nationalism became potent global forces, the zone appeared anachronistic. In the late 1950s, Panamanian professionals and students launched small-scale protests, planting Panamanian flags in the zone. Panamanian leaders saw greater possibilities in these displays and in 1959 they advocated a peaceful "invasion" of the Canal Zone. Marchers' confrontation with U.S. police turned violent and drew Washington's attention. Eisenhower's own Defense and Canal Zone bureaucracies neglected to act on his pronouncements that there should be a visual recognition of Panamanian sovereignty. A year later, on September 21, 1960, the Panamanian flag was raised for the first time alongside the American in Shaler Triangle, near Panama City.[19]

Panama's leaders had sought piecemeal revisions to the treaty, but that strategy ended in 1964. Pressed by President Roberto Chiari, John F. Kennedy allowed the two nations' flags to fly side by side at seventeen specified locations in the zone. Neither flag was to be flown at other official sites, including schools. A group of Balboa High School students protested the law in January 1964 by raising the U.S. flag several mornings in a row. Panamanian students marched from their school to Balboa High, insisting that both flags must be flown there. Two hundred young Panamanians collided with the Zonian students who surrounded the flag pole. U.S. police separated the sides, and eventually the angry Panamanian students marched out of the zone to a receptive audience. The group grew to thousands and turned violent, but President Chiari refused to employ the National Guard. They threw rocks and Molotov cocktails; they torched buildings. Police responded with tear gas, then carelessly with live ammunition, killing a young man. Some twenty-four Panamanians were killed during the clashes and riots, and became known at the "martyrs of 1964." At least five Americans, including three soldiers hit by snipers, were killed. President Chiari broke relations with the United States.[20]

As the two countries slowly moved to resume relations later that year, Lyndon B. Johnson yielded to Panama's pressure. McPherson argues that

---

[18] Jaén Suárez, *Las Negociaciones sobre el Canal de Panamá*, pp. 63–66.

[19] Ibid.

[20] Jorden, *Panama Odyssey*, pp. 32–66; Jaén Suárez, *Las Negociaciones sobre el Canal de Panamá*, Chapter 4.

Panamanian leaders' anti-colonial rhetoric and use of the Organization of American States (OAS) helped "try" the flag riots in "courts of world opinion." The riots reinforced Panamanian nationalism and turned the struggle over the canal into a moral crusade.[21] Johnson announced the United States would open the 1903 treaties to revision, designating former Treasury Secretary Robert B. Anderson as special envoy. On December 18, 1964, Johnson announced that the United States and Panama would not revise the existing treaties, but would replace them with entirely new agreements.[22] The concession opened nearly three years of negotiations, which culminated in the "three-in-one," Robles–Johnson Treaties of 1967. The treaty would abrogate the 1903 pact, create a joint, but U.S.-dominated canal administration and judicial system, and increase tolls to give a direct share to Panama. Most importantly, the treaty contained an expiration date, December 31, 1999. However, the treaty granted the United States free military bases and defense rights until 2004 – or if a new canal were built, until 2067.[23] Sensing opposition, neither Robles nor Johnson presented the treaty to their legislatures. Within a year, both were out of office. New Panamanian President Arnulfo Arias had campaigned against the treaty.

New Government, New Goals

On October 11, 1968, a cadre of young officers in the Panamanian National Guard plotted to overthrow the newly inaugurated President Arias, a protean populist elected despite "reports of widespread fraud and intimidation of voters."[24] It was Arias' third presidential victory, though his previous terms had been interrupted by coups. To preempt a third coup, Arias promised he would not alter the Guard's hierarchy, but within days of his election, Arias moved to purge the Guard of powerful officers, including Major Boris Martínez and Lt. Colonel Omar Torrijos. The two men decided to oust Arias as much to save their careers as their country. Their units swept into the city and surrounded the presidential palace while Arias was out. They captured radio stations and cut off the streets. With the Guard loyal to the coup plotters, Arias fled to the Canal Zone.[25] A year later, having wrested sole control from his fellow coup-plotter, Torrijos allowed himself a vacation to Mexico. Worried that Torrijos was moving too far left, three disgruntled colonels informed Torrijos he should stay in Mexico. Torrijos wrangled a private plane and flew to a Guard base near David, Chiriquí, that was controlled by his ally Manuel Noriega. With Noriega, Torrijos led a group of soldiers to Panama City, where the rank-and-file Guard showed its loyalty to Torrijos and briefly jailed the

---

[21] McPherson, "Courts of World Opinion."
[22] Jaén Suárez, *Las Negociaciones sobre el Canal de Panamá*, pp. 180–183.
[23] Jorden, *Panama Odyssey*, pp. 116–117.
[24] "Arias Panama chief," *Chicago Tribune*, May 31, 1968, p. 15.
[25] Jorden, *Panama Odyssey*, Chapter 6.

plotters, who soon made daring escapes to the Canal Zone. Torrijos blamed the Americans for the coup and the escapes. Unlike Panama's traditional elites, the general felt no loyalty to the Americans.

Torrijos decided from the beginning to create a different relationship with the United States. He also decided to pursue his goals, both domestic and regarding the canal, without permitting democracy. In his estimation, those goals justified the repression of political organization and expression. This included banning political parties, dismissing the legislature, and tightly controlling the media. Torrijos did not approach the levels of violence of his contemporaries in Argentina or Chile, but coercion was part of his undemocratic repertoire.[26] It included the forceful exile of prominent critics and vast patronage and cooptation. Though many of his former friends and followers believe Torrijos planned to allow a democratic opening after the Canal Treaties – having allowed greater free expression in 1980, allowing the return of some exiles, and holding relatively fair, though limited, legislative elections – the general's death in a plane crash makes the question unanswerable.[27] His government was followed by the brutality of Manuel Noriega, who had earned a feared reputation as Torrijos' intelligence chief.

Divergent Positions, Irreconcilable Goals?

To assess Torrijos' success, it is important to clarify Panama's goals and point of departure. Torrijos' government had three options regarding the 1967 treaties, wrote Foreign Minister Juan Antonio Tack. It could submit them for ratification, hoping the United States would do the same; use the treaty as a starting point to negotiate revisions; or reject the treaties and seek new negotiations under a *torrijista* foreign policy.[28] Recognizing the 1967 treaties was politically difficult for Torrijos, who promised to break the control of the old political guard. Torrijos decided early on that he would not settle for a partial solution of the canal issue, so Panama renounced the earlier treaties and pushed for a blank-slate approach. In the first few years, the decision yielded no results. The United States took a much harder line than it had in 1967. Memories of the 1964 riots had faded, and the new Republican administration of Richard Nixon and Henry Kissinger placed less emphasis on Latin America than their

---

[26] According to both a 1978 report from the Inter-American Commission on Human Rights (IACHR) and a 2001 Panama Truth Commission, the most serious violations came in the first years after the coup, 1969–1972, and included selected killings of supporters of President Arias. The IACHR report "The Truth Commission" is available from the U.S. Institute of Peace. Available online: www.usip.org/publications/truth-commission-panama-truth-commission-comisi-n-de-la-verdad-de-panam.

[27] Some in Panama continue to blame Noriega for Torrijos' death. Though various conspiracy theories exist, there is little evidence to support them.

[28] Juan Antonio Tack, "La Lucha de Omar Torrijos por la Recuperación de la Integridad Nacional," *Revista Lotería* agosto-diciembre, no. 305–309 (1981).

Democratic predecessors. "The developing world was significant for Nixon and Kissinger only to the extent that turmoil there might complicate the pursuit of their core geopolitical agenda," Mark Atwood Lawrence notes.[29] The administration's initial response manifested this lack of interest.

The Defense Department saw an opportunity to renege on the compromises Torrijos had deemed insufficient. In 1970, the Pentagon accepted renewed talks, but argued that "US control over canal and defense should be "nonnegotiable" for "the indefinite future."[30] Kissinger, who four years later signed a radically different set of principles, recommended the essential Defense position to the president.[31] Decision Memorandum 64 stated U.S. goals: "In any new negotiations three points are to be considered nonnegotiable: (a) effective U.S. control of canal operations; (b) effective U.S. control of canal defense; and (c) continuation of these controls for an extended period of time, preferably open-ended."[32] This was much more conservative than the 1967 treaties, maintaining U.S. control for fifty to ninety years depending on possible canal improvements.[33] For Panama, the U.S. reversion to the positions from before the flag riots was a slap in the face. The U.S. proposals set the stage for frustrating negotiations in 1971 and 1972, adding to Torrijos' deep suspicion of the United States.

Panama's principal goal was the immediate elimination of the Canal Zone. On this goal, the Panamanian government and population were united. On other issues, there was less internal agreement during 1970–1971. In a meeting with Nixon on October 25, 1970, Torrijos' handpicked president Demetrio Lakas seemed out of touch with his own foreign ministry's increasingly nationalistic positions. He told Nixon: "Panama does not want the Canal. [Lakas] regarded the United States not only as the defender of the Canal but as a 'big brother' to Panama and, indeed, to all the Americas. Panama did not want to operate the Canal either, he stated."[34] Foreign Minister Tack proposed more

---

[29]   Mark Atwood Lawrence, "Containing Globalism: The United States and the Developing World in the 1970s," in *The Shock of the Global: The 1970s in Perspective*, ed. Niall Ferguson (Cambridge, Mass.: Belknap Press of Harvard University Press, 2010).

[30]   Packard to Kissinger, "NSSM 68 – Panama Canal," May 4, 1970, *FRUS 1969–1976*, vol. E-10. Available online: http://history.state.gov/historicaldocuments/frus1969–76ve10/d534.

[31]   Kissinger to Nixon, June 1, 1970, *FRUS 1969–1976*, vol. E-10. Available online: http://history .state.gov/historicaldocuments/frus1969–76ve10/d535.

[32]   Nixon, "National Security Decision Memorandum 64," June 5, 1970. *FRUS 1969–1976*, vol. E-10. Available online: http://history.state.gov/historicaldocuments/frus1969–76ve10/d536.

[33]   William L. Furlong and Margaret E. Scranton, *The Dynamics of Foreign Policymaking: The President, the Congress, and the Panama Canal Treaties* (Boulder, Colo.: Westview Press, 1984), p. 48.

[34]   Arnold Nachmanoff, "Memorandum of meeting, Panama Canal Treaty negotiations," *FRUS, 1969–1976*, vol. E-10, doc. 539. Available online: http://history.state.gov/historicaldocuments/ frus1969–76ve10/d539. Accounts of this meeting vary substantially. William Jorden recalls it as a hastily planned coincidence that occurred when Nixon's planners needed to add a guest to a dinner. In a better-documented account, Omar Jaén notes that the visit coincided with the UN General Assembly and had been requested by Panama months ahead. Jorden, *Panama Odyssey*, p. 151. Jaén Suárez, *Las Negociaciones de los Tratados Torrijos–Carter*, pp. 96–97.

radical modifications, starting with an end to the "perpetuity" clause of the original treaty, the transfer of the canal to Panamanian control, the increase of economic benefits derived from the canal, and phasing out of the U.S. military presence in the country.[35] Tack's demands contradicted Lakas, but Torrijos was slow to make his position known. Increasingly, Torrijos' foreign policy statements emphasized autonomy from the United States. When the general named new negotiators in March 1971, he sided strongly with Tack's position. However, Torrijos doubted the United States would concede without further bloodshed.[36]

More specific Panamanian goals evolved during the negotiations of 1971 and 1972. Marked by frustrations, the talks benefited the most strident members of Torrijos' circle and added to suspicions of the United States, solidifying inflexibility on both sides. By the end of 1972, Panamanian goals enjoyed broader consensus. They included:

(1) an end to the "perpetuity" clause of 1903, with an end date of December 31, 1994;
(2) elimination of U.S. jurisdiction in the Canal Zone and the institution of Panamanian legal and political authority there;
(3) an immediate reversion of all lands and waters not needed directly for the operation or defense of the canal;
(4) immediate Panamanian participation in the administration of the canal, with 85 percent of the payroll destined to Panamanian citizens;
(5) the cessation of U.S. military activities not directly related to the canal, such as the School of the Americas, and stipulations and limits on U.S. military presence, and neutrality over the canal under a United Nations (UN) mandate;
(6) a dramatic increase in the revenue Panama derived from the canal;
(7) exclusive use of the Panamanian flag;
(8) neutral arbitration of disputes;
(9) Panamanian determination over the construction of a new or expanded canal, to be negotiated later.[37]

---

35 Panamanian Foreign Minister Juan Antonio Tack said that during the restarted negotiations "Panama manifested that *the negotiations had been restarted with the aim of eliminating one government inside of another government, so that the so-called Canal Zone could be integrated physically and politically into the rest of the territory of the Republic of Panama, under the full jurisdiction of the Panamanian government, and that our government has a profound interest in moving in that direction.*" Tack to Anderson, letter, October 26, 1972, folder Negociaciones, 1972–1974, no. 545, Archivo del Ministerio de Relaciones Exteriores, Panama City, Panama, (AMREP), sec. 2, pp. 5–6. Translation from Spanish, emphasis in original. Further references to this archive will use the abbreviation AMREP, from the Spanish initials, following Jaén Suárez.

36 Jaén Suárez, *Las Negociaciones de los Tratados Torrijos–Carter*, pp. 100–118.

37 "Posiciones básicas de Panamá en las principales materias," December 4, 1972, folder Negociaciones, 1972–1974, no. 545, AMREP, sec. 9, pp. 1–19.

Though Tack was the clear intellectual leader in defining these goals, Torrijos set the broad direction for a foreign policy that would demonstrate independence and challenge U.S. positions on the canal. Despite decades of negotiations, U.S. negotiators did not seem to grasp Panama's principal goal. For Panamanians, the real problem – the issue that gnawed at their national consciousness and wrecked their sense of sovereign dignity – was the strip of segregated land surrounding the canal. The Zonians ran and enjoyed a separate school system, grocery stores, post offices, and legal system in the center of the isthmus. The "state within a state" did not answer to the authorities of the country in which it territorially resided. It was the domain of a governor Panamanians did not appoint or elect. Its legal system was based on the state laws of Louisiana. "Panama was born in 1903 with a contradiction between the nation and the Canal Treaty of 1903," said Ahumada "This wasn't the result of the military bases, or that the canal was managed by the United States... The major problem was the existence of the Canal Zone. And it is difficult, if not impossible, to be an independent state with such an overwhelming presence in the middle of the national territory."[38]

Panama cared deeply about the negotiations, but the U.S. government was not particularly interested, and less in making concessions. Panama faced a steep climb. It needed to gain U.S. attention and get the United States to alter its hard-line policy. How, then, did Panama eventually achieve its goal? Panama scored several major wins in shaping the international agenda. During 1972 and 1973, Panama held a UN Security Council (UNSC) seat, and then held a UNSC meeting in Panama over U.S. objections. Capitalizing on that attention, Panama got the United States to agree to broad principles for the negotiations, including an end to perpetual U.S. control. In 1975, the countries negotiated a Status of Forces Agreement (SOFA) that regularized the U.S. military presence and lessened the Pentagon's opposition. Panama's ambitions were stalled by Nixon's political crises and Ford's political weakness, but Panama capitalized on the election of Jimmy Carter to achieve major goals while giving in on others to reach a deal.

Rejecting the Past and Crafting a Strategy

In late 1970, Presidents Lakas and Nixon agreed to restart conversations about the canal. These talks were plagued by Lakas' lack of understanding, Nixon's lack of interest, and chief negotiator Anderson's lack of influence. In 1971, the two sides were miles apart. Anderson insisted that Panamanian demands would never pass Congress and demanded permanent control over operations and defense.[39] Torrijos asked if Anderson was willing to end the Canal Zone,

---

[38] Ahumada, interview with the author. See also Rómulo Escobar Bethancourt, *Torrijos: Colonia Americana, No!* (Bogotá: C. Valencia Editores, 1981), p. 257.

[39] Anderson to de la Ossa, February 19, 1971, folder Negociaciones, 1972–1974, no. 545, AMREP, sec. 4, pp. 1–8.

and Anderson said no, he would only alter the 1967 arrangements – apparently not in the direction of Panama's wishes.[40] By July, Panama's initial hopes collapsed into disappointment. Panamanian negotiators filled sessions, speeches, and letters with drawn-out histories of grievances against the United States. Personal relationships that lacked rapport from the start turned venomous.[41] Though the Panamanian team did not know, their counterpart, Ambassador Anderson, operated from the wilderness of the Nixon administration. Anderson represented a secretary of state who played a faint second fiddle to Kissinger; he was further handicapped by President Nixon's dislike for him. Years before, President Eisenhower briefly considered replacing Nixon as his running mate with Anderson. Neither Nixon nor Kissinger met directly with Anderson.[42]

Tired and skeptical of the constant U.S. appeals to Congressional constraints, Torrijos announced that any treaty would face hurdles in Panama, too. First by proclamation, then later through a revision to the constitution, Torrijos decreed that any treaty would have to be approved by the Panamanian people in a plebiscite – and the people would not accept another treaty that maintained U.S. perpetuity, he intoned.[43] The frustrating talks led Torrijos to challenge the decades-long U.S. position that all canal matters were to be discussed bilaterally and confidentially if Panama wanted even modest concessions. Torrijos was not interested in modest concessions, but in a dramatically different relationship. As a senior Panamanian advisor wrote: "General Torrijos had told [Anderson] that so long as Panamanian aspirations were not fully met, Panama would not sign a treaty, even if it was necessary to wait for a new generation of Americans to achieve Panamanian demands, he would continue negotiating until a new generation had taken over the country's leadership."[44]

In late 1972, Torrijos appointed a twenty-seven-year-old, political loyalist as new ambassador to the United States. Torrijos told the new envoy, Nicolas González Revilla: "You are not being requested to go to Washington because you are an expert in either [the treaties or history]," González Revilla recalled. Torrijos wanted the young man to take "a fresh look." Upon his return, the ambassador told Torrijos: "Our problem simply does not exist in the agenda of U.S. problems. Not even in the State Department is it an issue."[45] Torrijos gathered his advisors, and they decided to adopt a new approach. "[Torrijos] realized that he needed to create an issue, and he did it brilliantly," González

---

[40] Jorden, *Panama Odyssey*, p. 154.

[41] Tack to Anderson, letter, October 26, 1972. Sec. 2, p. 5. Translation from Spanish.

[42] Jorden, *Panama Odyssey*, p. 159. Sol Linowitz also wrote that Anderson "had neither access nor influence in the White House." Sol M. Linowitz, *The Making of a Public Man: A Memoir* (Boston: Little, Brown, 1985), p. 147.

[43] Jorden, *Panama Odyssey*, p. 162.

[44] "Memorandum," Jorge Illueca to JA Tack, letter. December 7, 1972, folder no. 1118, AMREP, p. 5. Translation from Spanish.

[45] Nicolás González Revilla, interview with the author, September 20, 2011, Panama City, Panama.

Revilla added. "He went to the third world. Non-aligned... He started to travel a lot, within Latin America and out of Latin America."[46]

Panama had started internationalizing the canal issue even before González Revilla's report, first in international organizations, where Panama sought and obtained Latin American support for a UNSC seat. When the Security Council held an extraordinary meeting in Addis Ababa – the first in the developing world – Panamanian Ambassador to the UN Aquilino Boyd equated the U.S. presence in Panama with the colonialism faced by his African colleagues. The attack caught U.S. Ambassador George H.W. Bush off guard.[47] Boyd also suggested, as an improvisation, that a meeting be held in Panama.[48] Secretary of State William Rogers warned President Nixon of the potential for embarrassment.[49] The United States condemned Boyd's departure from bilateralism, with U.S. negotiator David Ward warning that "The Panamanian presentation of a complaint against the United States in the Security Council had provoked adverse reactions in many circles of the U.S. government, in the executive and legislative, which in his opinion would reverse progress by at least three years."[50] The Panamanian representative had put himself out on a limb, but Torrijos's support was just as strong as the resistance engendered in the United States.

Boyd gained support for the meeting from Latin American and African governments. In March 1972, Boyd invited UN Secretary General Kurt Waldheim to visit Panama to see how the stagnated negotiations threatened peace. Boyd wrote Tack: "I told Mr. Waldheim that if the current negotiations for a new treaty failed, the Panamanian government, with the goal of winning international public support for its just cause, had the intention of appealing to the United Nations."[51] U.S. representatives tried throughout 1972 to organize opposition to a meeting in Panama, or elsewhere outside New York,

---

[46] Torrijos made a similar point in a conversation with U.S. diplomat William Jorden. "The general said he based his strategy on a 'very simple principle.' That was: 'to resolve a problem, the first thing you have to do is *make* it a problem.' He was persuaded the only way to do that was to move the issue to the center of the world stage." Jorden, *Panama Odyssey*, p. 176. Torrijos also used similar language talking to a reporter in early 1975, saying, "The first thing was to get them to consider that it was a problem. Until very recently, they didn't even think it was a problem." Qtd. in "Panama's leader hopeful on canal," *New York Times*, February 4, 1975, p. 7.

[47] Jaén Suárez, *Las Negociaciones de los Tratados Torrijos–Carter*, pp. 228–229.

[48] Carlos Ozores, "Omar Torrijos y sus Proyecciones en la Política Internacional," *Revista Lotería* agosto-diciembre, no. 305–309 (1981).

[49] Rogers to Nixon, "Security Council meeting in Africa," February 10, 1972, *FRUS, 1969–1976*, vol. 5, doc. 124. Available online: http://history.state.gov/historicaldocuments/frus1969–76v05/d124.

[50] Jorge Illueca, "Informe de la Conversación," March 23, 1972, folder no. 1118, AMREP. Ward's account of the meeting concurs with the basic points presented by Illueca. David Ward, "Memorandum of conversation: Panama Canal Treaty negotiations," March 23, 1972, folder no. 1118, AMREP, 1–2.

[51] Aquilino Boyd to JA Tack, March 29, 1972, letter, folder no. 1118, AMREP, n.p.

arguing they were a fiscal strain, an organizational headache, and increased regional tensions.[52] The administration pressured the Panamanians directly, sending NSC aide William Jorden to dissuade Torrijos,[53] while Secretary Rogers warned Tack that the meetings would generate public opposition to improving relations with Panama.[54] Anderson told Boyd and foreign ministry advisor Jorge Illueca "that regardless of what happened in the Security Council or any U.N. organism, the United States would continue considering these problems as internal to the two countries."[55] Despite these pressures, Panama received favorable responses from most Security Council members, and by November was moving ahead with plans for a meeting in Panama City.[56]

The Panamanian strategy had two main objectives. The first was to raise the issue's profile on the international agenda, and thereby gain greater attention from U.S. foreign policymakers. The second was to increase the diplomatic costs to the United States of failing to resolve the problem. The gambit was a remarkable success. Rómulo Escobar Bethancourt, a leftist university rector who spent a decade as a lead negotiator, later reflected: "The United States of America began to feel a horsefly biting its leg, and there were more horse-flies coming. Panama had broken the isolation of its past and its obsequious foreign policy."[57]

On January 26, 1973, with eager support from China, the Soviet Union, France, Peru, and others, the Security Council approved Panama's initiative to host a meeting.[58] The United States recognized at least eleven of fifteen members would vote for the meeting. U.S. opposition would appear closed minded,[59]

[52] Rogers to all American Republic Posts, "Possible SC meeting in Panama," August 10, 1972, *FRUS, 1969–1976*, vol. 5, doc. 126. Available online: http://history.state.gov/historical documents/frus1969-76v05/d126; Armitage and Herz to Bush, "Possible Security Council meeting in Panama," October 3, 1972, *FRUS, 1969–1976*, vol. 5, doc. 131. Available online: http://history.state.gov/historicaldocuments/frus1969-76v05/d131.

[53] William J. Jorden to Henry Kissinger, "General Torrijos and Captain Villa, *FRUS 1969–1976*, vol. E-10, doc. 562. Available online: http://history.state.gov/historicaldocuments/frus1969-76ve10/d562; Jorden, *Panama Odyssey*, pp. 185–189.

[54] Rogers to Tack, "Proposed Security Council meeting in Panama," October 16, 1972, *FRUS 1969–1976*, vol. 5, doc. 137. Available online: http://history.state.gov/historicaldocuments/frus1969-76v05/d137.

[55] "Memorandum," Jorge Illueca to JA Tack, letter. December 7, 1972, folder no. 1118, AMREP, pp. 4–5.

[56] J.A. Tack to Kurt Waldheim, November 23, 1972, folder Reunión del Consejo de Seguridad, 1973, AMREP, n.p.

[57] Escobar Bethancourt, *Torrijos*, pp. 201–202.

[58] "U.N. council decides to meet in Panama," *New York Times*, January 27, 1973; Chi Ping Fei to J.A. Tack, January 14, 1973, folder Reunión del Consejo de Seguridad, no. 33, Archivo del Ministerio de Relaciones Exteriores; Boyd to Brin, c. January 1973, folder Reunión del Consejo de Seguridad, tomo II, Archivo del Ministerio de Relaciones Exteriores.

[59] William E. Schaufele, Jr., "Telegram from the Mission to the United Nations to the Department of State," December 27, 1973, *FRUS, 1969–1972*, vol. 5, doc. 146. Available online: http://history.state.gov/historicaldocuments/frus1969-76v05/d146.

so the United States eventually voted alongside all other members to hold the meeting in Panama. A host of U.S. representatives warned Panama that hot rhetoric or grandstanding in Panama City would ruin chances of any concessions. Instead, the meetings would prove a pivotal moment in Panama's struggle to change how the United States and the world saw the canal issue, while forcing higher-level U.S. policymakers to take the matter more seriously.

From Conflict to Cooperation

In the middle of March 1973, the attention of world leaders shifted to Panama. Panama was ready.[60] The Panamanian government had installed state-of-the-art telecommunications facilities, refurbished halls and government buildings, and added security to curtail unwanted protests, especially at the University of Panama. The government had honed its message, aimed both abroad and at buttressing Torrijos' image among the Panamanian people. Torrijos sought the "moral backing of the world," no less.[61] The United States was less prepared despite its fear the meeting would be an anti-Yankee propaganda event. George Bush had just been replaced by John Scali, a former reporter and relative diplomatic novice as U.S. permanent representative. While the Panamanians appealed to justice, decolonization, and fairness, Scali insisted: "Problems with the canal will be solved by very quiet and painstaking negotiations and not by speeches in any international forum."[62]

In the Council's opening session on March 15, Omar Torrijos took the stage of the freshly remodeled (though still disbanded) National Assembly to welcome the delegates. The general compared his country's struggles with those of everyone who suffered injustice. "Panama understands the fight of countries that suffer the humiliation of colonialism," Torrijos proclaimed. "Highest leaders of North America, it is nobler to amend an injustice than to perpetuate an error."[63] Early in the week, the United States opposed any draft resolution on the grounds that the United Nations should not be involved in bilateral affairs.

---

[60] For a more complete treatment of the March 1973 UNSC meeting, see Tom Long, "Putting the Canal on the Map: Panamanian Agenda-Setting and the 1973 Security Council Meetings," *Diplomatic History* 38, no. 2 (2014).

[61] Eric Morgenthaler, "UN Security Council is Meeting in Panama amid Anti-U.S. chorus," *Wall Street Journal*, May 15, 1973, p. 1. Quote from Richard Severo, "UN panel sits in Panama today," *New York Times*, March 15, 1973, p. 16; Sayre to State Department, "UN Security Council in Panama – GOP preparations," March 12, 1973. RG 59, Central Foreign Policy Files, Electronic Telegrams. NARA-AAD. Available online: http://aad.archives.gov/aad/createpdf?rid=8048&dt=2472&dl=1345. Reference to this collection of U.S. telegrams from Record Group 59, published online by the NARA, will henceforth be referenced as NARA-AAD, RG59.

[62] Qtd. in Marlise Simons, "Panama's leader hits U.S. on Canal," *Washington Post*, March 16, 1973.

[63] Speech of Omar Torrijos at U.N. Security Council inaugural session, March 15, 1973, folder Reunión del Consejo de Seguridad, no. 17, 1973, AMREP, 1–6.

The State Department instructed the U.S. delegation to prevent the Security Council from "passing resolutions on subjects that are not properly of its concern." State did not expect any resolution could secure a majority, so elected to play defense. "For us, Panama will essentially be a damage-limiting operation," Secretary Rogers wrote Scali before the meetings.[64] Once in Panama, it became obvious that the climate was propitious to anti-U.S. resolutions. Scali publicly warned that the United States would veto any resolution that did not adequately consider its interests, while also saying that the United States had no intention of introducing its own resolution.[65]

On the second day, Panama and Peru introduced a resolution that demanded the abrogation of the 1903 treaty, reaffirmed Panama's sovereignty over the Canal Zone, and called for immediate Panamanian jurisdiction. Panama showed some willingness to compromise, but the United States sought to block any text on the canal, claiming the UN had no place in the matter.[66] Panama and Peru found cosponsors for a revised resolution with softer language, including China and Russia. The United States was isolated and belatedly considering a counterproposal.[67] On March 19, Scali went to Foreign Minister Tack's office. The U.S. diplomat told the Panamanian that the United States "would prefer no resolution at all. Tack replied that he was aware that was our preference, but indicated that there would, of course, have to be a resolution." Scali pushed for a vague resolution that only urged the continuation of negotiations, without any statement of specific goals. Tack listened quietly and told the U.S. delegation that he would check with Torrijos.[68]

Many in Torrijos' circle had concluded that forcing the United States to veto in isolation would be a major public relations victory.[69] Despite that, the Panamanians did not stop seeking U.S. support for their resolution. The U.S. delegation repeatedly insisted on including a phrase referring to U.S. "legitimate interests" in the canal in any resolution. Panama, knowing it had the support of nearly the full council, refused to compromise on the point. The Panamanian

---

[64] Rogers to Scali, "For Ambassador Scali from the Secretary," March 9, 1973, NARA-AAD, RG59. Available online: http://aad.archives.gov/aad/createpdf?rid=147&dt=2472&dl=1345.

[65] Francis B. Kent, "U.S. warns of UN veto on Panama issue," *Los Angeles Times*, March 17, 1983; Simons, "UN body ways Canal Zone stand," *Washington Post*, March 17, 1983, p. 8; Sayre to State Department, "Panama SC Mtg Amb Scali Press Conf," NARA-AAD, RG59. Available online: http://aad.archives.gov/aad/createpdf?rid=5529&dt=2472&dl=1345.

[66] These included Guinea, India, Indonesia, Kenya, Sudan, and Yugoslavia. "Proyecto de resolución revisado," n.d., 1973, folder Reunión del Consejo de Seguridad, no. 17, 1973, AMREP, 1–2.

[67] Kent, "China, Russia Endorse Panama's canal stand," *Los Angeles Times*, March 20, 1973, p. 11.

[68] U.S. Delegation to State Department, "UNSC meeting – Canal resolution," March 20, 1973, NARA-AAD, RG59. Available online: http://aad.archives.gov/aad/createpdf?rid=5324&dt=2472&dl=1345.

[69] Jaén Suárez, *Las Negociaciones de los Tratados Torrijos–Carter*, p. 247; Jorden, *Panama Odyssey*, p. 195.

delegation offered Scali a third, revised resolution that incorporated some of his complaints from the previous night – something Tack emphasized. When Scali reiterated his veto threats, the issue was closed.[70] To drive home the point, Manuel Noriega, second in command of the National Guard, made an ominous call to the U.S. delegation, telling Scali that if he planned on casting a veto, "it would be best to do it from Panama's Tocumen airport." The call, Torrijos later told the U.S. ambassador was "not sent as blackmail or threatened violence," but was just a helpful piece of close U.S.–Panamanian cooperation on security for the meeting.[71]

The United States offered its first counterproposal on the conference's last day.[72] It was too little, too late. Thirteen members voted to approve Panama's resolution. The United Kingdom abstained, on the grounds that given U.S. opposition, the resolution did nothing to advance the issue. Ambassador Scali cast the third Security Council veto in U.S. history on direct orders from the White House,[73] saying that though "there is so much in it [the resolution] with which we agree," the matter was not the business of the United Nations and "the present resolution addresses the points of interest to Panama but ignores those legitimate interests important to the United States."[74] Foreign Minister Tack closed the meetings, saying, "The United States has vetoed Panama's resolution, but the world has vetoed the United States."[75]

Before and during the meetings, the Nixon administration repeatedly warned that any public displays would set the negotiations back for years. This was the main bargaining chip the United States sought to employ, and it failed spectacularly. Panamanian historian Omar Jaén Suárez reflected: "The Nixon administration had faced a small, military-led country without a trained civil or diplomatic service, without any economic or military power, and it had been beaten on difficult ground."[76] Why? The Panamanians had decided that negotiations were stalemated, and they had little to gain there. The piecemeal concessions granted to previous Panamanian governments would not satisfy Torrijos, but the Nixon administration had not yet grasped the difference. The Security Council meeting produced an immediate breakdown, but it also provoked a reevaluation on the U.S. side. A year earlier, Henry Kissinger and

---

[70] Scali to Rogers, "Ref: Panama 1491," March 14, 1973, NARA-AAD, RG59. Available online: http://aad.archives.gov/aad/createpdf?rid=5321&dt=2472&dl=1345.

[71] Scali to Rogers, "Panama SC meeting," March 21, 1973, NARA-AAD, RG59. Available online: http://aad.archives.gov/aad/createpdf?rid=729&dt=2472&dl=1345.

[72] Draft resolution submitted by the United States, March 21, 1973, folder Consejo de Seguridad, no. 28, AMREP, sec. 15.

[73] Jorden, *Panama Odyssey*, pp. 195–196.

[74] Speech by John Scali before the UN Security Council, March 21, 1973, folder Consejo de Seguridad, no. 28, AMREP, sec. 15.

[75] Speech of J.A. Tack to UN Security Council, March 21, 1973, folder Reunión del Consejo de Seguridad, no. 17, 1973, AMREP, 1–4.

[76] Jaén Suárez, *Las Negociaciones de los Tratados Torrijos–Carter*, p. 250.

U.S. Ambassador to Panama Robert Sayre yielded to the Pentagon's positions with little thought. In the wake of the UN debacle, both took fresh looks at the costs of U.S. intransigence. On April 6, Sayre wrote to the State Department that Torrijos was a nationalist who would not accept the previous relationship. The U.S. ambassador criticized the United States' lack of clarity over the importance of the canal and its inconsistent negotiating positions.[77]

A month before the meeting, Kissinger had told Scali that he did not "have any very clear views on [Panama]."[78] The meetings succeeded on the world stage and got Kissinger's attention. Jorden, Kissinger's assistant for Latin America, later reflected: "I believe that what really made Kissinger understand he was sitting on a potential powder keg was the U.N. Security Council meeting in early 1973."[79] The meeting empowered Jorden, who was predisposed to a treaty, to advance his views. At Jorden's suggestion, Nixon's address to Congress included the president's most prominent mention of the issue:[80]

Another important unresolved problem concerns the Panama Canal and the surrounding Zone. U.S. operation of the Canal and our presence in Panama are governed by the terms of a treaty drafted in 1903. The world has changed radically during the 70 years this treaty has been in effect. Latin America has changed. Panama has changed. And the terms of our relationship should reflect those changes in a reasonable way... It is time for both parties to take a fresh look at this problem and to develop a new relationship between us – one that will guarantee continued effective operation of the Canal while meeting Panama's legitimate aspirations.[81]

Panama seized upon Nixon's call for a "fresh look."[82] González Revilla met with State Department official Morey Bell before returning for consultations with Torrijos. The Panamanian inquired about replacing written exchanges with informal talks, suggesting that both sides might be more flexible.[83] Others were less optimistic. Juan Antonio Stagg, an astute observer of the United States who served many years as consul in New York, told Tack that Nixon's growing political crisis made the possibility of successful negotiations remote.[84]

---

[77] Ibid., p. 252.

[78] Meeting request from John Scali, February 22, 1973, Kissinger Telephone Conversations, Digital National Security Archive. Henceforth, online database referred to as DNSA.

[79] Jorden, *Panama Odyssey*, p. 206.

[80] Ibid., pp. 198–199.

[81] Richard Nixon: "Fourth Annual Report to the Congress on United States Foreign Policy," May 3, 1973. The American Presidency Project. Available online: www.presidency.ucsb.edu/ws/?pid=3832.

[82] Jaén Suárez, *Las Negociaciones de los Tratados Torrijos–Carter*, p. 277.

[83] Bell to Sayre, "Panamanian ambassador comments on USG-GOP relations and treaty negotiations," May 7, 1973, NARA-AAD, RG59.

[84] J.A. Stagg to J.A. Tack, "Respuesta al cuestionario sobre las proyecciones de la reunión del Consejo de Seguridad en las negociaciones del nuevo tratado," May 8, 1973, folder Consejo de Seguridad, no. 27, AMREP, n.p

Panamanian negotiators moved from polemic criticisms to push for specific goals. Many saw long-time negotiator Robert B. Anderson as a problem and advocated for his removal. The UN meeting had exacerbated divisions within the U.S. government. Panamanians concluded that continuing negotiations with a stubborn and isolated Anderson was useless. Bell even told his Panamanian counterpart that Anderson would be replaced.[85] Summarizing conversations with Bell, an advisor wrote Tack that "Ambassador Robert B. Anderson is an unyielding exponent of the U.S. position, and while he remains at the front of the U.S. delegation, it will be very difficult to achieve any change in the U.S. position that would facilitate an understanding with Panama."[86] That Panamanians related the stalled negotiations to Anderson personally set the stage for progress upon his removal.[87]

Tack tried to capitalize on Nixon's "fresh look" by appealing directly to Secretary Rogers. The opportunity materialized when Rogers announced he would attend the investiture of the new Argentine president, with a stop in Brazil.[88] Seeking to answer criticisms that Panama sought concessions while offering none, the negotiators proposed the end of the century as the termination of U.S. control, backing off its previous position of December 1994.[89] On May 24, 1973, at the Plaza Hotel in Buenos Aires, Tack handed Rogers a letter that included eight principles, which largely reiterated Panama's key demands: (1) the abrogation of the 1903 treaty, (2) an end to perpetuity, (3) the complete end of U.S. jurisdiction at treaty's end, (4) elimination of the Canal Zone, (5) a fair share of economic benefits, (6) limiting U.S. activities to the maintenance, operation, and defense of the canal, (7) limitation of U.S. military activities, and (8) mutually agreed-upon options for any new construction.[90] The men also discussed the make-up of the U.S. negotiating team, with Rogers indicating, in a veiled reference to Anderson, that certain changes would be desirable.[91]

Though Rogers discussed the proposal directly with President Nixon, the timing could hardly have been worse.[92] Congressional hearings on Watergate had started a week before the meeting. Still, Tack's complaints about

---

[85] Manfredo to Tack, "Memorandum," April 17, 1973, folder Negociaciones 1973, no. 546, AMREP, sec. 8, pp. 1–9.

[86] de la Rosa to Tack, "Memorandum," April 23, 1973, folder Negociaciones 1973, no. 546, AMREP, sec. 8, p. 2.

[87] J.A. Tack, "Cuestionario sobre las proyecciones de la reunión del Consejo de Seguridad en las negociaciones del nuevo tratado," April 25, 1973, folder Consejo de Seguridad, no. 27, AMREP, n.p.

[88] Tack to Gibson Barboza, May 10, 1973, folder Negociaciones 1973, no. 546, AMREP, sec. 5.

[89] Bell to Sayre, "Panamanian foreign minister's request for interview with secretary in Buenos Aires," May 17, 1973, NARA-AAD, RG59. Available online: http://aad.archives.gov/aad/createpdf?rid=23694&dt=2472&dl=1345.

[90] Tack to Rogers, May 21, 1973, folder Negociaciones 1973, no. 546, AMREP, sec. 2, 1–7.

[91] Ricaurte Antonio Acheen, "Puntos fundamentales de la conversación de Rogers con Tack," May 27, 1973, folder Negociaciones 1973, no. 546, AMREP, sec. 3.

[92] Jorden, *Panama Odyssey*, p. 206.

Anderson sped the negotiator's demise. A month after the meeting, word leaked that veteran diplomat Ellsworth Bunker was being considered as a new chief for the delegation.[93] Bunker was just returning from a long stay in Vietnam, where he helped negotiate the war's conclusion. The energetic seventy-nine-year-old was internationally recognized and well respected in the Department of Defense. Panama told U.S. officials that Bunker would be an "excellent choice."[94] Anderson resigned a few days later, on July 2. His term had started with the negotiations for the 1967 "three-in-one" treaties, but ended in estrangement. Rogers' own time was short. He had stridently criticized the break-ins at Watergate and against whistleblower Daniel Ellsberg. By the time Rogers answered Tack's letter, rumors of Rogers' impending departure swirled around Washington. Still, Rogers' reply showed a shift in the administration's tenor regarding the canal, stating that he "read these principles with great interest and find important elements in them that my government is prepared to accept," including abrogation of the 1903 treaty.[95] Rogers' resignation, announced August 22, did little to change the locus of decision-making, which rested squarely between Nixon and Kissinger.[96] Bunker and Kissinger were confirmed to their new positions as negotiator and Secretary of State, respectively, in September.

After a few months of relative quiet, Torrijos continued his international grandstanding. The general spent September in Spain, ostensibly on vacation, but also meeting with General Francisco Franco and making announcements to the press, in which he equated the British presence at Gibraltar with the U.S.-run Canal Zone. Torrijos' suspicion of the United States had been piqued by allegations in *Newsweek* from imprisoned Nixon crony John Dean that E. Howard Hunt and others involved in Watergate had put Torrijos on a hit list in 1972 because of his alleged involvement in drug smuggling. Though Dean's allegations were highly suspect, they angered Torrijos all the same.[97] Upping the rhetoric, Torrijos called the Canal Zone "a time bomb in the heart of Panama."[98] Torrijos went on to visit Marshal Josip Tito in Yugoslavia and Pope John VI.[99]

---

93 "Bunker Is Expected to Get Panama-Negotiations Post," *New York Times,* June 30, 1973, p. 14.

94 Bennett (USUN) to Rogers, "U.S.–Panama relations," August 1, 1973, NARA-AAD, RG59. Available online: http://aad.archives.gov/aad/createpdf?rid=50915&dt=2472&dl=1345.

95 Rogers to Tack, August 6, 1973, folder Negociaciones 1973, no. 546, AMREP, sec. 1, 1–2.

96 So much so that a *New York Times* column on Kissinger's nomination as secretary of state was titled simply, "Kissinger gets the title, too."

97 Jaén Suárez, *Las Negociaciones de los Tratados Torrijos–Carter,* p. 273. The allegations again made news while the treaties were being debated. Jack Anderson, "Watergate plotters set assassination of Torrijos," December 16, 1977, United Features Syndicate.

98 Rivero to State, "Panama's 4862," September 13, 1973, NARA-AAD, RG59. Available online: http://aad.archives.gov/aad/createpdf?rid=70129&dt=2472&dl=1345; Sayre to State Department, "Torrijos on Canal and conspiracy," September 21, 1973, NARA-AAD, RG59. Available online: http://aad.archives.gov/aad/createpdf?rid=74073&dt=2472&dl=1345.

99 Jaén Suárez, *Las Negociaciones de los Tratados Torrijos–Carter,* p. 276.

On November 26, Bunker arrived at the tranquil island of Contadora off Panama's Pacific coast. The island would be the site of many rounds of talks. Panama's decision to host Bunker there instead of in the city was intended to melt the frigid style that had characterized talks with Anderson. Having learned that Bunker was a boating enthusiast, the Panamanians put President Lakas' yacht at his disposal.[100] Tack greeted the new negotiator by recalling how they had met ten years before at the OAS, for the most part eschewing the historical diatribes often recounted by the Panamanian team.[101] Bunker told Kissinger the meeting had gone better than hoped and relayed greetings from Torrijos, who said "for the first time he has faith and hope that all will turn out well." The two sides came to near-total agreement on seven of the eight principles. Bunker suggested they serve as a joint declaration between the two presidents.[102]

Bunker understood Panamanian sensitivities regarding jurisdiction and treaty duration. The United States should try to take advantage of the "euphoria... of long-disheartened people being extremely glad that there is at last a decent climate for forward movement."[103] After Bunker's departure on December 3, Morey Bell stayed on Contadora to hammer out language on the principles with González Revilla, whom he knew from frequent consultations in Washington. They worked for two weeks through several drafts of the eight points, which had evolved from Tack's proposals to Rogers through Bunker's modifications to become a joint document. There were many changes in wording from Tack's letter – for example, to clarify that the 1903 treaty would be abrogated with a new treaty, not before – but the primary effect of the eight points remained the same.[104] Bell felt that the Panamanian team was being flexible on issues of jurisdictional rights during the treaty.[105] One of the main changes in the U.S. position was the recognition that Panama would "grant" U.S. rights for operation and defense of the canal, something the United States had often claimed it inherently possessed.[106] The principles contained

---

[100] Jorden, *Panama Odyssey*, p. 214.

[101] "Salutación: Embajador Bunker," November 26, 1973, folder Negociaciones 1973, no. 546, AMREP, sec. 11.

[102] President Nixon quickly signed off on Bunker's request. Bell to Sayre, "Announcement of U.S. unilateral actions," December 27, 1973, NARA-AAD, RG59. Available online: http://aad .archives.gov/aad/createpdf?rid=109449&dt=2472&dl=1345.

[103] December 2, 1973 – Bunker recommends adopting "joint presidential declaration on principles." Bunker to Kissinger, "Resumption of Panama–U.S. treaty negotiations," December 2, 1973. Available online: http://aad.archives.gov/aad/createpdf?rid=108252&dt=2472& dl=1345.

[104] Jaén Suárez writes, "A comparison of the eight principles proposed by Tack with the U.S. proposal does not show great differences." Jaén Suárez, *Las Negociaciones de los Tratados Torrijos–Carter*, p. 281.

[105] Bell to Bunker, "Resumption of U.S.–Panama treaty negotiations," December 4, 1973, NARA-AAD, RG59. Available online: http://aad.archives.gov/aad/createpdf?rid=108581& dt=2472&dl=1345.

[106] "Ocho principios," December 19, 1973, folder Negociaciones 1973, no. 546, AMREP, sec. 14.

substantial ambiguity and failed to address major questions such as the length of the treaty.[107] Perhaps for the first time, however, Tack and Torrijos saw a treaty as a possibility, and they sought to accommodate the United States with flexibility and patience. Panamanian interlocutors acknowledged the Congressional and political constraints Nixon faced, with Torrijos telling his ambassador, "If they want a treaty in a few months, that is good, but if they want to have it next year or even later, that's good too, and we will wait."[108]

At Bunker's urging, Kissinger planned a whirlwind visit to Panama. Torrijos met Kissinger at the airport, joining his motorcade to the Palacio Justo Arosemena, where Tack and Kissinger signed the eight principles at a lively ceremony. The Panamanian crowd roared at the second principle, declaring an end to the hated "perpetuity" clause of 1903. Kissinger's speech was directed beyond Panama's borders to demonstrate a "new dialogue" with Latin America.[109] The eight principles, elaborated by Bunker, Tack, and their assistants, now bore the name Tack–Kissinger.[110] After the signing, Kissinger met Torrijos at the Panama City apartment of Rory González, a friend whose home often served as a getaway for the general. Torrijos wanted to break each of the eight principles into several smaller issues to allow for "successive stages of achievement" to build trust between Panamanians, Americans, and Zonians. Both men evinced frustration with the Zonians' ability to stymie progress. Torrijos stressed how he had kept the peace in the Canal Zone. He negotiated constantly, Torrijos said, and listened to students' speeches for as long as six hours. Both men faced a similar problem. "There is a large group of people, however, whose mission is to see to it there is no agreement. They live off this problem," Torrijos said. This was a challenge Kissinger would soon appreciate.[111]

The trip, along with Kissinger's warm reception at a ministerial in Mexico City,[112] fed Panamanian hopes for a quick treaty, but the signing spurred loud opposition in the United States. "Tack used to say, if we have these eight points, the treaty, we will write it down in a couple of months," González Revilla reflected. "This conceptual agreement, it's got everything."[113] It would

---

[107] In a later NSC meeting, Kissinger referred to the principles as deliberately ambiguous "platitudes."

[108] Bell to Bunker, "U.S.–Panama treaty negotiations: report on developments," January 24, 1974, NARA-AAD, RG59. Available online: http://aad.archives.gov/aad/createpdf?rid=1382&dt=2474&dl=1345.

[109] David Binder, "U.S. agrees to yield sovereignty of canal to Panama," *New York Times*, February 8, 1974, p. 2; Jorden, *Panama Odyssey*, pp. 219–222.

[110] They are often given the reverse name, Kissinger–Tack, in the United States.

[111] Memorandum of conversation between Torrijos and Kissinger, February 7, 1974, DNSA.

[112] Martin to American Republics, "MFM: Discussion of agenda item 4: Panama Canal," March 6, 1974, NARA-AAD, RG59. Available online: http://aad.archives.gov/aad/createpdf?rid=33949&dt=2474&dl=1345.

[113] González Revilla, interview with the author. Shortly after the signing of Tack–Kissinger, Tack told a Danish diplomat he expected a treaty draft by September or October. Daniels to Kissinger, "Canal Treaty negotiations," March 20, 1974. NARA-AAD, RG59. Available online: http://aad.archives.gov/aad/createpdf?rid=33742&dt=2474&dl=1345.

not be so easy. The day after the ceremony, a Congressional campaign began, opposing the transfer of the canal. Democratic Representative John Murphy alleged that the Torrijos government was unstable and linked to drug trafficking – even warning that a coup was in the offing. Senator Strom Thurmond continued his bombastic opposition, called the Tack–Kissinger principles "a pseudotreaty which will cause grave harm to United States' interests." The South Carolinian told his colleagues, "There is nothing of consequence left to negotiate once we surrender our rights, even only in principle."[114] The following month, Thurmond introduced a resolution, cosponsored by thirty-four senators, insisting that the United States maintain sovereign rights over the Canal Zone.[115]

After the signing, the teams confronted the complex task of filling in the details conveniently omitted to arrive at an agreement. On the Panamanian side, the negotiations had been handled mostly by Tack and González Revilla. Now the rest of the foreign policy cadre, including the official negotiators, tried to grasp the meaning of the principles. These advisors, including Jorge Illueca and Juan Antonio Stagg, along with former negotiators Carlos López Guevara and Diógenes de la Rosa, met on March 5 to study the agreement. They generated a forty-eight-page list of questions deconstructing nearly every word of the agreement. The meetings on Contadora were notable for their relaxed tone and lack of heated historical diatribes, while the document was full of references to decades-old UN and OAS resolutions.[116] Torrijos had said he wanted to avoid just that, but the weight of history and the ingrained tendency of the Panamanian foreign ministry to appeal to it was hard to overcome. Having been left out of the process, the advisors did not hesitate to cast stones, while also insisting against the advice of their own team that the entire treaty be conducted under the United Nations.[117]

The principles were brief and general, but the final treaty would necessarily be complex. Tack and Torrijos' strategy was to address easier points first to build trust and increase various factions' investment in reaching an agreement. The next phase of negotiations would require a larger and more specialized team. A specific agreement would also be more open to criticism, and Torrijos was concerned about attacks from the left. Those two facts led to the inclusion of a broader array of men. Some were selected largely for technical expertise as lawyers or engineers, while others, such as Illueca, represented factions of the left. When the negotiators, including Bunker, reconvened on Contadora after Kissinger's departure, the amount of work remaining eroded some of the

[114] "A campaign starts in Congress to keep control of Panama Canal," *New York Times*, February 9, 1974, p. 4.

[115] S.Res. 301, 93rd Congress.

[116] Illueca, Stagg, de la Rosa, and López Guevara, "Cuestionario formulado por el grupo de negociadores y asesores," March 5, 1974, folder Negociaciones 1972–1974, no. 548, AMREP, i-ii, 1–47. Translation from Spanish by author.

[117] Jaén Suárez, *Las Negociaciones de los Tratados Torrijos–Carter*, p. 293.

optimism. Tensions surfaced between Tack and the young González Revilla. Tack's prestige had been bolstered by the accords, but this also made him a potential challenger.[118] To complicate matters, despite the principles, U.S. negotiators were still working under essentially unchanged guidelines, including for a fifty-year treaty, with longer options for a sea-level canal. Bunker understood the importance of duration to the Panamanians, noting it after his first trip to Contadora. Without authorization to change the termination date, Bunker avoided the issue over the course of the next year, fearing that a mention of fifty years would scuttle the talks.[119] The inflexible instructions frustrated both sides. Years later, González Revilla felt Nixon and Kissinger had used the eight principles as a way to prolong the negotiations without making progress. He recalled:

After the eight points, the first round of negotiations was absolutely ridiculous. The position of the US had gone back to the worst position in the last ten or fifteen years... And at that point it was an absolute frustration from everyone in the government. Torrijos – very, extremely frustrated. Because we all thought we had it done and Tack thought two months to develop the full treaty. We were so far away, that it was not even worth it to negotiate.[120]

González Revilla pointed to the old guidelines as evidence. "What Kissinger was doing, I think, was playing with the same guidelines, but with more brilliance."[121]

In fact, it appears Kissinger did want to conclude the treaties. In April, he urged Tack to make a "negotiating breakthrough" before further opposition was able to mobilize. However, they were not his top priority, and he needed the president to sign new instructions on duration.[122] For Nixon, the negotiations were never of more than marginal importance.[123] As the teams on Contadora tried to take the next steps, the House Judiciary Committee discussed impeachment and a special prosecutor prepared a request for the White House tapes. Many senators and representatives had made their hostility to a canal treaty known. Nixon faced an ever-growing battle with Congress, and he did not want to open another front.

With their president consumed by other matters, the dated guidelines tied the U.S. negotiators' hands in replying to Panamanian grievances they saw as just. Both pushed for greater latitude. With progress on the main issues out of

---

[118] Ibid., p. 295.

[119] Jorden, *Panama Odyssey*, p. 277.

[120] González Revilla, interview with the author.

[121] Ibid.

[122] Bell, "Secretary's conversation with Foreign Minister Tack," April 23, 1974. NARA-AAD, RG59. Available online: http://aad.archives.gov/aad/createpdf?rid=51979&dt=2474&dl=1345.

[123] For example, Nixon's only mentions of Panama in his memoirs mention the country in passing while talking about travels during his vice presidency.

reach, the teams focused on conceptual agreements and on listing the matters that would need to be addressed under each principle. Tack and Bunker "agreed that the duration and expansion issues should be put aside until all other issues are resolved to our mutual satisfaction."[124] In March, the Panamanian team presented a thirty-eight-page list of questions. Some of the most incendiary questions had been removed from the earlier draft, but it still pressed for more specific answers. What will be the date of termination? Will that date be in this century?[125] Tack employed comments from outside advisors to position himself as a moderate while generating pressure on Bunker and Bell by demonstrating that many Panamanians were less inclined to compromise. The question of duration hung over the teams' progress.[126]

As late as November 1974, Bunker noted Panamanian cooperation and thought he could get a treaty by March 1975.[127] Panama had eased its position on operations through accepting a joint structure to run the canal. The United States would retain ultimate control during the treaty, but Panama would have increasing responsibilities to permit training and accommodation.[128] The teams were fruitfully progressing through major issues. To get a treaty, however, decisions needed to be made on issues dear to Congress and the Department of Defense. Panamanian frustration grew over the evasive responses on duration, as they had offered concessions. In early 1975, Bunker suggested the Pentagon accept the end of the century as a termination date – echoing Panama's position. The Pentagon answered that it could stomach twenty-five years for operation of the canal, but demanded forty years for defense. Bunker and Bell knew it was a nonstarter with Panama, and fought to change it, precipitating an interagency struggle. Having been left out of the Contadora negotiations, the Pentagon demanded a stronger voice.[129]

Bunker pressed for a presidential decision in the summer of 1974 to settle the disagreement with Secretary of Defense James Schlesinger. Nixon was nearing a choice between resignation and impeachment. Wiretapping scandals threatened Kissinger, too. It is not clear whether the Nixon administration made an explicit decision to postpone a treaty, but rumors circulated in Panama that it had.[130] Regardless, Nixon had lost authority. The *New York Times*

---

[124] Bunker to Kissinger, "U.S.–Panama treaty negotiations: Report of chief negotiator-level talks," April 5, 1974, NARA-AAD, RG59. Available online: http://aad.archives.gov/aad/createpdf? rid=52247&dt=2474&dl=1345.

[125] "Principales materias vinculadas a los ocho principios," March 19, 1974, folder Negociaciones 1972–1974, no. 548, AMREP, sec. 3, pp. 1–38.

[126] Bell to González Revilla, "Deputies working paper," April 13, 1974, folder Negociaciones 1972–1974, no. 548, AMREP, sec. 15, 1–8.

[127] Bunker to Kissinger, "U.S.–Panama treaty negotiations: Report of chief negotiator-level talks," April 5, 1974.

[128] Bunker to Kissinger, "U.S.–Panama treaty negotiations: Chief negotiator talks," June 30, 1974.

[129] Jorden, *Panama Odyssey*, pp. 277–289.

[130] Jaén Suárez, *Las Negociaciones de los Tratados Torrijos–Carter*, pp. 296–297.

summarized: "[N]o one who knows Mr. Nixon's thinking believes the new Canal treaty will be concluded. The reason is simply stated: Senator Thurmond and his 34 conservative colleagues represent the President's last barrier against impeachment... So forget a new canal treaty for a while."[131]

After years of intrigue and months of daily drama between the White House and Congress, President Nixon announced on August 8 that he would resign rather than face trial on articles of impeachment. Even as the news was breaking in Washington, Kissinger sent Ambassadors Bunker and Jorden an urgent note to Tack to assure him that the resignation "will not in any way affect the negotiation" and that Kissinger intended to "press ahead" for a new treaty.[132] Nixon's departure reopened the possibility of progress, but President Gerald Ford's position was not clear. Negotiations continued through August 1974, with a decision to negotiate the SOFA.

Frustrated by the pace and feeling pressure from the left, Torrijos responded by going on the offensive – shaking the monkey's chain, as he liked to put it. Torrijos had made common cause with Cuba nearly since he took power, giving the Cuban ambassador a prominent platform at the UN Security Council, for example, but he stopped short of causing real alarm in Washington. After waiting months to hear a proposal on duration, Torrijos wanted to cause alarm. He approached democratic Latin American leaders about reinstating diplomatic ties with Cuba en masse.[133] Jorden noted: "Clearly, [Torrijos] looked on the opening to Cuba as a way to shake Washington out of its lethargy."[134] As with Torrijos' previous gambits, the United States tried to block cooperation. In this case, it had greater success getting other countries to back down. The U.S. administration warned that closer ties with Cuba could ruin negotiations, but the pressure steeled Torrijos' determination to demonstrate his independence. While rapprochement with Cuba would placate students and other leftists, Torrijos did not want to spook Panamanian businessmen and investors with the specter of Cuban-style nationalizations, and he knew Washington was watching. The general played to both sides. To open relations with the hemisphere's only communist state, Torrijos' delegation was headed by well-known free-market economist Nicolás Ardito Barletta. Accompanying Ardito Barletta

---

[131] David Binder, "Impeachment's effect on foreign policy is growing," *New York Times*, August 4, 1974.

[132] Kissinger to Tack, "Secretarial message," August 9, 1974, NARA-AAD, RG59. Available online: http://aad.archives.gov/aad/createpdf?rid=124886&dt=2474&dl=1345.

[133] Jaén Suárez questions Jorden's interpretation of the ties with Cuba being driven by Torrijos' frustration with negotiations. Instead, he emphasizes that Torrijos had slowly built ties with Cuba since 1971 and had previously considered establishing relations, Jaén Suárez, Las Negociaciones de los Tratados Torrijos–Carter, p. 306. Others, including González Revilla, made this connection, however, in an interview with the author. It seems clear that the move was made in part to help Torrijos with the left, which was clearly frustrated with the pace of the canal talks.

[134] Jorden, *Panama Odyssey*, p. 259.

were people from across the political spectrum, including student leader and lawyer Adolfo Ahumada and businessmen.[135] Tack insisted to U.S. diplomats that Castro served as a moderating influence on Panamanian leftists who looked to the revolutionary for guidance.[136] The delegation announced diplomatic ties on August 27, 1974, in Havana. The decision helped Torrijos shore up his left flank just as the negotiations turned to the sensitive questions of neutrality and defense.

The major dispute on defense concerned what would happen upon the treaty's expiration. Panama argued it should be solely responsible for defense and believed the United States had agreed to this in the Tack–Kissinger principles.[137] Bell did not believe Panama was capable of defending the canal alone.[138] The real sticking point for Panama was the massive U.S. military presence; for the United States, the worry was the Cold War and assuring the canal would remain open. That did not require the physical presence of U.S. troops on Panamanian soil, as González Revilla wrote Torrijos.[139] Future president Aristides Royo called the U.S. proposal "unacceptable," saying that the U.S. idea of joint defense was to "turn the whole country into a military base."[140] Negotiators López Guevara and de la Rosa argued that the U.S. military presence in Panama should be regulated the same way U.S. bases were treated in Spain, Iceland, Japan, and elsewhere.[141] The argument appealed to Panamanians and offered a model negotiators could point to in talks.

Despite the U.S. Department of Defense's opposition to a wider treaty, the SOFA was handled swiftly, based on texts used elsewhere.[142] This was more surprising given Torrijos' choice to head the SOFA negotiating team – Rómulo Escobar Bethancourt, the rector of the Universidad de Panamá and

---

[135] Ibid., pp. 256–260, María Mercedes de la Guardia de Corró, *Hasta la Última Gota: Gabriel Lewis Galindo* (Cali: Cargraphics, 2009). Ahumada and Ardito Barletta, interviews with the author.

[136] Ahumada recounted how in 1976 Fidel Castro insisted to Torrijos that he continue negotiating despite the frustrating pace. Also see Jaén Suárez, *Las Negociaciones de los Tratados Torrijos–Carter*, pp. 306–307.

[137] Nicolás González Revilla to Morey Bell, August 11, 1974, folder Negociaciones del nuevo tratado del canal, agosto 1974, no. 550, AMREP, sec. 3, pp. 1–3. Emphases in original.

[138] Bell to González Revilla, August 14, 1974, folder Negociaciones del nuevo tratado del canal, agosto 1974, no. 550, AMREP, sec. 5. Emphases in original.

[139] "Comentario verbal hecho por Morey Bell," August 16, 1974, folder Negociaciones del nuevo tratado del canal, agosto 1974, no. 550, AMREP, sec. 5, n.p; Nicolás González Revilla to Omar Torrijos, August 17, 1974, folder Negociaciones del nuevo tratado del canal, agosto 1974, no. 550, AMREP, sec. 5, n.p.

[140] Aristides Royo, "Opiniones de los negociadores estadounidenses," September 12, 1974, folder Negociaciones del nuevo tratado del canal, agosto 1974, no. 550, AMREP, sec. 7, pp. 1–3.

[141] López Guevara and de la Rosa to J.A. Tack, "Punto 7 de la declaración Tack-Kissinger," September 17, 1974, folder Negociaciones del nuevo tratado del canal, agosto 1974, no. 550, AMREP, sec. 8, n.p.

[142] Bunker to Kissinger, "U.S.–Panama treaty negoaitions (sic): Reports of chief negotiators' session," November 7, 1974. NARA-AAD, RG59. Available online: http://aad.archives.gov/aad/createpdf?rid=171119&dt=2474&dl=1345.

famed critic of U.S. policy. The choice played well domestically. "Torrijos concluded that, if a leftist like Rómulo could work out a SOFA with the Americans, Panama's Marxists and activist students would not likely oppose it."[143] The teams addressed problems of wording and finished the drafts in late January, allowing Bunker and Tack to finalize the accords on March 6.[144] "[T]he SOFA opened the doors to the rest of the negotiations," Ahumada said. "The negotiations took off when the U.S. military could breathe calmly about their presence in Panama." At the same time, Panama had started a process of reducing the fourteen military bases on the isthmus to an interim number of four. However, the SOFA also postponed the question of duration.[145]

President Ford's lack of engagement created major problems for the U.S. team. Following Bunker's earlier request, Kissinger sent a draft memo asking for new negotiating guidelines that would allow as little as twenty-five years for both operation and defense of the canal.[146] The Defense Department restated demands for a fifty-year minimum for defense rights. Jorden criticized the proposal:

At this point in history, to seek another 50 years of U.S. responsibility for canal defense is folly. To say this 'may be a little too much for Panama to swallow' is a considerable understatement. In fact, Panama will choke on such a proposal... For three-quarters of all Panamanians now living, 50 years is, repeat is 'perpetuity.' General Torrijos and probably all others involved in this negotiation will almost certainly be gone before the expiration of such a period, and they are acutely aware of that fact.[147]

Despite impassioned pleas from Jorden, Bell, and Bunker, Ford offered nothing new. Kissinger pressed him, too, but Ford dodged the matter. Ford's ambivalence led to another frustrating year. Panama became more assertive, especially on issues of lands and waters and economic compensation. The Panamanian lands and waters team was led by the architect Edwin Fábrega, whose knowledge of the Canal Zone far exceeded that of his U.S. counterparts.[148] Fábrega's assistants included the geographer Omar Jaén Suárez, a detail-minded man who would later become the preeminent Panamanian historian of the canal.

The team's premise was that Panama would temporarily grant the United States the use of territories truly necessary for the canal's operation and defense. In January 1975, Fábrega began presenting detailed proposals that questioned U.S. justifications for keeping long-idle parcels. Panama insisted the defense of

---

[143] Jorden, *Panama Odyssey*, p. 268.

[144] Ahumada, interview with the author. Jorden to Kissinger, "Negotiation of Status of Forces Agreement," January 21, 1975, NARA-AAD, RG59; Jaén Suárez, *Las Negociaciones de los Tratados Torrijos–Carter*, pp. 328–329.

[145] Ahumada, interview with the author. Translation from Spanish by author.

[146] Jaén Suárez, *Las Negociaciones de los Tratados Torrijos–Carter*, pp. 328–329.

[147] Bell and Jorden to Bunker, "U.S.–Panama treaty negotiations: Proposed change in presidential instructions," March 2, 1975, NARA-AAD, RG59. Available online: http://aad.archives.gov/aad/createpdf?rid=45180&dt=2476&dl=1345.

[148] Jorden, *Panama Odyssey*, pp. 466–468.

the canal required only three military bases – one on each coast and another in the middle.[149] The initial U.S. proposal offered to return about 200,000 acres, less than 60 percent of the Canal Zone. It excluded sites Panamanians considered essential.[150] The low-key, technocratic team continued to bargain. The Panamanians were far more prepared than the Americans, who were hampered by poor guidelines, bureaucratic resistance, and lesser knowledge.[151] Given that much of the land was occupied by military facilities, the talks were closely linked to defense. For years, Panama had argued that the headquarters of the U.S. Southern Command (SOUTHCOM), the School of the Americas, and training zones had no relation to canal defense. The bases not only violated Panama's sovereignty, they contravened the hated treaty of 1903![152] Sites the United States labeled essential had "not been used for many years" and were retained "for contingency planning."[153] Panama hoped to free up land around Panama City and Colón, which had been constrained by the Canal Zone and military installations.[154] Torrijos saw the cities' expansion as central to his social and economic policies.

In the negotiations, Panamanian leaders influenced U.S. policy despite their country's small size through persuasion, ideas, and information. Panama often argued that "the creation of a friendly environment [is] indispensable to effective defense."[155] That is, the best way to ensure the security of the canal was through a content, proud Panamanian population. The Panamanian negotiators wrote: "The only true guarantee for the security of the canal is that it is surrounded by a friendly population, which protects the canal of its own desire because it feels like a participant in it and because the canal will be transferred to it at the end of the treaty."[156] Panamanians redefined the problem of the canal, and the idea gained currency with U.S. officials. In his plea to Bunker and Kissinger for more flexible instructions, Jorden repeated the

[149] "Puntos de vista de los negociadores de la república de Panamá sobre materia concerniente al use y tierras y aguas," January 21, 1975, folder Negociaciones del nuevo tratado del canal, agosto 1974, no. 554, AMREP, pp. 1–5. See also Jaén Suárez, *Las Negociaciones de los Tratados Torrijos–Carter*, pp. 333–359.

[150] Jorden, *Panama Odyssey*, p. 276.

[151] Meeting summary, February 5, 1975, folder Negociaciones del nuevo tratado del canal, agosto 1974, no. 554, AMREP, n.p.; "Resumen de las discusiones del uso de tierras y aguas," February 6, 1975, folder Negociaciones del nuevo tratado del canal, agosto 1974, no. 554, AMREP, n.p.

[152] The former negotiator Carlos López Guevara published a pamphlet making that case in legal terms in 1971. Carlos López Guevara, "Panamá Tiene Derecho a Denunciar la Convención del Canal Ístmico de 1903 por Violaciones a la Misma por Parte de Estados Unidos" (Panamá: Centro de Impresión Educativa, 1971).

[153] "Minutes of the meetings on lands and waters," February 10, 1975, folder Negociaciones del nuevo tratado, no. 554, AMREP, n.p.

[154] "Minutes of the meetings on lands and waters," February 7, 1975, folder Negociaciones del nuevo tratado, no. 554, AMREP, 1–3.

[155] "Minutes of the meetings on lands and waters," February 10, 1975, folder Negociaciones del nuevo tratado, no. 554, AMREP, n.p.

[156] "Defensa," February 11, 1975, folder Negociaciones del nuevo tratado, no. 554, AMREP, 1–5. Translation from Spanish by author.

argument, noting that three Panamanians on a dark night could destroy the locks and close the canal for years.[157] Bunker told Kissinger and Ford at a May 15 NSC meeting that a treaty would provide "more real security than we have today." Kissinger added that "failure to conclude a treaty is going to get us into a *cause célèbre,* with harassment, demonstrations, bombing of embassies."[158] In a May 22 speech, Bunker went further, mentioning the possibility of sabotage or other attacks: "We would find it difficult if not impossible to keep the canal running against all-out Panamanian opposition."[159] Panama's argument gradually became the conventional wisdom regarding the canal's security.

When Bunker returned to Contadora in March, it was increasingly clear he had exhausted his authority. As Bell confided to Bunker, Panama had made concessions in the SOFA and expected U.S. flexibility in return. "The trouble is that we have nothing to take our turn with at this point."[160] Tack said it was time for a "real and visible advance regarding lands and waters and to initiate conversations about the duration of a new treaty."[161] Bunker was stuck. His requests for twenty-five-year duration had gone unanswered, and Bunker returned to Washington in mid March to seek concessions from his own government. Torrijos sensed the stalemate and turned to his closest allies for help. The year 1974 saw the election of several democratic presidents who viewed the canal's status as a matter of justice: Daniel Oduber in Costa Rica, Carlos Andrés Pérez in Venezuela, and Alfonso López Michelsen in Colombia. Two weeks after Bunker left Contadora, these three presidents joined General Torrijos on the island. While appeals to the Non-Aligned Movement and to Cuba had strengthened Torrijos' image of independence, these presidents' proximity to the United States made them important advocates. Upon the conclusion of the meetings, they drafted a long letter to President Ford. Highlighting the "great interest for all of Latin America" in the canal dispute, the leaders criticized the U.S. position:

The Government of Panama hopes to agree on a fixed term for the duration of the new treaty which will put an end, in unequivocal terms, to the unlimited concession over the Canal established by the Treaty of 1903 between the United States and Panama. The term should not extend beyond December 31 of 1994. The Government of the United States, on the other hand, has demanded a longer term, originally fixed at a minimum of fifty years, a time lapse not in agreement with the trends of the times.

---

[157] Bell and Jorden to Bunker, "U.S.–Panama treaty negotiations: Proposed change in presidential instructions," March 2, 1975, NARA-AAD, RG59.

[158] Minutes, Part II, National Security Council meeting, May 15, 1975. Ford Presidential Library (FPL). Available online: www.fordlibrarymuseum.gov/library/document/0312/1552390.pdf.

[159] "Bunker is fearful of Panama conflict if canal talks fail," May 23, 1975, *New York Times*, p. 3.

[160] Bell to Bunker, "U.S.–Panama treaty negotiations: Report of developments, February 23–March 1," March 2, 1975. NARA-AAD, RG59. Available online: http://aad.archives.gov/aad/createpdf?rid=45860&dt=2476&dl=1345.

[161] Tack, "Exposición hecha por el ministro Tack al Embajador Bunker," March 12, 1975, folder Negociaciones del nuevo tratado, no. 554, AMREP, n.p.

It is obvious that if the government of the United States insists in maintaining the existing situation, this position would create a serious problem of unpredictable political consequences for the Government of Panama, and may even lead to threats of public unrest and threats against the security of the Canal itself.[162]

Ford took a discourteous three months to respond with brief, platitude-filled notes to the three presidents.[163] A five-month feud, almost entirely about treaty duration, continued between State and the recalcitrant Pentagon.[164] Many in the Pentagon, including Secretary of Defense James Schlesinger, preferred a breakdown in treaty talks – maybe even a permanent one.

In May, Kissinger told Ford that an NSC meeting on Panama was needed. When Ford expressed his worries about Congress, Kissinger warned of "massive riots" in Panama and diplomatic beatings for the United States.[165] Kissinger recognized the political sensitivities; he suggested negotiating but delaying signing and ratification until after the election. "If these negotiations fail, we will be beaten to death in every international forum and there will be riots all over Latin America."[166] In an NSC meeting on May 15, Bunker told Ford that a treaty was "within reach." He asked for flexibility on lands and waters and duration, starting at fifty years, but with the option to fall back to twenty years as the shortest term. Failure would provoke a "confrontation" that would lead to worldwide condemnation and "hamper the operation of the waterway." Kissinger pointed out that the failed 1967 treaties had offered thirty-three years, much better than the current terms. Ford fretted about the domestic political repercussions.

Defense's hard-line was clear. "Flexibility" was just a giveaway, and once the United States sacrificed its "sovereignty," Panama would bargain down the timeline. "When the U.S. shows strength and determination, it receives respect. When it recedes from its position, it whets appetites," Schlesinger said. Trying to gain the president's approval, Kissinger argued that with flexibility to go as low as twenty-five years on defense rights, the negotiators could actually get forty or forty-five years. "This is no issue to face the world on. It looks like pure colonialism," he said.[167] Facing discord, Ford again postponed a decision. The delay frustrated Torrijos, and the Panamanians began "toughening their position" so the general could "protect his political flanks should the talks break down." Torrijos and Tack increasingly believed the State Department had lost to the Pentagon, and that Bunker, Bell, and Jorden's good

---

[162] López Michelsen, Odúber, and Pérez to Ford, March 24, 1975, folder Negociaciones, no. 529, AMREP, n.p.

[163] Jorden, *Panama Odyssey*, p. 280.

[164] Ibid., pp. 278–289.

[165] Memorandum of conversation between Ford, Kissinger, and Scowcroft, May 5, 1975, DNSA.

[166] Memorandum of conversation between Ford and Kissinger, May 12, 1975, DNSA.

[167] Minutes of National Security Council meeting, Part II, May 15, 1975, FPL.

intentions were hollow.[168] Pressure from Congress and Defense was unabated, and fear of domestic backlash paralyzed Ford. In June, Representative Dan Snyder attached an amendment to the State Department appropriations bill to prohibit funds from being used to negotiate a canal treaty.[169] Torrijos cordially offered the U.S. negotiators a loan to continue their work![170] Though the Senate later struck the provision, its passage in the House was a clear signal regarding a treaty's unpopularity. Only Kissinger's insistence kept the matter on the agenda.

In mid July, Kissinger pressed Ford to make a decision in the upcoming NSC meeting. "If we don't settle Panama, I fear we will have a Vietnam in the Western Hemisphere. Our Army will be engaged in guerrilla warfare, pilloried in international forums – all for something we will give up eventually, and on worse terms if we wait."[171] Ford wanted a treaty if it were "something we have bargained for which will protect our rights." Ford wanted to limit political costs, while avoiding violence in Panama. "We want the situation under control here and certainly not a renewal of the fighting from 1964 there where people were killed and we had a hell of a mess."[172] A presidential order, signed on August 18, authorized not less than forty years for defense rights and twenty for operations, though U.S. negotiators were told to seek longer periods.[173]

The "new" position was one the U.S. ambassador had told his superiors months earlier would be unacceptable in Panama. Furthermore, between the NSC meeting and the signing of the order, Torrijos flatly stated: "[I]t cannot go one day beyond the year 2000." Torrijos blamed U.S. domestic politics and questioned the appeals to Congress and the Pentagon whenever the "crucial moment" arrived. Pressure was building in Panama, too, and his ability to keep the peace around the canal was based on a sense of hope among the population. "I haven't lost hope, but I cannot live just on hope."[174] Torrijos warned Jorden that he feared rioting, and that students and activists were growing

---

[168] Jorden to Bell, "Canal negotiations: Local atmosphere cooling," May 8, 1975, NARA-AAD, RG59. Available online: http://aad.archives.gov/aad/createpdf?rid=86746&dt=2476&dl=1345.

[169] Graeme S. Mount and Mark Gauthier, *895 Days That Changed the World: The Presidency of Gerald R. Ford* (Montréal: Black Rose Books, 2006), pp. 172–173.

[170] Bunker to Tack, via Jorden, personal letter, June 27, 1975. NARA-AAD, RG59. Available online: http://aad.archives.gov/aad/createpdf?rid=105249&dt=2476&dl=1345.

[171] Memoranda of conversations between Ford and Kissinger, July 7 and July 21, 1975, FPL. Available online: www.fordlibrarymuseum.gov/library/guides/findingaid/Memoranda_of_Conversations.

[172] Minutes of National Security Council meeting, July 23, 1975, FPL. Available online. Kissinger discusses, and quotes widely from, the NSC meetings in *Years of Renewal* (New York: Simon & Schuster, 1999), pp. 761–765.

[173] Gerald Ford, Presidential Decision Memorandum no. 302, August 8, 1975.

[174] Qtd. in Binder, "Panama leader says U.S. politics stall canal talks," *New York Times*, July 28, 1975, p. 3.

impatient.[175] Panama kept up its frenetic diplomatic pace, both to pressure the United States and to give Panamanian leftists something to cheer about. In addition to joining the Non-Aligned Movement, Panama won another term on the Security Council despite having occupied one of two Latin American spots two years prior.[176]

After a six-month absence, the longest breakdown since Tack–Kissinger, Ford ordered Bunker to return to Panama in September. Torrijos said that the sooner the ambassador could get to Panama and counter widespread pessimism, the better.[177] Bunker's return to Contadora disappointed. The U.S. position seeking at least forty years for defense with options for a post-treaty presence and guarantees regarding new canal construction still had a ring of perpetuity. The frustration was clear in the Foreign Ministry's public statement, even after Bunker and Jorden's pleas: "The Foreign Ministry feels that there has been very little progress in this stage of the negotiations."[178] Stagnation, combined with harder-line, public comments from Kissinger, provoked demonstrations and an attack on the U.S. embassy, where the crowd railed not just against the *gringos*, but against Torrijos.[179] Torrijos insisted talks continue – though he was far from starry-eyed about their prospects. He often stressed the threat from the left, implying that any government that replaced him might lean decisively to the Soviet bloc. His challenges went beyond the ideological. After solid growth, the Panamanian economy was foundering, with high unemployment and growing fiscal deficits. A treaty would offer legitimacy for Torrijos, but in the meantime, he sought the transfer of land for development and the employment of more Panamanians in canal operations. Even as Torrijos resigned himself that a treaty would not be done before the U.S. elections, he pressed for near-term, concrete concessions. Transferring land required Congressional approval, and the Ford administration did not wish to stir the pot.[180]

<hr>

[175] Jorden to Rogers and Bunker, "Talk with Torrijos," July 7, 1975, NARA-AAD, RG 59. Available online: http://aad.archives.gov/aad/createpdf?rid=124700&dt=2476&dl=1345.

[176] Binder, "The canal is more than a two-nation problem," November 9, 1975, *New York Times*, p. E3; Jaén Suárez, *Las Negociaciones de los Tratados Torrijos–Carter*, pp. 381–383.

[177] Jorden to Bunker and Rogers, "Message to Torrijos," August 11, 1975, NARA-AAD, RG59. Available online: http://aad.archives.gov/aad/createpdf?rid=144714&dt=2476&dl=1345; Jorden to State Department, "Canal treaty negotiations: Local atmosphere," August 14, 1975, NARA-AAD, RG59. Available online: http://aad.archives.gov/aad/createpdf?rid=144701& dt=2476&dl=1345.

[178] Qtd. in "Foreign ministry communique on negotiators' departure," September 18, 1975, NARA-AAD, RG 59. Available online: http://aad.archives.gov/aad/createpdf?rid=165793& dt=2476&dl=1345. Also in Jaén Suárez, *Las Negociaciones de los Tratados Torrijos–Carter*, p. 389.

[179] Jorden, *Panama Odyssey*, pp. 298–299.

[180] Jorden, Bunker, and Rogers, "Talk with Torrijos," NARA-AAD, RG59. Available online: http://aad.archives.gov/aad/createpdf?rid=165774&dt=2476&dl=1345.

Bunker returned to Contadora in November, with bleak prospects for progress. Jorden wrote: "[Bunker] knew the hard-line stand he was being asked to push reflected not military reality but domestic politics." As he saw it, the danger to the canal was exacerbated by a large, continued troop presence.[181] Retired Lt. General Welborn Dolvin joined the U.S. team in early November to help with the Pentagon and Congress.[182] Torrijos' inner circle questioned the will of the United States to come to any conclusion and criticized the electorally motivated delays. Bunker offered the shortest allowed duration: a December 31, 1999 expiration for U.S. operational control and forty years for defense rights.[183] In mid December, the Panamanian team flew to Washington, hopeful of improving on Bunker's offer. But the political climate in Washington was cooling. A once-obscure California governor challenged Ford for the Republican presidential nomination. Election season had arrived early, and the negotiations fell apart.[184] A frustrated Omar Torrijos boarded a plane to Havana.

Elections: Anticipation and Doubt

Torrijos' trip to meet Fidel Castro, in response to an invitation issued when relations were reestablished, included a large group involved in the negotiations: Ardito Barletta, González Revilla, Escobar Bethancourt, Ahumada, and Illueca. Economic, church, cultural, and military figures went, too, including Colonel Manuel Noriega.[185] Some 200 people joined Torrijos' entourage, which was greeted by white-and-red clad crowds. Torrijos had gotten friendly advice from Jorden and U.S. Senator Jacob Javits about moderating his message while in Cuba. The general told reporters that while he admired its social progress, the Cuban system would not work in Panama.[186] Ahumada related that Castro advised Torrijos to be patient, to continue negotiating, and to deter aggression in the zone during the U.S. campaign.[187]

---

[181] Jorden, *Panama Odyssey*, p. 307.

[182] Bell to Jorden, "U.S.–Panama treaty negotiations: Unilateral actions," November 3, 1975. Available online: http://aad.archives.gov/aad/createpdf?rid=204496&dt=2476&dl=1345.

[183] Bunker to Kissinger, Clements, and Brown, "Panama negotiations: Status report," November 26, 1975.

[184] In November, a front-page *New York Times* article called Reagan a 2-to-1 favorite to win the Florida primary, while also noting the rise of a "boyish-looking Georgian." In fact, Ford would win the Florida primary, though by a relatively narrow margin. R.W. Apple, Jr., "Reagan is termed Florida favorite," *New York Times*, November 17, 1975, p. 1.

[185] Jorden, "Panamanian delegation accompanying Torrijos to Cuba," January 8, 1976, NARA-AAD, RG59. Available online: http://aad.archives.gov/aad/createpdf?rid=275345&dt=2082&dl=1345.

[186] Binder, "Panama's leader hailed in Havana," *New York Times*, January 11, 1976, p. 8. See also Jorden, *Panama Odyssey*, pp. 310–314.

[187] Ahumada, interview with the author. Jorden also makes this point.

Whereas 1975 had been characterized by slow, technical progress, 1976 saw little progress at all. In early 1976, the teams had reached conceptual agreements on three of the eight Tack–Kissinger principles. Once hopeful of concluding a treaty in early 1975, Bunker resigned himself to completing the remaining conceptual agreements in October 1976 – as a best-case scenario.[188] Panamanians listened anxiously to U.S. politicians' statements that deployed the republic's name as a shibboleth. The campaign brought little courage from Ford, who delayed action for fear of criticism. In response to candidate Ronald Reagan's attacks, Ford took tougher stances on Panama – tougher, in fact, than his own presidential guidelines. "The United States, as long as I am President, will do nothing to give up the control of the operations of the canal and will do nothing to give up the military protection of the canal," Ford told reporters.[189] In the final stretches of the primaries, Ford told a questioner: "[U]nder no circumstances will I ever do away with our right, our authority, our national defense usability of the Panama Canal... And we will get that kind of canal right and it will be for at least 50 years."[190] The statements put U.S. diplomats and negotiators in an impossible situation. Torrijos discounted a certain amount as campaign rhetoric, but the reports soured the public mood. Having bet heavily on the pacts, Torrijos struggled to withstand the long freeze. He set 1977 as the new, public target for a treaty, adding, "Patience has its limits."[191] The negotiations went on, and Bunker made several trips to Contadora, but his presence was mostly symbolic. The White House withdrew from the issue.[192]

By June, Georgia Governor Jimmy Carter emerged as the favorite to challenge the Watergate-plagued Republicans. During the primaries, Carter's position on the canal had been ambiguous, but his public statements gave little reason to hope for a significantly different policy. In response to a question early in the campaign, Carter said he would not give up control or defense rights for the canal. During a debate with Ford, he stated: "I would never give up complete control or practical control of the Panama Canal Zone, but I would continue to negotiate with the Panamanians."[193] As his positions solidified, he recognized in a June speech that Panama retained sovereignty under the

---

[188] Jaén Suárez, *Las Negociaciones de los Tratados Torrijos–Carter*, pp. 519–521.

[189] Ford, "The President's news conference," March 13, 1976, The American Presidency Project. Available online: www.presidency.ucsb.edu/ws/?pid=5703.

[190] Ford, "Remarks and a question-and-answer session at the Abilene Jaycees bicentennial celebration," April 30, 1976, The American Presidency Project. Available online: www.presidency .ucsb.edu/ws/?pid=5918.

[191] "Panama's leader calls for new pact on canal by 1977," *New York Times*, April 10, 1976, p. 9.

[192] Gwertzman, "GOP leaders tell Ford he's harmed as criticism of Kissinger's moves rises," *New York Times*, May 7, 1976, p. 30.

[193] Carter, "Debate with Ford," October 6, 1976, in *Public Papers of the President, Gerald Ford, 1976*, p. 2430.

1903 treaty; the United States gained "control as though we had sovereignty." The distinction, perhaps lost on many Americans, was not lost in Panama. In general, though, Carter's stated desire for "open and continued negotiations" resembled Ford's, especially earlier in 1976.[194]

The stalemated negotiations and personal rivalries caught up with Panama's foreign minister, Juan Antonio Tack. Known as a fierce critic of the United States prior to the Tack–Kissinger announcement, Tack was replaced less for policy than politics. Tack had lost influence to close friends of the general and representatives of leftist movements – Nicolás González Revilla on the one hand and Rómulo Escobar Bethancourt on the other. Aquilino Boyd, who spearheaded the international campaign at the United Nations, replaced Tack in the foreign ministry but never dominated the negotiating table as had Tack in his hey-day.[195]

With talks frozen, Panama tried a much riskier tactic. In late summer, U.S. negotiators received an ominous warning from Escobar Bethancourt that Torrijos had opted for direct actions. In October 1976, several bombs exploded throughout the Canal Zone, the first destroying the car of an anti-treaty Zonian.[196] The United States privately protested that the Panamanian National Guard was behind them. Torrijos, in a letter to Kissinger, vehemently denied it.[197] The authorship of the October bombings was never explicitly claimed,[198] with U.S. officials holding that the Guard, and likely Noriega, was involved. Panama insisted otherwise, but Torrijos later admitted he considered similar tactics. The National Guard had a plan called *agua potable* to destroy the canal's locks if the treaties failed in the Senate.[199] The October 1976 explosions briefly threatened to derail the bilateral relationship, but the United States largely dropped its assertions of official Panamanian involvement. Meanwhile, the U.S. presidential campaign came to a close. Panama played a smaller role in

---

[194] "Excerpts from Carter's speech and his replies," *New York Times*, June 24, 1977, p. 22.

[195] Jaén Suárez, *Las Negociaciones de los Tratados Torrijos–Carter*, pp. 509, 557.

[196] Jorden, *Panama Odyssey*, pp. 332–335; John Dinges, *Our Man in Panama: How General Noriega Used the United States and Made Millions in Drugs and Arms* (New York: Random House, 1990), pp. 83, 86.

[197] Torrijos to Kissinger, November 29, 1976, folder Negociaciones, no. 529, AMREP, n.p.

[198] In an account of questionable veracity, Noreiga claims that the attacks were led by a Central Intelligence Agency trained team of Panamanian explosive experts. Furthermore, he recalls the plan as having been hatched by the CIA station chief and approved by the Director of Central Intelligence George H.W. Bush. Of course, Noriega penned this account from a jail cell after being arrested in an invasion ordered by then-President Bush. Jorden offers a very different account of this same meeting, arguing that the United States was hoping to drop the issue. Manuel Antonio Noriega and Peter Eisner, *America's Prisoner: The Memoirs of Manuel Noriega* (New York: Random House, 1997), pp. 43–48.

[199] This plan is mentioned by Escobar Bethancourt and José de Jesús Martínez. It was also confirmed in interviews with the author. Ardito Barletta, for example, did not know about the plan at the time, but later told Torrijos it was a disastrous idea. The most detailed and credible description is Escobar Bethancourt, *Torrijos*.

the general election than during the Republican primary, but voters frequently raised the issue. Carter rode Southern support and his promise of renewal after a scandal-plagued decade to unseat the unelected incumbent.

Enter Carter

The election of a Democratic president brought hope to the Panamanian negotiating team, despite Carter's cautious campaign statements. Carter and his team decided before inauguration to address the canal negotiations early. Panamanian and U.S. participants credit Carter's political will to tackle the issue early in his term as crucial to the treaties' ratification. What is sometimes lost, however, is that Carter's team was able to conclude the treaties with several months of hard work because of the significant advances made during the previous years. That the treaties figured so high on Carter's agenda was a testament to a long Panamanian struggle to put them there.

After his election, Carter took interest in the negotiations. In mid November meetings with Kissinger and Ford, the president-elect asked both men about the talks. Carter "hoped we would settle Panama," Ford told Kissinger. They agreed "it was very doubtful."[200] Panamanian pressure, aided by friendly Latin American presidents, continued in the preinaugural period. News stories in Panama and the United States noted nervousness in the Panamanian government over Carter's intentions. Days after the election, Venezuelan President Carlos Andrés Pérez emphatically called on Carter to quickly address the impasse.[201] Pérez raised the issue in his congratulatory letter to Carter, saying Carter must "approve the new treaty which will put an end to a situation which identifies a great nation with colonial practices."[202] Foreign Minister Boyd traveled to Washington to press the outgoing Ford administration and sound out Carter's plans – including in a meeting with Sol Linowitz, who served as U.S. ambassador to the OAS under Johnson.[203] Linowitz had grown even more interested in Panama while chairing a commission on inter-American relations during the campaign. Boyd met with Kissinger on December 3 in a meeting made tense by discussion of the canal bombings. The outgoing secretary said 1977 was propitious for negotiations, that he would encourage Cyrus Vance to make Panama a priority, and that "he would do all he could to keep the

---

200 Memorandum of conversation: Ford, Kissinger, and Scowcroft, November 23, 1976. FPL. Available online: www.fordlibrarymuseum.gov/library/document/0314/1553567.pdf.

201 Jaén Suárez, *Las Negociaciones de los Tratados Torrijos–Carter*, p. 569. "Venezuelan: Canal a test for Carter," *Washington Post*, November 11, 1976, p. A23.

202 Pérez to Carter, transmitted in Pete Vaky to State Department, "Message of congratulations from President Perez to President-elect Carter," NARA-AAD, RG59. Available online: http://aad.archives.gov/aad/createpdf?rid=301725&dt=2082&dl=1345.

203 Binder, "Panama presses for commitment by Carter on canal negotiations," *New York Times*, December 3, 1976, p. 5.

matter from becoming a partisan one in the United States."[204] In late December, Bunker flew to Contadora. No one expected major changes, but the visit served as a symbol of continuity and kept the talks in the press.[205]

In the days before inauguration, Carter's intentions were becoming clearer – and more favorable to Panama. A president who three years prior was "vaguely aware" of the dispute was now making the negotiations a priority. Carter described his decision as a matter of justice and as necessary for the canal's safety – using an argument similar to Panama's about the importance of a friendly population.[206] In private meetings, Carter told Congress that the canal would be among the first foreign policy challenges he addressed. Torrijos noted he had received optimistic signals from the incoming administration.[207] Carter's appointment of former Kennedy administration official Cyrus Vance as secretary of state was seen as a positive sign. Vance had emphasized late in the campaign and after the election that the next president would need to address Panama.[208] Panamanian actions over the preceding years had created a problem for U.S. policymakers, placed it on the agenda of a U.S. president, and advanced ideas that Carter seized upon to solve the problem.

Once in office, Carter signaled the issue's importance in two ways. The first NSC meeting was on Panama, and his first presidential directive ordered a review of U.S. policy on the canal negotiations. Second, Carter appointed Linowitz as a temporary, special envoy for the negotiations. Linowitz had recently chaired the Commission on United States–Latin American Relations. Its first report, in October 1974, called the Canal Zone an "anachronism" and recommended the conclusion of a new treaty under the Tack–Kissinger principles.[209] The second report, issued in December 1976, was more direct, urging "the new President to exercise prompt, vigorous, and decisive leadership in negotiating an acceptable compromise."[210]

Panama also was reviewing its position. The foreign ministry was increasingly open to an arrangement in which the United States and Panama guaranteed the neutrality of the canal under a "cooperation treaty" that would be

---

[204] Bell, "The secretary's bilateral with foreign minister Boyd," December 10, 1976, NARA-AAD, RG59. Available online: http://aad.archives.gov/aad/createpdf?rid=312995&dt=2082&dl=1345.

[205] Don Oberdorfer, "U.S., Panama explore 21st century canal neutrality," *Washington Post*, December 25, 1976.

[206] Carter, *Keeping Faith*, pp. 154–155.

[207] Juan de Onís, "Panamanian leader hopeful on new canal pact," and Gwertzman, "Carter will pursue early canal pact and Cyprus accord," *New York Times*, January 14, 1977, p. 1.

[208] Linowitz, *The Making of a Public Man*, p. 150.

[209] Sol M. Linowitz and Kalman H. Silvert, *The Americas in a Changing World: A Report of the Commission on United States-Latin American Relations* (New York: Quadrangle, 1975), pp. 31–32.

[210] Commission on United States-Latin American Relations, *The United States and Latin America, Next Steps: A Second Report* (New York: Center for Inter-American Relations, 1976), pp. 5–6.

renewed periodically.[211] Not everyone in the government was onboard with this compromise. Two weeks after the inauguration, Boyd shuttled to Washington to meet the new secretary and review the main issues in the negotiations. Boyd insisted the treaties expire by 2000. Vance said this was a possibility if the United States retained certain defense rights beyond that date. Boyd considered this as a feasible compromise, but the idea had not yet gained Torrijos' approval. Many in Panama's government insisted on a guarantee by Panama alone or through the United Nations.[212] Boyd was undercut by González Revilla when Panama's embassy stated the next week that Torrijos would support neutrality under a UN framework, but not a U.S. guarantee. Torrijos added, in declarations made on live television, that the foreign minister would no longer be a permanent member of the negotiating team.[213] Boyd, who five years prior had launched the internationalization of Panama's cause at the UNSC, quit in disgust – on TV without warning Torrijos. The highly visible scuffle in part resulted from Rómulo Escobar Bethancourt's machinations to control the negotiations.[214]

The neutrality issue had not been solved within the U.S. government, either. General Dolvin wrote Robert Pastor, the twenty-nine-year-old NSC advisor for Latin American affairs, to say that the NSC memorandum on the topic "was being interpreted by some . . . to include a unilateral right by the United States." Secretary of Defense Harold Brown and Joint Chiefs Chair George Brown had, Dolvin believed, agreed on more ambiguous phrasing.[215] Juan Antonio Stagg, then serving as Panama's consul in New York, wrote Boyd, summing up a meeting with Pastor:

Robert Pastor noted that the discussion of the Panama Canal issue in the National Security Council had been animated, and that not everyone was in agreement with [all the details of] the new treaty, though he didn't give details for obvious reasons. Pastor's main worry was related to the guarantees that Panama could offer the United States regarding the Canal's neutrality and safe transit of U.S. ships after the treaty's termination. A multinational accord on neutrality, or one under the auspices of the United Nations, is not considered sufficient, unless the United States obtained certain rights of unilateral action that permit it to defend said neutrality if its interests are affected.[216]

---

[211] "Alternativas sobre duración y garantías de la neutralidad del canal," n.d., folder Negociaciones 1973, no. 529, AMREP, n.p. Though the document is not dated, events mentioned place it in late 1976 or early 1977.

[212] Carter, *Keeping Faith*, p. 157; Jaén Suárez, *Las Negociaciones de los Tratados Torrijos–Carter*, pp. 573–575.

[213] Embassy of Panama, "Press release," February 9, 1977, AMREP.

[214] Jaén Suárez, *Las Negociaciones de los Tratados Torrijos–Carter*, pp. 577–578; Jorden, *Panama Odyssey*, pp. 348–349.

[215] This became known as the Brown–Brown language. Welborn C. Dolvin to Robert Pastor, "Policy Review Committee meeting," January 31, 1977, Declassified Document Retrieval System (DDRS).

[216] Stagg to Boyd, February 6, 1977, folder Negociaciones, no. 531, AMREP, n.p.

The new administration's preparations intensified with Linowitz's appointment as special representative. Linowitz declined a full-time position because of personal business and because he refused to displace Bunker, an old friend. On February 8, 1977, Carter designated Linowitz "part-time conegotiator." Though he had met the president only once, he would become Carter's conduit for information on the negotiations.[217]

The first negotiations under the Carter administration began in mid February on Contadora. They started poorly. The Panamanian team was unsettled by Boyd's departure. He had been replaced by González Revilla, who was known and liked by many in the U.S. government, but his new role was unclear. Second, Bunker and Linowitz's initial offer did not meet Torrijos' expectations. The presentation of U.S. defense after the treaty's expiration sounded too much like perpetuity for the general to accept. The two sides were testing one another. Did Torrijos want resolution or a constant issue to harp on? Was Carter ready to back away the "never" he articulated in the campaign? The meetings began with delays and absences from Panama, which upset the business-minded Linowitz. Once the formal meetings began, the Panamanians launched a fiery denunciation of the U.S. stance. Only right before the U.S. team's departure did they receive encouraging words from Escobar Bethancourt, who hoped for a quick resumption of talks.[218] The February breakdown led Linowitz to reconsider the treaty format, and helped produced the final and successful approach. He later wrote:

The cornerstone of the strategy would be to divide one treaty into two. The first of the two treaties – and we would insist on agreement on this treaty before we would proceed to the second – would deal solely with security questions, the authority of the United States to protect the canal from armed challenge of any kind, in partnership with Panama or, if necessary, unilaterally. We called it the "Neutrality" Treaty, because in form it was proclaimed as a way of protecting universal access to the canal. The second treaty would deal with Panamanian sovereignty in the Canal Zone, money matters, control of the company that operated the canal, the rights and privileges of American citizens working for the canal company (an immensely complicated question, and very emotional for the individuals concerned), and the logistical details of the presence of American forces on Panamanian soil. The two documents had to be separate because key elements of the first would be permanent, while the second would provide a fixed cutoff date, after which the canal operation would belong to Panama.[219]

Both sides reported to their leaders. Carter called the update "not very encouraging." While he refused to give way on post-treaty defense rights, he signaled

---

[217] Linowitz, *The Making of a Public Man*, pp. 150–152. Jimmy Carter: "Special Representative for the Panama Canal negotiations designation of Sol M. Linowitz," February 8, 1977, The American Presidency Project. Available online: www.presidency.ucsb.edu/ws/?pid=7677.

[218] The frustrating round is described in Jorden, *Panama Odyssey*, pp. 349–356; Jaén Suárez, *Las Negociaciones de los Tratados Torrijos–Carter*, pp. 579–586; Linowitz, *The Making of a Public Man*, pp. 155–158; Escobar Bethancourt, *Torrijos*, pp. 23–26.

[219] Linowitz, *The Making of a Public Man*, p. 153.

a willingness to meet Panama on duration.[220] Carter mentioned the year 2000 to the press, an apparent slip after a decision to use the termination date to gain concessions on neutrality.[221] The leverage was diminished.

Impatient with the laid-back style of Contadora, Linowitz pushed for the next meetings to be held in the United States, at the residence of Panama's ambassador in Washington. An exchange of letters between Carter and Torrijos had improved the disposition of both teams, seeming to convince each that the other truly wanted a treaty. Carter noted "common interests" and called for a "balanced agreement." He told Torrijos he looked forward to meeting him to sign the accords.[222] The March meeting marked the inclusion of Aristides Royo. The negotiators remained distant on many issues. Linowitz spoke of a treaty lasting until 2000; Escobar Bethancourt now pressed for 1990. When the U.S. team sought to clarify questions of neutrality, Panama pushed for the transfer of lands and facilities like the railroad, the ports of Balboa and Colón, and Ancón Hill. The university rector said, "there cannot be a treaty if these don't pass to [Panama's] direction and ownership."[223] At times, the talks collapsed into arguments about who had been flexible. Escobar Bethancourt invoked Carter's letter, saying Carter had "proposed a new spirit for arriving at a treaty. That's the spirit that should be reflected in this meeting."[224]

After a tough morning session, the teams returned to the table. Though Escobar Bethancourt kept up a rigid line, Linowitz's new position on neutrality included significant concessions, including the withdrawal of U.S. troops from the Canal Zone unless a new arrangement had been agreed to. He proposed joint responsibility, without an explicit U.S. unilateral right to intervene.[225] Bunker realized that the president he now represented would take risks to see an accord through. Near the end of the meeting, the old statesman said, "We know what you consider essential. Both the canal and the zone are going to be turned over to Panama, much earlier than had been contemplated."[226] In response to a letter signed by eight Latin American presidents, Bunker and Linowitz planned trips to Colombia and Venezuela.[227] Carter stoked hopes

---

[220] Jimmy Carter, *White House Diary* (New York: Farrar, Straus and Giroux, 2010), p. 29; Jorden, *Panama Odyssey*, pp. 386–387.

[221] Zbigniew Brzezinksi, "Weekly national security report #5," March 18, 1977, DDRS.

[222] Carter to Torrijos, March 9, 1977, DDRS.

[223] The move of the negotiations to Washington also provided an improvement in recordkeeping, with embassy and State personnel on hand. "Informe de la reunión," March 13, 1977, folder no. 47, AMREP. See especially, p. 19.

[224] Ibid., p. 23.

[225] Ibid., p. 15.

[226] Ibid., p. 28.

[227] The visit was mentioned to the Panamanians, who were pleased with the idea, at the end of the March meeting.

for a treaty when he addressed the OAS on April 14, saying: "I am firmly committed to negotiating in as timely a fashion as possible a new treaty which will take into account Panama's legitimate needs as a sovereign nation and our own interests and yours in the efficient operation of a neutral canal, open on a nondiscriminatory basis to all users."[228]

Away from the negotiating table, González Revilla's move from the Panamanian embassy in Washington to the foreign ministry left the position of ambassador to the United States open at a crucial moment. Torrijos' choice for ambassador in 1977 could hardly have been more different than his choice in late 1972. Whereas González Revilla entered as a twenty-seven-year-old neophyte known for his leftist leanings and reliance on the general, Gabriel Lewis Galindo was an established businessman from a wealthy family. Despite his upbringing and confessed admiration for the United States, he was close friends with the general. Lewis Galindo could get through to Torrijos quickly, and "He could say 'no' to Torrijos, something that a lot of people could not do."[229] U.S. Ambassador Jorden gave Lewis Galindo his enthusiastic recommendation.[230] On May 5, the businessman arrived at Washington, D.C. Along with his wife, Nita, he moved into the diplomatic residence, where he had lived decades earlier when his father served as Panama's representative to the United States.[231]

Lewis Galindo's reception also differed from that accorded to González Revilla, who got the distinct impression when he arrived that the Panama Canal was not a problem anyone in Washington was trying to solve. Lewis Galindo was received the day after his arrival by Warren Christopher, acting secretary in Vance's absence. Christopher told Lewis: "I hope that we will have a new treaty before the first snowfall."[232] The State Department made arrangements for Lewis Galindo to present his credentials as soon as Carter returned to the country. On May 16, Lewis Galindo entered the White House with his son Samuel – then a Georgetown University student – and his wife, Nita. Though Lewis Galindo had been advised that the meeting would be brief and limited to formalities, as he shook Jimmy Carter's hand in the Oval Office, the ambassador broached the subject of the negotiations.[233] Carter took up the conversation. He asked a staffer to take Lewis Galindo's wife and son on a White House tour and called in his national security advisor, recalled Samuel Lewis. The meeting marked the beginning of a close relationship between

---

[228] Jimmy Carter, "Organization of American States address before the Permanent Council," April 14, 1977, The American Presidency Project. Available online: www.presidency.ucsb.edu/ws/?pid=7347.

[229] Ricardo Bilonick qtd. in de la Guardia de Corró, *Hasta la Última Gota*, p. 89.

[230] Jorden, *Panama Odyssey*, pp. 363–364.

[231] de la Guardia de Corró, *Hasta la Última Gota*, pp. 87–88.

[232] Jorden, *Panama Odyssey*, p. 366.

[233] de la Guardia de Corró, *Hasta la Última Gota*, pp. 90–91.

Carter and Lewis Galindo, and later with members of the president's team such as Hamilton Jordan and Robert Pastor.[234] When the ambassador called Torrijos about the meeting, Torrijos told Lewis Galindo to fly to Panama that afternoon. At Torrijos' beach compound, Lewis Galindo described the tone of Carter's message, indicating the president would fight for the treaties early in his presidency. Lewis Galindo returned to Washington, where he made an early morning "urgent" meeting with National Security Advisor Zbigniew Brzezinski. The message from the general was, in fact, quite similar to previous messages, though the urgency and the access signaled a change.[235] Lewis Galindo would have a significant impact on the negotiations and during the ratification battle.

Days after Lewis Galindo's arrival, the negotiations resumed. Linowitz again pushed for the meetings to be held in Washington, where he thought the teams would be more productive.[236] As the sessions opened, the same problems that dominated the March meeting rose to the surface. The United States announced on the first day, May 9, that it would accept December 31, 1999 as the conclusion of the U.S. operation and defense arrangement, without demanding a long-term military presence in the treaty. While the United States saw this as a major change, it had been assumed by Panama since Carter mentioned the year 2000 to the press. Panama was pleased, and for the most part, Escobar Bethancourt stopped pushing to revise it to 1990 or 1995.[237]

Panama insisted on addressing high-profile land they wanted returned, like Ancón Hill, which looms over Panama City. Escobar Bethancourt wanted these resolved before addressing what the United States considered "big" issues. "[C]onsidering . . . the reality of a small country negotiating with a great power, we sincerely believe that to begin our discussion on lands and waters allows us to give our government some information on the scope of the solution being worked toward and would allow us to use it as a gauge for the solution of other problems," he said.[238] The treatment of Ancón Hill was a litmus test for how the United States would treat Panama on a range of topics. To the Panamanian team, that was the "big" issue, but it took some time for the United States to grasp why Panama continued to return to it. To the great frustration of the Panamanian team, the Americans said they were not yet prepared to discuss the matter, which had to be dealt with by higher authorities.

---

[234] Samuel Lewis Navarro would go on to become Panama's vice president, running-mate of Omar Torrijos' son Martín. Samuel Lewis Navarro, interview with the author, September 15, 2011, Panama City, Panama. Translation from Spanish by author.

[235] de la Guardia de Corró, *Hasta la Última Gota*, pp. 92–93.

[236] Linowitz, *The Making of a Public Man*, p. 160.

[237] Jaén Suárez, *Las Negociaciones de los Tratados Torrijos–Carter*, pp. 597–599.

[238] "Memorandum of conversation: Second general meeting of the negotiators, May 1977," transcript, May 10, 1977, folder Negociaciones, May 1977, no. 178, AMREP, 1–13.

The solution of Ancón is emblematic of how many questions, after years of divergence, were finally solved. Panama insisted on the return of the whole hill, while the United States needed parts to operate communications and other facilities. The two sides were talking past one another. If the United States would give Panama the whole hill, Panama would "give you all the necessary facilities for the operation and defense of the Canal." Royo told Linowitz and Bunker, "our aspiration and your interests are wed happily." Escobar Bethancourt explained that jurisdiction over all of Ancón was a matter of pride for the Panamanian people – something not affected by having U.S. experts work there for some years.[239] The Panamanians coincided in this – give us the territory and we will let you use it during the treaty period. What the U.S. team saw as marginal mattered deeply to Panama.[240] During the May 10 meeting on the hill, the Pentagon's representative admitted he did not know, after months of talks, what Ancón Hill was.[241]

In response to misunderstandings regarding Linowitz's two-treaty proposal, Ambassadors Lewis Galindo and Jorden began meeting in the Panamanian's living room to assess the day's negotiations, helping work through issues that threatened to derail the May round. The Panamanian told Jorden that Torrijos was about to recall his team. In response, Bunker and Linowitz announced, to the great joy of Royo and Escobar Bethancourt, that the United States would accept Panama's spirit of cooperation and return Ancón, the railway, and the country's principal ports to Panamanian jurisdiction as soon as the treaty entered into force, with select facilities open to U.S. operators. The Panamanian was happy with the U.S. position on particular lands, but worried about neutrality. Royo reminded the U.S. team that any declaration of neutrality would limit sovereignty and face tough criticism. Panamanians feared that a U.S.-affiliated canal could make Panama a target in a superpower war. Royo proposed the following language: "The Republic of Panama and the United States are in agreement to maintain the neutrality regime established in this treaty."[242] With this understanding, the two sides worked toward an agreement that served as the basis of the Neutrality Treaty. Carter wrote: "By May 18, after much argument, the Panamanians agreed to the neutrality issue, with the understanding that our right of defense applied to external threats only, and that Panama would protect the Canal from danger from within."[243]

---

239 Ibid., pp. 2–5.

240 Jorden gives an explanation of this "a-ha!" moment, with an emphasis on his role in it. Jorden, *Panama Odyssey*, pp. 372–381.

241 This was General Dolvin. "Memorandum of conversation: Second general meeting of the negotiators, May 1977," transcript, May 10, 1977, p. 8.

242 "Acta de la reunión celebrada," transcript, May 18, 1977, folder Negociaciones May 1977, no. 127, AMREP, pp. 4–6.

243 Carter, *Keeping Faith*, p. 157. See also, Linowitz, *The Making of a Public Man*, p. 163.

With neutrality solved in principle, several items remained: the new canal authority, on which there was substantive agreement; lands and waters, on which there had been much progress; and financial compensation, which was tabled in 1975 by Torrijos' personal decision. Torrijos was concerned that if compensation were made an early issue, the United States might try to buy the agreement it wanted on other matters.[244] The two sides had exchanged position papers on finances in early 1975, but since that point, the issue had been off the table. Canal administration was sensitive to the Zonians, but also reminded Panamanians of a history of labor discrimination. In principle, Panama's practical control should grow gradually instead of being transferred suddenly. A Panamanian would become subdirector of the canal authority from the treaty's initiation until 1989. Over the next ten years, a Panamanian would direct the canal, with a U.S. citizen serving as subdirector. Similar arrangements would take place throughout canal operations, with Panamanians assuming jobs once reserved for U.S. citizens. The formula had been proposed by the Panamanian delegation, and Royo was satisfied enough to present the U.S. version to Torrijos.[245] Meetings on May 24–26 were amicable as the two sides worked through language and regulations for questions like commercial activities in the Zone, the make-up of the canal's board of directors, and the canal authority's political independence.

The calm did not last. On May 29, Escobar Bethancourt met Linowitz for a Sunday lunch in Washington's Mayflower Hotel. The Panamanian dropped a bomb: a demand for an up-front payment of over $1 billion as compensation for seven decades of nearly free use of Panama's land and waters. Panama calculated that the United States actually owed Panama more than $6 billion, but in the spirit of cooperation and out of respect for President Carter, they lowered the total. Panama also wanted a massively increased annual payment of $300 million. The negotiations returned to crisis mode.[246] Escobar Bethancourt detailed the myriad items for which Panama should be compensated – use of their geographical resource, land for military bases, and the exclusion of Panamanian businesses from Zone commerce. Linowitz did not try to disagree with Panama's case. Instead he insisted that a treaty in which the United States paid Panama to take the canal would not stand a chance.

---

[244] Ardito Barletta, Ahumada, Royo, and González Revilla, interviews with the author. Also, Escobar Bethancourt, *Torrijos* , p. 257.

[245] "Negociaciones del tratado del Canal de Panama," transcript, 3:07 p.m., May 23, 1977, folder Negociaciones, May 1977, no. 127, AMREP, pp. 1–42.

[246] Accounts of the lunch and Escobar's proposal largely coincide. However, explanations of the origin of the proposal diverge. Jorden describes the demand as the product of a booze-fueled, late-night bull session. Jaén Suárez, as well as Panamanian interviewees, describe it as the result of more careful planning. Jaén Suárez, *Las Negociaciones de los Tratados Torrijos–Carter*, pp. 602–603; Jorden, *Panama Odyssey*, pp. 392–395; Linowitz, *The Making of a Public Man*, pp. 164–167; Escobar Bethancourt, *Torrijos*, pp. 278–279.

Carter later wrote: "[T}he Panamanians dealt the negotiations an almost fatal blow. They demanded enormous payoffs from the United States . . . This was a ridiculous request, which we never seriously considered, but it was great news to the treaty's opponents."[247]

The request should be seen in the context of the Panamanian economy. Facing high oil prices since 1973, economic growth had slowed. Ardito Barletta says that worldwide stagflation, poorly considered social legislation in Panama, and uncertainty over the canal generated the economic malaise. Torrijos' decision to exile a group of businessmen hurt confidence and reduced investment. The country's debt was getting less manageable.[248] Torrijos insisted on massive compensation in part as economic stimulus. For the Senate and U.S. public, the concept would be a deal breaker. The United States would be turning over an asset of incredible value. Why pay for the privilege? Bunker and Linowitz accepted a main point: over the life of the canal, Panama had been drastically undercompensated. Both agreed – indeed the United States had assumed during years of talks – that Panama should derive greater benefits from canal tolls. This point had been uncontested in 1975, and broadly accepted even in the Nixon administration's 1971 policy review. On previous issues, Panama had been willing to risk the treaty talks to call the U.S. bluff. Now, with a largely acceptable draft of the treaty nearing completion, Panama had more to risk. Would Panama again face down the United States?

The lump-sum question hung over the negotiations. On June 3, Torrijos gathered the Panamanian Council of State to discuss the talks.[249] When the negotiators returned to Washington, the stalemate continued. Two members of the Panamanian team believed their compensation demand would kill the treaty. The first was Lewis Galindo. The second was Ardito Barletta, who began work on another economic proposal in cooperation with U.S. negotiators. He argued that a more economically secure population would better protect the canal – extending Panama's security argument into the economic sphere.[250] In mid June, the United States responded with an offer that combined a toll increase with substantial loans from the Export-Import Bank and the U.S. Agency for International Development. It included about $200 million generated from the interest on funds that had been paid to the Treasury Department for the original cost of construction. The sides haggled over tolls; eventually Ardito Barletta settled on 32 cents per canal ton, but added that the U.S. military should compensate Panama for the use of its land during the new treaty. Even so, Torrijos insisted on lump-sum payment. The month of June had faded with

---

[247] Carter, *Keeping Faith*, p. 158.

[248] Ardito Barletta, interview with the author, September 21, 2011.

[249] Frustratingly, little documentation exists explaining this period inside the Panamanian government.

[250] Ardito Barletta, interview with the author.

no agreement. July threatened to go the same way. Sol Linowitz's six-month appointment, and the clout he brought to negotiations, was set to expire.

The United States turned to the same Latin American leaders, who had pressed Panama's case in the past – reversing Torrijos' strategy. At the end of June, Venezuelan President Carlos Andrés Pérez made a two-day visit to Washington, meeting with Carter and both teams of negotiators.[251] Pérez and Colombian President Alfonso López Michelsen "thought [the demand] was a serious mistake on Torrijos' part."[252] Initially, the Panamanians were not persuaded. At the beginning of July, the negotiators flew to Panama for further consultations with Torrijos. "As the weeks passed, it seemed the negotiations had reached a stalemate," Carter wrote.[253] Carter and Torrijos tried to break the deadlock in different ways. Torrijos prepared to meet with Latin American presidents in Bogotá in early August, while Carter gathered the negotiators in the Oval Office on July 29 to seek an end to the dispute. Carter stressed to Escobar Bethancourt, Lewis Galindo, and Royo[254] that the payment they sought was impossible. They convinced Carter that only direct communication with Torrijos, who held Carter in high esteem, could convince the general to back away from what he saw as a just demand. Carter recalled in his memoirs: "I personally wrote a letter to Torrijos for the Panamanian negotiators to deliver, stating in effect that we were making our last offer, and that it was 'generous, fair, and appropriate.'"[255] Carter's letter highlighted the "major concessions" the United States had made on land-use and insisted he had given as much as he could.[256] Administration officials told the *New York Times* that a treaty would be quickly concluded if Panama "would scale down to reasonable levels" its financial demands.[257] Carter's letter was a crucial element in convincing Torrijos to scale back his demand. While Escobar Bethancourt continued pressing for billions, Ardito Barletta had hashed out a compromise including higher tolls, a package of loans, U.S. investment for public housing, and some cash.

President Carter inadvertently dropped another unresolved issue into the negotiations. Based on meetings with Alaska Senator Mike Gravel, who was

<hr>

[251] "Venezuelan leader praises Carter's foreign policy," *Los Angeles Times*, June 29, 1977, p. 2.

[252] Jorden, *Panama Odyssey*, p. 415.

[253] Carter, *Keeping Faith*, p. 158.

[254] The meeting participants are listed, with unfortunate mistakes and misspellings for the Pana-manians, in Carter, "Digest of other White House announcements week ending Friday," July 29, 1977, The American Presidency Project. Available online: www.presidency.ucsb.edu/ws/?pid=7894.

[255] Carter, *Keeping Faith*, p. 158.

[256] The text of the letter was printed in: Graham Hovey, "Carter draws the line in talks on canal," *New York Times*, August 2, 1977, p. 9.

[257] Hovey, "President exhorts chief negotiators on a Panama treaty," *New York Times*, July 30, 1977, p. 1.

eager to ship his state's oil riches, Carter mentioned that the United States should have an option to build a sea-level canal.[258] The idea had a long history. During the 1960s, the U.S. government studied the idea of excavating with nuclear explosions, but deemed the idea risky, unsound, and expensive. The idea of the sea-level canal, prominent in 1967, had not been a factor a decade later until the president's comments. To those who had studied the issue, a sea-level canal was not a serious possibility. However, the president's public mention of it meant that it would have to be addressed, and Panama was not willing to countenance the possibility that the treaty would grant new or extended rights to the United States.

During the first week of August, Bogotá hosted an ad hoc summit of regional leaders – all nominally democrats, except Torrijos. Instead of unfettered support, Torrijos heard cautious advice. After presentations from Escobar Bethancourt and Ardito Barletta, the leaders urged Panama to finalize negotiations. Torrijos decided to press for a conclusion to the treaty talks that very day so the leaders could announce the success together. The chief negotiators and ambassadors of both countries gathered at the embassy, where they talked for hours while getting input from the leaders in Bogotá – including Pérez, Oduber, López Michelsen, President José López Portillo of Mexico, and Prime Minister Michael Manley of Jamaica.[259] Torrijos accepted Ardito Barletta's curtailed economic proposal. Yesterday's issue was solved, but now the sea-level canal loomed. Carter was willing to back away from his off-the-cuff comments that the United States should have a right to build a new canal and accept that the United States and Panama should agree. The White House worried that another country – perhaps the Soviet Union – could build a new canal. Torrijos reacted harshly to the perceived impingement on his country's sovereignty. It was unacceptable for the United States to retain the right to build a canal elsewhere in the Americas over Panama's objections if Panama could not build a canal with a partner of its choosing. With Torrijos calling from Bogotá and Carter telegramming from Plains, Ga., the leaders agreed on vague, open-ended treaty language.

Even with the major issues laid to rest, much work remained in drafting the treaties. The U.S. team headed to Panama City with an impending deadline. Sol Linowitz's appointment would expire on August 10. The final days were tense, with Panama testing the United States to get any final advantage, and then retreating to previous agreements. In the late afternoon of Linowitz's final day, the two sides emerged from the Holiday Inn, where they had been

---

[258] Carter, "Yazoo City, Mississippi remarks and a question-and-answer session at a public meeting," July 21, 1977, The American Presidency Project. Available online: www.presidency.ucsb.edu/ws/?pid=7854.

[259] Jorden, *Panama Odyssey*, pp. 5–15, 425–426; Jaén Suárez, *Las Negociaciones de los Tratados Torrijos–Carter*, pp. 618–619.

working. Linowitz, Bunker, Escobar Bethancourt, and Royo announced to a throng of reporters that the "basic elements" of the treaties were ready.[260] After seven years of negotiations with three presidents, General Omar Torrijos had gotten much of what he started out seeking. However, without approval in the U.S. Senate and in a plebiscite in Panama, the draft treaty would mean nothing. A significant group in the United States opposed the very basis of the treaty, and some Panamanian groups protested the announced U.S. military presence until 2000, the residual defense rights, and the relatively modest payment.[261]

Torrijos and Carter sought to gain momentum from the conclusion of the treaty, and they independently arrived at a similar idea. Latin American leaders had played crucial roles at many stages of the process, from the UNSC meeting through the hectic telephone negotiations of August 5–6. Both men wanted to send a message that the canal treaties went beyond bilateral relations. Immediately after the August 10 agreement, Bunker and Linowitz went to meet Torrijos – the first time Linowitz had done so. Torrijos proposed "to invite all the Presidents of the Latin American nations to come to Panama as witnesses to the signing," a wish Lewis Galindo had already conveyed to Carter. Though he wanted an impressive ceremony in Panama, Torrijos understood it could become a political punching bag for U.S. treaty opponents.[262] Carter decided to invite leaders to Washington for a signing ceremony. The idea of a hemispheric meeting appears to have originated in Panama, but was held in Washington as a concession to Carter. The OAS offered a neutral setting that allowed Torrijos to recognize the support he had enjoyed.[263] To attract the strongest attendance possible, Carter offered private meetings to any head of state who attended. Eighteen presidents and prime ministers, from Canada to Chile, accepted.[264] Preparing for so many meetings, which ranged from twenty minutes to an hour, represented a major commitment for Carter.[265]

Even before the final agreements, the Carter administration and the Panamanian government had been planning for a difficult fight on Capitol Hill. Carter tried to gain Republican support, talking with Ford and Kissinger on

[260] Hovey, "U.S. and Panama reach accord to transfer canal by 2000," *New York Times*, August 11, 1977, p. 1; Linowitz, *The Making of a Public Man*, pp. 173–175.

[261] "Leftists and nationalists say Panama has made too many concessions," *New York Times*, August 11, 1977.

[262] Linowitz, *The Making of a Public Man*, p. 175.

[263] Jordan to Carter, "Panama Canal announcement checklist," August 5, 1977, DDRS. See also, de la Guardia de Corró, *Hasta la Última Gota*, p. 104.

[264] Consultations with the governments had been ongoing throughout mid August. The invitations from Carter to all thirty-three heads of state, excepting Fidel Castro, in the Western Hemisphere are available through DDRS.

[265] Peter Tarnoff to Brzezinski, "Proposed schedule for President Carter's bilateral meetings," August 31, 1977, DDRS.

August 9. The president telegrammed every senator to ask them to wait until seeing the treaties before passing public judgment.[266] Panama contributed in three main respects. First, Panama engaged in direct lobbying. Lewis Galindo was a frequent and effective presence in Congress, meeting dozens of senators. At times he was accompanied by Ardito Barletta, who estimated he met with fifty U.S. senators in Washington and Panama. Lewis Galindo had almost daily contact with the Carter administration, often with the president himself.[267] Second, Panama employed the support of other countries. In the past, backing from Latin America, the nonaligned world, and other developing countries forced the United States to pay attention or put pressure on U.S. positions. Panama now turned to the industrialized world's connections in Congress. As hearings took place in the Senate, Torrijos toured Europe and the Mediterranean, where he met with the British Prime Minister James Callaghan and the Israeli Prime Minister Menachem Begin, among others.[268] In a letter to Torrijos on November 2, Carter noted: "The statement by Prime Minister Begin that he will ask Senators who are friendly to Israel to vote favorably on the Canal treaties is an important one."[269] Third, Panama hosted numerous Congressional delegations to make its case. Most of these delegations met with Torrijos, who at times patiently weathered insults. Many senators expressed concerns about democracy and human rights. Though Panama engaged with the U.S. Congress, Torrijos was frustrated with the emphasis on it. He did not appear to fully grasp the separation of powers, nor the very real limitations on Carter's ability to pressure individual senators. The time spent in the U.S. capital convinced Ambassador Lewis Galindo and even the skeptical Escobar Bethancourt of the threat that the U.S. Senate would scuttle the treaties.

Torrijos convinced many skeptics, in and out of Congress. One such skeptic was John Wayne, who encapsulated conservative American pride. After meeting, the general and "the Duke" became friends. During the ratification debate, Wayne wrote senators and treaty opponents – including the most visible opponent of all, Ronald Reagan. The Duke told his erstwhile Hollywood friend he would "show [Reagan] point by God damn point in the Treaty where you

---

266 Jordan to Carter, "Panama Canal announcement checklist," Office of the Chief of Staff Files, Hamilton Jordan's Confidential Files, Panama Canal Treaty 8/77 [1], Container 36, Carter Presidential Library, August 5, 1977. Available online: www.jimmycarterlibrary.gov/digital_library/cos/142099/36/cos_142099_36_02-Panama_Treaty_8_77_1.pdf; Carter, *White House Diary*, p. 80.

267 After ratification, Carter wrote to Lewis Galindo: "I doubt if there has been an Ambassador in the history of our country who has accomplished more for peace and the mutual interests of the United States and his own country than you have on behalf of the people of Panama during your brief service here in Washington." Carter to Lewis Galindo, June 5, 1978, personal letter. On display in the Fundación Gabriel Lewis Galindo, Panama City, Panama.

268 Jaén Suárez, *Las Negociaciones de los Tratados Torrijos–Carter*, pp. 662–663.

269 Carter to Torrijos, November 2, 1977, DDRS.

are misinforming people…you are not as thorough in your reading of this Treaty as you say or are pretty damned obtuse when it comes to reading the English language."[270]

While Torrijos dedicated much of his time, somewhat reluctantly, to pleasing U.S. Senate delegations, his government mobilized a campaign across Panama to support the treaties in the referendum, scheduled for October 23, 1977. Jaén Suárez wrote: "The regime's entire public relations and propaganda apparatus was placed at the service of Torrijos-Carter treaties in a giant national campaign that also opened space to those who opposed the pact."[271] The campaign began with an assembly of local representatives, where negotiators explained the treaties to town-level officials from across the country. To promote the treaties, Torrijos opened an "Office for the Publicity of the New Treaty." This agency printed and distributed tens of thousands of copies of the Torrijos–Carter pact in advance of the referendum. It also hosted speeches that explained the advantages of the new arrangement and tried to undermine criticisms.[272] On October 23, about 800,000 Panamanians headed to the polls, with 506,805 of them, more than 67 percent, voting to approve the new treaties.[273] The only province to vote against the treaties was San Blas, home to the autonomous Kuna tribe, which has historically seen the United States as an important protector against encroachments of the Panamanian central government. The Panamanian people gave the treaties their stamp of approval less than two months after the two leaders had signed them at the OAS. The Senate would take considerably longer to do so. Its leaders refused to rush the treaty ratification, and long hearings dragged into 1978.

The Carter administration, with help from Panama, had collected about sixty votes by early March 1978, when Arizona Senator Dennis DeConcini proposed a reservation that gave the United States the right to renegotiate a military presence after 2000. More offensive to Panama, the amendment said the United States retained the right to intervene to protect the canal – violating the spirit of the Neutrality Treaty. Without this, DeConcini warned, Carter would lose his support along with a crucial handful of others. The amendment violated the spirit of partnership Torrijos viewed as essential. The infuriated general threatened to renounce the treaties if they included the amendment. Torrijos and Noriega had planned to sabotage the canal if the treaty was rejected, and he considered enacting the plot in response to the amendment's passage.

---

[270] John Wayne to Ronald Reagan, November 11, 1977, folder Negociaciones de los tratados Torrijos-Carter, no. 191, AMREP, ff. 26.

[271] Jaén Suárez, *Las Negociaciones de los Tratados Torrijos–Carter*, p. 660.

[272] Lucho Bejarno, Oficina de Divulgación del Nuevo Tratado, "El concepto de perpetuidad y el tratado Torrijos-Carter," September 22, 1977, folder Negociaciones de 1977, no. 119, AMREP, n.p.

[273] For full results at a province level, see Jaén Suárez, *Las Negociaciones de los Tratados Torrijos–Carter*, p. 671.

Carter, Lewis Galindo, and former Linowitz aide Ambler Moss convinced Torrijos to interpret the amendment in a less offensive manner. On March 16, the Senate passed the amended Neutrality Treaty with sixty-eight votes. The ratification was the longest and closest treaty fight in U.S. history. In the following weeks, the Carter administration appealed to the secretary general of the OAS, the president of Venezuela, and Panamanian intermediaries to calm Torrijos. Had Panama lost a war?, the general mused, adding: "The U.S. didn't ask this much of Japan after the Second World War." The statement of interventionism sounded alarms across Latin America, harkening to the canal's creation. Carter promised to neutralize the language in the second treaty. The Senate approved an amendment to the second treaty that reduced the interventionist sting of DeConcini's reservation. Carter continued intense personal appeals in the Senate – including offering numerous pet projects – to win wavering votes. The general backed down, essentially choosing to ignore DeConcini. On April 18, the Senate approved the Panama Canal Treaty by the same margin, with sixty-eight votes in favor.[274]

Conclusions

One of Latin America's smallest countries had attained its goals of territorial integrity, control of the canal, and enhanced economic benefits. In exchange, it would have to wait during the gradual transfer, which Torrijos referred to as walking "for twenty-three years with a pebble in our shoes [as] the price we have to pay for getting the dagger out of our heart."[275] Panamanian leaders were able to sway U.S. policy peacefully only through years of determination, spanning three U.S. presidencies. The process was variously marked by cooperation, conflict, and compromise. Panama challenged the United States carefully, searching for and creating opportunities to change the agenda, assembling friends through international institutions and diplomacy, and advancing new understandings about how to enhance the canal's security.

Omar Torrijos' government began assessing its options regarding the canal in late 1970. After deciding to reject the 1967 treaty, it vigorously pursued the abolition of the Canal Zone and a transfer of the canal to Panamanian authority. While Panama was persistent in its pursuit of these goals, its leaders altered their strategies in response to domestic conditions, the requirements of divergent stages of negotiations, and foreign events – especially political events in

---

[274] The above summary is based on ibid., pp. 678–724; David N. Farnsworth and James W. McKenney, *U.S.–Panama Relations, 1903–1978: A Study in Linkage Politics* (Boulder, Colo.: Westview Press, 1983), pp. 189–224; Carter, *Keeping Faith*, pp. 164–178, Furlong and Scranton, *The Dynamics of Foreign Policymaking*, Chapter 5; Pastor, *Exiting the Whirlpool*, Chapters 3, 7.

[275] Qtd. in Pastor, *Exiting the Whirlpool*, p. 6.

the United States. There were several significant periods during the negotiations that required new approaches. To make fruitful negotiations possible, Panama decided it needed to gain higher-level attention from U.S. policymakers. It radically altered the bilateral approach that had dominated U.S.–Panama relations from their inception. Panama made the canal an international issue, using narratives such as decolonization and discrimination against the Global South. Panama linked its struggle with those of its neighbors and a host of unlikely allies across the globe. The key event was the March 1973 UNSC meeting in Panama City, though the campaign began when Panama gained the support of its neighbors for a UNSC seat. All the while, Panama walked a careful line of nudging the United States without provoking too harsh of a reaction. Panama called the U.S. bluff and the meetings achieved their goal, raising the stakes of failing to address the issue and gaining attention from a higher echelon of U.S. policymakers. Panama achieved a framework for achieving goals with the Tack–Kissinger principles.

On every item of the Tack–Kissinger principles, the U.S. stance gradually gravitated to Panama's position. This was a slow process, often stymied by political conditions in the United States. Progress on the most crucial issues, especially treaty duration, was stalled by the U.S. leaders' unwillingness or inability to make tough political decisions. U.S. political problems – feuds between State and Defense, the Watergate scandal, Ford's weakness – bogged down the negotiations. In response, Panama first adopted a much more accommodating tone, suggesting it would take the U.S. political context into account. However, these delays created domestic challenges for Torrijos. The general responded by strengthening ties with Cuba and the Non-Aligned Movement as a show of independence, while also hoping it would pressure the United States to make decisions. Panama balanced ties with controversial countries with warm relationships with Latin America's democratically elected leaders.

Panama sought to reframe the question of the canal's security. The canal was not a military asset best protected by bases, but a geographical resource that was impossible to defend without the engagement of the Panamanian population. The understanding harkened to the violence of the flag riots, and does not seem to have been cynical or purely instrumental. Even as Panama's interpretation of the problem became the conventional wisdom for some Americans, the small country faced a constant struggle to overcome U.S. inaction. The power of the smaller country, especially one led by a military dictator whose control was rarely in doubt, was its single-minded focus. The Panamanian leadership exhibited an ability to learn from U.S. responses and improve its understanding of the U.S. political process. Echoing some of the literature on asymmetrical wars, a small and focused country can negate some of the advantages of a larger country whose power is more diffuse. However, the canal issue entailed steep political costs for U.S. leaders, which makes Carter's presence a critical factor. Though Kissinger – and Bunker to an even greater degree – were willing to conclude a treaty, they did not have the backing of a president willing to take political risks. In that climate, Panama made incremental progress, but its leverage to initiate change was limited by U.S. domestic politics. It seems unlikely the United States would have transferred control of the canal without the sustained and vigorous Panamanian effort. The canal remained a unique and popular asset, even if it was no longer essential to U.S. naval planning.

Comparing Torrijos's goals in 1972 with the final treaty, it is clear that Panama attained most of its objectives. The treaties eliminated "perpetuity." Panama began seeking a full transfer of the canal by 1995. After more than five years of negotiations, Panama's fallback position of 2000 was accepted – a remarkable concession from the 1972 U.S. goal of perpetual defense rights, or a ninety-year extension. Panama achieved an immediate elimination of the Canal Zone, with de facto jurisdiction transferred over three years. There was an immediate or short-term reversion of the vast majority of zone lands, including high-value sites such as the ports, the railroad, and Ancón. Panama gained direct and immediate participation in canal operations. Panama demanded an end to U.S. military activities not related to canal defense, naming the School of the Americas, which was moved three years after ratification. U.S. military activity was regularized under the SOFA. Panama's original demand for neutrality was largely secured, though the United States refused Panama's preference for a UN mandate. Instead the neutrality guarantee was held in the OAS, where the United States did not contend with the Soviet Union or China. Regarding compensation, Panama's goals early in the 1970s were less clear. The final package did not approach the massive totals Panamanians felt they were owed, but resulted in a major increase in revenue derived from tolls. Panama insisted that it should determine where and whether a new canal was constructed. In August 1977, Torrijos and Carter agreed to broad phrasing on the issue. After the expiration of the treaty, Panamanians voted in a referendum to expand the canal on their own, without U.S. participation. The huge investment will build new sets of locks to accommodate larger ships and ensure the canal's importance to world shipping for years to come.

U.S.-focused accounts of the negotiations have missed the extent to which policy agendas, definitions of interests, and eventual outcomes resulted from an interactive process. Most scholarly accounts have focused on Carter's arrival as a single, transformative moment in the negotiations. Certainly, Carter played a crucial role in closing the negotiations and ratifying the treaties. However, Panama had escalated its struggle over the canal four years prior to Carter's arrival. This consistent approach allowed Panama to build a coalition of allies who helped raise the canal's profile on the U.S. agenda while increasing costs for leaving the matter unaddressed. Years of interaction and negotiation primed the issue. Carter's inauguration and his emphasis on renewing U.S. policy presented another opportunity that Panamanians used to conclude a treaty that included compromises by both parties. Through the force of its ideas and arguments, Panama shaped the understanding of the canal by stressing elements of sovereignty and justice; Panama turned its smallness into a source of strength, convincing the United States that a new approach to the canal was needed.

4

A Recalculation of Interests

NAFTA and Mexican Foreign Policy

No event since the Mexican Revolution has had such a dramatic effect on relations between the United States and Mexico as the North American Free Trade Agreement (NAFTA). NAFTA has often been understood as the result of expansionist U.S. trade policy at a triumphal historical moment – a victory for the U.S. international economic agenda even as the Soviet Union collapsed. This interpretation largely ignores Mexico's role in initiating talks. NAFTA fed hopes for a "free trade zone stretching from the port of Anchorage to Tierra del Fuego," in the words of President George H.W. Bush.[1] This initiative had started with Canada a few years prior. However, it received its most important boost when the United States and Mexico decided in early 1990 to pursue an agreement that would, for the first time, tightly link the world's largest economy with that of a much lower-income country.

Despite the congruence with announced U.S. policies – President Reagan had similarly dreamed of free trade from "Yukon to Yucatan"[2] – the pact hinged not on U.S. pressure but on Mexican leaders' profound reevaluation of their own country's interests. NAFTA reflected a realization that Mexico could best pursue its interests by engaging the United States in institutional arrangements instead of by rhetorical counters. Even before NAFTA, Mexico relied on exports of oil and light manufacturing from *maquiladoras*, overwhelmingly to the United States. The rules governing these exports were open to constant negotiations and the frequent threat of countervailing duties on Mexican products. With NAFTA, Mexico's leaders sought to eliminate

---

[1] "Remarks announcing the Enterprise for the Americas Initiative," June 27, 1990, Public Papers of the President. Available online: http://bushlibrary.tamu.edu/research/public_papers.php?id=2041.

[2] Even in November 1988, Mexican leaders told the *New York Times* they had little interest in such an idea.

uncertainty, convincing the United States to make commitments and bind itself to dispute settlement mechanisms. The shift could not have happened without Mexico's recalculation of its national interest vis-à-vis the United States and Mexico's aggressive pursuit at key moments. To be sure, Mexican actions do not provide the entirety of the explanation. However, Mexican leaders' initiatives took advantage of a coincidence of other factors to dramatically alter the nature of the U.S.–Mexico relationship.

Brandishing the scars of territorial loss in 1848 and U.S. interventions during Mexico's bloody revolution, Mexico's ruling Partido Revolucionario Institucional (PRI) based its foreign policy on the desirability of maintaining autonomy from the United States in defense of Mexican sovereignty. President Carlos Salinas de Gortari (1988–1994) dramatically revised that stance, while gradually discarding the rhetoric. While Salinas' economic reforms followed the trail blazed by his predecessor, Miguel de la Madrid (1982–1988), his recalculation of Mexican foreign policy was previously almost unthinkable. It reversed one of the central tenets of the PRI legacy. Though NAFTA has been discussed largely in economic terms, both in relation to international trade and as a mechanism to "lock in" liberal reforms that dismantled Mexico's import substitution apparatus, its foreign policy significance is of equal importance. The increase in interdependence the agreement produced led to still-greater changes. This was just as NAFTA's architects, Mexican and American, wished. The decision to pursue a free trade agreement (FTA) was a major shift in *how* Mexican leaders sought to influence the United States.

While this decision had much to do with the worldviews of President Salinas and his coterie of U.S.-trained economists, it is too narrow to interpret the agreement only in personalistic terms. NAFTA was a watershed moment for Mexico, not an aberration. The shift started more cautiously before Salinas' presidency, and it has proved remarkably durable. The North American strategy guided Mexican economic and foreign policy through the historic collapse of the long-ruling PRI, two *sexenios* of the Partido Acción Nacional (PAN), and now a reemergence of the PRI. The decision immediately changed the tenor of Mexican policy toward the United States. Mexico quietly handled irritants – including an embargo on its tuna exports, the invasion of Panama, and the kidnapping of a citizen to stand trial in the United States – that might have derailed improved relations.

While a tremendous amount has been written about NAFTA, there are considerably fewer works that examine the actual negotiations. Frederick F. Mayer offers a detailed account as a test for frameworks of political analysis.[3] Maxwell Cameron and Brian Tomlin build on dozens of interviews and a thorough review of mostly U.S. sources to assess the importance of power asymmetry, political institutions, and negotiating positions on the process and

---

[3] Frederick W. Mayer, *Interpreting NAFTA: The Science and Art of Political Analysis* (New York: Columbia University Press, 1998).

final agreement.[4] A few scholars have examined the agreement more broadly in terms of how it has affected relations between Mexico and the United States. Jorge I. Dominguez and Rafael Fernández de Castro argue that Salinas and Bush shifted the trajectory of bilateral relations from its historical patterns of "conflict" or "bargained negligence" to a new cooperative path.[5] Two Mexican scholars argue that this led to a dramatically new level of interaction between Mexican foreign policy and the U.S. political system – something that would have been both unthinkable and unacceptable just a decade earlier.[6]

This chapter builds on newly available Mexican and U.S. archival sources. There has not, to my knowledge, been a study of the NAFTA negotiations that incorporates significant Mexican documentation, which I obtained at the Secretaría de Economía (formerly the Secretaría de Comercio y Fomento Industrial, or SECOFI, the agency that led the Mexican negotiating team). Building on these documents, as well as on interviews with key members of the negotiating team, this chapter seeks to contextualize and explain crucial Mexican decisions. Why did Mexico decide to open its economy, and, in a second step, tie itself more closely to the United States? How was this decision seen in relation to Mexican foreign policy? How did Mexico define what issues it was willing to include and what needed to be excluded from an agreement? Why did Mexico reverse its traditional stance regarding involvement in other countries' internal politics by engaging in an intense lobbying effort in the U.S. Congress? How did Mexico relate to Canada during the negotiations? In closing, I examine the effects of NAFTA on U.S.–Mexico relations.

Background

In the 1970s, Mexico's discovery of the massive Cantarell oil reserve, coupled with high international prices for oil, offered a sudden windfall, which Mexico used to fund government programs and enhance its international role. The country took on significant loans from private lenders, on the expectation of continued high oil prices, to spur rapid development. When oil prices dropped and interest rates climbed in 1981, Mexico suffered climbing debts, a fiscal

---

4 Maxwell A. Cameron and Brian W. Tomlin, *The Making of NAFTA: How the Deal Was Done* (Ithaca, N.Y.: Cornell University Press, 2000). In addition to Mayer and Cameron and Tomlin, a handful of other books focus on NAFTA, but I do not review them in depth here. For a detailed look at four sectors of the negotiations, see Maryse Robert, *Negotiating NAFTA Explaining the Outcome in Culture, Textiles, Autos, and Pharmaceuticals* (Toronto: University of Toronto, 2000). The book suffers from a forest-for-the-trees approach that ignores much context and well as trade-offs across sectors. It gives little attention to why Mexico sought the agreement.

5 Jorge I. Domínguez and Rafael Fernández de Castro, *The United States and Mexico: Between Partnership and Conflict* (New York: Routledge, 2001).

6 Rodolfo O. De la Garza and Jesús Velasco, *México y su Interacción con el Sistema Político Estadounidense* (México: CIDE, Centro de Investigación y Docencia Económicas: M.A. Porrúa Grupo Editorial, 2000).

crisis, and a painful recession. In 1982, the Mexican government announced it could no longer service its debt; shortly afterward, the Mexican government shuttered and nationalized the country's major banks. That year, Mexico's GDP plummeted by 4.2. Mexico was obliged to accept structural adjustments in a deal with the International Monetary Fund and the U.S. Federal Reserve, but that brought only fleeting stability. Internally, the Mexican government created the Secretaría de Comercio y Fomento Industrial (SECOFI), which came to be dominated by liberal economists.

In 1986, another recession inflicted a 3.7 percent drop in GDP.[7] Much of Mexico's political class interpreted the dual recessions as evidence that the old PRI economic model had reached its limit. Oil prices remained low and Mexico had little access to credit markets. Government subsidies to unproductive, state-controlled sectors were no longer fiscally viable. In February 1985, President de la Madrid announced a new policy in which Mexico would begin seeking foreign direct investment – something it had long limited. De la Madrid said he would consider closer trade relations with the United States – though a free trade agreement (FTA) was never on the table.[8] In a major turnaround, Mexico joined the General Agreement on Tariffs and Trade (GATT) in July 1986.[9] Growth remained sluggish. The economic picture was complicated by ongoing debt negotiations with commercial banks, the United States, and international financial institutions. Throughout the mid 1980s, Mexico rescheduled payments, but the stopgap measures led to a greater overall debt burden. Creditors resisted calls for debt reduction. Mexican leaders again threatened default.

President Carlos Salinas took office in these inauspicious circumstances. Salinas' powers were extensive, and political competition was circumscribed. The PRI dominated the compliant Mexican Congress, which had little input in trade policy and almost no input in foreign policy. The PRI influenced media coverage and organized both labor and business interests into supportive coalitions dependent on the state.[10] As president, Salinas stood atop this hierarchy for six years. Salinas, who had a Ph.D. from Harvard, surrounded himself with Mexicans educated in elite, U.S. doctoral programs. These included his economy and trade minister Jaime Serra Puche and his deputy Jaime Zabludovsky; finance minister Pedro Aspe; Herminio Blanco Mendoza, who became chief trade negotiator; and Salinas' close advisor, José María Córdoba Montoya. All had backgrounds in liberal economics and they largely trusted freer markets to spur economic growth.

---

[7] World Bank database.

[8] "President de la Madrid defines Mexico's policy on foreign investment," February 1985, *Mexico Today*, p. 1.

[9] Cameron and Tomlin, *The Making of NAFTA*, p. 59.

[10] Weintraub notes that Salinas was able to massively sway public opinion in Mexico, and "He probably could not have achieved the turnaround in Mexican public opinion that he did had he not been an authoritarian leader." Sidney Weintraub, *Unequal Partners: The United States and Mexico* (Pittsburgh, Pa.: University of Pittsburgh Press, 2010), p. 32.

The weak economy and debt crisis was only one part of the turbulent situation that Salinas encountered. His government faced doubts about Salinas' own legitimacy and ability to govern. Though the PRI remained formidable, Salinas' election had been the most bitterly contested in the PRI's decades of one-party rule. He had faced opposition candidate Cuauhtémoc Cárdenas, the son of revolutionary hero and former President Lázaro Cárdenas. The younger Cárdenas had defected from the PRI to create his own political movement, and many Mexicans who had previously accepted one-party rule saw Salinas' victory as marred by electoral fraud. That de la Madrid had chosen Salinas to be his successor confirmed the PRI's intention to continue liberal reforms. Salinas had served on de la Madrid's cabinet and was a vocal supporter of lowering tariffs, privatizing industry, and reducing state involvement in the economy. Salinas appointed liberal reformers to the upper echelon of his team, including U.S.-trained economists Aspe and Serra Puche. Their major priorities were to address the debt, control inflation, and begin dismantling protectionist barriers.[11]

Liberalization began well before Salinas decided to pursue an FTA with the United States: "Salinas accelerated initiatives to open up the Mexican economy, reducing tariffs and restrictions on imports, mainly quotas. By 1989, Mexico's average weighted tariff was 6.2 percent, and 96 percent of Mexican imports were free of quotas." In many cases, tariff reduction went well beyond what was required by Mexico's GATT accession.[12] For Salinas, economic liberalization was a means to economic growth, which was itself a means to boost the popularity of the PRI to the point it could continue to win elections, even as they became increasingly fair. Salinas' views were further shaped by historical global changes. As Salinas took office, the Soviet Union was in the midst of remarkable transitions. Salinas saw Mexico's own changes in a global context.

From the beginning of his term, it was clear that George Bush would have to manage grand global changes. The Berlin Wall tumbled down during his first autumn in office, setting off a quick succession of events leading to the speedy reunification of Germany and the shocking collapse of the Soviet Union. In that context, it might be surprising that relations with Mexico received frequent, high-level attention, especially since Bush also launched military interventions in Iraq and Panama. What accounts for the Bush administration's consistent interest in Mexico? It is often noted that the Mexican leadership team held many advanced degrees from U.S. universities. The backgrounds of influential members of the Bush administration drew them to Mexico. In an interview, Bush's Ambassador to Mexico John Negroponte noted: "The administration really cared about the relationship...it was a bunch of Texans. They understood that the relationship was important. No one had to convince them. This

---

[11] Carlos Salinas de Gortari, *México: Un Paso Difícil a la Modernidad* (Barcelona: Plaza & Janés Editores, 2000), p. 9.

[12] Cameron and Tomlin, *The Making of NAFTA*, p. 59.

was a national decision, and made at a political level."[13] Trade negotiations would be a high priority for both the Mexican and the U.S. administrations. Bush's base was built on his close relationship with the business sector, most of which strongly supported increased trade with Mexico, though many in Congress opposed his trade policies.

Bush and Salinas, Starting Together

Bush and Salinas met in Houston, both presidents-elect, on November 22, 1988. Bush had intimated during the campaign that he would like to extend the recently approved U.S.–Canadian free trade deal into a North American agreement. Candidate Bush told a business luncheon in Chicago: "We need to build on our agreement with Canada by developing a new, special economic relationship with Mexico."[14] Though Bush's comments attracted little attention in the United States, Salinas' close political advisor Córdoba Montoya recalled in an interview that Bush had been the first to put the idea of free trade on the table.[15] The bulk of the preinaugural meeting centered on Mexico's debt, then more than $100 billion. Salinas recalls in his memoirs that Bush mentioned free trade during that meeting: "To start, President Bush proposed the establishment of a free trade zone between Mexico and the United States . . . Bush's proposal came in an unexpected moment . . . He did not insist on free trade, but he had proposed the topic, and I would recall that as time passed."[16] There is some disagreement about the nature of this proposal. Neither Negroponte nor Serra Puche was at the meeting, but neither believes Bush proposed it. James Baker, who was present, wrote in his memoirs: "The subject of a free-trade agreement was not raised."[17] Córdoba Montoya was present, and referenced the proposal in an interview in the same manner as Salinas. Despite the disagreement about whether an FTA was mentioned, trade and debt were clearly on the agenda. At the time of the meeting, Salinas saw an FTA as too great a leap for Mexico as the country dealt with debt and banking crises. All agree that an FTA was not mentioned again until Salinas took the initiative. In a March 8, 1990 phone call, after the Mexican government had made its momentous decision to seek an FTA, Salinas reminded Bush of the proposal "of a possible FTA" made in Houston. Bush simply responded, "Yes."[18] During the

---

[13] John Negroponte, telephone interview with the author, April 20, 2012. See also Stuart Auerbach, "Mexico comes calling for free trade," *Washington Post*, June 10, 1990, p. H1.

[14] "Excerpt of remarks of Vice President Bush," at the Executive's Club in Chicago, Ill., September 13, 1988, via *Federal News Service*.

[15] José Córdoba Montoya, interview with the author, May 3, 2012, Mexico City, Mexico.

[16] Salinas de Gortari, *México*, p. 12.

[17] James Addison Baker and Thomas M. DeFrank, *The Politics of Diplomacy: Revolution, War, and Peace, 1989–1992* (New York: Putnam, 1995), p. 607.

[18] "Telephone conversation with President Salinas de Gortari of Mexico," March 8, 1990, George Bush Presidential Library (GBPL). Available online: http://bushlibrary.tamu.edu/research/pdfs/memcons_telcons/1990-03-08-Salinas.pdf.

Houston meeting, the two presidents-elect and their key advisors established positive personal relations – they would later refer to the "the spirit of Houston." The leaders held numerous phone calls and meetings during their presidencies. Bush invited Salinas for suppers at the White House and weekends at Camp David and Kennebunkport. The rapport seemed genuine, based on perceived shared interests.

Salinas took office days after the Houston meeting, on December 1, 1988. Debt was the top priority, and Salinas charged finance secretary Pedro Aspe with addressing it. Continuing discussions from Houston, Aspe insisted to U.S. Treasury Secretary Nicholas Brady that additional rescheduling was not an option. Constant negotiations cast uncertainty over Mexico's economic future. If Mexico did not obtain significant write-offs of its commercially held debt, it would be forced to stop servicing it.[19] These talks led to the U.S. announcement of the Brady Plan on March 19, 1989, with Mexico expressing immediate interest.[20] The plan gave Mexico a framework for its negotiations with commercial creditors, with the banks accepting either long-term, low-interest payments or markdowns in exchange for U.S. Treasury-backed bonds. By August 1989, Mexico had completed negotiations for a significant part of its debt.

That autumn, Mexico turned its attention to trade. The Salinas government argued that its tariffs reductions had not led to corresponding improvements in market access for Mexican exports. The government's May 1989 development plan noted: "Mexico has undertaken an important process of commercial opening to increase the efficiency and competitiveness of national production. However, this opening has not been adequately reciprocated in terms of access to international markets."[21] Though Salinas had moved aggressively to open the economy, there was not a consensus inside the Mexican government that an FTA with the United States was in Mexico's interests – or that it was politically desirable. Negroponte said that during 1989, talk of an FTA was not seen as realistic. "My honest recollection at that time is that it was considered too hard. We'd have to stick to a more gradualistic approach, sector by sector. That was the prevailing wisdom."[22] Salinas favored incremental increases in U.S.–Mexico ties through agreements to strengthen trade and investment in limited industrial sectors, increasing quotas for Mexican exports of steel and textiles, for example.[23] The two countries sought to expand the 1987 framework agreement on trade and investment to provide a mandate for broader negotiations.

---

[19] Pedro Aspe, interview with the author April 27, 2012, Mexico City, Mexico.

[20] President Salinas called Bush almost immediately after the plan was announced. "Telephone conversation with President Salinas," March 10, 1989, GBPL. Available online: http://bushlibrary.tamu.edu/research/pdfs/memcons_telcons/1989-03-10-Salinas.pdf.

[21] "Extractos del Programa Nacional de Modernización Industrial y del Comercio Exterior, 1990–1994," in Carlos Arriola, ed., *Documentos Básicos* (México: SECOFI, Grupo Editorial Miguel Ángel Porrua, 1994), doc. 4.

[22] John Negroponte, interview with the author.

[23] Cameron and Tomlin, *The Making of NAFTA*, p. 60.

Mexican leaders pressed the United States for larger quotas and lower tariffs on particular products, but eschewed a more comprehensive agreement.[24]

Salinas made a state visit to Washington in October 1989, where he and Bush presented sectoral agreements and highlighted improved bilateral cooperation.[25] The Mexican president pressed for expanded Mexican exports, arguing it would stimulate trade and improve the overall bilateral relationship.[26] Trade was central to the agenda throughout the visit. Shortly after the state visit, Commerce Secretary Robert Mosbacher told a Senate committee he thought a U.S.–Mexico trade agreement was likely, and that the United States should pursue it incrementally. Other officials noted that Salinas had continually rejected the idea of an FTA.[27] Publicly, Mexican officials insisted they had no plans to pursue a comprehensive agreement. Even Jaime Serra Puche, personally committed to free trade, denied an agreement was in the offing. Shortly after the state visit, Serra Puche addressed Mexican news media to explain the new sectoral trade agreements. When asked, he said that a trade agreement between Mexico and the United States was not feasible:

You will remember that on the topic of whether we would develop a common market between Mexico and the United States, we have said that the difference in levels of development between the two countries is still of the nature that it would not be natural to establish a free trade agreement between the two countries; but it is possible and we have to study the possibility of making sectoral agreements between the two economies.[28]

Serra noted years later: "I could not give the slightest hint on an FTA without creating antibodies."[29] Salinas was concerned about the reactions of Mexican society, including major segments of his political base, to the idea of overly close cooperation with the United States. While he struck a cooperative tone on trade, he was less openly cooperative on issues like counternarcotics. Salinas refused to allow U.S. agents to pursue suspects across the border in "hot pursuit," citing concerns about Mexican sovereignty. Salinas wanted closer ties with the United States, but he was eager to signal the limits to that cooperation.

---

[24] "Salinas hails better U.S. ties," *The Washington Times*, October 3, 1989, p. A6.

[25] George Bush, "Remarks at the signing ceremony for the Mexico-United States environmental and trade agreements," October 3, 1989, The American Presidency Project. Available online: www.presidency.ucsb.edu/ws/?pid=17610.

[26] Adela Gooch, "Bush, Salinas hail pact to boost mutual trade," *Washington Post*, October 4, 1989, p. A 12.

[27] Clyde Farnsworth, "Mosbacher sees a free-trade pact with Mexico," *New York Times*, October 15, 1989, p. D9; Karen Riley, "Free-trade pact with Mexico advocated," *The Washington Times*, October 19, 1989, p. C1.

[28] Jaime Serra Puche, press conference, October 10, 1989, classification 10.01.00.00, caja 1, exp. 2, Archivo General de la Nación, Mexico, D.F., pp. 1–18.

[29] Serra Puche, email correspondence with the author, May 3, 2012.

Sea Change: Mexico Proposes an FTA

Just three months after Salinas and Serra had publicly rejected an FTA, they would propose a pact to U.S. Trade Representative Carla Hills, leading to much greater economic interdependence and an historic shift in the nature of the U.S.–Mexico relationship. What happened between October and January to provoke the changed Mexican position? First, Salinas was affected by the dramatic shifts in the international environment. A month after Salinas' return from Washington, the Berlin Wall fell. The opening of Eastern Europe seemed to signal the triumph of democracy and open markets – an argument Salinas made to Bush the first time he directly presented the idea of an FTA.[30] Along with the unwinding of Central American conflicts, the global shift shook the pillars of the PRI, which had exhibited its "revolutionary" nature through (often symbolic) support of leftist causes abroad and nationalist, historically focused appeals for autonomy from the United States.[31]

With the debt negotiations largely complete, Salinas' government turned toward generating economic growth. The top leadership was convinced that Mexico needed to move toward freer trade, using foreign investment and stronger exports to create employment. Mexican leaders hoped to balance their ties with the United States with links to the rest of the world. Salinas and others believed that the path to economic growth, without greater dependence on the U.S. market, led to Japan, whose growth through the 1970s and 1980s drew great admiration. Mexican citizens held the Japanese in higher esteem than Americans, according to polls in 1988. In September 1989, Mexico hosted a visit from the Japanese prime minister. The visit ended cordially, but without any specific agreements. Economic ties between the two countries grew, but they were never very large.[32] Mexican hopes for major Japanese investment, aid, and debt relief failed to materialize. The perception grew that Japan was interested first in building an East Asian trading bloc, and second in maintaining trade with the United States. The Japanese touted the visit as a demonstration that Japan would assist the United States with global problems.[33]

Having failed to make inroads with Asia's economic power, Mexico's officials met on January 8, 1990 in the *gabinete económico*, or economic cabinet – the central forum in the Salinas government. Mexican leaders again emphasized the need to promote export-led growth to generate employment for a young, growing population and earn foreign exchange. With oil prices low, Mexico's traditional source of exchange was insufficient. The economic team had hoped

---

[30] "Telephone conversation with President Salinas de Gortari of Mexico," March 8, 1990, GBPL.

[31] Salinas' changed stance did not mean unquestioning support of the United States. Mexico, along with the rest of Latin America, loudly decried the U.S. invasion of Panama on December 20, 1989.

[32] Domínguez and Fernández de Castro, *The United States and Mexico*, p. 23.

[33] Karl Shoenberger, "Japan, Mexico pledge closer economic ties," *Washington Post*, September 6, 1989, p. C4.

for short-term gains after the resolution of the debt crisis, but improvement had been slow.

Mexico had failed to attract serious attention from Japan, so the Salinas administration decided to pursue investment and trade deals with Europe.[34] In late January 1990, the Mexican team, including Salinas, Serra, Córdoba Montoya, and Aspe, set off on a tour of Europe. Salinas met with Mario Soares of Portugal, Margaret Thatcher of the United Kingdom, and Helmut Kohl of Germany. All noted that attention and investment would likely turn to Eastern Europe, and that Mexico needed to focus regionally to attain growth. Kohl told Salinas that Mexico would "only be attractive as part of one of the three great blocs of international commerce."[35] As they traveled across Europe, and tried in Davos to position themselves among global political and business elites, Salinas came to a realization. The end of communism in Eastern Europe was not simply a victory for free markets. The sudden changes meant that the number of middle-income countries looking to attract foreign investment had suddenly exploded. The former Soviet republics were competing with Mexico for international capital, and they had the advantage of being much closer geographically – and more important geopolitically – to Western Europe. Reducing its debt and enacting economic reforms was not enough to put Mexico on the agenda of the turbulent European continent. Serra explained: "When we went to Davos, we were not in the investment map . . . [W]e realized that the opening up of Eastern Europe and so on, was really leaving us behind in terms of being able to attract foreign direct investment, which the country needed and needs badly. And also our trade flows weren't growing like they should."[36] Experience with the Japanese forced the realization that Asia would not offer a quick economic solution. The trip to Europe drove home the point that Mexico could not count on the old continent, either.

A Watershed Recalculation of Interests

Mexico's decision to reverse decades of policy intended to keep the United States at arm's length came suddenly. There had been cautious steps since 1985, but the decision to propose an FTA was made between the president and two or three ministers, Serra said. As Salinas recounts the story, he woke up Serra during a restless night in Davos. As Serra sat on the side of the bed, Salinas told him that he had talked with Aspe and wanted to approach the U.S. trade representative in the morning to propose free trade talks. Serra, as Salinas knew, supported the idea.[37] Serra and Hills already had a meeting scheduled

---

[34] Salinas de Gortari, *México*, p. 45.
[35] Ibid., pp. 47–48.
[36] Jaime Serra Puche, interview with the author, May 2, 2012, Mexico City, Mexico.
[37] Salinas de Gortari, *México*, pp. 50–51.

to finalize an agreement on textiles. The pair left that to their deputies while Serra made the unexpected gambit.

Though the idea of a U.S.–Mexico free trade area had been in circulation since the mid 1980s in political and academic circles, it had not gained political traction during the de la Madrid administration and was scarcely discussed during the first year of the Salinas government.[38] Free trade with the United States was not seen as politically feasible or particularly desirable. Mexico feared that economic openness would make it vulnerable to U.S. pressures. However, even without an FTA, more than 77 percent of Mexican exports were being sold to the United States.[39] Mexican leaders did not give up the notion of reducing dependence on the United States, but they recognized that in the status quo, Mexico was already dependent. Mexico was more vulnerable when these exports relied on short-term agreements. Mexican exporters depended on the Generalized System of Preferences (GSP), under which Mexico could export under low or zero tariffs – if those exports stayed under set quotas. Serra noted that some of the large, export-driven industries shut down before the end of the year as they approached GSP quotas for preferential access to the U.S. market. Businesses were reluctant to make large investments when their market access depended on frequent quota negotiations. The Mexican team accepted many of the arguments made by European leaders: as part of a North American market, Mexico would be an interesting economic partner – a gateway to U.S. consumers. Serra and Salinas did not relinquish their goal of diversifying Mexico's economic ties, but they adopted a radically new strategy.[40]

On the one hand, Salinas' core goals had not changed. His priority was to spur economic growth to maintain PRI popularity in the face of increasing democratization. On the other, the decision represented a major shift from the longtime Mexican goal of autonomy from the United States through the avoidance of dependence. The Salinas administration saw the goal of autonomy differently, as a question of interdependence instead of dependence. Dependence made Mexico more vulnerable to U.S. pressures, but an understanding based on interdependence meant that Mexico could gain leverage, too. This was particularly true on economic issues, where Serra Puche was eager to guarantee market access. Political advisor Córdoba Montoya saw interdependence as the best way to pursue Mexico's long-term political interests, as well. Mexico's geographical proximity to the United States was not going to change,

---

[38] Interviews with Serra Puche and Aspe.

[39] The United States imported $27.186 billion dollars in goods from Mexico in 1989, out of a total of $35.171 billion of total Mexican exports. Foreign Trade Division of the U.S. Census Bureau and WTO Statistics Database, respectively.

[40] In fact, Mexico has remained stubbornly dependent on the U.S. market to buy its exports. In 1990, nearly 70 percent of Mexican trade was with the United States. This figure has stayed fairly steady and only declined slightly starting in 2005.

but the understanding of it shifted dramatically. The shifting international land-scape weighed heavily. In 1990, Salinas mentioned privately that the world was moving to "an apparent reliance on blocs" and that Mexico would need to join or be passed by.[41]

The U.S. Reaction

U.S. Trade Representative Carla Hills' first response to Serra was ambivalent. She was glad that Mexico wanted to lock in reforms and lower tariffs; how-ever, her near-term priority was to conclude the Uruguay Round of GATT negotiations. Serra argued that the two sets of negotiations were "not incom-patible." While Hills agreed, she was cognizant of the limited attention of high-level officials and the U.S. Trade Representative's (USTR) limited resources to attack two simultaneous, complex negotiations. Hills told Serra she would have to consult with her president. The Mexican proposal converged with long-standing U.S. goals of opening markets, but the U.S. preference had long been for global trade regimes – namely the GATT – instead of regional blocs that it might be shut out from. At Canada's request, the Reagan administration took a step away from the globalist position and agreed to negotiate a bilat-eral trade agreement. The ongoing Uruguay Round of the GATT was bogged down in disputes between the United States and Europe on agriculture, ser-vices, and intellectual property. However, USTR hoped to break the stalemate and achieve a number of major U.S. trade priorities.

Having taken the decision to approach the United States, Mexican lead-ers did not wish to wait for the completion of the Uruguay Round to start bilateral talks. Making concessions or liberalizing in the GATT negotiations could lower their bargaining leverage at the bilateral level. Plus, they needed to quickly establish macroeconomic stability and attract investment. While they saw the GATT as useful, it did not offer Mexico the unique, high-profile bene-fits of securing access to the world's largest economy. The Mexican leadership was betting that expectations created by FTA negotiations would spur an eco-nomic boost. Mexico appealed to the highest levels of the Bush administration to prevent any delay. Serra talked with Secretaries Baker and Mosbacher – both Texans. Baker wrote in his memoirs that "even while we had been nego-tiating the Canadian FTA we had thought about the benefits of expanding it to a continent-wide free-trade zone." Baker held Salinas in high regard.[42] Córdoba Montoya developed a relationship with National Security Advisor Brent Scowcroft. U.S. Ambassador Negroponte provided a sympathetic ear and pathway to President Bush. Shortly after the Mexican proposal, a group of American officials gathered with Bush to discuss the possibility of negotia-tions with Mexico, and how this might relate to the GATT talks. If there was

---

[41] Carlos Salinas, in conversation with Robert A. Pastor, July 28, 1990. Robert A. Pastor personal papers.
[42] Baker and DeFrank, *The Politics of Diplomacy*, p. 43.

any serious thought of delaying trade negotiations with Mexico until after the Uruguay Round, Bush ended it. For the United States, long-term foreign policy interests trumped multilateral trade goals.

In early 1990, Salinas called Bush and said: "I think now that what's happening in the world and in Mexico suggests that we should speed up and broaden the scope of negotiations. So Mexico is willing to initiate a negotiation for a free trade agreement with the United States." Europe would be gaining an advantage from the cheaper labor in the opening eastern bloc. Salinas added that "in Mexico I want to consolidate the new policies for a market-oriented economy." Bush responded warmly to the idea, which he had already heard from Hills and others. The two presidents agreed they would quietly explore free trade, but that they would wait until they met in June to make any public statements.[43] With the strong personal commitment of the two presidents, the administration quickly accepted the Mexican proposal. As Serra's remark about "antibodies" indicates, the Mexicans were concerned that opposition to the negotiations would quickly mobilize in Mexico and the United States. When Bush and Salinas talked in February, they agreed to lay significant groundwork for the agreement before making it public. Secrecy lasted only a month before word leaked to the *Wall Street Journal*.

The leak was followed by more infelicitous news. Mexican doctor Humberto Álvarez Machaín, suspected of involvement in the torture and killing of U.S. Drug Enforcement agent Enrique Camarena, was kidnapped from Mexico and deposited in the United States to stand trial. In other times, the two events might have halted any talks. While the Mexican government condemned the kidnapping, it did not let the brazen act sour the overall relationship or derail the preliminary talks. Salinas set about convincing the PRI, business leaders, and the public that an FTA with the United States was the best course for the country's future – something they had rejected in October. The Mexican cabinet set up forums across the country, and Salinas traveled the country to advocate the policy. Initially, several large unions opposed the idea. However, the PRI's control over labor remained tight. Nearly all of Mexican labor was led for decades by one man, Fidel Velázquez, head of the Confederación de Trabajadores Mexicanos, which was closely linked to PRI. Once Velázquez was brought on board, labor ceased to be an obstacle.

In September 1990, SECOFI decided to create a forum for consultation with Mexican industry, called Coordinadora de Organismos de Comercio Exterior (COECE), headed by influential businessman Guillermo Güemez. COECE served four main purposes. First, it was an important source of information for Mexican negotiators about what specific Mexican industries needed in terms of market access and transition time to a more open economy. Second, the group got business leaders to buy into the FTA and turned many into advocates. Third, the businessmen used their networks in the United States to help convince U.S.

---

[43] "Telephone conversation with President Salinas de Gortari of Mexico," March 8, 1990, GBPL.

counterparts to support NAFTA. Last, members of COECE later traveled to negotiations, garnering the nickname of "the side room," or *el cuarto de al lado*. There, they provided information, opinions, and a visible constraint on Mexican positions. With Mexican labor and business both supportive, approval from the PRI-dominated Mexican Senate to seek the agreement was a formality. The Senate concluded its brief debate and recommended on May 21, 1990, that Mexico seek a trade agreement – months before Bush presented his own notification to the U.S. Congress.

Mexico's leaders initially wanted to include Canada in the negotiations – and briefly considered requesting admission to the already signed U.S.–Canada pact instead of starting new negotiations.[44] Some in SECOFI hoped that by making the negotiations trilateral, they could blunt domestic criticism that the pact represented a capitulation to the United States. They also hoped to learn from the Canadian experience. In May 1990, Serra met with his Canadian counterpart John Crosbie and told him that Canada would have a seat at the table if it wished. Initially, Crosbie rebuffed the offer. The U.S.–Canada pact had been a contentious issue in the recently completed Canadian elections, and the Canadian government hoped to avoid a politically costly repeat. In addition, the Canadians had mixed feelings about helping Mexico achieve an FTA with the United States and sharing their advantageous access to the U.S. market. However, just weeks after Serra's visit to Montreal, Canada suddenly changed its stance. A SECOFI memo noted: "During the last days, there has been a radical change in the position of the Canadian government regarding the FTA. After emphatically expressing its desire to remain on the sidelines, they have recently approached the Mexican government expressing a desire to engage in the negotiations."[45] Canada's about-face triggered an argument over the costs and benefits of including Canada. Serra was skeptical. Figuring that the Canadians might now want to join just to act as spoilers, Mexico opposed expanding the talks. SECOFI argued: "Canada already has its agreement; therefore, the cost of failure in the FTA is much less (almost zero) than for Mexico. This means that Canada could be inflexible regarding Mexican interests."[46] SECOFI argued that the U.S.–Mexico agreement should be completed first, and then the three countries could look to create a free trade area based on the two bilateral agreements.[47] On September 25, 1990, Bush noted to Salinas that "The Canadians came on like a ton of bricks on this thing, but

---

44 Bush told Salinas in their March 1990 conversation that it would be better to have bilateral negotiations because of political complications in Canada. Mulroney visited Mexico City the week after the Bush–Salinas phone conversation, and Bush suggested that Salinas sound out the Canadian position.

45 SECOFI, "ATC," May 30, 1990, SECOFI, Subsecretaría de Comercio Exterior, n.p.

46 Ibid.

47 Mexico adopted this argument starting in September 1990 when Canada confirmed its interest in joining trilateral talks. SECOFI, "Canada y el ABC," January 23, 1991, SECOFI, Subsecretaría de Comercio Exterior, n.p.

late." While the United States would "consult" with Canada, it was willing to proceed to bilateral discussions with Mexico "if these consultations [with the Canadians] get complicated." Baker agreed that trilateral negotiations would be unduly complex. Mexico, Salinas insisted, preferred the bilateral track.

SECOFI pressed USTR to formally notify Congress, hoping the announcement would coincide with Salinas' trip to Washington in mid June 1990. Notification would start a period of sixty legislative days for hearings and comment before talks could begin. USTR maintained it would not be ready at least until December.[48] Despite Bush's embrace of the idea, USTR's attention to GATT and the disagreement over whether Canada would participate kept the talks from beginning as quickly as the Mexican team would have liked. When the two presidents met for a private dinner on June 10, they agreed in principle to seek an FTA and ordered Hills and Serra to study the possibility and return with recommendations.[49] USTR and SECOFI had, of course, been studying the agreement for some time, and the decision to proceed had already been made. The presidents' announcement bought time for preparations and consultations at USTR's request. The White House, along with Baker, pressed USTR to speed the start of negotiations in deference to Mexico. Serra and Hills returned their recommendations in early August that an FTA would be beneficial. After receiving a formal letter from Salinas requesting trade talks, Bush notified Congress in late September that he would seek extension of fast-track negotiating authority for both the Uruguay Round and the trade talks with Mexico. Bush emphasized both the economic and the foreign relations rationales for the agreement in a letter to Salinas:

I share your conviction that such an agreement would provide an historic opportunity to expand trade and investment, thereby contributing to sustained economic growth and greater economic prosperity for our peoples. This would be an important milestone in further enhancing our relationship and meeting the new challenges and opportunities posed by the sweeping changes occurring throughout the globe.[50]

The question of Canadian participation remained. In January 1991, Prime Minister Brian Mulroney appealed directly to Bush, who preferred to accommodate Canadian wishes. With Bush pressing for Canadian inclusion, Serra backed down. Before doing so, he obtained a letter signed by all three sides stating that if one party became an obstacle to the completion of the talks, the other two would be free to continue bilateral negotiations. Serra later said: "That is a letter that I pushed for, because for a moment I thought the

---

[48] SECOFI, "Estado de las pláticas del ABC," June 4, 1990, SECOFI, Subsecretaría de Comercio Exterior, n.p.

[49] Clyde Farnsworth, "Free-trade talks seen with Mexico," *New York Times*, June 11, 1990, p. D1.

[50] George Bush to Carlos Salinas, letter, September 25, 1990, in "Informe de los trabajos del TLC," SECOFI, Subsecretaría de Comercio Exterior, annex 2.

Canadians were going to be party poopers. But they weren't."[51] Serra wrote his Canadian counterpart:

"The Canada–U.S. Free Trade Agreement will not be used as a means to frustrate that objective or delay the conclusion of a North American free trade agreement responsive to the needs and aspiration of all three Parties; nor are the trilateral negotiations intended as a means to renegotiate the provisions of the Canada-United States Free Trade Agreement."[52]

Salinas and Bush were both personally involved in launching the negotiations, and they shared concerns that Canadian participation could slow negotiations. The two presidents' commitment marked the initiation of negotiations and would be crucial when the talks got stuck. Bush privately told Salinas: "I want this Free Trade Agreement to be one of the major accomplishments of your and my presidencies. You've got my personal commitment to the success of the negotiation."[53]

Lobbying: Redefining Nonintervention

In the early 1990s, Mexico's economic team boasted sterling academic credentials but very little experience in international trade negotiations. This lack of firsthand experience was a legacy of Mexico's decades of relative separation from the world economy, and it meant the Salinas government faced a steep learning curve. Though many key policymakers had studied in the United States, several were slow to understand the depth of the U.S. Congress' involvement and the potential for hostility. Mexico traditionally proclaimed an aversion to foreign interference in domestic politics, and the Foreign Ministry avoided close involvement in other countries' political processes, particularly with the United States. Mexico typically followed formal diplomatic channels, eschewing direct contacts with the White House. It was even less engaged with the U.S. Congress. Unlike many other countries, Mexico had not maintained a staff of lobbyists – or even a congressional liaison office in its embassy.

Mexico dramatically altered these behaviors in pursuit of a trade agreement. It was quickly clear that the fate of the FTA could be decided before negotiations with USTR began. In order to effectively negotiate a trade agreement with Mexico and to continue the Uruguay Round, Bush needed an extension of fast-track negotiating authority from Congress. There was little opposition to the ongoing GATT talks; however, the notion of free trade with Mexico spurred resistance from some labor and environmental groups. Mexican leaders

---

[51] Serra Puche, interview with the author.

[52] Serra Puche to John C. Crosbie, letter, February 5, 1991, in annex to "Seguimiento de los trabajos del TLC," February 12, 1991, SECOFI, Subsecretaría de Comercio Exterior.

[53] Bush, "Telephone conversation with President Carlos Salinas de Gortari of Mexico," February 5, 1991, GBPL. Available online: http://bushlibrary.tamu.edu/research/pdfs/memcons_telcons/1991-02-05-Salinas.pdf.

worried that labor's Congressional allies would split fast-track approval into two votes, one for Mexico and the other for GATT. Passage of fast-track for multilateral talks coupled with a denial for Mexico would be an intense political blow for Salinas – an approval of free trade but an explicit rejection of Salinas' gamble for closer ties to the U.S. economy.

A second factor led Mexico to adopt a different approach regarding the U.S. Congress. Salinas tapped SECOFI as the secretariat directly responsible for trade negotiations, largely sidelining the Foreign Ministry and Secretary Fernando Solana from the discussion. A more traditional Mexican diplomat, Solana was more skeptical of such close ties with the United States. Solana was rarely included in meetings of the economic cabinet, where key decisions about the negotiations were made. The Foreign Ministry was further marginalized from the trade talks because Salinas had named Gustavo Petricioli, an economist and former finance secretary, as ambassador to the United States. According to an official who worked with Petricioli during the NAFTA negotiations, on trade matters the embassy reported to SECOFI and not the Foreign Ministry.[54]

SECOFI recommended hiring lobbyists and legal advisors in the United States as early as June 1990, shortly after Salinas' meeting with Bush.[55] Based on studies of the U.S.–Canadian trade negotiations and fast-track procedures, SECOFI recognized fast-track was a "fundamental piece of achieving approval of the final agreement." At first, SECOFI planned to coordinate with the Mexican embassy in Washington to hire a legal advisor and a lobbying firm. As the fast-track debate unfolded, SECOFI created its own office in Washington to direct lobbying efforts. Announced on September 5, 1990, it was led by Herman von Bertrab, a former Jesuit professor of Herminio Blanco, Mexico's chief negotiator and Serra Puche's key deputy. Von Bertrab wrote that individuals at Washington think tanks advised the Mexican team that it was customary and important for foreign countries to hire lobbyists to deal with the U.S. government. Eventually, the Washington office would hire five lobbying firms, several legal advisors, and a number of public relations consultants. Von Bertrab wrote: "If lobbyists did not exist, we would have had to invent them, for we could not participate in a game without understanding its rules."[56] One of the first people the Mexican government hired was Robert Herzstein, an influential Washington lawyer and former undersecretary in the Department of Commerce. From the outset, Herzstein advised the Mexican team that their negotiations would be not just with USTR but with 535 members of Congress. "They took that to heart," he said.[57]

---

54 Manuel Suárez-Mier, interview with the author, April 6, 2012, Washington, D.C.

55 SECOFI, "ABC estrategia," June 25, 1990, SECOFI, Subsecretaría de Comercio Exterior, n.p.

56 Hermann von Bertrab, *Negotiating NAFTA: A Mexican Envoy's Account* (Westport, Conn.: Praeger, 1997), p. 15.

57 Robert E. Herzstein, interview with the author, April 16, 2012, Washington, D.C.

USTR's frequent and early references to Congress as a source of delays and as a constraint on the U.S. position further focused SECOFI's attention on legislators.[58] Mexican leaders saw maintaining a single fast-track vote as a top priority, with high political costs for failure. The bureaucratic players mostly likely to oppose the new strategy were not at the table. There was little room for serious dissent in Mexico's political system after the decision was made – though there was some criticism in the Mexican press over the spending for and role of foreign lobbyists. Mexican deputy negotiator Jaime Zabludovsky noted that the slower start to fast-track proceedings and negotiations was a disguised blessing for the Mexican team, which was eager, but in truth, not prepared to begin negotiations in 1990.[59] In February 1991, Serra and von Bertrab visited influential Democratic Representative Bill Richardson, who warned them that as things stood, they were in real danger of losing the fast-track vote. Mexico stepped up its visits to Congress, tried to mobilize sympathetic business inter-ests, hosted Congressional delegations to Mexico, and sought support from the Hispanic community.[60] This represented a significant change in how the Mexican government had related with its citizens in the United States. Mexico had eschewed any sort of attempts to organize emigrants: it would violate its foreign policy tenet of nonintervention, and it was not clear how the migrants saw the PRI.[61]

In another first, the Mexican government launched a U.S. public relations campaign. The debate on trade was peppered with uncomplimentary images of Mexico as a country of poverty, corruption, drugs, violence, and hordes of unskilled laborers. Mexico approached this on two fronts. The Mexican gov-ernment organized a "road show" in which Mexican officials traveled across the United States to make public presentations on the benefits of the trade agreement, sometimes in conjunction with U.S. officials, including Treasury Secretary Mosbacher. More broadly, Mexico launched an effort to present Mexican history and culture, with museum exhibits and events in thirty-one key U.S. media markets.[62]

On the Fast Track

The level of Mexican participation in U.S. domestic politics would have been hard to fathom just a few years earlier. Lobbying from Mexico, the Bush administration, and business allies improved fast-track's prospects in Congress. Both governments sought to placate Congressional concerns on labor and the

---

[58] USTR stressed that it needed to complete consultations with Congress before sending formal notification. SECOFI, "ABC estrategia," June 25, 1990, SECOFI, Subsecretaría de Comercio Exterior, n.p.

[59] Jaime Zabludovsky, interview with the author, May 14, 2012, Mexico City, Mexico.

[60] von Bertrab, *Negotiating NAFTA*, p. 13.

[61] Alexandra Delano, *Mexico and Its Diaspora in the United States: Policies of Emigration since 1848* (New York: Cambridge University Press, 2011), Chapter 4.

[62] von Bertrab, *Negotiating NAFTA*, p. 25.

environment by providing plans and assurances to influential members such as Illinois Representative Dan Rostenkowski and Missouri Senator Richard Gephardt. The fast-track process put the Mexican government in close cooperation with USTR and other parts of the administration – even though they would soon be across the negotiating table. A SECOFI analysis advised that until fast-track authority was approved:

The lobbying program will take particular care to closely coordinate everything with the Bush administration. In particular, all the meetings or discussions with U.S. Congress people will take place in close contact with USTR to maintain a coordinated, univocal message, and to avoid exaggerating the Mexican presence in the U.S. Congress.[63]

In early April, as Congress prepared for the vote, Salinas and Bush again met in Houston to promote the FTA. Salinas was also there to support Mexico's public relations and lobbying campaign, making a seven-city tour through the United States to press for fast-track approval.

While the focus before negotiations was primarily economic, sectors of the Mexican government recognized the negotiation's importance to U.S. foreign policy. Serra said he tried to limit the negotiations to economic questions, but they unfolded in a political context. Mexico emphasized the negotiations' importance to U.S. national interests when threats surfaced. The Mexican government knew Mexico's stability was of paramount importance to the United States, and that it was salient to the cohort of Texans in the White House. In preparation for the Salinas–Bush meeting, Mexico made clear the immense importance of the fast-track vote and implicitly linked the negotiations to bilateral relations:

It would be convenient to take advantage of the meeting [between Salinas and Bush] to reiterate how much is at risk in this process. The Mexican government has come to the United States in a gesture of confidence and friendship, which is not without risks. The rejection by the U.S. Congress of the Mexican initiative to negotiate an FTA would have a very negative effect on national public opinion. The great advances made in the bilateral relation would be seriously threatened by a de-authorization of the negotiation with Mexico.[64]

It has been argued that before NAFTA, Mexico opposed linkages between different issues on the bilateral agenda, out of concern that this would weaken its position. A number of authors have argued that Mexico's more recent acceptance of linkage is a result of NAFTA.[65] In fact, during the earliest stages of

---

[63] "Informe de los trabajos del TLC," March 27, 1991, SECOFI, Subsecretaría de Comercio Exterior.

[64] Ibid.

[65] For a general argument, see Miles Kahler, *Liberalization and Foreign Policy* (New York: Columbia University Press, 1997). On the link between NAFTA and Mexico's approach to migration, see Delano, *Mexico and Its Diaspora in the United States*.

NAFTA negotiations, Mexican officials saw the connections between enhanced trade relations and other foreign policy issues and sought to use them to their advantage.

The Mexican team argued that Mexico had made major, recent improvements to environmental and labor legislation. It tried to combat critics, who noted that Mexico's legislation was fine on paper, but laxly enforced. With an eye on the negotiations, Mexico stepped up inspections and prosecutions of environmental violations and addressed problems that affected U.S. border cities. Mexico convinced Gephardt, who drew his support from labor, to back the fast-track extension. Gephardt's lukewarm approval provided cover for other Democrats. In late May 1991, the House and Senate re-authorized Bush's fast-track authority for North American negotiations and the ongoing Uruguay Round, without adding any specific environmental or labor riders.[66] More than a year after Salinas phoned Bush with the proposal, talks to form a North American free trade area could begin in earnest.

Negotiations: Mexico's Goals and Strategy

As the fast-track debate came to an end, the Mexican team – lead by Serra Puche, Zabludovsky, and Blanco – began to enunciate its opening negotiating positions while also considering how to strategically cede ground. Many in Mexico, including supporters, argued that the developing country should receive special consideration. However, the overriding goal for Mexican policy makers was to secure access to the U.S. market. The United States and Canada would not concede an across-the-board transition period for Mexican producers without extraordinary protections for key U.S. and Canadian goods – what the Mexican team termed "excessive compensation."[67] The Mexican team rarely worried about the agreement going too far in lowering tariffs – though they wanted to exclude labor, environmental, and political matters.[68]

The Mexican team was extremely optimistic about how quickly an agreement could be concluded. This stemmed in part from a lack of experience, but also because they were willing to use the Canada–U.S. Free Trade Agreement (CUSFTA) as a base. In mid June 1991, they expected an agreement could be ready by January 1992, or even earlier. The Mexican team was attentive to the U.S. electoral calendar. The fast-track debate had vividly illustrated that the negotiations could ignite a political firestorm. Nonetheless, President Bush

---

[66] On labor and environment, the House passed nonbinding resolutions, noting the importance of the topics, but they had no legal force. Cameron and Tomlin, *The Making of NAFTA*, p. 76, Salinas de Gortari, *México*, pp. 104–105.

[67] "Aranceles," draft, June 7, 1991, SECOFI, Subsecretaría de Comercio Exterior, p. 1.

[68] "Informe GE junio 10, 1991," June 10, 1991, SECOFI, Subsecretaría de Comercio Exterior, pp. 1–58.

was enjoying sky-high approval ratings in the wake of the Gulf War; it did not appear the trade debate would pose a serious threat. As negotiations got under way, problems became more evident. However, the Mexican negotiators often said they believed the remaining differences could be resolved quickly, with Zabludovsky noting that for months he thought each major meeting could be the final one. Their initial optimism befuddled Americans Jules Katz and Chip Roh. Cameron and Tomlin note: "Incredibly, on some issues the Mexicans were acting, at least in the American view, as though they were actually on the verge of a deal, when in fact the two parties remained far apart."[69]

One of Mexico's top priorities was to secure access to the United States (and Canada to a much lesser degree) for fruit and vegetable exports. U.S. tariffs on Mexican goods were generally low, but this was not the case for many agricultural products in which Mexico directly competed with U.S. growers. Tariffs were not the only issue. Mexican produce was sometimes prohibited from entering the United States at all, or suffered from what Mexicans saw as arbitrary health and sanitary restrictions. When prices on some products fell, Mexican products could be excluded under U.S. laws meant to "safeguard" U.S. agriculture from influxes of imports. A SECOFI position paper stated: "Mexico will seek the immediate drawdown of tariff barriers that affect its [agricultural] exports."[70] Mexican negotiators realized this position was inconsistent with their own protections for corn and beans, crops that were dominated by small producers who lacked the scale, technology, capital, and in many cases, the favorable environmental conditions of U.S. farmers. The Mexican team knew how politically and socially dangerous reforming agriculture would be, noting that more than two million Mexicans relied on corn production.[71] Serra Puche believed that the Mexican countryside was in desperate need of reform and that eventually Mexican *campesinos* would have to face global market prices. The reforms would require the PRI to roll back what many saw as gains of the Mexican revolution. "It had a huge ideological background behind it and not much economic rationality," Serra Puche said. "We had already started [eliminating] the *precios de garantia* and the *ejidos*.[72] It was necessary for the countryside in Mexico."[73] Necessity did not make the process easy.

Despite prior changes to domestic policy, Mexico was slow to make internal decisions about how to approach corn in the talks. This indecision slowed the progress of the agricultural group, where the United States pressed for broad access. The Mexican team realized that requesting special treatment for

---

[69] Cameron and Tomlin, *The Making of NAFTA*, pp. 95–96.

[70] "Aranceles," draft, June 7, 1991, SECOFI, Subsecretaría de Comercio Exterior, p. 27.

[71] Ibid., p. 22.

[72] *Campesinos* is often translated as peasants; it refers to rural agricultural workers. The *ejidos* is a system of common land ownership and management granted largely in Mexican indigenous communities. *Precios de garantía* was a system of minimum prices and prices supports that supported small production in Mexico.

[73] Serra Puche, interview with the author.

corn would undermine its arguments for other products. Any significant action on agriculture would require the direct involvement of President Salinas. On September 4, 1991, Serra Puche made his case to Salinas in an economic cabinet meeting "that if we refused to open up to corn imports, the U.S. would refuse to open up its horticultural products." Other cabinet members noted the potential for "tremendous social upheaval" if the PRI tried to rapidly change the Mexican countryside. Salinas pressed the cabinet for forms of social support that could be compatible with trade liberalization and economic modernization.[74]

For manufactured goods, Mexico wanted to move beyond the GSP to encourage investment. The United States and Canada worried about third-country companies using Mexico as a tariff-free export platform. The Mexican industrialists represented in COECE largely favored replicating CUSFTA's rules-of-origin content requirement that 50 percent of a product's value had to originate within the region to earn tariff-free status. In most industries, a 50-percent rule would not require substantial changes in manufacturing practices. A summary of a *gabinete económico* meeting from mid June 1991 concluded: "The establishment of integration requirements of less than 50 percent seems undesirable from the Mexican point of view, as they would not create incentives to invest in the country."[75] For automobiles, Mexico adopted a different stance. Initially, its producers – dominated by Ford and General Motors – wanted national content standards as high as 70 percent. This was even higher than the U.S.–Canada trade pact, and would benefit Mexican auto parts producers. Conversely, companies like Nissan, which had recently invested in Mexican production, requested lower requirements or long transition periods.[76]

In addition to setting goals, the Mexican team sought to identify what it would not give up and what it considered bargaining chips. Mexico had long controlled certain sectors through import permits, which the Mexican team had decided as early as July 1991 would be incompatible with an agreement that gave Mexico the market access it sought. In a draft position paper on tariffs, SECOFI officials noted: "In the FTA it is clear that the possibility of eliminating restrictions on our exports will largely depend on our own willingness to eliminate the system of advance permits in the sectors where there is an exporting interest for the U.S. and Canada (grains, dairy, some fruits, poultry, autos, pharmaceuticals, among others)."[77] Despite that realization, Mexican negotiators argued for months that the permitting system was needed in some sectors – primarily to trade it for later concessions.

Perhaps the most crucial area where Mexico held back in the hope of making trade-offs was in banking and financial services. The debt crisis of the

---

[74] Salinas de Gortari, *México*, p. 116.
[75] "Informe del GE del 17 de junio de 1991," June 17, 1991, SECOFI, Subsecretaría de Comercio Exterior, p. 15.
[76] "Aranceles," draft, June 7, 1991, SECOFI, Subsecretaría de Comercio Exterior, p. 19.
[77] Ibid., p. 7.

early 1980s prompted the Mexican government to nationalize the banking sector. The Salinas administration did not believe it could effectively enter the world economy with a government-controlled banking sector, so Salinas directed finance minister Pedro Aspe to privatize financial institutions early on. The troubled banking sector made access to capital expensive for Mexican businesses, making the Mexican team eager to reform banking. However, the newly privatized banks were weak and politically vulnerable, given that connected individuals had bought banks without the expectation of facing foreign competition. For SECOFI, the promise of broader benefits and U.S. concessions outweighed those concerns. The tariffs position paper continued:

In financial services, the FTA represents an opportunity to receive important concessions in exchange for an opening that, under the right conditions, could generate substantial economic benefits, including in the short term. The cost of financial inputs, of great importance in the whole economy, could be substantially reduced as a result of the arrival of foreign institutions, without a major displacement of national ones... The FTA with Mexico in financial services has a great value to the United States, above all as a precedent for multilateral negotiations, to the point that the absence of substantial concessions in the topic would make the treaty unacceptable for the U.S.[78]

The approaches to agriculture and financial services illustrate the central tenet of the Mexican negotiating strategy. Serra Puche, Zabludovsky, and Blanco believed that Mexico independently needed to make most of the reforms that would be considered "concessions" in negotiations. The negotiations presented the advantage of receiving something in return for difficult reforms while also making them more politically palatable. A summary for the *gabinete económico* noted the widespread possibilities offered by an FTA: "The FTA creates a unique possibility to carry out wholesale trade liberalization both of ourselves and of our primary trading partner, which will create fundamental benefits for the country."[79] Mexico's position reflected a belief that economic liberalization was worth the costs, and that those costs could be reduced by including reforms as trade-offs in the FTA.

The *gabinete económico* discussed Mexico's "red lines" early on, saying that Mexico would not grant anything that would require changes to the constitution. Salinas announced on November 26, 1990 that the constitutional prohibitions on the energy sector would not be on the table – though there was considerable diversity of opinion within Mexico about what could be liberalized short of a constitutional revision. In Mexico, nearly all activities tied to petroleum were controlled by state-owned Petróleos Méxicanos, or Pemex. Pemex's revenues constituted a substantial portion of the Mexican federal budget; its powerful union was a major employer and political force. Beyond that, state control of petroleum had important historical roots as a

---

[78] Ibid., p. 31.
[79] "Informe del GE del 17 de junio de 1991," June 17, 1991, SECOFI, Subsecretaría de Comercio Exterior, p. 13.

rejection of what many saw as excessive foreign control and exploitation of Mexican resources under the long reign of Porfirio Diaz. The nationalized oil industry was a major legacy of the PRI. Before the first official trilateral session, Mexican negotiators maintained that there should not be a specific negotiating group for energy. Such a move would stir too much controversy within Mexico, they feared, and strengthen the hand of critics. During the prenegotiation phase, the United States had accepted Mexico's position, but during the June 12, 1991 meeting, Carla Hills insisted that "respecting the Mexican constitution, there was still room to discuss the topic in the FTA."[80] Given that energy had been a major point of debate in the U.S.–Canada deal, neither of the northern countries was ready to give Mexico a free pass. Though Mexico eventually acquiesced to having an energy group, it maintained a hard line on the energy issues on which the United States pressed it – guaranteed emergency supplies; foreign investment in production, distribution or sales; and no shared-risk contracts.[81] Oil was perhaps the only real deal breaker for Mexico, so long as the United States guaranteed market access, agreed to restrict protectionist responses, and was bound by an adequate dispute resolution mechanism.

Mexico's concerns about the strength of dispute resolution mechanisms were tied to its new conceptualization about how to approach relations with its powerful neighbor. Whereas Mexico had long tried to exclude U.S. influence from its politics or U.S. domination of its economy, the Salinas government decided that Mexico should instead bind the United States into institutional arrangements. Mexico's concern was not U.S. power, which was an undisputed fact, but the arbitrary use of that power. In trade issues, Mexico realized U.S. actions were often driven by domestic politics. The Mexican team took aim at U.S. anti-dumping laws or other measures that could undermine in practice the benefits it had gained at the negotiating table. U.S refusal to curtail these practices probably constituted the biggest threat to the negotiations from the Mexican perspective, as SECOFI officials noted in an update on the progress of talks:

Failing to achieve significant protections from anti-dumping could not only nullify in practice the other accomplishments made in the negotiation, it would also miss an exceptional opportunity to obtain substantial agreement in the matter. Because of that, we suggest that obtaining major concessions on anti-dumping should be designated as a minimum requirement (deal-breaker) for the FTA itself. This designation would place anti-dumping in the same level of importance that the Americans grant to foreign investment and financial services in the agenda with Mexico, or intellectual property in the negotiations with Canada.[82]

---

[80] "Informe de la reunión ministerial celebrada en Toronto, Canada," June 17, 1991, SECOFI, Subsecretaría de Comercio Exterior, pp. 1–6.

[81] Mexico's conditions on petroleum were not completely defined in June 1991, but would coalesce into the "five no's," all of which were excluded from the final agreement.

[82] SECOFI, "Informe de los trabajos del TLC," July 22, 1991, SECOFI, Subsecretaría de Comercio Exterior, pp. 1–38.

USTR insisted that Congress would not accept any change, and it refused to create a group dedicated to the matter. Negotiator Jules Katz publicly insisted in early July 1991 that the United States would not adjust its laws. Eventually, Hills and Katz agreed to table a group that included anti-dumping, along with subsidies and unfair trade practices. The group made little progress through 1991 due to "U.S. intransigence on discussing seriously the possibility of trilateral agreements." In response, Mexico toughened its positions in other groups, even where its industries privately said they preferred immediate liberalization.[83]

The Mexican negotiators viewed Carla Hills as tactical and patient, willing to move slowly in order to gain concessions. She and Katz were also balancing the FTA negotiations with the stop-and-go talks of the Uruguay Round. Mexico clearly wanted to move quickly, as did some in the U.S. government, such as James Baker, Robert Zoellick, and Brent Scowcroft. Ideally, they wanted Congressional approval well before the U.S. presidential elections.[84] USTR saw this as unlikely. USTR pressed for draft treaty texts that could be directly compared to drive the point home on how far apart the sides were. After a late October meeting in Zacatecas, the ministers declared that the stage of exchanging viewpoints was over, and they would create drafts of each treaty chapter by December 1991.[85]

When Bush invited Salinas to visit Camp David in mid December, the Mexican cabinet hoped to use the occasion to gain Bush's direct intervention. Mexican negotiators believed the delays were largely a function of USTR's strategizing or their preference for the Uruguay Round. SECOFI wrote: "It seems possible to conclude the negotiations during the first months of 1992 and to submit the text for Congressional approval before the elections, which demands a presidential mandate to USTR to give the FTA the necessary priority."[86] Baker also wanted to use the meeting to speed the talks and pressure his own team; U.S. negotiators had the sense that higher ups failed to grasp the distance separating the three parties.[87]

The two presidents came together for a friendly meeting on December 14. Bush stressed to his own officials that he and Salinas "want a NAFTA agreement and we want it as soon as possible." Bush noted that despite political pressure and criticism, "we will not move an inch back." Serra Puche remained optimistic that an agreement could be reached in six weeks, while Hills argued

---

83 SECOFI, "Informe GE 2a reunión ministerial," August 16, 1991, SECOFI, Subsecretaría de Comercio Exterior, pp. 1–28; SECOFI, "Propuesta arancelaria," c. September 1991, SECOFI, Subsecretaría de Comercio Exterior, pp. 1–4.

84 SECOFI, "Informe de los trabajos," October 25, 1991, SECOFI, Subsecretaría de Comercio Exterior, pp. 1–6.

85 Cameron and Tomlin, *The Making of NAFTA*, pp. xii, 95–96.

86 SECOFI, "Gabinete económico: Temas para la entrevista presidencial del 14 de diciembre de 1991," November 26, 1991, SECOFI, Subsecretaría de Comercio Exterior, pp. 1–9.

87 Mayer, *Interpreting NAFTA*, p. 130.

she needed an agreement that Congress would approve. Each side laid out the key remaining problems as it saw them. For Mexico, these lay in agriculture, textiles, autos, and anti-dumping. President Bush brought up energy, which Mexico was still reluctant to discuss. Bush wondered why Mexico would not allow foreign-owned gas stations. Hills raised several other issues, like import permitting and foreign investment in financial services.[88] The Mexican team had privately decided it would dismantle most of the advance permitting system and allow significant investment in banking. However, Mexico held these concessions to strike bargains on the final deal. They promised Bush and Hills that they would narrow the list of exceptions.

At the end of December, the parties compiled the different texts to create a version where disagreements were in brackets. These were extensive. The bracketed text pushed the Mexican team to more clearly define its positions on energy, foreign investment, and financial services. Though much of the energy sector remained off the table, they expanded the allowable fields of petrochemicals where foreign investment would be constitutionally acceptable. Though they continued barring risk-sharing contracts, the Mexican team placed procurement for energy giants Pemex and the Comisión Federal de Electricidad on the agenda.

Mexico hoped the negotiations would gain steam following those concessions. As late as the January 14, 1992 meeting of the economic cabinet, Mexico hoped to conclude the FTA in February.[89] When Mexico reiterated its desired timeline in a January 28 meeting with Katz, it drew the consternation of the veteran negotiator, who argued that there had been almost no progress in recent months. Mexico was still postponing a final decision on corn, too, which led Katz to argue that "exceptions are exceptions." Any Mexican limitations on corn would lead to U.S limits on vulnerable agricultural products.[90] Removing the major exemptions would require concessions from Mexico, the least open economy. While they realized that, Mexican negotiators were hesitant to be the party giving in on point after point.

To jumpstart talks, the three sides scheduled a plenary session in Dallas. The heads of individual negotiating groups would bring their disagreements to the chief negotiators and ministers, who would try to settle as many as possible. The Mexican team exhibited new urgency, reflecting Salinas' desire to conclude the treaties with the supportive President Bush instead of taking his chances on the U.S. elections. Because the ratification calendar required months for public comment, debate, and lobbying, the treaties needed to be signed by March.

---

[88] George Bush, qtd. in "Memorandum of conversation: Meeting with President Carlos Salinas of Mexico," December 14, 1991, GBPL. Available online: http://bushlibrary.tamu.edu/research/pdfs/memcons_telcons/1991-12-14-Salinas.pdf.

[89] SECOFI, "Gabinete económico: Informe de los trabajos del TLC," January 14, 1992, SECOFI, Subsecretaría de Comercio Exterior, pp. 1-36.

[90] SECOFI, "Gabinete económico: Informe de los trabajos del TLC," January 28, 1992, SECOFI, Subsecretaría de Comercio Exterior, pp. 1-9.

Their worry grew especially keen as Bush's approval ratings fell along with the weakening U.S. economy. Salinas pressured his team for advances. Before the Dallas meetings, chief negotiator Herminio Blanco sent instructions to each of the negotiating teams instructing them to be more flexible and conclude what they could.[91] The Mexican team was eager to show progress – ideally a concluded text – for another presidential meeting scheduled for February 27 in San Antonio.

The talks leapt ahead in the February 17–21 meetings, which the negotiators referred to as the "Dallas jamboree" for the free-wheeling style of bringing in a series of negotiating teams. Exhibiting this sense of urgency, Serra Puche and Blanco unveiled major concessions. Perhaps most significant, they agreed to remove the permitting and quota system on corn imports, replacing it with tariffs. These tariffs would be gradually phased out during implementation. This placed corn within the framework used in the rest of negotiations. Different products were sorted into categories labeled A, B, C, and eventually C+, designating how long the tariff phase-out would last. "A" products would be tariff free as soon as the agreement went into effect, while the C+ category would continue to enjoy some level of protection for over a decade. In financial services, the Mexican team opened its position to allow for U.S.-owned subsidiaries. The meeting succeeded in pushing many of the negotiating groups to remove brackets and near common texts, while highlighting the significant disagreements that remained. However, it fell well short of Mexico's goal of completing agreements for Salinas and Bush's meeting.

Bush used the meeting, held on the margins of a summit on counternarcotics cooperation, to restate his support for the agreement, telling Salinas, "I think it's good for the country and I think it's good politics." Both presidents wanted a broad agreement in order to distribute costs and benefits – that is, they would not solve disagreements by excluding those chapters from the final treaty. Salinas told Bush he thought it was possible to initial the agreements by March 12, allowing for them to be sent to the U.S. Congress before it recessed in August. The Mexican team's reading was that support in Congress was likely to wane as November neared. Serra and Salinas pushed for March completion. Mexico's haste was influenced by two other factors. First, the team hoped an agreement would spur interest in the Mexican economy, attracting investment and lowering bond yields. Second, if the U.S. team felt political pressure to move quickly, they might compromise on issues that were politically delicate for Salinas. In contrast, Hills pleaded for more time to consult with Congress and the private sector. After months of being relatively agreeable, the Canadians began insisting on protections for dairy and poultry,[92] threatening to pull out

---

[91] Cameron and Tomlin, *The Making of NAFTA*, p. 107.

[92] Canadian reticence on these products had much to do with their importance in politically restive Quebec. "Memorandum of conversation: Breakfast meeting with Carlos Salinas, President of Mexico," February 27, 1992, GBPL. Available online: http://bushlibrary.tamu.edu/research/pdfs/memcons_telcons/1992-02-27-Salinas.pdf.

of talks on agriculture and textiles in favor of separate agreements. By June, frustration with the Canadians boiled over into a shouting match between Jules Katz and Canadian negotiator Michael Wilson about whether Canada truly wanted to be engaged in a trilateral negotiation.[93]

After the meeting with Bush and Hills, it was clear that the agreements would not be initialed in mid March. From the Mexican perspective, seven of the ten negotiating groups were essentially concluded, with SECOFI reporting to the cabinet that they could be completed in a day of negotiation. Government procurement, energy, and investment remained more troublesome. Having made a number of concessions, Mexico felt that the United States and Canada should show more flexibility. Córdoba Montoya planned a trip to the White House to ask supportive members of the Bush administration to press USTR.[94]

While the list of exceptions was gradually narrowed, the United States began pressing for a special, C+ category that would allow for a longer tariff phase-out on brooms, glass, shoes, and ceramics. This created an odd dynamic, in which the United States was asking Mexico for greater protections. Mexico accepted the extended category, but wanted to shorten the transition time, which U.S. negotiators initially placed at 15–20 years. In a meeting in Toronto, U.S. negotiators even proposed a C++ category. In exchange for the longer transition time, Mexico gained an extraordinary phase-out of its corn tariffs, starting from very high levels, along with a quota at the initiation of the agreement. Blanco insisted the United States reduce the number of items – particularly agricultural ones – in the C+ category to a maximum of ten. Mexico was prepared to increase its quota proposal on corn to 2.5–3 million tons during NAFTA's initial years in exchange for greater liberalization on its exports.[95]

Mexico arrived to each major meeting with the strong desire to make it the last. SECOFI noted with frustration: "Mexico arrived to the meeting of chief negotiators in Toronto prepared to conclude the majority of remaining topics, leaving three or four subjects to be closed by the secretaries at the last moment ... However, the first day in Toronto, it was evident that the U.S. delegation did not share the Mexican mandate."[96] Meanwhile, Mexico's initial fears that Canada might play spoiler in the trilateral talks seemed to be vindicated, and the United States and Mexico for the first time threatened to drop

[93] SECOFI, "Acuerdo: Informe de los trabajos del TLC," June 8, 1992, SECOFI, Subsecretaría de Comercio Exterior, p. 21.

[94] SECOFI, "Acuerdo: Informe ministerial Montreal," April 10, 1992, SECOFI, Subsecretaría de Comercio Exterior, pp. 1–2.

[95] SECOFI, "Reporte de la reunión ministerial bilateral," July 2, 1992, SECOFI, Subsecretaría de Comercio Exterior, pp. 1, 4–5.

[96] SECOFI, "Informe de los trabajos del TLC," May 25, 1992, SECOFI, Subsecretaría de Comercio Exterior, pp. 1–6.

Canada from the agreement. Increasingly, Mexico felt USTR's request for time for consultations was a negotiating ploy. "Everything indicates that [Katz's] strategy consists of not showing any hurry, denying the existence of dates or deadlines . . . At the same time, he has increased pressure on Mexico, demanding concessions that, supposedly, had been agreed upon as excluded and denying any flexibility to Mexican interests."[97] Katz pressed Mexico, telling Blanco it did not seem the Mexicans were prepared to conclude the negotiations. Blanco responded that they were, but that did not mean giving the United States everything it demanded.

The dynamic of negotiation began to change in July 1992, owing in large part to Bush's flagging political fortunes. Bush hoped to make a splash with the U.S. business community at the Republican National Convention to gain momentum in the campaign's final stretch. Bush and Salinas met in San Diego on July 14, attending the Major League Baseball All-Star Game, along with their ambassadors. Bush asked Salinas for the final time about including petroleum in the FTA. U.S. Ambassador Negroponte interjected that the Mexicans were quite sincere that including oil could make the whole deal politically unpalatable in Mexico. Salinas reiterated that he had said since 1990 that petroleum would be a "deal breaker." Afterward, the United States dropped broad demands on oil and sought focused concessions in petrochemicals and procurement to placate the U.S. oil industry and induce it to support the agreement in Congress. The major remaining disagreement on oil regarded whether Mexico would commit to supplying the United States in the event of another oil crisis. Salinas and Serra believed this implied a U.S. right to oil in the ground, an argument that made little sense to the Bush administration. Mexico stayed firm on keeping this out of the agreement, and eventually the United States accepted informal assurances that oil contracts would be honored.

With the Republican convention scheduled for August 17, the U.S. team now faced a time crunch. Bush wanted to sign the agreements before the election. However, U.S. law required a ninety-day public comment period after the conclusion of talks before the president could sign – to say nothing of Congressional ratification. That meant getting an agreement in the first days of August. Feeling economic pressures, Mexico was also eager to get a deal. In San Diego, Salinas told Bush: "The market expects that there will be an agreement, and that it will be finished and signed before the elections. We worry that if we give a number of signals to the market that this is not the case this would be very bad."[98] Both sides began to move more quickly. Mexico moved closer to the

---

97 SECOFI, "Reporte de la reunión entre HBM, JK, y JW," June 15–20, 1992, SECOFI, Subsecretaría de Comercio Exterior, p. 6.

98 "Memorandum of conversation: Meeting with Carlos Salinas, President of Mexico, July 14, 1992, GBPL. Available online: http://bushlibrary.tamu.edu/research/pdfs/memcons_telcons/1992-07-14-Salinas%20%5B1%5D.pdf.

U.S. and Canadian positions on rules of origin for the auto industry while also agreeing to dismantle parts of its complex laws governing the auto industry in Mexico. Salinas and Bush were increasingly engaged in the negotiations by late summer. Bush badly wanted to sign NAFTA. "The Americans were getting anxious. The Bush administration wanted the president to be able to sign an agreement before the presidential election in November 1992."[99] While Katz and Hills had often stated that the timeline would not dictate their agreements – Hills frequently insisted that the United States must have a "good agreement" and not a quick one – that posture weakened under presidential pressure.

On August 2, the three teams arrived at Washington's Watergate Hotel. The Mexicans and Americans were determined to finish the FTA if at all possible. The remaining disagreements centered on government procurement and dispute resolution. Though many of the chapters were nearly resolved, the meetings became a marathon as the Canadian and Mexican teams sensed an opportunity to gain concessions. As Cameron and Tomlin conclude: "Our analysis of the negotiations process at the Watergate makes it clear that U.S. negotiators felt the presidential pressure to get agreement, that their Mexican and Canadian counterparts were aware of it, and that negotiating strategies were changed accordingly." Mexico, which had been ready to give broad access to Pemex's sizable procurement budget, sought to reserve some of it for Mexican firms. Canada held firm on the cultural exemptions it had gained in CUSFTA, though the United States had hoped to set a North American precedent that it could take to the GATT. Serra Puche had insisted that no part of the agreement should be considered closed until the entire deal was finished, and he tried to use that to improve Mexico's position.

The Mexicans remained concerned that weak dispute settlement mechanisms and a lack of protection from U.S. anti-dumping laws could undermine its market access gains. Early on, Mexico had proposed using CUSFTA as the model for NAFTA's dispute resolution mechanism. That chapter of CUSFTA established binational panels to hear disputes, instead of directing suits to national courts. While CUSFTA was a successful model in many other parts of the agreement, its dispute-resolution mechanisms had drawn considerable criticism from the U.S. Congress, and USTR stressed that it saw them as temporary.[100] The chapter in CUSFTA included a five-year sunset provision, to be superseded by a permanent arrangement. The Canadians saw CUSFTA's panels as beneficial and wanted to make them permanent, at least bilaterally. Both Canada and Mexico wanted strong mechanisms to curtail arbitrary U.S. protectionism – it was one of the few times the two countries teamed up. There was an additional complication from Mexico's *ley de amparo*, a constitutional provision that allowed Mexican citizens to challenge government decisions. The United

---

[99] Cameron and Tomlin, *The Making of NAFTA*, p. 151.
[100] Dispute resolution was handled in Chapter XVII on the CUSFTA.

States worried *amparo* could force trade disputes into Mexican courts, which it would not accept. Though Mexico had insisted it would not consider constitutional reforms during the negotiations – primarily to protect its energy sector – it offered major domestic legal changes to satisfy U.S. concerns. However, the issue stalled on the U.S.–Canadian dispute over the mechanism for implementing those changes, leading the Mexican team to privately call for a suspension of the Watergate meetings.[101] Cameron and Tomlin note: "[the Mexicans] did not want the gains they were making on other issues to be undone by failure on the part of the United States and Canada to reach agreement on Chapter Nineteen ['Review and dispute settlement in antidumping and countervailing duty matters']."[102]

The breakdown was the first time Mexico had moved so aggressively, and it came at a sensitive time for the Bush administration. With some reluctance, the U.S. team agreed to extend the CUSFTA dispute resolution mechanism with minor adjustments regarding implementation of legal changes in Mexico. The framework for dispute settlement is contained in Chapter XX, though important mechanisms are included in other chapters on investment disputes (Chapter XI), and unfair trade practices, including anti-dumping and subsidies (Chapter XIX). Chapter XX created a Free Trade Commission to oversee NAFTA's implementation, composed of members designated by the countries' Cabinet secretaries. Dispute resolution includes three stages: consultations, mediation through the commission, and finally a trinational arbitration panel, which could permit "retaliation through withdrawal of compensating benefit."[103]

Unfair trade practices had been crucial to the Mexican team from the beginning, when it pushed the question onto the agenda over U.S. objections. Mexico remained skeptical of U.S. positions on anti-dumping, "snapback" tariffs to protect against import surges, and the use of nontariff barriers. Von Bertrab later wrote: "From a foreign point of view, the United States enters trade agreements only when it retains the ability to carry a big stick if conditions run against its interests. Although no one had the power to take away the stick, it was at least possible to limit its arbitrary use."[104] The debate continued into the Watergate meetings, as USTR appealed to Congressional constraints. As the United States insisted, Chapter XVIII allows each country to maintain its own anti-dumping and countervailing duty laws. However, these laws

---

[101] This was referred to as a special review mechanism. Though this was eventually included, it was done so under strict Canadian conditions. On dispute resolution mechanisms, see Cameron and Tomlin, *The Making of NAFTA*, pp. 47–49, 168–171; Georgina Kessel, *Lo Negociado del TLC: Un Análisis Económico sobre el Impacto Sectorial del Tratado Trilateral de Libre Comercio* (México: McGraw Hill, 1994), Chapter 10.

[102] Cameron and Tomlin, *The Making of NAFTA*, p. 171.

[103] Gilbert R. Winham, "Dispute Settlement in the NAFTA and the FTA," in *Assessing NAFTA: A Trinational Analysis*, eds. Steven Globerman and Michael Walker (Vancouver: Fraser Institute, 1993), pp. 256–260.

[104] von Bertrab, *Negotiating NAFTA*, p. 69.

cannot be applied on a unilateral basis. As Canada insisted, the NAFTA chapter did not include a sunset provision. In many respects, this chapter extended CUSFTA's framework, including mandatory consultations on any changes to domestic trade laws and binational advisory panels in the event of conflict. The chapter required substantial changes in Mexican law, though the participants saw the changes as necessary to improve Mexico's trade and investment climate, noting: "The great majority of these changes were modifications that we planned to undertake anyway, but they had been postponed to have chips in the negotiations."[105]

Agreements on dispute resolution and unfair trade practices largely settled the disagreements between the United States and Mexico. However, the exhausted negotiators were growing bitter over sticking points between the United States and Canada over autos, textiles, and the Canadian cultural exemption. The United States, pressed by its powerful film and recording industries, wanted to eliminate the special exemption for Canadian cultural industries that had been granted in CUSFTA. USTR did not want to restate the precedent for future agreements, particularly GATT talks with the Europeans. Mexico did not fear U.S. media exports as deeply as the Canadians,[106] so the Mexican team was willing to allow Canada an exemption it did not get itself to complete the deal. At the Watergate, the United States and Canada went to the mat until President Bush decided, in conjunction with Hills, that he would not risk the agreement to break the exemption. Patience had been USTR's key weapon earlier in the negotiation, but now that the U.S. team felt presidential time pressures, Canada and Mexico made gains. Just after midnight on August 12, 1992, the three sides shook hands and completed the agreement.[107]

In its immediate, internal assessment of the talks, the Mexican team was extremely pleased. Mexico had gotten a broad agreement while maintaining its red lines on energy. Though the negotiators had not used divergent levels of development as a basis for negotiations, they felt Mexico had achieved substantial advantages through an immediate consolidation of the Generalized System of Preferences, which allowed Mexico access at lower tariff rates to the U.S. and Canadian markets than those two countries immediately received in Mexico. Mexico gained immediate, tariff-free access to the U.S. market for 84 percent of its nonpetroleum exports, while granting the same to 43 percent of imports from the United States. The Mexican negotiators argued the immediately lifted tariffs were on goods that Mexico needed as inputs – factory machinery or tractors. SECOFI concluded: "The consolidation of the

---

[105] SECOFI, "Informe final de la negociación del TLC," August 17, 1992, SECOFI, Subsecretaría de Comercio Exterior, p. 32.

[106] This was in part due to the language differences. Mexican negotiators also saw potential to cater to Spanish-speaking consumers in the United States.

[107] Cameron and Tomlin, *The Making of NAFTA*, pp. 173–174.

GSP permitted a result that is highly asymmetrical in favor of Mexico."[108] While Mexico would open sensitive agricultural sectors, it would do so under a fifteen-year transitional period, slowly lifting tariffs and quotas.[109] In financial services, Mexico made significant concessions late in the negotiations; however, internal documents show that the Salinas government was prepared to make most of these at the beginning of the negotiations, but withheld them to make trade-offs. For Mexico, completion of the agreement outweighed particular concessions. The FTA signaled to the world that the Mexican economy was open for business.[110]

Side Agreements: A Bitter Pill

The negotiations had taken much longer than the Mexicans had hoped, meaning that President Bush could not sign them before the election. Instead, on October 7, 1992, Bush, Salinas, and Mulroney stood behind their chief negotiators at a table in San Antonio as they initialed the documents.[111] The ceremony did not generate the political splash Bush and Salinas had hoped. The agreement would not go to the U.S. Congress during the current term, meaning Mexico and Canada needed to deal, at the least, with a new Congress. Bush's prospects were sinking along with the U.S. economy. The Mexicans began planning for the possibility of a new administration. In April 1992, Salinas privately said he was hopeful about getting candidate Bill Clinton's support, in part because organized labor hesitated in backing Clinton in the Democratic primaries.[112] After months of ambiguity, Clinton offered a clearer position in a speech on October 4 at North Carolina State University. Clinton argued that NAFTA alone was insufficient, but that he would support it if it were accompanied by side agreements on labor and the environment, as well as support for displaced American workers. Clinton hoped to have it both ways, getting the backing of the business community without losing support from unions and

---

[108] SECOFI, "Informe final de la negociación del TLC," August 17, 1992, SECOFI, Subsecretaría de Comercio Exterior. Years later, Serra Puche noted, "The Americans and the Canadians opened much faster than we did, and so that is where we captured the asymmetry." Serra Puche, interview with the author.

[109] NAFTA failed to make a dent in U.S. and Canadian agricultural subsidies, as they were unwilling to do so without corresponding changes from Europe in the GATT.

[110] Mexico was not particularly happy to have granted a handful of agricultural exceptions to the United States, particularly in orange juice and sugar, but Serra Puche said those exports were not important enough to risk the agreement.

[111] Though negotiations were completed August 12, the treaty texts still needed to undergo legal revision and translation, as noted in endnote 2, Cameron and Tomlin, *The Making of NAFTA*, pp. 248–289.

[112] Salinas, conversation with Robert A. Pastor, "Memorandum of conversation," April 24, 1992, Mexico City. Robert A. Pastor personal papers.

environmental activists.[113] The Mexican response was tepid, reflecting a feeling that these issues had been addressed during the fast-track debate. They had no interest in dealing with them again – and even less in reopening negotiations when they were pleased with the final product.

On November 2, Clinton won a comfortable victory over Bush, though third-party candidate Ross Perot meant that Clinton finished well below 50 percent. The Democrats retained majorities in the House and Senate. After fast-track, the Mexican team had largely halted its lobbying and promotion of the agreement in the United States. It now needed to restart those efforts, while also convincing skeptics on Clinton's transition team. In Serra Puche's eyes, the exceptions advocated in Clinton's North Carolina speech originated with campaign staff members, namely Mickey Kantor and individuals who had come over from Richard Gephardt's union-backed primary campaign.[114]

The day after the election, Salinas called the president-elect to "urge him to move ahead with the ratification of the NAFTA, without any renegotiation of its provisions."[115] In a show of concern, the Mexican ambassador flew to Little Rock to meet with the transition team. Later that month, Córdoba Montoya flew to Washington on a closely guarded mission to push the Clinton team to prepare for a fast ratification. The Mexican team was concerned that despite Clinton's stated support, the treaty could stagnate. From early on, it was clear Mexico would not enjoy the same sort of relationship it had with Bush. Gone was the personal chemistry between the two presidents. Clinton never viewed U.S.–Mexico relations in the same light as Bush and his team of Texans. The channels of communication between Mexico and the United States were more limited and formal. When word came in late December that Mickey Kantor would be named the USTR, Mexican officials feared the worst. Kantor was close to Clinton, having managed his campaign, but he was inexperienced with trade at a time when the U.S. trade agenda included NAFTA and the Uruguay Round. Kantor presented different challenges for Mexico than Carla Hills, a tough negotiator, but one who believed in the benefits of trade. Kantor was a political operator who "essentially looks at trade issues in terms of how many votes they could win in Congress or the next election," a *New York Times Magazine* profile noted.[116]

Salinas went to meet the president-elect personally in Texas, where Clinton restated that he would seek ratification with side agreements. Despite the intense skepticism of his negotiators, Salinas agreed in principle to open negotiations on the side issues. Salinas pressed Clinton and Bush to agree that Bush

[113] George W. Grayson, *The North American Free Trade Agreement: Regional Community and the New World Order* (Lanham, Md.: University Press of America, 1995), pp. 109–136; Cameron and Tomlin, *The Making of NAFTA*, pp. 180–183.

[114] Serra Puche, interview with the author.

[115] Cameron and Tomlin, *The Making of NAFTA*, p. 182.

[116] Keith Bradsher, "Mickey Kantor," *New York Times Magazine*, December 12, 1993.

should sign NAFTA before leaving office, which Bush did on December 17, 1992. Since NAFTA was negotiated under fast-track authority, if it was signed before June 1993, the agreement was guaranteed a floor vote in Congress within ninety days of its submission.[117] Salinas' gamble on the agreement was too great to risk letting it die, while it allowed Clinton to keep NAFTA under fast-track without adding his own signature. To try to limit any eventual side agreements, Salinas began mentioning other "side issues" Mexico might ask to add to the talks, such as a development investment fund. Salinas hinted that if labor and environment, which he saw as nontrade issues, were brought in, Mexico might try to insert migration in the negotiations. Salinas knew this was a political bombshell that even Bush had refused to touch, but he meant to signal that if the United States crossed Mexico's red lines, Mexico was prepared to do the same. In early meetings, Mexico set out three negatives: no reopening of the completed NAFTA text, no hidden protectionist measures, and no compromising Mexican sovereignty.[118]

Questioning the new administration's commitment to NAFTA's economic merits, Salinas and his subordinates argued quietly that delaying ratification had real consequences in Mexico. Salinas did not want a drawn-out ratification debate to creep into the PRI's candidate selection and election. Mexican officials intimated that the delay could be detrimental for Mexican stability, pushing the country toward economic stagnation, debt crisis, and political unrest. The looming prospect of instability at the southern border seemed to convince Clinton that he could not let the deal fail.[119] As Paul Krugman wrote at the time, "Mexico's government needs NAFTA, and the United States has a strong interest in helping that government."[120] Those concerns convinced Clinton he could not let NAFTA die, but they did not compel his administration to tackle NAFTA immediately. Though Kantor was quickly confirmed as USTR, the administration was slow to specify its positions on the side agreements. Coming off the intensive, White House attention that the negotiations had received under Bush, the relative inattention during the first months of the Clinton administration jolted Mexico. Herman von Bertrab, who coordinated Mexico's lobbying efforts wrote: "NAFTA was certainly not one of their priorities, and to our regret they would need time to establish a negotiating position... The Mexican team became nervous because of the delay in the further negotiations for NAFTA."[121] This concern was amplified when Kantor was unprepared

---

[117] For a helpful summary of fast-track law, see J.F. Hornbeck and William H. Cooper, "Trade Promotion Authority and the Role of Congress in Trade Policy," November 4, 2010, RL33743, (Washington, D.C.: Congressional Research Service, Library of Congress, 2010). Available online: http://fpc.state.gov/documents/organization/152034.pdf.

[118] Mayer, *Interpreting NAFTA*, pp. 168–169.

[119] Cameron and Tomlin, *The Making of NAFTA*, p. 182.

[120] Paul Krugman, "The Uncomfortable Truth about NAFTA: It's Foreign Policy, Stupid," *Foreign Affairs* 72, no. 5 (1993), p. 18.

[121] von Bertrab, *Negotiating NAFTA*, p. 82.

to establish the Clinton administration's opening position in his first meeting with Serra Puche and Canadian minister Wilson.[122] Serra Puche said Kantor was "not a very good counterpart for negotiations."[123] Salinas shared Serra's doubts throughout the side agreement talks.[124]

As the Clinton administration defined its positions, Labor Secretary Robert Reich became an outspoken advocate for a labor agreement "with teeth," which in practice meant trade sanctions and an independent secretariat. In a March 1993 meeting in Washington, Mexico and Canada immediately rejected the proposal. Frederick Mayer writes: "Kantor was convinced that the Mexicans wanted NAFTA badly enough to accept whatever the United States demanded and that Congressional approval would require side agreements strong enough to sell to Democrats like Gephardt. Strong enough meant sanctions."[125] Kantor was mistaken. Mexico, now often aligned with Canada, proved a tough negotiator. A month later, when the United States presented written draft side agreements, Canada and Mexico rejected them. With the United States insisting on sanctions, negotiations appeared stuck, leading White House chief of staff Leon Panetta to tell the *Washington Post* that NAFTA was "dead." The comment prompted an uproar from Mexico and supportive members of the U.S. Congress. Senator John Danforth and a host of cosigners pressed Clinton to move more quickly and to avoid side agreements that would "undermine the benefits."[126] Mexico insisted that it would only accept consultations on labor and environment, but would not permit intervention in its PRI-allied labor unions.

In June, the two sides began to soften their positions somewhat. Salinas feared that uncertainty about NAFTA was hurting the Mexican economy.[127] Mexico still opposed sanctions but could accept a system that levied fines for violations, and Canada seemed to agree. Both countries identified any possibility of sanctions as thinly disguised protectionism, which they feared the United States might use arbitrarily. USTR shifted its emphasis to the secretariat, which should independently apply international standards. Mexico wanted any secretariat only to monitor the enforcement of national laws. Negotiations on environment were less contentious, with Mexico and Canada showing more flexibility regarding the independence of trilateral environmental commissions.[128] A number of moderate environmental groups offered lukewarm backing for

---

[122] Mayer, *Interpreting NAFTA*, p. 171.
[123] Serra Puche, interview with the author.
[124] Salinas de Gortari, *México*, p. 173.
[125] Mayer, *Interpreting NAFTA*, pp. 183–184.
[126] John Danforth et al., to Bill Clinton, letter, April 28, 1993, carpeta Documentos Tratado de Libre Comercio, Control de Gestión, Subsecretaría de Comercio Exterior, Secretaría de Economía de México, México, D.F.
[127] Salinas de Gortari, *México*, p. 171.
[128] Mayer, *Interpreting NAFTA*, p. 195.

the agreement, easing the pressure on the Clinton administration.[129] Unions remained strongly opposed, and that opposition threatened to translate to "no" votes in Congress.

By August, USTR realized that the opposition from Canada and Mexico to strong sanctions was not going to evaporate, no matter how badly Mexico wanted NAFTA. The parties began working on a face-saving solution that would ensure the United States could not utilize the side agreements for backdoor protectionism, but would allow enough pro-union senators to vote for the agreement. The agreement nominally included sanctions, but made their application highly unlikely. First, a weak commission would observe the application of national laws, as Mexico wished. If those were not applied, fines could be applied after a lengthy process. Only if the violating country refused to pay the fines could sanctions be assessed. Kantor was glad to have sanctions nominally included; Mexico was satisfied they would never be used. Canada seemed to agree until new Prime Minister Kim Campbell publicly announced that any eventuality of sanctions was not acceptable. Grudgingly, Mexico and the United States granted Canada an exception, knowing that U.S. Congressional opponents really had their eyes on Mexico. Late on August 12, 1993, the three sides settled on the side agreements on environment and labor, one year after the close of the talks at the Watergate Hotel.

Mexico's key goal was to block any protectionist measures. Though skeptical about the side agreements, Serra Puche recognized the need to address U.S. political realities. He was pleased with the outcome of the negotiations: "The side agreements, paradoxically enough, I think we made complicated enough to avoid any protectionism."[130] The agreement on environment created a trilateral council of ministers and a public advisory committee to oversee implementation of the agreement. It also established rules for the creation of arbitration panels if a member showed a "persistent pattern of failure to effectively enforce an environmental law."[131] That panel could eventually assess fines, which would be used to improve environmental problems. Only if those were not paid and the problem was not addressed could punitive tariffs be used. The labor agreement established supranational organizations, including an international secretariat, but most of the responsibility was designated to nationally controlled offices. The agreement largely limits the various institutions' powers to consultation and exchange of information. Labor issues in nontrade-related industries are excluded from consideration. An amendment to the side agreements, pressed by Congressman Lloyd Bentsen to ensure Hispanic support, created a small development bank to fund health and environmental

---

[129] Organizations including the World Wildlife Fund, Audubon Society, and Natural Resources Defense Council decided that, on balance, a more developed Mexico would pollute less.

[130] Serra Puche, interview with the author.

[131] Qtd. in Grayson, *The North American Free Trade Agreement*, p. 142.

community improvement projects on the U.S.–Mexico border.[132] Though some hailed the side agreements for bringing "new" issues into a trade discussion, the effect of the side agreements was mostly political. They provided Clinton cover to pursue Congressional ratification.[133]

Engaging Congress: A Watershed

The fast-track debate drew the Mexican government further into U.S. domestic politics than it had ever gone. Trying to get NAFTA approved with a second, less enthusiastic, administration would pull Mexico in further. NAFTA, and Mexico itself, had been major issues in the U.S. presidential campaign because of anti-NAFTA crusader Ross Perot's candidacy. Relying largely on protectionist rhetoric and his substantial fortune, the technology entrepreneur won nearly 19 percent of the national vote – despite temporarily quitting the race over the summer. Perot argued NAFTA would create a "giant sucking sound" as U.S. employers headed for cheaper Mexico, and he was not hesitant about emphasizing Mexican poverty, desperation, corruption, and crime.[134] Even more eager to do so was far-right Republican Pat Buchanan. Both men commanded grassroots support, which they used to mobilize mass mailings to Congress opposing NAFTA. For the PRI, which had not entirely overcome its aversion to other countries' domestic politics, the intense scrutiny of the U.S. presidential campaign was uncomfortable. However, with ratification pending after years of discussions and negotiations, Mexico decided to double down on its lobbying strategy.

Mexico had partnered closely with USTR and President Bush during the fast-track debate to influence members of Congress. During the negotiations, USTR became an adversary. Now, the Mexican team needed to coordinate with a less friendly USTR to promote the agreement. Mexico had largely halted its lobbying activities throughout the negotiations. U.S. business had taken a wait-and-see approach to assess NAFTA's contents before throwing their weight behind it. NAFTA critics had taken no such break, and the forcefulness of Perot and Buchanan had sapped U.S. public support.

With the change of administration in the United States, Salinas replaced Ambassador Gustavo Petricioli with Jorge Montaño. Over four years, Petricioli had dramatically altered Mexico's diplomatic presence in the United States – including moving the embassy to a new building near the White House. He increased the size of the mission, establishing a congressional liaison office. In

---

[132] The bank remained a pet project for Bentsen when he moved into the Clinton administration as Treasury secretary.

[133] On the negotiation of the side agreements, see Cameron and Tomlin, *The Making of NAFTA*, Chapter 9.

[134] The other significant part of Perot's platform was a plan to eliminate the U.S. deficit with sharp budget cuts and tax increases. Grayson, *The North American Free Trade Agreement*, pp. 113–117.

addition to those changes, SECOFI had established an office to coordinate Mexico's newly hired Washington lobbyists, lawyers, and public relations firms.[135] Mexico's lobby effort included some of K Street's highest-priced talent, with a tab of some $30 million.[136] Salinas wrote: "In many occasions, our lobbyists guided us through the complicated paths of the U.S. legislative process. We did not have time to explore it on our own."[137] The Washington office served as a central point of contact during the ratification debate, though it was on a tight leash from Mexico City, where both Serra Puche and Salinas kept close tabs on likely vote counts in Congress.[138]

Mexico's lobbying strategy had several main components, with negotiator Herminio Blanco in residence in Washington for the debate's final chapter. On one side, Mexico utilized business contacts through COECE to help coordinate with U.S. corporate backers. Corporate coordinating organizations like USA*NAFTA helped ensure Republican backing. Mexico coordinated with White House special liaison William Daley to court reluctant Democrats.[139] Mexico attempted to organize Hispanics voters, particularly Mexican-Americans, who had not been deeply engaged in advocating U.S. foreign policy, into the Hispanic–American Alliance for Free Trade. Other Hispanic–American groups also spoke in support of the agreement. Mexico and its lobbyists gathered reams of information about potentially swayable members of Congress. They identified district-level groups and businesses that might support the agreement and urged them to contact their representatives. They invited members to take part in congressional trade delegations and visit Mexico.

The Clinton administration advanced several supportive arguments: that NAFTA would boost U.S. exports and competitiveness, lead to greater employment, reduce illegal immigration, create an economic bridge to Latin America, and spur completion of the GATT.[140] It largely fell to Daley and his deputy Rahm Emanuel to press individual members and round up votes. The two coordinated an extensive lobbying effort by Cabinet officials and business groups.[141] Nonetheless, anti-NAFTA calls and letters overwhelmed supportive messages to Congress. Attacks continued from the right (Buchanan) and the left (AFL-CIO, Sierra Club, and Ralph Nader). Perot released a polemical book in

---

[135] On Mexico's lobbying efforts, see von Bertrab, *Negotiating NAFTA*; Grayson, *The North American Free Trade Agreement*, Chapter 7; Todd Eisenstadt, "The Rise of the Mexico Lobby in Washington: Even Further from God and Even Closer to the United States," in *Bridging the Border: Transforming Mexico–U.S. Relations*, eds. Rodolfo O. De la Garza and Jesús Velasco (Lanham, Md.: Rowman & Littlefield, 1997).

[136] Mayer, *Interpreting NAFTA*, p. 236.

[137] Salinas de Gortari, *México*, p. 94.

[138] Serra Puche, interview with the author.

[139] Serra Puche noted that he stayed in frequent contact with Daley.

[140] Grayson, *The North American Free Trade Agreement*, pp. 168–169.

[141] Ibid., p. 203.

August 1993, *Save Your Job, Save Our Country: Why NAFTA Must Be Stopped – Now!*, provoking a point-by-point rebuttal from the administration. Mexico had specifically hoped the side agreements would convince House Majority Leader Richard Gephardt, but he now denounced NAFTA and said he would oppose the agreements.

Clinton had been cautious for months, but shortly before the Congressional vote, the president threw himself into the fray. The White House coordinated several high-profile events to support ratification. Both Serra Puche and Clinton administration officials talked with Henry Kissinger, asking the former secretary of state to make the foreign policy argument for NAFTA. On an even bigger stage, Presidents Ford, Carter, and Bush joined Clinton as he signed the NAFTA side agreements. Vice President Al Gore said NAFTA "transcend[ed] ideology." Bush stressed the bipartisan nature of NAFTA, saluting members of his team who were on hand. Carter stressed the democratization of Latin America and said NAFTA was the "single most important factor" to advance democracy in Mexico. Ford stressed the negative consequences for Mexico if NAFTA was not ratified, including spurring a wave of illegal immigration. Ford said: "If you defeat NAFTA, you have to share the responsibility for increased immigration to the United States, where they want jobs that are presently being held by Americans. It's that cold-blooded and practical. And members of the House and Senate ought to understand that."[142] The administration circulated a supportive letter bearing the signatures of all living U.S. presidents. The White House set up a televised debate between Vice President Gore and critic-in-chief Ross Perot. Gore artfully dispatched the Texan billionaire, giving NAFTA a public boost one week before the Congressional vote and neutralizing Perot's threats to turn his supporters and funding against NAFTA supporters. Clinton took his time, but once the president made his move, he gave ratification his enthusiastic backing.[143]

The administration relied on key supporters in each party to round up votes. Despite his strong dislike of Clinton, Republican Minority Whip Newt Gingrich supported NAFTA and pressed his own party for votes. Texas Democrat Lloyd Bentsen had been an important supporter from the first, and served as a contact for the Mexican team. Bentsen worked to convince skeptics in his own party and from border states of NAFTA's merits. Democratic Representative Bill Richardson served as a contact for the Mexicans and carefully counted Democratic votes. Meanwhile, Daley and Kantor made aggressive deals in Congress to address grievances and build support. From a Mexican point of

---

[142] "Remarks by President Clinton, President Bush, President Carter, President Ford, and Vice President Gore in signing of NAFTA side agreements," September 14, 1993, National Archives and Records Administration, Clinton Presidential Materials Project. Available online: http://clinton6.nara.gov/1993/09/1993-09-14-remarks-by-clinton-and-former-presidents-on-nafta.html.

[143] Grayson, *The North American Free Trade Agreement*, pp. 203–215.

view, the most frustrating were "understandings" that USTR pushed Mexico to accept. Kantor shored up the support of Floridians by offering greater protections for sugar and citrus. Serra Puche and his SECOFI colleagues were angered at being asked to cede market access they had negotiated a year earlier, and they feared these concessions might be the beginning of a series of "urgent" requests to win votes that would nibble away at Mexican exports. A call from Senator Bentsen helped convinced the Mexican team that the votes of nineteen members from Louisiana and Florida, and NAFTA's passage, might hang in the balance.[144] "Really, the final decision was, are we going to break this down because of sugar and oranges?" Serra Puche reflected. Nevertheless, these final adjustments were more sour than sweet for Mexico's negotiators.

On November 17, Salinas and Serra Puche watched live on C-Span to see the House pass the agreement 234 votes to 200. Mexicans had spent months making economic contingency plans for how to respond if the agreement were rejected. They could now relax. The vote garnered nearly a three-quarters majority of GOP representatives and four of ten Democrats. The Senate passed NAFTA 61 to 38 on November 20. In both chambers, members from southwestern border states were key supporters. The dealing drew intense criticism from treaty opponents, who highlighted some $2 billion of concessions and earmarks made in exchange for votes. Clinton and Salinas shared congratulations in a brief phone call. Between the House and Senate votes in the United States, the Mexican Senate opened debate on NAFTA on November 18. With the overwhelming PRI majority and the support of the business-minded PAN, the Mexican Senate passed the agreement on a 56 to 2 vote.

Conclusions

While several scholars have noted the impact of NAFTA on later Mexican foreign policy, NAFTA itself is usually analyzed from an economic or international negotiations perspective. This chapter argues that NAFTA was also the result a profound recalculation of Mexican national interests, which affected the decision to pursue an FTA, the process of negotiations, and Mexican strategy on issues such as lobbying. Salinas defined Mexican goals in terms of guaranteed market access, foreign investment, limits on U.S. protectionist measures, and the exclusion of a handful of issues – primarily oil and PRI–labor relations. The Mexican decision reflected changing international conditions, a different perception of the United States, and domestic political and economic factors. The 1982 debt crisis convinced Mexico's leaders that the country's previous economic model had reached its limits. This prompted a move toward liberalization and to joining the GATT, but these decisions predated serious consideration of U.S.–Mexico free trade. Though President Miguel de la Madrid joined

---

[144] Salinas de Gortari, *México*, pp. 181–183.

the GATT, he considered a U.S.–Mexico FTA to be undesirable and politically impossible. Multilateral liberalization did not force de la Madrid to sacrifice the nationalist plank of PRI politics.

Salinas' recalculation of the Mexican national interest went deeper than de la Madrid's. It was broader than just economics. Salinas also responded to dramatic shifts in global politics, using NAFTA as a geopolitical and geoeconomic instrument to improve relations with the United States and position Mexico in the emerging post-Cold War environment. The Treaty of Maastricht shaped Salinas' view that the post-Cold War world would be defined by emerging regional blocs that were both political and economic in nature. Salinas argued that if Mexico were going to matter, it would need to achieve influence through interdependence and not just autonomy. This implied a reorientation not just of Mexico's economic policy, but also of its approach to international relations. Even before he decided to seek an FTA, Salinas already was pursuing a closer relationship with the United States. This intensified after attempts to build ties and draw investment from Europe and Japan fell short. His warm personal relationship with President Bush might have represented a liability for his predecessors, who over the past decade had tried to counter U.S. policy in Central America. Some of this change seems to be attributable to a generational shift in the PRI; new leaders saw the United States in a different light based on their experiences there. The leadership also believed that the reflexive impulse to isolate Mexico from the United States had outlived its usefulness. Nor had it stopped Mexico from becoming dependent on the United States, which was already Mexico's top trading partner, source of tourists, and destination for migrants. Decisions made unilaterally by U.S. officials on trade and other issues had major consequences for Mexicans, even though they had no seat at the table. Mexico's standoffishness in Washington had not stopped the U.S. government from what PRI traditionalists saw as meddling in Mexico's domestic affairs. Both the economic and the foreign policy models that had shaped Mexican policy for decades were failing to produce results.

This recalculation produced a new Mexican strategy. As an active participant in the world economy, and then in a regional free trade scheme, Mexico would have a voice in shaping rules and institutions. Given the predominance of the United States as an export market, the Salinas government decided that it could ill afford seemingly arbitrary U.S. decisions. It would be more advantageous to lock the United States into clear economic arrangements through an FTA. The objective explains why Mexico placed such heavy emphasis on achieving clear dispute resolution mechanisms, why it held out for clear rules to restrain anti-dumping measures, and why it fought hard against sanctions in the side agreements. For Mexico, the top priority was binding the United States into predictable arrangements. This recalculation governed the Mexican negotiating strategy, which was marked by a cooperative attitude instead of skepticism about U.S. goals. Mexico's decision to actively engage Congress and U.S. domestic politics was a significant departure, made even more surprising by the close coordination with the U.S. executive. Mexico's decision to lobby was seen as necessary to better understand what was happening in the U.S. Congress and advance its top priority there. Salinas' felt his gamble on the FTA was too big to leave Congress to chance. An FTA presented other advantages. It allowed Salinas to make a number of important reforms in one blow, which otherwise would have necessitated constitutional changes that required two-thirds approval from the Senate and Cámara de Diputados. NAFTA required only ratification by the Senate, which was friendlier to Salinas.

The U.S. interest in establishing a free trade area with Mexico was not particularly surprising and had been mentioned in vague terms by President Reagan and Vice President Bush. However, Mexico had previously rebuffed these mentions. The key change came in Mexico's decision to propose an agreement itself, which reversed the dynamic normally associated with U.S.–Latin American economic relations. Bush, Baker, and Mosbacher saw NAFTA as a way to promote stability and economic growth in Mexico, advance broad economic policy goals, and perhaps slowly advance democratization. When negotiations reached impasses, foreign policy goals triumphed over particular interests, even the preferences of the oil industry. Domestic political concerns were most visible at three moments. First, during the fast-track debate, various domestic groups wanted to divide the fast-track vote on Mexico from the GATT. However, the Bush administration was less concerned about environment and labor lobbies, and minimized their influence. Second, U.S. domestic politics conditioned the timeline of negotiations. Bush and Salinas made optimistic projections about how quickly talks could be completed to minimize the issue's salience in the U.S. campaign. Last, domestic politics clearly mattered in negotiations over side agreements and in seeking ratification. Clinton was highly attuned to striking a balance between labor, environment, and business to get the agreements through Congress. Domestic industry demands affected particular U.S. positions, but these were less important than foreign policy goals for both Bush and Clinton. There was a concern, frequently mentioned outside the negotiating table, that Mexico's stability would be undermined by failed negotiations. Mexican documents demonstrate that Mexico understood this U.S. concern and sought to reinforce it. Salinas and Bush discussed it directly, and it manifested itself in warnings from Gerald Ford and others that NAFTA's failure would provoke waves of millions of desperate immigrants.

Why did Mexico decide to involve itself so deeply in U.S. domestic affairs? Despite the decades-long tradition of noninvolvement, the answer seems fairly simple. Necessity was the mother of intervention. Once Salinas made the decision to break Mexico's and the PRI's traditional isolation from the United States, he needed his primary gambit to succeed. Salinas and Bush were on the same side of the fast-track debate, meaning their administrations would be working together. Without Congressional approval of trade promotion authority, NAFTA would not be negotiated. Mexico could stand by, as it traditionally had, while others debated the country's core interests in Washington, or it could join the debate. This was much easier for Salinas and his largely U.S.-educated team to accept than it was for some PRI traditionalists. However, the traditionalists had been bureaucratically sidelined. Having taken the step of seeking an FTA, rejection carried political risks too great for Salinas to leave to chance. Given the historical lack of direct political involvement – the ambassador had to establish a congressional liaison's office – the Mexican government did not have the contacts or know-how to create its own operation in the months available. Outsourcing these duties to U.S. lobbyists was not risk-free. Mexico's considerable spending drew criticism in Mexico and from U.S. treaty opponents. Given USTR's frequent references to Congress, Mexican negotiators soon realized that connections on the Hill were helpful for more than passing the agreement; Mexico needed "intelligence" about what was happening in Congress to make independent decisions about what concessions USTR actually needed to win Congressional votes and which were less crucial. In this way, Mexico tried to manage the United States' "two-level game."

Asymmetry mattered, but often not in the obvious sense. At times, Mexican negotiators felt the United States used the size of its market to bully them into concessions. However, Salinas also privately said, "The problem is that they [U.S. negotiators] treated us like equals, but we are not."[145] Mexican negotiators wanted asymmetry in development to be recognized, and Serra Puche argues that it was through gradual tariff reductions and GSP consolidation. Asymmetry was an implicit focus of the negotiations – particularly on dispute resolution. In the past, asymmetry had led to U.S. decisions on economic policy with outsize effects on Mexico, made without consultation. NAFTA was a way for Mexico to reduce the economic effects of asymmetry through institutions, rules, and interdependence.

Salinas' decision to pursue an FTA allowed for dramatic shifts in policy, even as U.S. interests were stable. Mexicans had previously shunned the suggestion, and without their decision there would have been no NAFTA. Even earlier, it was largely Mexican initiative that led to a changing climate for relations – though as the Camarena incident showed, this was not uniform. At the same time, the Bush administration exhibited great openness to Mexican proposals, particularly on trade and debt. During the negotiations, there was considerable overlap in goals between the United States and Mexico. Both Bush and Salinas had made strong, personal commitments to the success of the talks. Mexico's effort, at times bypassing USTR for consultations with Baker, Scowcroft, and Bush, helped ensure that NAFTA received equal or greater attention than the GATT talks. At the same time, Mexico made clear that it would not make large-scale transformations in its oil sector in order to secure agreement. Though the United States also had exceptions, Mexico's were almost certainly greater.

---

[145] Salinas, conversation with Robert A. Pastor, April 24, 1992, Mexico City. Robert A. Pastor personal papers.

It was obvious to Salinas – as was made clear by his close advisor Córdoba Montoya – that NAFTA would rewrite the rules for U.S.–Mexican relations just as it would for the Mexican economy. Though NAFTA created only weak institutions, it multiplied mechanisms for consultation across many levels of the three governments. The sweeping changes in bilateral relations that resulted from Mexican leaders' recalculation of national interests illustrate how the stance adopted by a Latin American state can be just as influential as the United States' orientation. Latin American leaders possess the ability to change the countries' relationship while pursuing their interests – though this is certainly easier when there is convergence. Beyond trade, Salinas showed more willingness to work with the United States on other issues, including as a mediator in the Central American conflicts and with Cuba. The legacy of NAFTA, unfortunately, is not that it catapulted Mexico into the first world. It is that it dramatically altered the way in which the United States and Mexico relate to one another, playing a major part in converting the two countries from "distant neighbors" to close partners.

5

An Urgent Opportunity

The Birth of Plan Colombia

As Andrés Pastrana prepared to take the oath of office, many of the institutions of the Colombian state were crumbling around him. The government exercised only titular control over much of the national territory. A host of armed groups – guerrillas, paramilitaries, and drug traffickers – operated nearly unchecked. Colombia's principal cities, including Bogotá, had previously been largely isolated from the decades-long conflict. By 1998, armed fronts of the Fuerzas Armadas Revolucionarias de Colombia (FARC) moved closer to the capital, while urban bombings brought the danger home. Head to head with the FARC, the Colombian Army often seemed overmatched. Towns slipped out of the control of the Colombian state. The FARC were adding soldiers and amassing weapons. They seemed to have little trouble obtaining sufficient resources, unlike the government troops they faced. Colombia faced a sharp recession and approached a balance-of-payment crisis, problems that were exacerbated by the violence. In addition to the troubling material situation, the Colombian government faced a crisis of legitimacy. Drug-money scandals had engulfed Pastrana's predecessor Ernesto Samper after audio tapes surfaced proving his campaign had taken millions of dollars from the kingpins of the Cali drug cartel.[1] His denials (later recanted) fell on deaf ears in Colombia and increased the ire of a hostile U.S. ambassador. The Colombian Army was seen as irreparably tainted by ties to paramilitary groups, which were guilty of massacres, forced displacements, torture, and other human rights violations on an increasing scale. The connections further eroded the legitimacy of the central government. As a result of opposition to Samper and concern about human rights, U.S. aid had plummeted. Most of the aid that remained was funneled directly to the Colombian National Police, with the conspicuous purpose of

---

[1] Pastrana played a role in bringing these tapes to light, and he actively lobbied for Samper to step down.

174

marginalizing Samper, but with the side effect of weakening other institutions. The army's morale was disastrously low and its conditions pitiful, with only a handful of functioning helicopters to traverse the country's mountainous jungles. Facing overwhelming challenges and lacking the tools to address them, President Pastrana surveyed his options and crafted a domestic and international strategy. That strategy involved intense collaboration with the United States and led to the creation of Plan Colombia.

Set against the background of hostility that engulfed U.S.–Colombian ties during the Samper administration, it is perhaps surprising that under Colombia's next president, the country became the third-largest recipient of U.S. aid. More surprising is that much of that aid went to the Colombian military, which a U.S. official said in late June 1998, "doesn't pass the test with human rights groups, the US Congress, or the media."[2] The thesis of this book offers a new lens through which we can understand the origins of Plan Colombia and explain this puzzle. Though "Plan Colombia" has been used to describe a wide swath of U.S.–Colombian cooperation from the late 1990s to the present, I focus on the overlapping mandates of the Colombian President Andrés Pastrana and U.S. President Bill Clinton from 1998 to 2001. I ask, how did the Colombian government approach Clinton administration policy to Colombia? What goals did Pastrana set, what did he wish to obtain from the United States, how did he pursue those objectives, and at what cost?

This case is set at the height of the United States' "unipolar moment," with its power unrivaled on the international stage, and is important in examining how that international context affected Latin American strategies. In the post-Cold War period, there has been a focus on "transnational" issues, of which drug trafficking is a paradigmatic example. This chapter explores how weaker countries deal with the effects of transnational issues on their relations with the United States and on their own domestic political situations. The case explores a process of influence that occurs not through a dramatic recalculation of interests or through conflict, but through a largely cooperative process – in which weaker-state leaders tend to be considered imperial lackeys.

In the face of that portrayal, the case illustrates that Pastrana's government had considerable influence in the creation and shape of Plan Colombia. Characterizations of the plan as either an imperial design foisted upon a reluctant but desperate Colombia or as a perversion of Pastrana's initial, more benevolent program misconstrue the process. That is not to claim that Plan Colombia can accurately be described as a purely Colombian proposal adopted by the Clinton administration – and much less by the U.S. Congress. Pastrana altered his policies in response to conditions in Colombia and to U.S. and Colombian policymakers' perceptions of the conflict. The actors' ways of seeing the conflict and its actors mingled across borders. Colombians achieved several of their initial priorities in their foreign policy toward the United States. Those priorities

---

[2] David Passage to Roberta Jacobson, "Consultations with SOUTHCOM," June 1, 1998, DNSA.

included a broad vision of *responsabilidad compartida*, or shared responsibility, to use the term of the Colombian foreign minister Guillermo Fernández de Soto, that encompassed not just the drug war, but the Colombian conflict itself. Contrary to the flawed accounts of some critics, the Colombian government clearly sought, from Pastrana's first days as president-elect, a substantial increase in U.S. military aid, accompanied by stronger social programs. Pastrana maintained aspects of his policies that were unpopular with important sectors in the United States, particularly negotiations with the FARC until these had abjectly failed to produce results. To facilitate this incipient peace process, Pastrana maintained the *zona de distensión*, also called *el despeje*, a significant geographic area in which the army was forbidden from pursuing the FARC, and which served as a safe haven for conducting peace talks. Both the peace process and the *despeje* were routinely criticized in the U.S. Congress.[3] Pastrana had warm relations with Cuban President Fidel Castro, visiting him on several occasions and appealing for the Cuban's intercession with Colombian guerrilla groups.[4] Plan Colombia combined the Pastrana administration's top goals while allowing the United States to address a perceived source of regional instability.

Divergent Interpretations of Plan Colombia in the Literature

There are three major strands in the case literature on Plan Colombia. In the United States and Latin America, many critics of Plan Colombia portray the initiative as the new face of U.S. imperialism in Latin America. One volume of Colombian academic essays asks: "How can we explain that the Colombian government has accepted as its most visible policy something that is a U.S. law... precisely one of the specific, localized expressions of the new configurations of empire?"[5] Many critics link Plan Colombia to dependency theory critiques. Germán Rodas argues that the plan is a pretext for "rich countries in the framework of their neoliberal strategy... to consolidate at any cost their project in the Andean region."[6] Likewise, Jairo Estrada sees the plan as aimed "to consolidate the hegemony of the empire and its local allies."[7] In this telling, Colombian leaders are at most imperial lackeys. Others see the final Plan Colombia as a perversion of a pacific Colombian initiative. A Colombian

---

[3] It is worth noting that they also had many detractors in Colombia, especially in the Colombian military. The ultimate failure of these two policies has left Pastrana with a rather unpopular legacy in Colombia.

[4] Andrés Pastrana Arango and Camilo Gómez, *La Palabra Bajo Fuego* (Bogotá: Planeta, 2005), pp. 145–155.

[5] Jairo Estrada Álvarez, ed., *Plan Colombia: Ensayos Críticos* (Bogotá: Universidad Nacional de Colombia, 2001), p. 14. Translation by author.

[6] Germán Rodas Chaves, *El Plan Colombia: Análisis de una Estrategia Neoliberal* (Quito: Ediciones Abya-Yala, 2002), pp. 30–31. Translation by author.

[7] Estrada Álvarez, ed., *Plan Colombia*, p. 14.

scholar argued in 2001 that "the currently unfolding project is a transformed version of the initial idea formulated by President Pastrana"[8] Similarly, Grace Livingstone argues that the original Colombian concept of Plan Colombia was not a military initiative: "Its focus [was] on achieving peace and ending violence," adding, "The United States' redesign of Plan Colombia turned it from a peace plan into a battle plan."[9] Other critics have focused more on the U.S. interests at play in creating the plan. For example, some argue the plan's military focus has given the U.S. defense establishment generally, and Southern Command (SOUTHCOM) in particular, a new *raison d'etre*.[10] It also provided an opportunity for Congressional largesse to the military–industrial complex, exemplified by Senator Christopher Dodd's support for sending the Colombian military Connecticut-built Blackhawk helicopters.[11] The plan's intellectual supporters have emphasized the U.S. role, largely ignoring Colombian policymakers. Arguing for the plan's expansion in 2003, Gabriel Marcella wrote, "Common wisdom prevails that little of magnitude happens in the Western Hemisphere without the leadership of the United States, especially on such a controversial, sovereignty-laden issue as fighting the scourge of narcotics at the international level."[12] Juan Gabriel Tokatlian argued that "Plan Colombia – designed in Casa de Nariño [home of Colombia's president] by the suggestion of the White House – was launched after an intense debate in Washington, a tenuous discussion in Bogota, and a worrying silence in the hemisphere."[13] Russell Crandall, citing an anonymous interview with a U.S. State Department official, writes that "The ostensibly comprehensive 'Colombian' Plan Colombia was basically a Washington creation." Crandall focuses on how Plan Colombia fit into the U.S. political context, with little attention to events in Colombia.[14] These divergent explanations have one thing in common: all focus on U.S. motives for launching Plan Colombia, whether they refer to it as an invasion and a breach of Colombian sovereignty or a bold American success story.

[8] Jaime Caycedo Turriago, "Una Guerra Social de la Globalización," in *Plan Colombia: Ensayos Críticos*, ed. Jairo Estrada Álvarez (Bogotá: Universidad Nacional de Colombia, 2001), p. 183.

[9] Grace Livingstone, *Inside Colombia: Drugs, Democracy and War* (New Brunswick, N.J.: Rutgers University Press, 2004), pp. 124, 128.

[10] William M. LeoGrande, "From the Red Menace to Radical Populism: U.S. Insecurity in Latin America," *World Policy Journal* 22, no. 4 (2005); Dean A. Cook, "U.S. Southern Command: General Charles E. Wilhelm and the Shaping of U.S. Military Engagement in Colombia, 1997–2000," in *America's Viceroys: The Military and U.S. Foreign Policy*, ed. Derek S. Reveron (New York: Palgrave Macmillan, 2004), pp. 127–162.

[11] Crandall, *The United States and Latin America after the Cold War*, pp. 92–93.

[12] Gabriel Marcella, *The United States and Colombia: The Journey from Ambiguity to Strategic Clarity* (Carlisle Barracks, Pa.: Strategic Studies Institute, U.S. Army War College, 2003), p. 33.

[13] Juan Gabriel Tokatlian, "Colombia, el Plan Colombia y la Región Andina: Implosión o Concertación?," *Nueva Sociedad* 173 (2001), p. 137. Translation by author.

[14] Crandall, *The United States and Latin America after the Cold War*, p. 124.

There is another perspective from which to view the development of Plan Colombia. Rather than seeing it as a solution to a U.S.-defined problem (e.g., the absence of a post-Cold War military mission or cocaine flows), Plan Colombia can be seen through the lens of Colombian policymakers who were seeking to address the massive problems they faced in the late 1990s. From this perspective, Plan Colombia is the outcome of interactions between U.S. and Colombian policymakers. The United States occupied a dominant position in terms of military and financial resources; however, Colombia held important cards. Evidence from archives and interviews in the United States and Colombia indicates that the essential elements of the final version of Plan Colombia were priorities sought by the Pastrana administration starting early in his presidency and even as president-elect. These include large U.S. military assistance, enhanced counternarcotics cooperation, alternative development programs, and political backing for the negotiations with the FARC. Pastrana's initial attempt to end the Colombian conflict did indeed stress pacific solutions such as dialogue and development; however, Pastrana and his administration saw the rebuilding of the military as a necessary complement. This chapter will describe the background in which Plan Colombia was launched before turning to the interactions between U.S. and Colombian policymakers during the years in which Plan Colombia was born.

Background

Colombian foreign policy has traditionally centered on the United States, with a secondary focus on neighboring countries. Sometimes called the "Suárez doctrine," after Colombian president Marco Fidel Suárez, the Colombian foreign policy elite considered the United States to be the "north star" that oriented their country's interests.[15] Beginning in the 1960s, Colombia diversified its foreign relations and became an important regional actor, involved in the Panama Canal Treaty negotiations and later the Contadora initiative. However, as Colombia's importance in the global drug trade grew, relations with the United States – along with aspects of its domestic politics – became "narcotized."[16] The U.S. market for international drugs emerged as servicemen returned from Vietnam, provoking President Richard Nixon's domestic narcotics control act in 1969. Nixon also pressured foreign governments to curb narcotics production. Initially, these policies focused on heroin and opium. However, cocaine supplanted heroin as a drug of choice during the 1970s, drawing the Andean

---

[15] Juan Gabriel Tokatlian, "The Political Economy of Colombian–U.S. Narcodiplomacy: A Case Study of Colombian Foreign Policy Decision-Making, 1978–1990," Ph.D. thesis, Johns Hopkins University (1991). Randall, *Colombia and the United States*.

[16] Tokatlian, "The Political Economy of Colombian–U.S. Narcodiplomacy," pp. 40–43. See also Russell Crandall, *Driven by Drugs: U.S. Policy toward Colombia*, 1st edn. (Boulder, Colo.: Lynne Rienner Publishers, 2002), pp. 26–32.

region, native soil of the coca leaf, into the drug trade.[17] Still, with the exception of a $95 million program in Bolivia, counternarcotics assistance to the Andean region remained minimal throughout the 1970s.[18]

During the 1970s, Colombian cartels based in Cali and Medellin forced out other narcotics traffickers, notably Corsican and Sicilian mafias.[19] The massive amount of U.S. currency generated by the sale of drugs swelled the accounts of Colombian banks, which were often knowingly complicit in laundering drug profits. U.S. authorities estimated drug exports as 16 percent of Colombian gross domestic product by the late 1970s, with financial flows large enough to boost inflation.[20] By 1979, the glaring growth of the Colombian narcotics industry led Colombia's government to respond with a military campaign. The U.S. government offered $3.8 million in counternarcotics aid to the effort.[21] And while the United States claimed credit for the Colombians' initial success against drug trafficking organizations, President Julio César Turbay acted because traffickers and insurgents "had reached the point of threatening democratic institutions and perhaps even its tradition of civilian government."[22] By 1981, Colombia had become the major producer and transit point for coca leaf grown in Bolivia and Peru, the major grower of marijuana, and a major player in the production of other drugs.[23] U.S. funding increased under the Reagan administration, which paired an intensive escalation of "war on drugs" rhetoric with a militaristic approach in the hemisphere. This was encapsulated in Presidential Directive 221 of 1986, which stated that narcotics trafficking was a threat to the integrity of Latin American democracies, noting that some insurgent groups funded themselves by involvement in the drug trade. The president called for increased involvement of the U.S. military in counternarcotics operations abroad.[24]

U.S. attention to Colombia intensified dramatically with the 1989 assassination of Luis Carlos Galán, a presidential candidate for the Liberal Party who was viewed favorably in Washington.[25] From 1989 to 1999, the United States granted Colombia counternarcotics aid totaling $1.1 billion, with much of this destined for the Colombian National Police.[26] This total, however,

---

[17] William L. Marcy, *The Politics of Cocaine: How U.S. Foreign Policy Has Created a Thriving Drug Industry in Central and South America* (Chicago, Ill.: Lawrence Hill Books, 2010), pp. 8–10.

[18] Ibid., p. 18.

[19] Ibid., pp. 12–14.

[20] Ibid., p. 21.

[21] Richard B. Craig, "Colombian Narcotics and United States-Colombian Relations," *Journal of Interamerican Studies and World Affairs* 23, no. 3 (1981), p. 255.

[22] Ibid., p. 257.

[23] Ibid.

[24] "Narcotics and National Security," National Security Decision Directive no. 221. Available online: www.fas.org/irp/offdocs/nsdd/nsdd-221.htm.

[25] Crandall, *Driven by Drugs* (2002), p. 34.

[26] Tokatlian, "Colombia, el Plan Colombia y la Región Andina," p. 138.

obscures significant shifts in the tenor of U.S.–Colombian relations during the decade preceding Plan Colombia. The George H.W. Bush administration largely coincided with Colombian President César Gaviria. Gaviria pushed Colombia through a violent struggle against Pablo Escobar's Medellín cartel.[27] At the same time, Gaviria attempted to address Colombia's conflicts with the guerrilla through peace dialogues. Hosted in Venezuela and Mexico, the dialogues proved largely ineffectual, and gave the FARC a respite in which to grow more militarily potent, later handing the military a series of defeats.[28] Sandra Borda argues that Gaviria was the first Colombian president to exploit the U.S. concern about drugs to gain an advantage in Colombia's civil conflicts. Borda notes Colombian rhetorical strategies:

By conflating the illegal drug business with insurgent activities, the Colombian government was able to skillfully construct arguments to convince Washington to militarily support governmental counterinsurgent strategies. The construction of this frame allowed the emergence of a common course of action between Washington's war on drugs and Colombia's concern with the growth of insurgency.[29]

While some Colombian governments benefited from increased U.S. involvement, the issue inflicted severe costs on President Ernesto Samper. Even before his 1994 inauguration, Samper was tarnished by allegations that his presidential campaign had been directly funded by drug traffickers, corroborated by cassette recordings of major kingpins. The scandal would lead to the dismissal and resignation of top Colombian officials. Samper faced a harsh response from the United States, along with domestic opposition, which intensified as embarrassing details about administration corruption came to light.[30] Ironically, as Crandall points out, the scandal pressured a weak Samper to comply with U.S. wishes to adopt a hard line against traffickers, especially the Cali cartel.[31] In 1996 and 1997, the Clinton administration "decertified" Colombia under U.S. counternarcotics aid laws, signaling that the Colombian government was not cooperating in the war on drugs. Decertification triggered a cutoff of most U.S. aid programs. Remaining aid, given under a national security waiver, was channeled around the president through the head of the Colombian National Police. The Clinton administration even denied a visitor's visa to sitting President Samper.[32]

---

[27] Mark Bowden, *Killing Pablo: The Hunt for the World's Greatest Outlaw* (New York: Atlantic Monthly Press, 2001); David P. Thompson, "Pablo Escobar, Drug Baron: His Surrender, Imprisonment, and Escape," *Studies in Conflict & Terrorism* 19, no. 1 (1996).

[28] Sandra P. Borda, "The Internationalization of Domestic Conflicts: A Comparative Study of Colombia, El Salvador and Guatemala," Ph.D. thesis, University of Minnesota (2009), pp. 55–57.

[29] Ibid., p. 57.

[30] Crandall, *Driven by Drugs* (2002), pp. 101–106; Borda, "The Internationalization of Domestic Conflicts," pp. 59–61.

[31] Crandall, *Driven by Drugs* (2002), pp. 114–115.

[32] Cook, "U.S. Southern Command," p. 131; Crandall, *Driven by Drugs* (2002), Chapter 4.

Attempts to embarrass Samper and the aid cuts that accompanied decertification "helped weaken the Colombian state at precisely the most inopportune time."[33] The natures of the country's drug trafficking, armed groups, and decades-old conflict were rapidly changing. For the first time, in the 1990s, coca plants began to be cultivated in Colombia on a large scale. The fall of the Cali and Medellín cartels created an opening. Initially, armed groups, both guerrilla and paramilitary, began to draw on drug revenue by levying taxes or offering protection to growers and traffickers. Some scholars argue that it was precisely the success of the U.S.-backed drug war that offered the FARC opportunities to deepen its involvement in the drug trade.[34] By the late 1990s, while the Colombian government was starved of revenues because of a deep recession and a sharp reduction of international aid, the FARC captured hundreds of millions of dollars in funding from drugs. Three Colombian scholars summarize:

The participation of the FARC in the drug-trafficking economy, starting in the second half of the 1990s, caused a shift in organizational structure in their areas of influence. The period from 1996 to 1998 corresponded to the largest FARC offensive against public forces, and this demanded significant financial resources to obtain arms and new members. As a consequence, the FARC intensified its activities in the region known as the "coca belt."[35]

Goals and Context: A New Administration Faces Immediate Crisis

The son of a president and a longtime leader of Colombia's Conservative Party, Pastrana took office with a thorough understanding of Colombian politics. However, his government faced profound threats. Three factors created the immediate and difficult context in which Andrés Pastrana took office: the military's failures against the FARC, widespread domestic calls for peace during Colombia's elections, and the intense strain on U.S.–Colombian relations during the presidency of Ernesto Samper.

The Colombian conflict, which had long been seen as a peripheral problem for the country's urban elites, came to occupy the center of national life as it threatened Colombian cities and the state itself.[36] A boom in drug production gave the FARC massive new resources against the Colombian government. In

---

[33] Crandall, *Driven by Drugs* (2002), p. 131.

[34] Mark Peceny and Michael Durnan, "The FARC's Best Friend: U.S. Antidrug Policies and the Deepening of Colombia's Civil War in the 1990s," *Latin American Politics and Society* 48, no. 2 (2006).

[35] Arlene Tickner, Diego García, and Catalina Arreaza, "Actores Violentos No Estatales y Narcotráfico en Colombia," in *Políticas Antidroga en Colombia: Éxitos, Fracasos y Extravíos*, eds. Alejandro Gaviria Uribe and Mejía Londoño (Bogotá: Universidad de los Andes, 2011), pp. 413–445.

[36] Even in early 1998, a report noted that many commentators "argue that Colombian elites and urban residents – relatively insulated from the political violence that is rife in the countryside – are 'in denial' about the seriousness of the guerrilla problem," in "Intelligence report," Central

1998, Colombia was estimated to be the source of 90 percent of the cocaine entering the United States, and as much as half of this came from coca leaf cultivated in areas under FARC control.[37] It became clear that drug money was facilitating the major gains in FARC military capacity. A report by the U.S. Joint Chiefs in February 1998 noted: "Security situation in Colombia has worsened – right-wing paramilitaries and narco-guerrillas have effectively taken over large parts of the country."[38] Indeed, in the months before Pastrana took power, the Colombian military was in retreat, a point driven home when the FARC routed the army's supposedly elite unit in March 1998.[39] The combination of a U.S. president trying to appear tough on drugs and Samper's weakness proved a poisonous combination that drove relations to their nadir, while undermining the Colombian state at home and abroad.[40]

Violence was the central theme in the 1998 presidential campaign, surpassing the failing economy and Samper's legacy of scandal. The run-off election pitted Horacio Serpa, who had been a major figure in the Liberal Samper administration, against Pastrana, a previously unsuccessful Conservative presidential candidate and former mayor of Bogotá. The early stage of the campaign was dominated by groups advocating for peace. The *Mandato Ciudadano por la Paz*, or the Citizens' Mandate for Peace, organized demonstrations against the violence, instructing voters to deposit a white card alongside their ballot in a 1997 municipal election as a demand for peace. Though the cards were not officially counted, Pastrana and others began citing "10 million votes for peace" as a pressing popular demand to address the conflict.[41] Pastrana tried to define himself as the "peace candidate" by proposing a multipronged peace plan at the Hotel Tequendama on June 8, 1998, shortly before the second round of voting. He emphasized peace negotiations with insurgents, rural development, and political reforms. One of Pastrana's main goals was to receive international funding for development and assistance to restructure Colombian sovereign debt – what Pastrana called a "Marshall Plan" for Colombia.[42]

Pastrana's key policy objectives almost demanded improved cooperation with the United States. His principal foreign policy goals, closely linked with

---

Intelligence Agency, Office of Asian Pacific and Latin American Analysis, January 20, 1998, DNSA.

[37] Arlene Tickner and Carolina Cepeda, "Las Drogas Ilícitas en la Relación Colombia-Estados Unidos," in *Políticas Antidroga en Colombia: Éxitos, Fracasos y Extravíos*, eds. Alejandro Gaviria Uribe and Mejía Londoño (Bogotá: Universidad de los Andes, 2011), pp. 211–212.

[38] "OC w/ Gen Locarno, Colombia CHOD," February 12, 1998, DNSA.

[39] Curtis W. Kamman to Secretary of State, "The Colombian Army pummeled at 'El Billar'," March 27, 1998, DNSA.

[40] Pastrana Arango and Gómez, *La Palabra Bajo Fuego*, p. 112.

[41] Given that this would represent nearly everyone who voted, the total is dubious, though it is cited by everyone from Pastrana to UNICEF. However, it is clear that the movement had a large impact on the tenor of the second-round campaign. Ibid., p. 31.

[42] Ibid., pp. 45–52.

the domestic situation, were to restore international respectability, to obtain fiscal and development aid, and to gain international backing for peace negotiations. Pastrana also emphasized the need to attack drug trafficking as a means to sap funding from the conflict and to strengthen the Colombian military in order to improve the government's positions vis-à-vis guerrillas and traffickers. Foreign Minister Guillermo Fernández de Soto summarized their goals as obtaining emergency social assistance, recovering a monopoly on the use of force, internationalizing the peace process, and finding "the solution of the problem of drug plantations as an essential step to end the armed conflict."[43] Given the historically central role of the United States in Colombian foreign policy, and the globally preeminent U.S. role in military aid, technology, and intelligence in the late 1990s, it seemed clear the Pastrana administration would place the United States at the center of its international strategy.

Pastrana had a robust peace agenda, but even as a candidate he did not see a negotiated solution as adequate on its own: Peace talks required a military strategy. In a meeting with Assistant Secretary of State Peter Romero at the U.S. embassy, Rodrigo Lloreda, a top Pastrana deputy who would later be appointed defense minister, stressed the difficulty of combining political and military realities in Colombia. The U.S. embassy in Bogotá reported: "On peace, Lloreda told us Pastrana knows the guerrillas must be weakened militarily before they come to the negotiating table, but this was not a popularly acceptable campaign theme."[44] Plus, the next president's options would be limited by the weakness of state institutions. Pastrana later wrote: "It was clear then, in the middle of 1998, that the Armed Forces were not capable of mounting a large offensive against the illegal groups because they did not have the means or human and logistical resources to do so. It was as simple as that."[45] Or as his principal advisor said, when Pastrana arrived, "*No tenía con qué ponerse bravo.*" – he did not have anything to get tough with.[46]

In addition, Colombia was in dire fiscal straits, with heavy foreign debt and an economy weakened by the violence.[47] One of Pastrana's main goals was to receive international funding for development and assistance from international financial organizations to restructure Colombian sovereign debt – a goal Pastrana encapsulated during the campaign by referring to first a "Marshall Plan" and later "Plan Colombia." In his inaugural address, Pastrana called Plan Colombia "a combination of alternative development projects that will channel the shared efforts of governments and multilateral institutions with those of

---

[43] Guillermo Fernández de Soto, *La Ilusión Posible: Un Testimonio sobre la Política Exterior Colombiana* (Bogotá: Grupo Editorial Norma, 2004), p. 93.

[44] Eva Weingold, "Parade of Candidates 1: Bedoya and Pastrana," April 6, 1998, DNSA.

[45] Pastrana Arango and Gómez, *La Palabra Bajo Fuego*, p. 85. Translation by author.

[46] Jaime Ruiz, in an interview with the author, May 16, 2011, Bogotá, Colombia.

[47] Marcelo Giugale, O. Lafourcade, and Connie Luff, *Colombia: The Economic Foundation of Peace* (Washington, D.C.: World Bank, 2003), pp. 39–49.

Colombian society."[48] However, alternative development was not the entirety of Pastrana's plan. He later summarized his goals: "It was urgent to reform and modernize the military forces, recover our international relations, launch a plan of social investments, fight drug trafficking and seek reconciliation."[49] This was not just post hoc rationalization: Pastrana had included these points in his Tequendama address, and he restated them at his inauguration on October 22, 1998. After reiterating his call for a Marshall Plan, Pastrana spoke at length about the problem of drug trafficking and its relationship to the conflict, arguing that the prolongation of fighting benefited only drug kingpins. Pastrana argued: "Colombia faced two clearly different wars," one against drug trafficking and the other against groups with social and political aims.[50]

Initial Approaches

Many in the Clinton administration seemed to realize that the harsh treatment of Samper had damaged U.S. interests in the region and diminished the institutions of the Colombian state by late 1997. However, rapprochement with Samper appeared unworkable and politically infeasible. Before the first round of the Colombian election, Pastrana's representative Rodrigo Lloreda told U.S. officials that improving bilateral ties was a top issue, and that Pastrana realized he needed development, counternarcotics, and military aid.[51] In early May 1997, Clinton's special representative for Latin America, Thomas McLarty, visited Bogotá to commemorate the founding of the Organization of American States. Though he had only a passing conversation with Samper, McLarty met with political campaigns, business groups, and civil society organizations. He had a long meeting with National Police General Rosso José Serrano, who stressed to McLarty the "increasing connection between narcotraffickers and guerrillas." Furthermore, "Serrano asserted that fighting drug trafficking in Colombia is the key to fighting the rest of Colombia's ills, from corruption to crime to the guerrillas."[52] On the same trip, McLarty met Pastrana's campaign chief Rafael Pardo and future foreign minister Guillermo Fernández de Soto. The latter emphasized the need for better cooperation with the United States not only on drugs, but to improve the economy and crack down on human rights violations. Neither Pardo nor McLarty thought narcotrafficker–guerrilla cooperation was as deep as Serrano argued. Pastrana's representatives emphasized the need for a national peace process and explored the possibility of U.S.

<hr>

48 Oficina del Alto Comisionado para la Paz, "El Momento de la Paz" October 22, 1998, APA 1998, Dirección Secretaria General, caja 3, carpeta Directivos Presidenciales, Archivo Presidencia de la República, p. 40.

49 Pastrana Arango and Gómez, *La Palabra Bajo Fuego*, pp. 34–35.

50 Oficina del Alto Comisionado para la Paz, "El Momento de la Paz," p. 40.

51 "Parade of candidates," April 6, 1998, DNSA.

52 Kamman, "Special envoy for the Americas Thomas McLarty visits Colombia in conjunction with 50th anniversary of the OAS," May 14, 1998, DNSA.

involvement. Later that day, McLarty was told that "any peace process would probably involve demilitarization of parts of Colombian territory, and that the police and military need to be strengthened in order to reestablish their legitimacy in much of the country."[53]

Once the election results determined Pastrana to be the victor, neither the president-elect nor the U.S. government awaited the end of Samper's mandate to begin changing policy. Pastrana had pledged during the campaign to sit face to face with FARC leaders to seek a negotiated peace. He wasted little time. Launching an elaborate ruse, the president-elect slipped past the media and most of his own bodyguards. With a handful of staff members, he boarded a small International Red Cross plane and flew to a hamlet near the FARC stronghold of San Vicente de Caguán for a secret meeting with the legendary FARC commander Manuel Marulanda, alias "Tirofijo," and the military chief known as Mono Jojoy.[54] According to Pastrana, the meeting served as an illustration of good faith to the guerrillas and the Colombian public. Several days before his inauguration, Pastrana traveled to Washington with designated ministers Fernández de Soto and Lloreda and Ambassador Luis Alberto Moreno. The incoming administration asked Clinton to back his Marshall Plan proposal. They also requested equipment and training for the Colombian military and help in stabilizing Colombia's fiscal situation.[55] Fernández de Soto said of the initial contacts: "President Clinton and the U.S. administration, people like Madeleine Albright, understood very well that we needed to turn the page on the relations with Colombia from Samper."[56] In a demonstration of Clinton's personal concern over the Colombian situation, the U.S. president issued an invitation, apparently improvised, for a formal state visit. That visit was speedily organized, and Pastrana returned with a larger delegation from October 26 to October 30. During the first meeting and the state visit, the two sides built an agenda that emphasized counternarcotics cooperation and included economics, strengthening of civil and military institutions, energy, and the unfolding peace process.

Pastrana was inaugurated on August 7, 1998, days after his return from Washington. The tone of his inaugural address was clear: "My top priority will be the recovery [*recuperación*] of our international relations and a frontal attack on the problem of drug-trafficking."[57] Four days later, while presenting his choice for the position of High Commissioner for Peace, the principal contact for negotiations with the guerrilla, the president outlined his plans for the *despeje*. He promised to root out ties to paramilitaries, and asked for

---

53 The name of the person who offered this key insight has been redacted from the document. Ibid., p. 4.
54 The meeting is described in Pastrana Arango and Gómez, *La Palabra Bajo Fuego*, pp. 60–73.
55 Ibid., pp. 120–123, 187–188; Fernández de Soto, *La Ilusión Posible*, pp. 93–95.
56 Interview and translation by author.
57 Pastrana Arango and Gómez, *La Palabra Bajo Fuego*, p. 75.

international cooperation with the "Marshall Plan for peace in Colombia."
Pastrana laid out a challenge to the guerrillas, the FARC in particular: "The
Armed Forces that I command could be armed forces for peace or for war.
In both cases, they need to be efficient. Paradoxically, that is the point of
departure for any serious negotiations."[58] Pastrana's focus on revamping the
military went beyond words. During the administration's first week in office, it
began seeking fourteen Blackhawk helicopters as a first step toward addressing
the army's inability to pursue guerrillas and traffickers.[59]

In the U.S. embassy in Bogotá, Ambassador Curtis Kamman greeted the
change of administration. Kamman had been designated early in 1998 to
replace Myles Frychette, whose animosity with Samper was widely known.
Kamman, a career diplomat who had been ambassador to Bolivia, worried
that victories by guerrilla forces during the months before Pastrana took office
had handed them momentum just as the government prepared to negotiate.
Noting that Pastrana and new military leaders were "intent on embarking on a
major program of internal reform and modernization," Kamman advised that
the United States should amplify its support beyond counternarcotics to include
advocacy in international financial institutions and backing for Pastrana's alternative development goals. Kamman wrote: "Effective military reform will be
essential to the success of the government's strategy. In fact, one political figure
close to Pastrana has told us that peace negotiations are necessary to buy time
to create a more effective military force." The role for the United States was
clear.[60] In Washington, the Clinton administration was increasingly concerned
about overall stability in the Andean region, with the ongoing Colombian
conflict seen increasingly not just as a local matter, but a broader risk. Starting during the summer of 1998, there was considerable division within the
executive branch about how, or whether, the United States should work with
the Colombian army. The Department of Defense, with a sizeable influence
from SOUTHCOM chief Admiral Charles Wilhelm, argued: "A modernized,
more professional military could more capably support counterdrug efforts
and the peace process."[61] In addition to U.S. willingness to reset relations with
Colombia, long-held beliefs among U.S. policymakers about the Colombian
civil conflict had started to erode. Visions of the FARC and the Ejército de
Liberación Nacional (ELN) as Marxist revolutionaries were replaced with a
focus on the nexus between these groups and drug trafficking. Initially, many

---

[58] Ibid., pp. 76–77.
[59] That Colombia was allowed to buy Blackhawks was emblematic of the shifting tone of U.S.–
   Colombian relations since the sale of these helicopters is restricted. Ruiz, interview with the
   author.
[60] Kamman, "The Colombian peace process: Implications for U.S. policy," September 9, 1998,
   DNSA.
[61] Assistant Secretary of Defense for Special Operations and Low Intensity Conflict to Secretary of
   Defense, "Read-ahead for July 7, 1998 Principals Committee Meeting on Panama-Colombia,"
   July 2, 1998, DNSA.

believed that the FARC role consisted of levying protection "taxes" on traffickers, but in a July 1998 meeting, U.S. officials said, "We are now convinced that some factions of the FARC and ELN are heavily involved in the production of illicit drugs."[62]

Pastrana aimed to convince holdouts in the U.S. administration of the importance of drug trafficking in financing armed groups, in part because he wanted to involve the Colombian military in attacking both traffickers and guerrillas. Colombia would not accept a "'narcotized' peace," Pastrana said.[63] Neither the peace process nor development projects would interfere with the drug war. Pastrana personally asked Clinton for $150 million in U.S. support to create a new counternarcotics battalion, which the Colombian military command had proposed weeks before the state visit. Colombian military chief General Fernando Tapias had already laid the groundwork with U.S. officials for the proposal, which merged Colombian and U.S. interests.[64] As a newly formed, handpicked group, the battalion could avoid the human rights concerns that dogged much of the Colombian military. The battalion would operate two dozen helicopters to enable rapid strikes, focusing on narcotics, but with the aim of disrupting guerrilla financing.[65] The Pentagon was receptive to the proposal, but advised Pastrana during his visit that the request for $150 million exceeded Defense's current spending authorization.[66] Pastrana's state visit signaled Colombia's importance to U.S. interests and produced a series of important agreements. In addition to the military plans, Pastrana gained Clinton's support for the passage of a fiscal package from the International Monetary Fund (IMF) that helped avert a balance-of-payments crisis with $1 billion in 1998 and another $1 billion in 1999. The deal went through shortly after the state visit, with decisive U.S. support. The visit allowed Pastrana to offer evidence to a domestic audience of international support, especially with Clinton's $280 million

---

[62] "Read-ahead for July 30, 1998 meeting with U.S. embassy Bogota deputy chief mission," n.d., DNSA.

[63] Oficina del Alto Comisionado para la Paz, "El Momento de la Paz."

[64] Dean A. Cook writes that SOUTHCOM Commander Charles Wilhelm pushed the Colombian military to take a larger role in attacking drug trafficking during Samper's final year in the presidency. Cook also says that Wilhelm met with Pastrana in September 1998 to convince the Colombian president that military pressure needed to be part of the peace process, and that it was a "hard sell." However, Pastrana and his advisors emphasized the role of the military during the presidential campaign, during the preinaugural visit, and immediately after his August 1998 inauguration. Wilhelm was an influential strategic voice and an advocate in the U.S. Congress for aid to Colombia, but to say he convinced the Colombians that they should involve the military against drug trafficking ignores that Pastrana had already made that decision.

[65] Kamman, "Despacho de la Viceministra de América y Soberanía Territorial," Ministerio de Relaciones Exteriores, Memoria al Congreso Nacional, 1998–1999 (Santafé de Bogotá: Fondo Editorial Cancillería de San Carlos, 1999), pp. 278–279; Kamman, "Colombian Army counternarcotics battalion proposed for USG assistance," October 15, 1998, DNSA.

[66] "Read-ahead for the October 29, meeting with Colombian President Andres Pastrana," October 28, 1998, DNSA.

commitment to Pastrana's social plans.[67] In the presidents' joint appearance, Clinton called the drug fight "our joint responsibility."[68] The U.S. Congress passed supplemental counternarcotics funding of about $160 million, destined for the Colombian National Police.

The two governments agreed to set up a high-level coordinating group through which the United States could assist Colombia with counternarcotics, the peace process, and economic challenges. The interagency group, under the auspices of the Colombian Foreign Ministry and the State Department, would be a central site for hashing out the programs and funding that would become Plan Colombia over the following eighteen months. The Pentagon and the Colombian Ministry of National Defense formed a separate working group for defense issues. Assistant Secretary Romero met with Colombian officials, including Pastrana, to establish its mechanisms shortly after the state visit. Mindful of how his predecessor had lost influence to the National Police, Pastrana insisted that the relationship be conducted through the Foreign Ministry, run by his old friend Fernández de Soto. The Colombians often stressed to their American counterparts that the peace process might lead in uncertain directions, and that its immediate impact on counternarcotics was uncertain. Colombian military and civilian officials, even in discussing the peace process, stressed the ever-closer connection between the guerrillas and drug production. Because U.S. military aid was restricted to use in counternarcotics operations, the guerrilla – narcotics nexus could lead to broader discretion in the use of U.S. assistance. Defense Minister Lloreda told his counterparts that if, after the initial ninety-day truce, talks with the FARC failed, "the guerrillas need to know that the government has other options ('Plan B'), and that the normalization of relations with the United States and the international community changes the dynamics." The U.S. team met with Colombians planning alternative development projects in Putumayo under the rubric of Plan Colombia, and showed cautious enthusiasm about assisting in the peace process.[69]

Peace Process

Pastrana's bold, preinaugural trip to meet FARC leaders was a media sensation. However, it was difficult for the administration to maintain the momentum. Upon taking office, Pastrana declared Colombian security forces would not pursue the FARC in the *zona de distensión* or *despeje*, in order to facilitate peace talks between the government and the guerrillas. Peace talks did not

---

[67] Kamman, "Despacho de la Viceministra de América y Soberanía Territorial," pp. 280–281.

[68] "The President's news conference with President Andrés Pastrana of Colombia," October 28, 1998, The American Presidency Project. Available online: www.presidency.ucsb.edu/ws?pid=55165.

[69] Kamman, "Acting A/S Romero's visit to Bogota," November 13, 1998, DNSA; Kamman, "Despacho de la Viceministra de América y Soberanía Territorial," pp. 282–283.

officially begin until January 7, 1999, nearly a month after the ninety-day order for the military to abandon the *despeje*. When Pastrana again flew to the *despeje* to launch talks, FARC commander Marulanda failed to show up, saying the meeting was unsafe. The sides struggled to establish trust and form a common agenda for the talks. Fighting between the FARC and the military continued unabated elsewhere in Colombia, since a ceasefire was not a condition for talks. Less than two weeks after talks began, the FARC sent an open letter accusing the government of complacency regarding attacks from paramilitaries and announced they would suspend the dialogues.[70]

Pastrana wanted to link peace negotiations with the international community, believing international involvement would lend credibility to the process while also helping it to continue beyond his four-year term.[71] Pastrana saw the United States as an essential participant, and he lobbied personally for U.S. participation. He argued that direct contact with the FARC might help the United States understand how complex Colombia's situation was – and how different from Ireland or Central America, to which U.S. officials sometimes compared it. The Clinton administration supported the peace process after Pastrana's preinaugural visit. Peter Romero approved an initial U.S.–FARC rendezvous, under the condition that it be held secretly in a third country. The FARC also showed interest in meeting with the United States.[72] In mid-December 1998, State Department officials met with Raul Reyes, the FARC's primary spokesman, in Costa Rica. U.S. officials stated they were there because of Pastrana's strenuous lobbying and stressed their intentions to continue counternarcotics efforts with the Colombian government.[73]

Two events scuttled Pastrana's plan for closer U.S. collaboration with the peace process. First, word of the initial meeting was leaked to *El Tiempo* in Bogotá, possibly by the FARC, drawing criticism from the U.S. Congress and making involvement more politically costly. Despite that, U.S. Ambassador Kamman accepted the invitation to witness the opening of negotiations on January 7. The murder of U.S. indigenous rights activists by FARC commandos was the final blow. On March 4, 1999, the bodies of two missing women

---

[70] Manuel Marulanda et al., "Open letter to the President of the Republic," January 18, 1999, APA 1999, Alto Comisionado para la Paz, caja 52, carpeta Ministerio de Relaciones Exteriores, Archivo Presidencia de la República, ff. 54.

[71] This was a new facet of the Colombian conflict. Previous talks, including successful negotiations with the M-19, had been almost entirely domestic. Diego Cardona, "La Política Exterior de la Administración Pastrana (1998–2002)," in *Relaciones Internacionales y Política Exterior de Colombia*, eds. Sandra Borda and Arlene B. Tickner (Bogotá: Universidad de los Andes, Facultad de Ciencias Sociales, Departamento de Ciencia Política-CESO, 2011), p. 208. Also, Fernández de Soto, interview with the author, May 15, 2011, Bogotá, Colombia; and Jaime Ruiz, interview with the author.

[72] Pastrana Arango and Gómez, *La Palabra Bajo Fuego*, pp. 130–135.

[73] Philip T. Chicola, "Memorandum of conversation between USG representatives and representatives of the Revolutionary Armed Forces of Colombia (FARC)," n.d., DNSA.

and one man were found. Their hands were bound, and their bodies showed evidence of torture. Several days later, the FARC admitted to the murders, saying it would discipline those responsible, but would not turn them over to law enforcement. The killings called into question the goodwill of the FARC, as well as its negotiators' control over the group's disparate "fronts."[74] Though the peace talks continued, the United States backed away from its previous contacts with the FARC and declared the group "terrorists." U.S. support for the talks was henceforth cool and cautious.

In Colombia and the United States, the talks were unpopular with many on the right. The Heritage Foundation labeled the *despeje* and peace talks a "white flag." Republicans in Congress, including Speaker Dennis Hastert, attacked the proposal and threatened to cut funding should the *despeje* lead to increased coca production.[75] While many in the United States viewed the *despeje* with trepidation, it provoked outrage among Colombian military brass.[76] Commanders saw the zone as a giveaway to the FARC, who, in their eyes, would be free to use it to train, produce cocaine, and launch attacks before retreating into the zone. Resistance to the peace talks, along with worries about Pastrana's designs to reorganize the military, provoked the first major crisis of the president's tenure. The Colombian military felt it was being left out. The conflict was worsened by tensions between Defense Minister Lloreda and Peace Commissioner Victor G. Ricardo. In protest of a rumored, indefinite extension of the *despeje*, Lloreda faxed Pastrana his resignation while Pastrana was at a summit with Latin American presidents. The resignations of a host of generals followed, sparking rumors that a coup might be in the offing. Though Pastrana accepted Lloreda's resignation, he calmed the generals in a daylong meeting at a military base.

The peace talks had been frozen for months because of the FARC's threat to break negotiations over continuing paramilitary violence. In early 1999, the government offered assurances about its respect for human rights and attempts to weed out links between the army and paramilitary groups. In a show of good faith, Pastrana extended the original ninety-day limit on the *despeje*, despite the activists' murders and complaints that the FARC was violating the zone's

---

74 Pastrana Arango and Gómez, *La Palabra Bajo Fuego*, pp. 134–135, 162–167. "Colombia rebels say own fighters killed 3," *New York Times*, March 11, 1999, p. A10.

75 For the original report, see John P. Sweeney, "Tread cautiously in Colombia's civil war," March 26, 1999, The Heritage Foundation. Available online: www.heritage.org/research/reports/1999/03/tread-cautiously-in-colombias-civil-war. For reactions from Colombia, see Oficina de Alto Comisionado para la Paz, "Informe semanal de coyuntura," March 26, 1999, APA 1999, Alto Comisionado para la Paz, caja 43, carpeta Informe Conyuntura, Archivo Presidencia de la República, ff. 15–11.

76 Diana Marcela Rojas Rivera and Adolfo León Atehortúa Cruz, "Ecos del Proceso de Paz y el Plan Colombia en la Prensa Norteamericana," in *El Plan Colombia y la Internacionalización del Conflicto*, ed. Universidad Nacional Instituto de Estudios Políticos y Relaciones Internacionales (Bogotá: Editorial Planeta Colombiana, 2001), pp. 122–123.

conditions. There was little visible progress until early May 1999, when the FARC and the Colombian government announced agreement on a broad twelve-point agenda for negotiations. It included the end of the conflict, political reforms, human rights, agricultural and natural resource policy, juridical reforms, foreign policy, and more. The agreement followed on the heels of another meeting between Pastrana and Marulanda, held on the president's initiative to salvage negotiations. However, the sides had not agreed on a ceasefire, and the guerrillas had launched more than 300 armed acts between the opening of the talks and the conclusion of the agenda.[77] Talks collapsed again in July when the FARC refused to allow international observers into the *despeje*. A U.S. analyst later summarized: "Throughout the first half of 1999, the FARC demonstrated an inability or unwillingness to take advantage of political space created for the peace process by the Pastrana administration, to recognize the significant political risks Pastrana had taken in making concessions, or to respond with reciprocal political gestures of real or symbolic importance."[78] Over the next year and a half, the two sides met frequently over this agenda, without reaching agreement on a single point.

Plan Colombia's Precursors

The peace talks progressed slowly, but U.S.–Colombian cooperation intensified much more quickly. U.S. Secretary of Defense William Cohen traveled to the port city of Cartagena for a hemisphere-wide meeting of defense ministers. At a breakfast meeting, Pastrana and Lloreda pressed Cohen with plans for the counternarcotics battalion, attack helicopters, and crop substitution and eradication. The U.S. ambassador wrote that Lloreda's "objective was to strengthen Colombia's military capability as a key tool for reinforcing the government's peace dialogue with the guerrillas." The new battalion gained strong support from Secretary Cohen.[79] As the Colombian Foreign Ministry prepared for the state visit and sought to reestablish the country's international credibility, much of the government's attention was focused on the creation of the *Plan Nacional de Desarrollo* (National Development Plan), a policy blueprint the presidency is required to present to Congress within six months of assuming office.[80] As early as December 1998, a draft of the *Plan Nacional* was circulating within the Department of National Planning. It stressed the "lack of governability" and the absence of the state, proposing "Plan Colombia" as a financing mechanism

---

[77] Oficina de Alto Comisionado para la Paz, "Informe semanal de coyuntura," May 7, 1999, APA 1999, Alto Comisionado para la Paz, caja 43, carpeta Informe Conyuntura, Archivo Presidencia de la República, ff. 62–55; Pastrana Arango and Gómez, *La Palabra Bajo Fuego*, pp. 170–189.

[78] Cynthia J. Arnson, ed., *The Peace Process in Colombia and U.S. Policy* (Washington, D.C.: Woodrow Wilson International Center for Scholars, 2000), p. 7.

[79] Kamman, "Pastrana breakfast and Colombia bilateral," December 22, 1998, DNSA; Kamman, "Despacho de la Viceministra de América y Soberanía Territorial," pp. 282–283.

[80] Law 152 of 1994, Chapter 4, Article 13, *Diario Oficial,* n. 41450, 19 July 1994, p. 18.

to promote investments to foster conditions for peace. The investments, both government and private, would target areas that were home to coca and poppy plantations and where the presence of guerrillas or paramilitaries had brought economic development to a halt.[81]

Director of Planning Jaime Ruiz led the drafting of the document, entitled *Cambio para Construir la Paz* (Change to Build Peace), which in large part focuses on social and economic development. Ruiz, eager to challenge the many critics of the Pastrana administration, argues that all the aspects of the eventual Plan Colombia were present in the government's early plans. Initially, the elements of the larger strategy were rolled out as separate policies. Alternative development programs, described as "a Marshall Plan for Colombia," during the campaign became Plan Colombia in the *Plan de Desarrollo Nacional*. Counternarcotics, judicial reform, and military reform are all present, but not explicitly linked.[82] The *Plan Nacional* calls Plan Colombia a "strategy of alternative development and state actions for zones affected by conflict and violence."[83] The next section of the plan focuses on the staggering level of violence in Colombia. While it calls for "negotiation with armed groups as a central part" of the search for peace, the plan declares that "ultimately, the recuperation of security depends on the armed institutions of the State recovering the monopoly over arms, and the full exercise of the authority and legitimacy of the State within a strict framework of human rights."[84] While the *Plan Nacional de Desarrollo* does not include the military under the programmatic name of "Plan Colombia," it makes ample references to the need to address violence that originates from drug trafficking, urban crime, and the larger conflict – initially targeting the most affected regions.[85] Large drug cultivations would be "eradicated without compensation," while small, peasant-held plots could benefit from alternative development. The *Plan* lays out a strategy for reorganizing military personnel and strengthening the military to address the conflict:

During the past several years, subversive elements have been developing a consistent strategic plan that has allowed them to grow and strengthen themselves economically and militarily, while the State has failed to confront them with a comprehensive plan. For that reason, it is imperative that we strengthen the country's defense sector... [to] confront the threat to public order.[86]

---

[81] Departamento Nacional de Planeación, "Cambio para la construcción de la paz: Plan Colombia," December 1998, APA 1999, Alto Comisionado para la Paz, caja 43, carpeta Plan Colombia 99, Archivo Presidencia de la República, ff. 23–17.

[82] Ruiz, interview with the author.

[83] Plan de Desarrollo Nacional: Cambio para construir la paz, p. 47. Available online: www.dnp .gov.co/QuiénesSomos/Misiónvisiónorigen.aspx.

[84] Ibid., p. 51, see also pp. 307–308.

[85] *Inter alia*, see pp. 305–308.

[86] Ibid., p. 399.

Many of the military issues targeted for improvement under the *Plan* would eventually be addressed with the U.S.-funded Plan Colombia – "intelligence capabilities, telecommunications, and mobility."[87] Pastrana and Ruiz's *Plan Nacional de Desarrollo* explicitly sought to "increase the offensive capability of the armed forces."[88] Given Colombia's fiscal constraints, it was clear the funding for military overhauls would have to come from outside Colombia.[89] The plan led to the creation of a high-level committee tasked with reforming the military hierarchy.[90] Key elements of the later Plan Colombia are in the *Plan Nacional de Desarrollo*, but are not yet tightly articulated. That process would come to fruition later with greater U.S. involvement.

During the first half of 1999, there were two parallel "Plans Colombia" developing inside the Colombian government. One was an interagency mechanism for social investments targeted to conflict and drug-producing regions, led by Rodrigo Guerrero under the auspices of High Commissioner Ricardo.[91] The other was led by a small group of advisers with personal proximity to the president, namely Jaime Ruiz, newly installed Defense Minister Luis Fernando Ramírez, Mauricio Cárdenas, and Guillermo Fernández de Soto, with the extensive consultation of the ambassador in Washington, Luis Alberto Moreno.[92] For Ruiz – who Pastrana called "the man chosen for the definitive design of Plan Colombia"[93] – the central goal of the plan was always to strengthen the Colombian state, and he saw the military, economic, social, and institutional components as complementary. The existence of these two tracks created bureaucratic tensions inside the Pastrana administration, spurring Guerrero's resignation as head of the coordinating entity in August 1999. In an acerbic letter to the president, Guerrero said he "understood that the integrated peace strategy had four, independent lines of action, closely coordinated under the president's authority: the political reform that was in Congress, the

[87] Given Colombian terrain, references to "mobility" essentially mean helicopters.

[88] Plan de Desarrollo Nacional, pp. 397–401.

[89] This point was made repeatedly in interviews with members of Pastrana's cabinet.

[90] "Decreto por el cual se crea una comisión consultiva" n.d., 1999, APA 1999, Secretaría Jurídica, caja 119, carpeta Ministerio de Defensa Nacional, Archivo Presidencia de la República, n.p.

[91] This is quite clear from the archives of the entity Plan Colombia and the notes from consultative group meetings it held throughout late 1998 and 1999. See, for example, the "Comité interinstitucional," APA 1999, Plan Colombia, caja 1, carpeta Alto Comisionado para la Paz, Archivo Presidencia de la República, n.p., and other folders for that entity, located in APA 1999 in the Archivo de la Presidencia.

[92] Ruiz, interview with the author; Fernández de Soto, interview with the author; and Luis Fernando Ramírez, interview with the author, May 26, 2011, Bogotá, Colombia. Published sources also mention these individuals as the key Colombian figures in the development on Plan Colombia. See Pastrana Arango and Gómez, *La Palabra Bajo Fuego*, p. 118; Marcella, *The United States and Colombia*, p. 39; Thomas R. Pickering, "Anatomy of Plan Colombia," *The American Interest*, vol. 5, no. 2 (2009).

[93] Pastrana Arango and Gómez, *La Palabra Bajo Fuego*, p. 118.

negotiated solution to the conflict, the *diplomacia para la paz*,[94] and Plan Colombia, a program of social and economic investment in critical conflict zones." However, he felt he had been shut out of an important part of the planning involving Fernández de Soto, Ruiz, Juan Camilo Restrepo, and Camilo Gómez. Guerrero felt he "was submitting himself to a futile waste, because he couldn't count on the interest or support of the high-ranking government to execute Plan Colombia."[95] More than being subject to U.S. domination, Plan Colombia was the object of bureaucratic politics within the Colombian executive branch. Different agencies had picked up on aspects of Pastrana's broad strategy that were in line with their missions, and which gave them a role moving forward.

Pastrana's solutions to the Colombian conflict required U.S. and international assistance for both security and development. The ministers who were closest to Pastrana increasingly turned their attention to security. This, in part, reflected the availability of resources from the United States for that purpose; it also reflected the stagnant peace negotiations with the FARC and a growing conviction that the revolutionary, political wing of the guerrillas had lost influence to those who controlled the purse strings. The latter group had no intention of extricating themselves from their lucrative drug-trafficking business. As Pastrana announced during his first days in office, he would build an army for peace or war.[96] By the time the U.S. package began to solidify, Colombian government officials believed the latter was more likely.

Writing a Bilateral Plan Colombia

The Pastrana administration felt pressure to combine its various programs "under the same umbrella." The purpose, as Ruiz explains it, was to better explain its plans domestically and internationally. Much of Pastrana's public rhetoric had concentrated on peace and development. In Colombia, there was criticism that the *despeje* and approach to the FARC had been naïve. Some in the United States, especially in Congress, echoed criticisms of the peace talks as soft on the FARC. Conversely, the FARC increasingly criticized U.S. military assistance as violating the spirit of the talks. Pastrana hoped to address these criticisms and take advantage of international funding opportunities. Ruiz argued that Plan Colombia unified related elements:

---

[94] The phrase was used to baptize the administration's foreign policy of repairing its international image and trying to involve the international community in the peace process. See Fernández de Soto, *La Ilusión Posible*, pp. 74–76.

[95] Ricardo Guerrero V. to Dr. Andrés Pastrana Arango, August 3, 1999, APA 1999, Alto Comisionado para la Paz, caja 43, carpeta Plan Colombia 99, Archivo Presidencia de la República, ff. 114–112.

[96] Pastrana used this phrase many times, starting in late 1998. He was asked about the phrase at length in interview with *Semana*. See "No hay Plan B," August 23, 1999, *Semana*. Available online: www.semana.com/especiales/no-plan/37934-3.aspx.

We knew all of these things were interrelated. That is, the idea of shared responsibility, the fight against drugs that we wanted, the strengthening of the army, and even though people did not perceive it there [in the United States], the hand extended to the guerrilla, the peace process. They were all related. They were pieces of a whole.[97]

To Ruiz it was obvious by 1999 that the United States would help strengthen the military, but that the Americans also could offer other programs for crop substitution, development, and institutional reform. "They also wanted to participate in the 'Marshall Plan'," he noted. During June and July 1999, Pastrana and his advisors began rhetorically linking the social programs, the peace process, the counternarcotics, and the security reform into one Plan Colombia.[98]

In recognition of the changed tone of U.S.–Colombian relations, the U.S. State Department gave Colombia full certification in the war on drugs. Under Samper, the certification process had consistently been rocky, with the United States either "decertifying" Colombia entirely or allowing it a partial waiver under a national security clause. Certification allowed the U.S. military to share real-time battlefield intelligence with the Colombian military starting in March 1999. Once this cooperation began, the Colombian military grew more effective at targeting FARC holdouts.[99] In response, the FARC launched a campaign aimed both at the government and at paramilitary groups who had captured territory from them. The number of killings spiked starting in May 1999. Violence increased further during a July 1999 FARC offensive. Paramilitaries responded with massacres aimed at anyone who might support the guerrillas. Military cooperation between the FARC and the ELN became more common, as they attacked police stations in small towns with the aim of pushing out the Colombian state and instituting their own governance. The strategy, some in the Colombian government believed, was aimed at gaining concessions during the negotiations and influencing upcoming elections.[100] The surge of violence increased public skepticism about the chances for a negotiated peace and led Pastrana and his advisors to emphasize counternarcotics and military strength.

Along with the apparent stagnation of peace negotiations, Colombia sensed an opportunity for even greater backing than had been promised in previous months. In late June 1999, the U.S. General Accounting Office (GAO)

---

97 Jaime Ruiz, interview with the author. Translation by author.

98 Ibid.

99 A former top advisor to the Gaviria administration stressed this point. Alfredo Rangel Suárez, "The Military and the Peace Process in Colombia," in *The Peace Process in Colombia and U.S. Policy*, ed. Cynthia J. Arnson (Washington, D.C.: Woodrow Wilson International Center for Scholars, 2000), pp. 52–53.

100 One of the most complete records of violence is available in Oficina de Alto Comisionado para la Paz, "Informe confidencial: Dinámica del conflicto armado y las manifestaciones de violencia en el primer año de vigencia de la zona de distensión," November 18, 1999, APA 1999, Alto Comisionado para la Paz, caja 43, carpeta Informe Conyuntura II 99, Archivo Presidencia de la República, ff. 22–1.

produced a report that painted a stark picture of drug production in Colombia, stating that coca cultivation had increased by 50 percent over the previous two years despite fumigation. The GAO projected another 50 percent increase during the next two years.[101] The report received intense public, Congressional, and Clinton administration attention. At the same time, internal Colombian government reports concluded that the original development plans were impossible to carry out given the level of conflict.[102] Between the violence and failing peace process, many advocated a new approach. High-level exchanges between the United States and Colombia intensified, with top State Department officials shuttling back and forth to Colombia.

The Colombian military came to the forefront. Luis Fernando Ramírez and General Tapias flew to Washington on July 16, seeking $500 billion in additional aid, primarily in the form of decommissioned UH-1H or "Huey II" helicopters that the United States would lend to a Colombian military severely lacking in air support. The two met Clinton's "drug czar" Retired General Barry McCaffrey. After Ramírez presented McCaffrey with the helicopter request, the American paused and "asked [Ramírez] a question [he] was not prepared for," Ramírez said. If the United States were ready to assist Colombia, how much would Colombia need? The new defense minister scrambled to make mental calculations, and told the drug czar that if Colombia were going to purchase instead of borrow all the equipment it needed, it would need about a billion dollars. McCaffrey looked at his notes and told the minister that according to his numbers, Colombia needed nearly $4 billion. Ramírez said, "Well, I am saying we'd need a billion per year."

"Now you're talking!" McCaffrey exclaimed.[103] From that point forward, McCaffrey became the administration's most visible advocate for aid to Colombia – no doubt contributing to Plan Colombia's drug-focused image. Colombia was clearly on the Clinton administration's agenda, but McCaffrey anticipated a fight in Congress. He framed Colombia as an "emergency" and a "near-crisis situation." He sent a letter to other administration officials advocating a massive, supplemental appropriation. After the meeting, Ramírez echoed Pastrana's line: "We are preparing modern armed forces that, if peace can be achieved, will guard our borders and natural resources. That is the country we dream of. But we are also preparing the armed forces for war if need be."[104]

[101] "Drug control: Narcotics threat from Colombia continues to grow," June 22, 1999, General Accounting Office.

[102] Oficina de Alto Comisionado para la Paz, "Informe semanal de coyuntura," August 13, 1999, APA 1999, Alto Comisionado para la Paz, caja 43, carpeta Informe Conyuntura, Archivo Presidencia de la República, ff. 306–300.

[103] Ramírez recounted the meeting, and his account squares closely with others'. Ramírez, interview with the author. Translated by author, with the exception of McCaffrey's exclamation, which was recounted in English.

[104] Larry Rohter and Christopher S. Wren, "U.S. official proposes $1 billion for Colombia drug war," *New York Times*, July 17, 1999, p. A7.

Ten days later, McCaffrey flew to Colombia, where he called for a $1 billion regional counterdrug effort, with the bulk of the money going to Colombia.[105]

Plan Colombia's backers often give U.S. assistance full credit for the later successes of the Colombian military against the guerrilla. While the equipment, training, and intelligence sharing played an important part, the role of internal reforms is underappreciated. From his candidacy, Pastrana pressed for the professionalization of the military. These efforts came to fruition under Pastrana's second defense minister, Luis Fernando Ramírez, who credits improvements in three categories. First, the military added "more and better men." The army had been crippled by the high number of conscripts circling through on year-long tours, of which they spent nearly half in training. Professionalization changed that. Second, there was an improvement in equipment, financed heavily by the United States. In early 1999, the military had just four combat helicopters. A U.S. military intelligence report noted that the Colombian Army's 5th Brigade had just one helicopter with one machine gun. Troops employed a mishmash of weapons that complicated logistics.[106] Finally, the administration made important legal reforms. It had been almost impossible for previous administrations to remove officers with over fifteen years of service – even those grossly incompetent or suspected of rights violations. Ramírez fired 5,000 for "corruption, human rights, and ineptitude." The military initially opposed these changes. At Ramírez's request, U.S. officers sat with Colombian generals to help convince them of the need to change. Their arguments were augmented by the growing strength of the guerrillas, who had shown themselves increasingly able to make large, frontal attacks on military outposts.

The breakdown in negotiations and the FARC offensive increased the Colombian government's need for a strong military while pushing many in the United States and Colombia to believe prolonged fighting was unavoidable. Some within the Peace Commission still resisted, arguing that a political solution with the FARC would end the guerrillas' motive for involvement with narcotics. Members of this camp continued to insist on a clear distinction between guerrillas and drug trafficking and argued that U.S. aid should be concentrated on support of the peace process.[107] But this view had lost favor within the Pastrana's inner circle. Even before the announcement of the huge Plan Colombia aid package, the U.S.-backed counternarcotics battalion began to put pressure on FARC operations. The increased military activity led the FARC to declare that the government did not truly want peace. The two sides were locked into a spiral that made a negotiated peace – a remote possibility even at the beginning of the administration – an ever-more-distant

---

[105] Bill Rodgers, "U.S.–Colombia drug war," July 29, 1999, *Voice of America*. Available online: www.fas.org/irp/news/1999/07/990729-col.htm.

[106] "DIA NMJIC intelligence summary," March 20, 2000, DNSA, p. 9.

[107] "Proceso de Paz," September 1, 1999, APA 1999, Alto Comisionado para la Paz, caja 53, carpeta Proceso de Paz documentos, Archivo Presidencia de la República, ff. 13–12.

mirage.[108] This set the context in which Plan Colombia would emerge as a bilateral policy, designed first by Colombian leaders with the goal of strengthening a weak state.

September 1999: A New Plan Emerges

Senior Clinton administration officials Thomas Pickering, Arturo Valenzuela, and Peter Romero flew to Bogotá on August 9, following the conversation between the Colombians and McCaffrey.[109] The Colombian Foreign Ministry wrote:

[T]hey discussed the modernization and professionalization of the military forces and the strategy the Colombian government has initiated regarding the peace process. The visit of Secretary Pickering constituted a fundamental piece to discuss the importance to Colombia of support from multilateral financial entities given the country's economic situation, to visualize multiple components of the peace process and to restate the government's compromise and initial actions in the fight against drugs.[110]

Pastrana went into the meeting with Pickering confident of Clinton's support, and the Colombian government planned to present Pickering with a one-year aid request. Pickering surprised them by saying the Clinton administration would back a three-year package, covering the rest of Pastrana's term. Assistance, Pickering said, could start that year if the Colombian government were to draft a plan quickly. Much of the planning had been done in different forms, but "what remained to be done was to reorganize the Plan in such a way that it would call together important U.S. assistance, along with aid from other countries and international organizations."[111] Pastrana chose Jaime Ruiz to begin designing a comprehensive aid request.[112]

Ruiz's favorite analogy for the situation in Colombia is not Vietnam, to which some in the United States forebodingly equated it, but Prohibition in the United States during the 1920s. Ruiz describes Colombia's violence in sweeping terms, saying that the world – not just the United States – has chosen a policy of prohibition. "A choice of policy is really a choice of consequences," Ruiz says,

---

[108] The Colombian government was aware of the effect the announced military aid was having on the peace process, but it also clearly needed the help to attain the basic goal of controlling the national territory. Oficina de Alto Comisionado para la Paz, "Informe semanal de coyuntura," September 24, 1999, APA 1999, Alto Comisionado para la Paz, caja 43, carpeta Informe Conyuntura, Archivo Presidencia de la República, ff. 252–236.

[109] Pickering, "Anatomy of Plan Colombia."

[110] "Subdirección de Estados Unidos y Canadá," Ministerio de Relaciones Exteriores, Memoria al Congreso Nacional, 1999–2000 (Santafé de Bogotá: Fondo Editorial Cancillería de San Carlos, 1999), p. 353. Translation by author.

[111] Pastrana Arango and Gómez, *La Palabra Bajo Fuego*, pp. 202–203. Also see, "Read-ahead for September 24, 1999 Principal's Committee meeting on Colombia," written for the Under Secretary of Defense for Policy, September 22, 1999, DNSA.

[112] Ibid., p. 118.

paraphrasing U.S. Senator Daniel Patrick Moynihan. A host of serious consequences stem from the worldwide choice to prohibit drugs, but those consequences are not distributed equally, falling heavily on the Andes and specifically on Colombia.[113] For Ruiz, it is a matter of basic fairness that the world should help Colombia address these monumental problems. The guiding light of Pastrana's policies was to build the Colombian state's capability to respond. "The primordial objective [of Plan Colombia] was to strengthen the state," Ruiz stressed. Ruiz believed Clinton understood this, though many in the U.S. Congress did not. Members' concern was to respond to constituents' fears of drugs in their communities. Ruiz opposed including what he saw as meaningless cultivation reduction targets in Plan Colombia, but he compromised. Congress wanted the unrealistic goal of 100 percent reduction. Ruiz picked the middle point – a reduction of 50 percent. "Without that, it would not have passed Congress, and I needed the military, technical, and human rights assistance," he said. Ruiz and Pastrana agreed that attacking drug trafficking needed to be part of the solution. Many in the United States, especially in Congress, saw counternarcotics as the goal of the plan. For Colombia it was a means to disrupt the financing of the FARC and paramilitaries, allowing the state to reassert itself in territory where it had lost influence.[114]

Early drafts of Plan Colombia, under the heading "Plan for Peace, Prosperity, and Strengthening of the State," were circulating between ministries in the Colombian government at least as early as September 12, 1999, when Defense Ministry economist Yaneth Giha Tovar sent a copy to Andrés Soto Velasco, chief of the justice and security unit in National Planning, with the note: "I send the attached document 'Plan for peace, prosperity, and the strengthening of the state' from Plan Colombia, written in the Division."[115] The detailed, Spanish draft was already moving between departments several weeks before the English version emerged, casting doubt on claims made by Russell Crandall that the plan originated in English in the United States. Crandall writes: "[M]any U.S. officials readily admitted that it was essentially devised by the US government and that a copy in Spanish did not exist until months after a copy in English was available."[116] This claim is repeated as a symbol of U.S. domination. In fact, it is more emblematic of how evidence

---

[113] Ruiz, interview with the author. Also see, "El poder detrás del trono," August 9, 1999, *Semana*.

[114] Thomas Pickering made this point independently, writing, "We understood that the drug problem and Colombia's internal decay were intimately connected…So we were mindful in shaping the policy that support for its drug-related aspects would have to be leveraged to accomplish more than met the Hill's eye." Pickering, "Anatomy of Plan Colombia," p. 71.

[115] Yaneth Giha Tovar to Andrés Soto Velasco, "Plan Colombia: Plan para la paz, la prosperidad, y el fortalecimiento del estado," September 12, 1999, ff. 332–339. Carpeta Plan Colombia, no. 2, código 124523053, Archivo DNP.

[116] Russell Crandall, *Driven by Drugs: US Policy toward Colombia* (Boulder, Colo.: Lynne Rienner Publishers, 2008), p. 124.

from Latin American sources can challenge assumptions in the study of U.S.–
Latin American relations.

The early draft of the plan emphasizes "the need to strengthen and consolidate the Colombian state" through four fundamental lines of action: "restart-
ing the economy, an anti-drug policy, juridical reform, and a strategy of social
development and the peace process." The draft put into law the argument that a
"mutually beneficial relation exists between the guerrilla and the drug traffickers, [and] it is of vital importance to break the links between these groups." This
particular draft, originating in the police and military divisions of the National
Planning Department, is nearly complete on plans to strengthen the police and
military, while also enforcing stricter human rights standards.[117] There is major
overlap between both the main points and the wording of the early draft and
the English version from October, which Jaime Ruiz, Luis Fernando Ramírez,
and Guillermo Fernández de Soto all insisted was written by Colombians.[118]
The Plan's introduction compares Colombia's violence to Prohibition in the
United States, as Ruiz had done. Sections of the English-language plan contain
uneven phrasing similar in structure to the Spanish draft.[119] In a comparison
of the draft and the English version, key sections are nearly identical, though
the later version expands on shorter points set out in the Spanish draft.

The refutation of the idea that the Plan was penned by the U.S. government is
not to suggest that Colombians wrote it in total isolation. Rather, the Plan was
the result of close collaboration between the two governments, starting with
Pastrana's preinaugural visit. It reflected many of Pastrana's original goals and
priorities, adjusted to changing conditions in Colombia. It also reflected U.S.
priorities, from both Clinton and Congress, about launching a visible response
to public concern about drugs. Pickering wrote: "Contrary to popular belief,
the United States did not design *Plan Colombia*. It was certainly discussed
with us. But it reflects a realization by the Colombian government that the
various strategies they had developed needed to be linked because so many,
if not all, the problems were inter-related."[120] The Pastrana administration

---

[117] "Plan Colombia: Plan para la paz, la prosperidad, y el fortalecimiento del estado," September
    12, 1999, ff. 332–339. Carpeta Plan Colombia, no. 2, código 124523053, Archivo DNP.
[118] In interviews, Ruiz and Fernando de Soto both said they considered insulting the readiness
    with which people assumed they could not write a paper in English.
[119] This was initially pointed out to me by Arlene Tickner, a top scholar at University of the Andes
    in Bogotá. It was also noted by Ruiz himself, who said that his wife helped him with sections
    of the English draft. For example, the English version reads: "With the FARC, a distention
    area was created as a safe haven for negotiations, and has helped both parties to formulate
    an agenda, a process completed in May, 1999," or "The international community can act as
    media for, overseer or, at a later stage, verifier of compliance with agreements made." Though
    Ruiz, who has a master's degree in engineering from the University of Kansas, where he met
    his wife, a U.S. citizen, speaks excellent English, he noted that the drafts hardly seem drafted
    by native English speakers.
[120] Chicola, reflections in *The Peace Process in Colombia and U.S. Policy*, ed. Cynthia J. Arnson,
    Working Papers of the Latin America Program, no. 246 (Washington, D.C.: Woodrow Wilson
    International Center for Scholars, 2000), pp. 32–37.

framed its priorities in language salient to U.S. policymakers and members of
Congress as a pragmatic response to the weakness of the Colombian state vis-
à-vis the FARC, paramilitaries, and drug traffickers, while also trying to boost
a struggling economy. Colombia was the smaller, poorer country, and it was
asking for billions of dollars. However, Pastrana's priorities and U.S. interests
were largely compatible. As Ruiz said, "*Se juntó el pan con la hambre*" – hunger
and bread came together. The Defense Department noted that the United States
"was actively involved in assisting the Colombians in drafting this plan."[121]
But Colombia did not accept a plan written for it by the United States. Rather,
Colombian policymakers actively sought resources and cooperation to address
problems they had identified.

President Pastrana decided he would present Plan Colombia in his address
at the United Nations General Assembly (UNGA) on September 20, 1999. He
planned to discuss it with Clinton on the same trip to New York. Colombian
officials presented their plans to Secretary Albright on September 16 at the State
Department. The next day, Pastrana delivered a televised address laying out
the plan to the Colombian people. He repeatedly spoke of drug trafficking as a
driver of conflict and corruption. Strengthening the state, including the police
and military, was a fundamental precondition for achieving lasting peace and
reinvigorating the economy. Pastrana argued that international cooperation
was needed for this, and that it was the responsibility of consuming countries
to help address the problems caused by drug trafficking. The strategy required
$7.5 billion over the next several years, and Colombia planned to appropriate
$4 billion, much of that dedicated to enhancing social programs. Pastrana
turned to the international community for the remainder, knowing that the
United States was likely to commit a substantial portion.[122] After the speech,
Pastrana flew to New York for the UNGA, also meeting with Clinton and
calling members of Congress.[123] Pastrana did not expect the United States to
cover all $3.5 billion, but hoped Clinton's leadership would convince European
countries.[124] In his UN address, Pastrana spoke about the plan in general terms
and admitted the peace process had struggled in the face of continuing violence.
He called for a "genuine partnership between the countries that consume and
produce illegal drugs, underpinned by the principles of joint responsibility,

---

[121] "Read-ahead for September 24, 1999 Principal's Committee meeting on Colombia," written
for the Under Secretary of Defense for Policy, September 22, 1999, DNSA.

[122] Pastrana and Ruiz calculate that Colombia spent more than $1 billion per year on fighting
drug trafficking, including the military and police. It had budgeted $900 million for new social
programs under "Network of Social Support" and $800 million for "peace credits" aimed
at conflict areas. Pastrana Arango and Gómez, *La Palabra Bajo Fuego*, pp. 204–209. On
the requests for international support, also see Larry Rohter, "Plan to strengthen Colombia
nudges U.S. for $3.5 billion," *New York Times*, September 18, 1999, p. A6; "Subdirección de
Estados Unidos y Canadá," (2000), p. 357.

[123] "Subdirección de Estados Unidos y Canadá," p. 357.

[124] "Necesitamos plata, Bill," October 18, 1999, *Semana*. Available online: www.semana.com/
nacion/necesitamos-plata-bill/39001–3.aspx.

reciprocity, and fairness."[125] Pastrana emphasized that Colombia's need for help was not limited to counternarcotics; economic and fiscal challenges further weakened the government.[126]

The English version of Plan Colombia was first publicly presented on October 6, 1999 to a hearing of the Senate Foreign Relations Committee. Many on the committee had been intensely lobbied by the Pastrana administration and its tenacious Ambassador Luis Alberto Moreno. Colombia persuaded many members of Congress and their staffs to visit. Senator Jesse Helms presided over the hearing, warning about the narcotic-financed power of Colombian guerrillas and the specter of narcotics "flooding American streets and school yards." Helms starkly framed the issue: "Without U.S. help, Colombia could lose this war." Lawmakers burnished their trips to Colombia as credentials, something Senator Paul Coverdell did repeatedly in supporting massive aid to Colombia. In the hearing, Republican senators expressed their support for the plan, while some Democrats such as Senator Paul Wellstone placed objections related to paramilitaries, human rights, and aerial fumigation. Senator Christopher Dodd expressed cautious support for the plan, so long as it balanced military support with other funding.[127] Because of his well-known interest in Latin America, Dodd was a particular target for Colombian persuasion.[128] Approval of the aid appeared to be on a fast-track after the hearing and the administration's embrace of the Plan Colombia draft. There was clear support in the Republican-controlled House, though the liberal wing of Clinton's own party tried to shift the funding to domestic drug treatment and prevention programs. In the Senate, it appeared Clinton might face some hurdles from Democrats, but they appeared surmountable.

Pastrana left for a tour of Europe, to "clear up doubts and concerns about the Plan and its initial presentation in the United States" while also "obtaining the support of the European Union."[129] Some criticized Pastrana for trying to sell different versions of the plan to different audiences. Fernández de Soto argued: "Europe had different strategic interests." His advisors did not expect major military aid from Europe. In his address to the European parliament, Pastrana

---

[125] "Address by Mr. Andrés Pastrana Arango," General Assembly, 54th session, September 20, 1999 (New York, UNGA Official Record #A/54/PV.5), pp. 8–10. Available online: www.un .org/documents/ga/docs/56/pv/a56pv45.pdf.

[126] Tim Golden, "Colombian leader says U.S. won't be drawn into war," *New York Times*, September 21, 1999, p. A3.

[127] "Crisis in Colombia: U.S. support for peace process and anti-drug efforts," Hearing of the Senate Foreign Relations Committee, October 6, 1999 (Washington, D.C.: Government Printing Office, 2000).

[128] Dodd was mentioned repeatedly in interviews with Colombian participants, and he gradually formed a personal relationship with Pastrana, whom he met on as many as a dozen occasions.

[129] "Visita del Señor Presidente de la República de Colombia a las instituciones de la Unión Europea," October 22, 2000, APA 1999, Dirección Secretaria General, caja 21, carpeta Despacho Señor Presidente, 2, Archivo Presidencia de la República, n.p.

was clear that a major goal of Plan Colombia was to tackle drug trafficking and production, though he stressed that "Plan Colombia is not a military plan, like some enemies of peace would have you believe."[130] The Colombian government had a harder time in Europe in part because the FARC had been very active there diplomatically, convincing many that they were "a bunch of Robin Hoods," said Fernández de Soto.[131] Pastrana's visit in late October 1999 helped convince many Europeans that the Colombian government was making a sincere effort in the peace process, though Europeans often disapproved of U.S. aid or felt left out of the formation of Plan Colombia.

By the time Pastrana returned to Colombia, the U.S. aid package had run into trouble in Congress. The Plan, put together hurriedly to gain emergency appropriations before the end of 1999, was caught in a quagmire of toxic executive–congressional relations. In part, this reflected lasting rancor over the Kenneth Starr investigation and Monica Lewinsky scandal. More directly, the branches were feuding over how to balance the budget. Major legislation came to a halt, and Colombia was caught in the middle. Colombians tried to push Plan Colombia through the logjam. Pastrana wrote: "Facing this situation, we started an intense lobby, and I gave Ambassador Moreno instructions to visit as many members of Congress as possible; I helped to pressure as much as I could, calling Congress people or inviting them to visit the country."[132] Moreno was a gregarious presence on Capitol Hill, often noted for his small stature, boyish appearance, easy charm, and sharp intelligence. He spent hours at the Capitol, where he would board the small, underground train that carries members and staffers between the office buildings and the chambers. As he waited, he would identify members of Congress and strike up a conversation. Before the ride ended, Moreno would often have extended an invitation to Colombia or set up a meeting. Then Moreno would hop back on the train and look for another opportunity to make his pitch.[133] The Colombians pressed the executive branch, too, making frequent appeals to advocates like McCaffrey and Attorney General Janet Reno.

Clinton phoned Pastrana in November, after U.S. legislation on Plan Colombia had stagnated for nearly two months. Pastrana was passing through dire straits. Unemployment sat near 20 percent, the peace talks appeared to have collapsed, the Colombian congress opposed him, and his popularity ratings were abysmal. He laid some blame at the feet of the United States, telling Clinton:

---

[130] Andrés Pastrana, "Palabras del señor Presidente de la República, Doctor Andrés Pastrana, con ocasión de su visita al Parlamento Europeo," October 26, 1999, APA 1999, Dirección Secretaría General, caja 21, carpeta Despacho Señor Presidente, 2, Archivo Presidencia de la República, n.p.

[131] Fernández de Soto, interview with the author.

[132] Pastrana Arango and Gómez, *La Palabra Bajo Fuego*, p. 205.

[133] This story was recounted by Minister of Defense Luis Fernando Ramírez, who accompanied Moreno on several occasions.

"It was not fair that when the Colombian government built a bridge to channel U.S. aid, Plan Colombia, we were left with only our side constructed."[134] Clinton responded to Pastrana's pleas with an address in which he spoke glowingly about the Colombian president and outlined items in the delayed foreign aid bill that would assist Colombia. However, this funding fell far short of the multi-billion-dollar package Pastrana needed to improve the situation in Colombia and his own political standing. That would be pushed back to the next budget cycle.[135] Later that month, Congress passed a supplemental that included an additional $165 million for Colombia, targeted to drug interdiction, the National Police, and some alternative development.[136]

The delay in U.S. aid was a major setback for Pastrana. Though his domestic agenda had been a constant struggle, until that point Pastrana's foreign policy had been fairly successful. Colombia had been able to reframe issues in a light favorable to its goals, but Pastrana and Clinton were fairly powerless when trying to get the U.S. Congress to take speedy action – even on a proposal with clear majority support. With Congressional action delayed, Colombia sought to influence the debate in Washington. Moreno continued to engage critical human rights NGOs and skeptical members of Congress, as he had since late 1998.[137] Moreno also became the point man for converting the version of Plan Colombia written by Ruiz and his team into a funding request from the U.S. Congress. In doing so, he collaborated closely with Undersecretary of State Pickering, who wrote that "support for its [Plan Colombia's] drug-related aspects would have to be leveraged to accomplish more than meets the Hill's eye."[138]

Meanwhile, the interagency debate continued. The State Department pushed for more economic and social assistance, but eventually concluded that large, upfront hardware purchases would skew the percentages heavily in favor of defense aid. Secretary Albright gave the package her OK in early January.[139] On January 11, Clinton announced his budget request for about $1.3 billion in additional funding for Colombia over the next two fiscal years. With previously appropriated money, that increased total aid to about $1.6 billion in U.S. funding for the Colombian government. Pending Congressional approval, Colombia

---

134 Pastrana Arango and Gómez, *La Palabra Bajo Fuego*, p. 206.

135 Bill Clinton, "Statement on funding for Colombian counternarcotics efforts," November 10, 1999, The American Presidency Project. Available online: www.presidency.ucsb.edu/ws/index
     .php?pid=56907.

136 For a breakdown of U.S. spending, see Nina M. Serafino, *Colombia: U.S. Assistance and Current Legislation* (Washington, D.C.: Congressional Research Service, 2001).

137 Luís Alberto Moreno to Guillermo Fernández de Soto, December 16, 1999, APA 1999, Alto Comisionado para la Paz, caja 47, carpeta Embajadas 99, Archivo Presidencia de la República, ff. 130–128.

138 Pastrana Arango and Gómez, *La Palabra Bajo Fuego*, p. 210; Pickering, "Anatomy of Plan Colombia," p. 71.

139 Ann Richard, Rand Beers, and Peter Romero to Madelaine Albright, "Colombian/Andean assistance package," January 6, 2000, DNSA.

would become the third-largest destination for U.S. aid after Israel and Egypt, a shocking turnaround from the near-total cutoff just three years earlier. Citing a "compelling national interest in reducing the flow of cocaine and heroin to our shores and in promoting peace, democracy, and economic growth in the region," Clinton said the aid would allow a push into the coca-producing south of Colombia.[140] In the ensuing press conference, Clinton admitted he would have liked to include even more economic aid, but balanced "good policy and likelihood of passage in the Congress." There was criticism in the United States and Colombia about the plan's military nature, but Pastrana and his advisors were thrilled that the U.S. aid package met important Colombian government and military needs. "The Plan should not have been less military. It should have had even more – but also more social," Ruiz said. He blamed Europe for failing to accept its share of responsibility.[141]

The announcement offered Pastrana a crucial political boost that neither the economy nor the peace process had. The most significant accomplishment in the peace talks since the agreed agenda was a "Christmas truce" declared by the FARC – a small concession compared with Pastrana's extensions of the *despeje* despite the violations of the terms.[142] Even that truce was partial, and it ended on January 10 with a surge of FARC attacks on towns, highways, and oil pipelines.[143] With U.S. aid in the offing, the dynamics of the talks changed. Some hoped the threat of an efficient, U.S.-trained and equipped Colombian military might persuade the FARC to make concessions they so far had avoided.[144]

The Pastrana and Clinton administrations cooperated to assure the Plan's passage through Congress. Three days after Clinton's announcement, Albright traveled to Cartagena to demonstrate U.S. support for Pastrana.[145] There was a spike in Congressional visits, pushing the total to nearly 120 members during Pastrana's term. Pastrana made another two visits to the United States in early 2000.[146] Defense Minister Ramírez said that during late 1999 and early 2000, so many Americans visited that he spent nearly half his time preparing for and guiding Congressional delegations. "It became 'fashionable' to visit

[140] Clinton's speech is available at "Statement announcing an assistance package for Colombia," January 11, 2000, The American Presidency Project. Available online: www.presidency.ucsb.edu/ws/index.php?pid=58066.

[141] Ruiz, interview with the author.

[142] "FARC declaran tregua navideña," December 20, 1999, *El Tiempo*.

[143] Kamman, "Colombia's armed actors return to work," January 21, 2000, DNSA.

[144] "Informe semanal de conyuntura, no. 26," January 14, 2000, APA 2000, Alto Comisionado para la Paz, caja 27, carpeta Proceso de paz con las FARC-EP, informes, Archivo Presidencia de la República, ff. 28–33.

[145] "Subdirección de Estados Unidos y Canadá," p. 354.

[146] Pastrana addressed the U.S. Conference of Mayors in January and the National Governors' Association in February. "Visits by foreign leaders of Colombia," U.S. State Department Office of the Historian. Available online: http://history.state.gov/departmenthistory/visits/colombia. Also see, Pastrana Arango and Gómez, *La Palabra Bajo Fuego*, pp. 255–256.

Colombia," he said. Most of those who opposed the Plan and visited changed
their opinion, Ramírez said, offering Senate Democrat Joe Biden as an example. "He listened and listened, and he became a great friend to Colombia."[147]
Despite the enthusiastic support from the administration and House Speaker
Dennis Hastert, the aid was subject to the normal pace of Congressional bud-
geting. There were battles – and lobbying – over exactly how the money should
be spent. Some of this was familiar pork-barrel politics, with powerful members sparring to include military equipment built in their jurisdictions. Another
group pushed to reallocate money from the Colombian military to the Colombian National Police. Some of these members were close to General Serrano,
who had become "a type of virtual ambassador" during the Samper years.
Others saw the police as more insulated from human rights problems and
paramilitary ties. Ramírez sought to convince these holdouts that the military
and police were, in fact, working as a team and that both needed assistance.
SOUTHCOM Commander Charles Wilhelm's testimony before Congress lent
critical support to the Colombian military. As the Senate considered the House
bill, Wilhelm accompanied Biden on a visit to Colombia, where the senator met
with Pastrana.[148] Visitors included high-profile opponents like Representative
Nancy Pelosi, who met with officials on February 21–22. Pelosi met with the
fiscal, Colombia's chief prosecutor, and pressed for more funding to be directed
to the fight against impunity.[149]

Critics frequently note that about two-thirds of U.S. support for Plan Colombia went to the police, military, counternarcotics, and justice. While true, the
Plan also represented an enormous increase in U.S. funding for so-called "soft"
programs like alternative development, civil society, and human rights. The
figure also takes the U.S. aid as the totality of Plan Colombia. In the eyes
of the Pastrana administration officials interviewed, U.S. assistance allowed
for items that needed to be bought with foreign exchange. The Colombian
government could fund many social programs with Colombian currency and
through development loans from the World Bank and IMF. These loans had
been granted on more generous terms and with more space for social programs
than was customary, in part because of the intercession of U.S. officials. As
the battle over the exact shape of Plan Colombia moved from the interagency
process to the Congress, Colombia tried to loosen the conditions for the use of
military aid. Traditionally, all U.S. aid had been tied to counternarcotics, often
going to special battalions vetted for human rights violators. The prevalent
belief that the insurgency and trafficking were becoming harder to differentiate
led the United States to be more accommodating in its "end-use monitoring"
agreement, revised in late January. Colombia hoped to loosen strictures while
arguing that it was improving respect for rights. The new attitude was reflected

---

[147] Ramírez, interview with the author. Translation from Spanish.
[148] Kamman, "Embassy Plan Colombia meeting," April 25, 2000, DNSA.
[149] Kamman, "Representative Pelosi's meetings in Bogota," February 28, 2000, DNSA.

in the embassy's recommendation for full drug-war certification and with visits from officials, including Army Secretary Louis Caldera, Pickering, and McCaffrey, during late January and February.[150]

The debate over aid happened in the middle of an ongoing conflict and nascent peace process. Colombian officials' idea of "negotiations in the middle of conflict" made little sense to the public, but Pastrana was determined to continue the peace process, on which he had bet his diminishing political capital. The lack of a FARC ceasefire subjected the talks to criticism from those who thought the government was making unilateral concessions. On January 29, 2000, the FARC denounced the proposed U.S. aid package, which they believed would be "invested in the war."[151] The combination of FARC reticence to U.S. involvement and public anger regarding the post-Christmas offensive once again put the peace process on the ropes. The government, seeking to improve its public relations with Europe as it sought development aid and trying to change the FARC's mentality, devised a plan for a joint European tour. Members of the Colombian government, led by Peace Commissioner Ricardo and Pastrana confidant Camilo Gómez Alzate, joined FARC leaders in discussions and visits to seven European countries. The government said it wanted to see these countries with the FARC as models for social reform. The government also wanted to demonstrate its good-faith attempt to make peace: "to present a more holistic vision of Colombia so the international community could understand the complexity of the conflict," Pastrana wrote. FARC spokesman Raul Reyes used the tour as an opportunity to criticize the Colombian government's fumigation and imply that it was subordinated to U.S. policy. Still, the high-profile tour offered hope that the peace process might yet yield benefits.[152]

Colombian Ambassador Moreno struggled to keep his country on Washington's agenda.[153] On March 9, the House Appropriations Committee approved an emergency supplemental bill that spread $1.4 billion in aid to Colombia over two fiscal years. The full House passed the aid package on March 30

---

[150] For Colombian visit summaries, see "Subdirección de Estados Unidos y Canadá," p. 355. On U.S. views, see Kamman, "EUM amendment: Signed, sealed, and delivered," January 25, 2000; "Embassy recommends certification," February 8, 2000, DNSA; Chicola, "ONDCP director McCaffrey's 2/23 mtg. w. Pastrana," February 25, 2000, DNSA.

[151] FARC communiqué, qtd. in "Informe semanal de conyuntura, no. 28," February 25, 2000, APA 2000, Alto Comisionado para la Paz, caja 27, carpeta Proceso de paz con las FARC-EP, informes, Archivo Presidencia de la República, ff. 65.

[152] For a full list of participants, see Adolfo Carvajal to Guillermo Fernández de Soto, "Gira de los negociadores," February 25, 2000, APA 2000, Alto Comisionado para la Paz, caja 27, carpeta Proceso de paz con las FARC-EP, informes, Archivo Presidencia de la República, ff. 94–103; Camilo Gómez Alzate to Mauricio González Cuervo, "Informe sobre los procesos de diálogos y negociación," July 17, 2000, APA 2000, Alto Comisionado para la Paz, caja 27, carpeta Proceso de paz con las FARC-EP, informes, Archivo Presidencia de la República, p. 4. See also Pastrana Arango and Gómez, *La Palabra Bajo Fuego*, pp. 221–228.

[153] "El hombre del Plan Colombia," July 24, 2000, *Semana*.

after attaching conditions that the military aid must comply with the Leahy Amendment on human rights. The Senate trimmed the package to $1.1 billion – largely by replacing some Blackhawks with reworked Hueys – and attached more human rights funding and conditions. The Senate passed the aid in a military construction bill. In June, the final conference bill passed, totaling $1.3 billion. It included five human rights-related stipulations, along with two other conditions. Since Colombia met only one of the seven conditions, President Clinton issued national security waivers for six conditions on August 22, allowing the aid to flow. The final package, contained in Public Law 106–246, tripled the human rights program support requested by Clinton.[154]

The final funding package was a product of complicated interagency and Congressional wrangling. President Clinton issued a decision directive that was clear in its support of Colombia's objectives. Almost quoting Colombian officials, the confidential directive said: "The Administration remains convinced that the ultimate solution to Colombia's long-standing civil conflict is through a successful peace process, not a decisive military victory, and believes that counterdrug progress will contribute towards peace."[155] In implementation, the U.S. government compromised with Colombian political demands: delaying aerial fumigation efforts in sensitive areas in favor of alternative development programs and protecting Pastrana's peace process. Following Ruiz's insistence, the plan would be enacted in such a way as to not jeopardize talks with the FARC. The Colombians insisted the next six months would be crucial, and that whether the talks succeeded or failed after that, they would have much greater latitude for action.[156]

Just as Pastrana seemed poised to take advantage of "the largest assistance ever received" by Colombia, he sank deeper into political crisis.[157] State Department polling found that just 21 percent of the Colombian population supported him.[158] Criticism mounted from several directions, but the most immediate problem was the president's disastrous relationship with the Colombian congress. Pastrana was frustrated by the legislature's inaction on his domestic and economic agenda, some of which was linked to IMF loans. He saw the body as corrupt and linked to drug money and paramilitaries.[159] On March 30, Pastrana called for a national referendum to reform the legislature followed by elections to replace its members. A leading news magazine wrote: "The parliamentarians received the recall like a declaration of war." Pastrana was forced to withdraw the referendum when the congress insisted that he, too, undergo a

154 Serafino, *Colombia.*
155 Clinton, "Presidential decision directive/NSC-73," August 3, 2000, DNSA.
156 Kamman, "Interagency planning team to visit Colombia," July 28, 2000, DNSA; Bob Brown to McCaffrey, "Report on U.S. planning team mission to Bogota," July 31, 2000, DNSA.
157 The quote is a chapter title from Pastrana's memoirs.
158 Romero, "Colombians dissatisfied with democracy, welcome U.S. help against counternarcotics," May 2, 2000, DNSA.
159 "Pastrana contraataca," May 1, 2000, *Semana.*

recall vote.[160] Because of the feud, Pastrana used the latitude granted to Colombian presidents in foreign affairs to largely exclude the legislature from Plan Colombia. Luis Fernando Ramírez concedes there was insufficient domestic debate about the direction of Plan Colombia.[161] When the Colombian legislature held discussions of the Plan in April 2000, it was already being debated in the U.S. Congress.[162] Human rights groups and other civil society members decried the lack of consultation with the Pastrana administration.[163]

The foundering peace process worsened Pastrana's political difficulties. In mid 2000, the FARC published a proposal for a ceasefire. Excitement was short lived because the FARC added that the truce would exclude kidnappings. In fact, there would be a new "tax" under which the rebels would kidnap for ransom anyone worth over $1 million and target a list of people they considered corrupt. Pastrana had to reject the ceasefire offer, given that it would allow the guerrilla force to continue its involvement in drug trafficking, extortion, and kidnapping. Additionally, the Colombian state would be prohibited from attacking these operations under the FARC's conditions. The FARC increased its demands to include more territory than had already been granted and even demanded payments from the Colombian government. It was a nonstarter that many interpreted as a ploy to get Pastrana to cancel negotiations and bear the blame for their failure. In late April, peace commissioner Victor G. Ricardo resigned, in part due to never-ending tension with members of the military who saw him as soft on the FARC regarding the *despeje*. In July, just a day before Clinton signed Plan Colombia into law, the unpopular Pastrana was forced to shuffle his cabinet and include more members of opposition parties.[164]

Pastrana again looked abroad to solidify his weak domestic position. He reiterated an invitation to President Clinton for a visit to Colombia, which he had first extended during the state visit in 1998. At the time, according to Fernández de Soto, Clinton told Pastrana he would go to Colombia once he had assembled bipartisan support for Plan Colombia.[165] On January 25, 2000, Clinton told Pastrana that once the aid was approved, he would visit Colombia with leaders of both parties "to make it clear that Plan Colombia could count on the bipartisan backing, which guaranteed its sustainability and permanence."[166] On August 4, Clinton announced that he would travel

---

[160] Larry Rohter, "Political turmoil adds to Colombian president's woes," *New York Times*, May 13, 2000, p. A3; "Póker peligroso," June 19, 2000, *Semana*.

[161] Ramírez, interview with the author.

[162] "Respuestas al cuestionario contenido el la proposición no. 245 de la plenaria del Senado de la República," n.d., n.p. Carpeta Plan Colombia, no. 4, caja 48, Archivo DNP; Manuel Antonio Salazar to Mauricio Cárdenas, letter, "Debate Plan Colombia," April 3, 2000, n.p. Carpeta Plan Colombia, no. 4, caja 48, Archivo DNP.

[163] Higgins Porter to Grace Shelton, email message, May 23, 2000, DNSA.

[164] Pastrana Arango and Gómez, *La Palabra Bajo Fuego*, pp. 230–232.

[165] Fernández de Soto, interview with the author.

[166] Pastrana Arango and Gómez, *La Palabra Bajo Fuego*, p. 256.

to Cartagena on August 30 with Speaker Hastert and Senator Biden. The trip included Clinton's daughter, Chelsea, and Albright, Reno, and National Security Advisor Sandy Berger.[167] Clinton presaged the trip with a televised address to Colombians, in which he countered the already prevalent criticisms that the plan was a U.S. creation. He stressed the increases in development, social, and human rights funding, and U.S. support for peace talks:

Of course, Plan Colombia will also bolster our common efforts to fight drugs and the traffickers who terrorize both our countries. But please do not misunderstand our purpose. We have no military objective. We do not believe your conflict has a military solution. We support the peace process. Our approach is both pro-peace and antidrug.[168]

The administration saw Clinton's trip as a way to boost Pastrana's flagging fortunes, since the United States had just made a billion-dollar bet on him. Secretary Albright wrote Clinton before the trip, saying it "present[ed] an opportunity to provide badly needed support for President Pastrana's peace initiative," which she admitted moved at a "glacial pace."[169] Clinton's presence on Colombian soil – the first U.S. presidential visit since John F. Kennedy went to support the Alliance for Progress – was a marked contrast from relations under the previous president, Ernesto Samper. Whereas Samper was stripped of his visa to enter the United States, Pastrana gained U.S. assistance and the most prestigious delegation the United States could assemble.[170]

Teams from both sides continued to work out the details of U.S. support through a host of implementation agreements after the high-level political goals had been accomplished, the aid approved, and the flashy visit concluded. Pastrana and his key deputies, starting with Jaime Ruiz, were intensely and personally involved in the formation of these agreements.[171] Colombia drafted an "interagency action plan" to coordinate U.S. aid. Pastrana named Gonzalo de Francisco as the point man for organizing Colombia's strategy for the south of the country, which had been targeted since the earliest Colombian drafts as a focus of Plan Colombia. Implementation agreements covered topics like counternarcotics and the strategy for increasing military and state presence in Putumayo as well as agreements between the U.S. Agency for International Development (USAID) and Colombian agencies to carry out development projects. Proposals were broad in the early stages, offering goals like "reduce

---

[167] Ibid., pp. 258–261. Clinton, "Statement announcing upcoming visit and further assistance to Colombia," August 4, 2000, The American Presidency Project. Available online: www.presidency.ucsb.edu/ws/index.php?pid=1493.

[168] Clinton, "Videotaped address to the people of Colombia," August 24, 2000, The American Presidency Project. Available online: www.presidency.ucsb.edu/ws/index.php?pid=1410.

[169] Albright to Clinton, "Your trip to Cartagena, Colombia," August 25, 2000, DNSA. On the trip, also see "Subdirección Estados Unidos y Canadá," p. 364; Clifford Kraus, "Clinton to herald a new era of ties on Colombia trip," *New York Times*, August 29, 2000.

[170] For a contemporary Colombian interpretation of the visit, see "El espaldarazo," September 4, 2000, *Semana*.

[171] Romero to Albright, "Expanded meeting with President Pastrana," August 30, 2000, DNSA.

the participation of the targeted population in illicit cultivation . . . generating favorable conditions for the peace process in Colombia."[172] Eventually, the proposals were concretized in manuals, glossaries of terms, and strategic plans. By October 2000, a U.S. interagency "ExCom" had "accepted the Colombian government's plan for implementing Plan Colombia as a valid basis for the USG to proceed with its own support planning."[173]

By the first quarter of 2001, bilateral defense groups had worked out arrangements for the modernization of aircraft in the Colombian Air Force, the training of hundreds of pilots, the weapons systems to be added to reworked Huey helicopters, and more.[174] To meet the human rights conditions of the aid, the United States supported the creation of mobile human rights investigative teams and training units to "strengthen and institutionalize a culture of respect for human rights."[175] Albright and Romero had been consistent in pressing for these sorts of teams. The Pastrana administration was receptive to the idea, but struggled to get compliance from the military, where entrenched officers saw proliferating human rights policies as threatening. State Department officials like Harold Koh pressed the Pastrana administration to be more engaged with human rights NGOs, to get their buy-in for at least some portions of Plan Colombia.[176] The State Department fretted that Pastrana was failing to build public support for the program, and that his unpopularity would undermine it. At the time, it appeared that failed presidential candidate Horacio Serpa had a strong chance of capturing the presidency – a possibility the United States did not welcome.[177] The continuation of U.S. support seemed assured, given its bipartisan support, even as Clinton's presidency entered its final months. More worrying was Pastrana's inability to translate the support of the international community into domestic political success.

While many aspects of this policy and of the closer bilateral cooperation endured, Pastrana's peace process would not. The Pastrana administration became more vocal about its intention to cut illegal armed groups off from drug revenues. Discussions between the FARC and the new peace commissioner grew tense. In late 2000, the FARC again suspended the talks over complaints

---

[172] "Convenio interinstitucional para fortalecer la capacidad del Ministerio de Defensa Nacional de Colombia en apoyo al programa bilateral sobre control de naróticos," August 14, 2000, caja 11, carpeta 3, doc. 34, Archivo Ministerio de Defensa Nacional, Unidad de Gestión Central, CAN, Bogotá (henceforth AMDN).

[173] James Mack, "Colombia initiative ExCom," October 6, 2000, DNSA.

[174] Eventually these details were contained in appendices to the agreement. See, mainly, Appendix 5. Many of these drafts and internal communications regarding the accords are held in Caja 11 at the Archivo Ministerio de Defensa Nacional, Unidad de Gestión Central, CAN, Bogotá.

[175] "Memorando de constancia," 4–5 June 2001, caja 11, carpeta 7, docs 87, 35, AMDN.

[176] Romero suggested to Albright that she bring this up in several meetings with both Pastrana and Fernández de Soto. See two August 28, 2000 briefing memoranda from Romero to Albright, DNSA; Peter Higgins to Harold Koh, "Your meeting with Plan Colombia southern coordinator Gonzalo de Francisco, September 20, 2000, DNSA.

[177] Romero to Albright, "Expanded meeting with President Pastrana," August 30, 2000, DNSA.

of paramilitary violence and to protest the increased U.S. role in counternarcotics. Instead of backing away from the peace talks, Pastrana doubled down, extending the *despeje*, though for a briefer period. He made two more visits to meet Marulanda in early 2001. In the second, Pastrana and Marulanda signed the "Agreement of Los Pozos," which, despite the administration's attempts to brandish it as a significant advance, contained few concrete measures.[178]

The mood of the talks improved briefly. In June 2001, the two sides agreed to the release of hundreds of captured soldiers and police.[179] However, the new George W. Bush administration saw the peace talks in a less favorable light than had Clinton, despite Pastrana's otherwise successful attempts to build a personal relationship. This was enhanced after September 11, 2001, though the change in U.S. policy after the attacks mattered less than the FARC's continued refusal to make significant concessions. It was no longer politically tenable in Colombia for Pastrana to continue extending the *despeje* to prolong a process that was almost universally seen as a failure. Finally, Pastrana called an end to the talks and the *despeje*. The final issue on which the FARC refused to agree was a seemingly preliminary one – a timetable for reducing the intensity of the conflict and trying to protect the civilian population. Pastrana administration officials decided the FARC had no real interest in extracating itself from drug trafficking. In Ruiz's formulation, the political elements of the FARC had lost influence to those who filled the coffers.[180] Pastrana ordered the negotiators to give the FARC stark proposals so they, not the president, would break off the talks. The FARC would not leave the negotiating table, nor would they give ground. When the FARC hijacked an airplane and kidnapped a Colombian senator during a commercial flight, it was the final outrage. He later wrote: "There were no more alternatives... I had bet with my whole soul on a process to reach peace, but the FARC, deaf and blind to the pain of their countrymen, preferred to bet on war."[181] Pastrana ordered the Colombian military, a far more efficient force than had retreated from the zone nearly three years prior, to reenter the *despeje*. Employing enhanced intelligence capabilities, Colombian pilots launched a two-day campaign against FARC locations inside the area.

Conclusions

From its roots with Pastrana, Plan Colombia grew into a signature, and highly controversial, U.S. policy. Under Pastrana's successor President Álvaro Uribe and President Bush, the rhetoric of the plan shifted to align with the post-September 11 "war on terrorism." The Colombian military, brandishing U.S.

---

[178] The agreement is contained in Appendix 4 of Pastrana Arango and Gómez, *La Palabra Bajo Fuego.*

[179] Ibid., Chapter 34, Appendix 36.

[180] Ruiz, interview with author.

[181] Pastrana Arango and Gómez, *La Palabra Bajo Fuego*, p. 474.

equipment and training, launched a much more effective assault on the FARC. Later investigations have unearthed links between Uribe's administration and allies in Congress with paramilitary groups. However, these events, and the greater strength of the Colombian government, are far removed from the situation Pastrana faced when he took office in 1998.

There are three predominant views of Plan Colombia in the case literature, which largely overlap with the "revisionist synthesis" and partisan wings of the establishment school. The first argues that Plan Colombia is a new expression of post-Cold War, U.S. imperialism meant to entrench U.S. hegemony through political and economic means. The second sees U.S. policies as a perversion of Pastrana's initially peaceful initiatives. A third, security-oriented triumphal view paints Plan Colombia as a model of successful U.S. state-building to be emulated elsewhere. A handful of Colombia-based scholars, finally, have hinted at an "internationalist" understanding of what Arlene Ticker calls "intervention by invitation."[182]

That "invitation" came directly from Pastrana, starting with the 1998 state visit. Pastrana fashioned foreign policy out of the executive branch, sidelining Colombia's congress. His right hand in creating Plan Colombia was Jaime Ruiz, who acted as a "super minister" to coordinate other agencies. Foreign minister Fernández de Soto was close to Pastrana and helped him advance his agenda with Colombia's allies. However, other agencies were not as fully on board. Because of his predecessor, Pastrana had to deal with a National Police command that was accustomed to acting on its own, even bypassing the president to work with the United States. The military was skeptical of Pastrana's peace negotiations as well as his plans to reform the officer corps. Pastrana was largely able to bring them around because Plan Colombia offered substantial benefits, and because the two sides agreed on their fundamental and urgent interest in strengthening the Colombian state. This guided Colombian policy and implied many second-order goals: stabilizing the economy, building state presence in rural Colombia, restoring territorial control, and reducing violence. In a different sense, the FARC were a constant player. Though the group interacted directly with U.S. policymakers only fleetingly, they sought to influence U.S.–Colombian relations through statements and actions. The failure of negotiations seemed to demonstrate their interests were incompatible with Pastrana's.

Colombia benefited from frequent, high-level U.S. attention. Pastrana did not need to do much to get on the U.S agenda – concern about cocaine and stability largely achieved that – but his actions set a new tone. Pastrana had substantive preinaugural meetings with Clinton and a state visit in the first months of his term. The Colombian government invited and coordinated frequent visits of high-level officials and members of Congress, another clear

---

[182] Arlene Tickner, "Intervención por Invitación: Claves de la Política Exterior Colombiana y de sus Debilidades Principales," *Colombia Internacional* 65 (2007).

expression of U.S. interest. This culminated in visits from the secretary of state and the president in 2000. Clinton's attention was important, but he was not the most significant player. Nor was the Pentagon, though its importance increased during implementation and later stages of planning. The most crucial U.S. actors were General Barry McCaffrey and Under Secretary Thomas Pickering. McCaffrey was central for his role in helping Colombians adapt their proposal to emphasize counternarcotics as a middle step to undermining the FARC in a way that was more politically salient in the United States. Pickering was crucial in frequent consultations with Colombians during the second half of 1999 in converting their Plan Colombia into a specific funding request. McCaffrey's office wanted drug supply reduction, and like many in the Pastrana administration, he saw that as inextricably linked with the Colombian conflict. Pickering was invested in Colombia's stability, and he stressed the risk that instability there could spread across the Andes. Both placed a high value on helping Pastrana.

During the creation of Plan Colombia, there was close intermingling between Colombian and American officials that affected how they defined their strategies and goals. Drugs and stability formed the two main U.S. interests in Colombia. For Colombians, the main goal was strengthening the state; for Americans, this was also crucial, though more as a means to reduce instability or drug trafficking than as an end on its own. This main Colombian interest was driven by domestic conditions, principally the interlocking crises Pastrana inherited. The FARC had gained considerable territory, the Colombian military was ineffective, the economy was suffering, and average Colombians were calling for respite. However, the strategies that Colombians pursed were closely related to perceptions of U.S. policy and the context of asymmetry. Colombia's position was greatly affected by the fact that it was a weak government making a large request for aid. On the one hand, the weakness made Colombia's situation a crisis for U.S. policymakers; on the other, its needs were great and its leverage limited. However, Pastrana's insistence on sticking with the peace talks and the *despeje* demonstrate that the strategy was not determined by the United States. The belief inside the Pastrana administration was that to weaken the FARC, it needed to cut into the group's financing, which was increasingly linked to cocaine. In 1998, the government was militarily unable to execute this strategy, but Colombians knew it squared with U.S. interests. Even before Plan Colombia, this led to cooperative initiatives like the formation of an elite counternarcotics battalion, largely equipped and funded by the United States. That served as a model for later cooperation, in which Colombia reframed its priorities in terms more amenable to U.S. actors. In doing so, it shifted the "issue area" from the unpopular question of involvement in the Colombian conflict to drug supply reduction, where there was more agreement.

Of the two U.S. interests, drugs and stability, the first has typically been understood as a domestically driven, "intermestic" issue, while the second is seen as a traditional U.S. foreign policy concern, particularly in Latin America.

While the administration, especially Clinton himself, was more concerned with stability, much of its public language reflected the drug issue. As much of the literature on Congress and foreign policy would suggest, the domestic concern about Colombian cocaine in U.S. "schoolyards," in Jesse Helms formulation, drew the greatest attention in Congress. Domestic politics invaded in a second way, when a stalemate about unrelated issues delayed Congressional consideration of Plan Colombia for several months. Power asymmetry was clearly a major factor in structuring the issue. The massive demand of the U.S. (and European) market created forces that the weak government of smaller Colombia was poorly equipped to handle. This structure meant that the Colombian government's main partners for addressing the consequences of drug trafficking on its internal conflict were the drug-consuming countries themselves. Because of that, Colombia was strategic in how it presented the problem. It employed the rhetoric of the U.S. war on drugs and worked within its confines by accepting limitations on military aid. However, it did not lose sight of its primary goal of strengthening the Colombian state and weakening the FARC. Colombian leaders did not seek to alter the twin U.S. concerns of drugs and instability. Instead, they pursued a strategy of adapting their interests in order to help shape U.S. policies to pursue their own goals.

If the United States had foisted its own policy on Colombia, as many critics assume, would that policy have been different than Plan Colombia? This question is perhaps more difficult to unravel in the case of Plan Colombia than in the other three cases because of how closely U.S. and Colombian officials interacted, even before Pastrana was inaugurated. Pastrana did not have to win a place on the U.S. agenda, nor was counternarcotics assistance something novel in U.S.–Colombian relations. However, the change in aid and in the relationship was dramatic compared with the previous administration. No significant new policy could be made with Samper at the helm. The U.S. government did not wish to work with him, and it was doubtful that he could have enacted major reforms. Instead, the United States began working with Pastrana as president-elect. Pastrana's pursuit of aid made the Clinton team feel as if it had a capable partner in Colombia after the disastrous Samper years.

However, there are several facets of the case where the effects of Colombia's efforts are more evident. Pastrana's policies on continued peace talks and the *despeje* are difficult to explain if one considers only U.S. interests; it is unlikely they would have formed part of U.S.-dominated policy. Likewise, the changed emphasis in U.S. aid from the Colombian National Police to the military altered previous U.S. policies. Many aspects might have looked similar, as they were designed to meld Colombian and U.S. priorities – an emphasis on drug-based financing versus an overall attack on the FARC (which also financed itself through extortion and kidnapping). Likewise, Colombian policymakers talked about coresponsibility, but did not make a point of assigning blame to the United States for its drug demand. All of these aspects reflect Colombia's weak position and its need to compromise to get U.S. assistance. Regardless of what exactly U.S. policy would have been, the outcome required intense cooperation from Colombian leaders. The U.S. government had worked with the Colombian National Police to avoid that worst-case scenario even with little cooperation from Samper, but the expanded war against the FARC that began in 2001 required the commitment of Colombian leaders even more than it required U.S. involvement.

U.S.-focused accounts have sought to explain why the United States created Plan Colombia, with explanations ranging from imperial designs to pork-barrel politics. Several authors have asserted, mistakenly, that the Plan was written in U.S. Department of State. These accounts have missed an essential aspect of the Plan's origin: the Pastrana administration actively pursued it and sought to shape it so that it helped achieve Colombian goals. At the same time, other accounts have tended to downplay Pastrana's peace process and misunderstand its role in later developments. The process, and the FARC's demands in its final stages, largely delegitimized the group as a potential political actor in the eyes of the Colombian public, and with many in the United States and Europe who still viewed the group through a Cold War, revolutionary lens. At the same time, Pastrana's actions in seeking to rebuild the Colombian military and Colombia's ties to the United States bequeathed his successor drastically different capabilities. As Pastrana himself later noted, in 1998, Colombians were exhausted by violence and voted for a peaceful, negotiated end to the conflict. Four years later, exhausted by the failed peace process, Colombians voted for Álvaro Uribe, who promised he would lead the assault on the FARC and initiate a period of "democratic security."

6

Conclusions

The cases of Operation Pan-America (OPA), the Panama Canal negotiations, the North American Free Trade Agreement (NAFTA), and Plan Colombia illustrate that Latin American leaders can, through certain strategies and under certain conditions, influence U.S. foreign policies despite their positions as weaker partners in asymmetrical relationships. As the cases demonstrate, Latin American leaders have often attempted to advance their own political goals in their policy with the United States. In these cases, they at least partially succeeded by affecting the U.S. policy agenda and the way in which the United States defined and pursued its interests in the region.

This concluding chapter will summarize the book's contributions to two different fields. First, using a cross-case comparison, I synthesize what my approach adds to the study of U.S.–Latin American relations that "establishment" and "revisionist" accounts omit or obscure. As argued in the introduction, this study advances the "internationalist" approach to the study of U.S.–Latin American relations by offering serious analyses of Latin American foreign policies. Previous internationalist scholars have argued that Latin American actors were not U.S. or Soviet "puppets," and were often able to maneuver around U.S. policy while non–Latin American actors struggled to control events in the region. This book builds on that point and demonstrates how Latin American leaders not only influenced events in their own region, but were at times able to influence U.S. behavior. Second, the book uses this evidence to advance theory on weaker-state foreign policy in asymmetrical relations. In particular, I develop an argument that the weaker states in asymmetrical relations can exercise a greater degree of influence in international affairs than a focus on divergent material capabilities indicates.

Cross-Case Lessons

By design, the four cases studied here vary tremendously. The countries involved range from tiny Panama to Brazil, South America's giant. The cases stretch across 45 years, encompassing periods of great bipolar tension, relative détente, and emerging and consolidated unipolarity. Demonstrating that Latin American leaders meaningfully influenced hemispheric relations in such diverse cases provides convincing evidence that these processes of influence should be at work more broadly. The cases are individually enlightening regarding the possibilities, limits, and means of influence. However, through comparison, we can examine the impact of different conditions and ask whether similar processes of influence are present.

Who are the most important actors in Latin America and the United States? How did each government define its interests, goals, and strategies? Latin American foreign policy is a highly presidential affair in all the cases. When Kubitschek developed OPA, the Brazilian Congress was an afterthought. Omar Torrijos had shuttered the Panamanian legislature and invented his own mechanism, a national referendum, to give the treaties legitimacy. The Mexican Senate held a vote on NAFTA, but the president's party, the then-dominant Partido Revolucionario Institucional (PRI), did not voice any serious objections. In the most recent case, Plan Colombia, President Pastrana was involved in such a row with his legislature that he tried to have all its members recalled, but legislators still had next to no involvement in the country's principal foreign policy endeavor. There were certainly other actors involved; the military was important in three of the four cases. However, executives were the most important Latin American actors in all four cases by a substantial margin.

The U.S. Congress was a much more salient force in every case than the legislature of the Latin American country – reflecting both asymmetry and the difference in governing institutions. NAFTA and the Panama Canal Treaties required U.S. Congressional ratification, with the latter requiring a supermajority in the Senate; OPA and Plan Colombia required substantial appropriations. Still, Congress' role did not exceed the U.S. executive's, in part because Congress' most important actions tended to come later in the cases, allowing the president to set the terms.[1] The much greater capabilities of the U.S. government also played a role. Latin American foreign policymaking usually centered on the president and a handful of close advisors. U.S. decisions often rose to the president, who delegated the execution of policy to the bureaucracy, though at times bureaucratic actors had substantial autonomy. Authority was spread much more broadly, with various actors sometimes offering different and competing approaches. U.S. pluralism offered avenues for Latin American influence.

---

[1] James Lindsay has noted, correctly, that the executive often anticipates Congressional concerns. However, the executive still retained an important first-mover advantage. For a discussion of executive anticipation of Congressional actions, see James M. Lindsay, "Congress and Foreign Policy: Why the Hill Matters," *Political Science Quarterly* 107, no. 4 (1992).

Regarding the definition of interests in the United States and Latin America, it is notable the extent to which domestic and foreign factors intermingled on both sides of the relationship. Jeanne Hey has argued that domestic factors are likely to be more pressing for small, less developed countries.[2] Certainly, domestic factors were important for Latin American leaders, with themes of economic development recurring in OPA, NAFTA, and Plan Colombia, and sovereignty and national dignity prominent in the Panama Canal case. Basic domestic political factors such as the continuance of the governing political regime mattered for the Latin American definition of interests in all four cases, too: Kubitschek believed that democracy needed to deliver growth in order to survive; Torrijos' popularity and power were linked to his nationalism and quest for the canal; Salinas hoped NAFTA would improve the Mexican economy and enable the PRI to win fair elections; and Pastrana wanted to regain control of much of national territory.

U.S. policymakers did not face that level of domestic influence in defining their interests and priorities. The U.S. concern about instability in the region is one of the primary continuities throughout the cases – starting with OPA, Latin American leaders tried to use this U.S. interest to their own advantage. However, while this interest does offer continuity in U.S. policy, the promotion of stability was understood in different ways, which Latin American actors sought to influence in all four cases. In OPA, Kubitschek stressed the connection between underdevelopment, instability, and communism. Torrijos argued that a stable and happy Panamanian population would guarantee the canal's safety. Salinas told U.S. officials that if NAFTA were rejected, it would undermine the government and send waves of migrants to the border. Pastrana and U.S. policymakers often stressed the effect that Colombian instability had on the export of cocaine to the United States and warned of spillover effects.

How was Latin America's definition of its interests, goals, and strategies affected by U.S. policy? How were these goals affected by domestic political factors? Latin American interests were primarily determined by domestic factors, with international factors, such as the goal of restraining U.S. unilateralism, in a secondary role. With the exception of the Panama Canal case, Latin American leaders invited a greater U.S. role in certain respects, though they often hoped to channel or contain U.S. power, as did Mexico's leaders when they prioritized binding the United States to NAFTA institutions and dispute resolution mechanisms. However, if Latin America's interests were rooted in domestic considerations, its goals and strategies were deeply affected by U.S. policy and the perception of U.S. power.

How was Latin America's ability to affect the outcome shaped by the issue area? As noted with regard to Panama, issue area was both important and

---

[2] Jeanne A.K. Hey, ed., *Small States in World Politics: Explaining Foreign Policy Behavior* (Boulder, Colo.: Lynne Rienner Publishers, 2003), p. 189.

somewhat malleable. For example, the core tenet of OPA was that an economic issue (development) was in fact a security issue (anticommunism) that weighed on the global balance of power.[3] Perhaps the more important factor had to do with *where* the issue took place. As might be expected, Latin American leaders were able to exercise more influence on issues and events that took place in Latin America. When those issues moved into the U.S. policymaking and especially legislative process, gaining influence was more difficult for Latin American leaders. That said, the cases exhibit a degree of learning by Latin American policymakers regarding the U.S. policy process and about Congress in particular. Although OPA's success depended in large part on Congressional appropriations, Brazil had no strategy for dealing with Congress. Torrijos and the Panamanian negotiators did not actively monitor Congress until the final stages, and then at the behest of Carter administration officials and Panama's astute Ambassador Gabriel Lewis. For Mexico, NAFTA was the beginning of a major break in its approach to the U.S. legislative branch. By the time of Plan Colombia, the Colombian government was cognizant of how it would need to approach Congress from the beginning of Plan Colombia planning. This process of adaptation and regional learning is a promising area for future study.

How were U.S. interests, goals, and strategies affected by domestic political factors, Latin American policy, or the asymmetry of power? As noted above, the most continuous U.S. interest was in promoting stability in the hemisphere; this broad interest is directly connected to the context of asymmetry. While any country would be concerned about the stability of its neighbors, the U.S. concern was global (though particularly acute regarding Mexico). Other U.S. interests and goals were affected by domestic political factors, such as the concern about drugs in Plan Colombia. U.S. strategy and the timing of U.S. actions were also often affected by domestic politics. For example, Eisenhower's Social Development Trust Fund was timed to address criticism aimed at Richard Nixon's presidential campaign. George H. W. Bush pressed to conclude NAFTA in time to announce it at the Republican Party nominating convention and put his rival on the defensive. Latin American leaders tried to shape the U.S. foreign policy agenda in order to gain greater levels of attention for their concerns. On the one hand, this could be done through cooperative, bilateral channels like presidential diplomacy, letters, and visits. On the other, it could mean more internationalized, confrontational approaches like Panama's 1973 United Nations Security Council (UNSC) meetings or Kubitschek's coalition of leaders who demanded economic concessions as a price for political cooperation in the Act of Bogotá.

---

[3] This dynamic of reframing issues through a process of "securitization" has been discussed by scholars in the Copenhagen School. Ronnie D. Lipschutz, ed., *On Security, New Directions in World Politics* (New York: Columbia University Press, 1995).

How would U.S. policy likely have been different in the absence of the Latin American effort? In all the cases, Latin American leaders had at least some influence on U.S. policy. This was perhaps smallest in OPA, at least when focusing on the Eisenhower administration. Even there, Brazilian and Latin American efforts paid off with the creation of the Inter-American Development Bank. Absent Latin American pressure, the Eisenhower administration had little reason to drop its long-standing opposition, but compared with the goals of OPA, it was a relatively minor concession. The U.S. policy in the early 1970s of maintaining control of the canal in perpetuity required a much greater shift, a change that would be incomprehensible without Panama's effort and its success in making the canal an issue with global resonance. The Mexican proposal of NAFTA coincided with U.S. interests in many respects and represents a very different path. The most crucial aspect of the case was Mexico's recalculation of its own interests, after which the negotiations could proceed on largely cooperative grounds – a sharp break from the past decades of U.S.–Mexico relations. The emergence of Plan Colombia was made possible in part by a change of administration in Colombia, after which the Clinton administration was eager to change its policies to help Pastrana. Previous U.S. policies focused almost entirely on fumigation and interdiction of illicit drugs by helping the Colombian National Police. Pastrana's ability to reframe the Colombian conflict led to changed policies. Fumigation and interdiction continued, with Pastrana's and later Uribe's blessings, but they were complemented by efforts to rebuild the Colombian Army into a force that could defeat the FARC, and supplemented by alternative development efforts and major increases in human rights and judicial reform funding. At the same time, Pastrana obtained Clinton's public support for the peace negotiations and the *despeje*, both of which elicited right-wing opposition in the United States. Taken together, these cases confirm that Latin American leaders have substantial room to maneuver around U.S. policies to pursue their own priorities in domestic and foreign policy. They also demonstrate that Latin American leaders have actively sought to shape how U.S. policymakers define and pursue their interests – a type of influence much different from that present in realism or even neoliberal approaches to bargaining. Below, I will discuss the types of strategies that these leaders used across the cases.

How would outcomes have been different if Latin American leaders had not vigorously pursued their interests? Changing U.S. policy in the preferred direction does not always lead to the desired outcome. Surely, the Inter-American Development Bank and ensuing Alliance for Progress did not spark the level of economic development and poverty reduction that Kubitschek and many of his Latin American counterparts sought. In other cases, the change in U.S. policy did lead to more propitious outcomes for Latin American leaders. The Panama Canal Treaties were executed as they were signed, with many aspects of the transfer and military withdrawal proceeding ahead of schedule – though the invasion to remove and arrest Manuel Noriega shows that U.S. intervention remained a concern for Panamanian leaders. NAFTA accelerated a long process of political opening in Mexico, but failed to spur enough immediate economic growth to salvage the PRI's slipping popularity. The 1994 financial crisis inflicted intense pain on the Mexican population and further undermined the incumbent party's legitimacy. The PRI lost power in 2000 before returning in 2012, boasting that NAFTA had led to significant macroeconomic growth and huge growth in trade and investment. Even with the PRI out of power, the governing PAN actively promoted trade with North America and beyond as the key to Mexican development. While NAFTA transformed bilateral relations, it did not lift Mexico to the first world as some of its promoters promised. Undocumented migration soared; drug trafficking and violence grew. Plan Colombia succeeded in strengthening the Colombian state and weakening the FARC, though not as quickly as Pastrana hoped. The peace negotiations failed, and Pastrana's promise that he would build "an army for peace or for war," took on a more ominous tone during a decade-long fight to reduce the FARC's influence and territory.

Dynamics of Asymmetry Revisited

This book contributes to the understanding of weaker states' foreign policies, particularly in asymmetrical relationships. Latin American leaders influenced U.S. policies and the outcome of these four cases in U.S.–Latin American relations. In that sense, they not only exercised "agency" but also, in Braveboy-Wagner's formulation, "foreign policy power." At times, weaker states can influence highly asymmetrical relationships – even when the partner is as powerful as the United States. The cases studied here indicate that while the leaders of the weaker states in asymmetrical relationships can exercise influence, they do so through strategies that are often outside traditional conceptualizations of the elements of national power. I categorize the strategies utilized by these states' leaders as constituting derivative, collective, and particularistic sources of foreign policy power.

It is important to note that these sources of foreign policy power do not negate broader asymmetries. Asymmetry shapes the aspirations of weaker states and affects their possibilities for action. To a greater extent, those with lesser material power must respond to the international conditions as they exist, whereas states with greater material power shape those conditions. This is stressed in work on hierarchy in International Relations (IR), where weaker states are seen as trading sovereignty for benefits. Though Lake notes the importance of "tying the suzerain's hands,"[4] it is not the weaker state that does the tying. Constraints on the great power are either external (great power rivalry) or made unilaterally. This book argues that, at least in some cases, the

---

[4] David A. Lake, *Hierarchy in International Relations* (Ithaca, N.Y.: Cornell University Press, 2009), pp. 122–131.

weaker state initiates changes in the terms of asymmetrical relationships, which could include a rejection of hierarchy. The leaders of weaker Latin American states will need to take advantage of opportunities to change U.S. policy. Here, I use "opportunity" to mean a temporally bound window for action. Often, these opportunities arise because of unexpected events that cast doubt on the efficacy of a particular U.S. policy or unsettle the policy agenda. Cognitive studies in Foreign Policy Analysis (FPA), note that policymakers tend to fit new information into preexisting "schema," but that momentous events are more likely to upset these patterns of understanding. Opportunities could also restructure political coalitions to facilitate actions. Without political actions, however, events and crises are not opportunities. To take advantage of these opportunities requires the astute use of a weaker state's derivative, collective, and particularistic foreign policy power.

Weaker states can compensate for their own limited capabilities by accessing the greater resources of more powerful states, through *derivative* power. In 1981, Michael Handel wrote, "The diplomatic art of the weak states is to obtain, commit, and manipulate, as far as possible, the power of other more powerful states in their own interests."[5] This had been characterized by Keohane as the "big influence of small allies," through bargaining, bureaucratic machinations, and public lobbying. At least some of this bargaining is captured within Lake's concepts of contracted relations of authority and subordination; however, this tends to be an extraction of benefits for domestic purposes as opposed to influence on the great power itself.[6] The weaker state inhabits a tenuous position where it is perceived by U.S. policymakers as a friendly country, but one that merits attention in order to maintain its cooperation. A slavishly pro-U.S. country might receive little attention and few resources. One that strays too far could attract the wrong kind of attention. These boundaries fluctuate and are not always easily discernable, as evidenced by the very different reactions from the Eisenhower administration to revolutionary regimes in Guatemala and Bolivia during the 1950s.[7]

Brazil sought to use OPA specifically as a plan to mobilize U.S. resources to address its domestic governance, but also to enhance its international position. A major part of its argument to the United States focused on Brazil's role as a crucial member of the West, and one that would be an even more effective partner if its democracy and economy flourished. However, it struggled to find a path between loyal anticommunist ally and autonomous, emerging power. Kubitschek's attempts to emphasize a communist threat were limited by his tenuous domestic political situation, as anticommunist generals watched

---

5 Michael I. Handel, *Weak States in the International System* (London; Totowa, N.J.: F. Cass, 1981), p. 257.
6 Lake, *Hierarchy in International Relations*.
7 Cole Blasier, *The Hovering Giant: U.S. Responses to Revolutionary Change in Latin America*. Pitt Latin American Series (Pittsburgh, Pa.: University of Pittsburgh Press, 1976).

closely over his shoulder. Sporadic hints that Brazil might establish ties with the Soviet Union came off as ham-handed. Brazilian diplomacy achieved only partial successes in mobilizing derivative power. As the leader of the smallest country in this study, Omar Torrijos seemed particularly aware of this balance as he sought to renegotiate Panama's impaired sovereignty and historic subordination to the United States. The March 1973 UNSC bolstered Panama's position internationally, but also created divisions within the U.S. government between State and Defense. Panama benefited from sympathetic diplomats who took much more supportive positions than U.S. generals. A strong domestic political consensus backed Torrijos position regarding the Canal Zone, which, combined with his solid, dictatorial control, allowed Panama to maintain a single-minded, long-term focus on the issue. Given the overwhelming U.S. presence, Panama had little choice but to engage directly in various forms of bargaining. Plan Colombia provides the clearest example of derivative power among the four cases. Colombian leaders were able to exploit a perceived commonality of interests to "obtain, commit, and manipulate" U.S. power and concerns for their own domestic political ends.

The ability to exercise influence on U.S. policy will often depend on the ability to win international allies and to work with other small and medium states, which I refer to as *collective* foreign policy power. In situations where the U.S. government rebuffs or ignores an initial weaker-state demand, international allies will play a more significant role. Successfully internationalizing an issue can accomplish several goals. First, it will increase the salience of an issue on the U.S. policy agenda. Allied countries can raise an issue in bilateral diplomacy, lend support in international institutions, and give a greater sense of legitimacy. Weaker states can also use international institutions as a megaphone for their concerns and as a forum for winning allies. Second, internationalization can raise the costs to a great power of refusing of deal with an issue. Supportive allies could create linkages between the issue and other great power interests where their cooperation is desired. A country's ability to mobilize these allies and effectively internationalize an issue is a demonstration of collective foreign policy power.

Brazil's Kubitschek clearly understood the importance of this power if Latin America was to overcome U.S. opposition to a development bank and heterodox economic policy. Brazilian diplomats prioritized building Latin American solidarity around their goals. Their early successes largely owed to the successful deployment of collective power. Panama likewise owed a considerable amount of its success to the support it garnered from Latin American and nonaligned states. As noted above, these coalitions raised the profile of the canal and increased the diplomatic costs of leaving it unresolved. Because of the initial, positive response to the proposal of a free-trade agreement, Mexico was less dependent on collective power; however, Mexican leaders' ability to make common cause with Canada during the side agreement negotiations helped counter protectionist sentiments in the Clinton administration and the Congress. Like Mexico, Colombian leaders placed less emphasis on collective power strategies, due to the success of their derivative power. The contrast between the two cases highlights an important aspect of collective power. Weaker states are more likely to turn to it when more direct options are lacking.

While the leaders of weaker states, by definition, lack the economic and military capabilities associated with coercive power, many hold *particular* resources that can be quite useful. Despite its small size, Panama's unique resource – a canal running across the heart of the country – meant that it would never be a strategic backwater. Brazil's size granted it inherent importance, though it was otherwise at the margins of the Cold War. As the Kennedy administration later surmised, "losing" Brazil would not be like losing Cuba; it would be like losing China.[8] Mexico's long, shared border likewise give it inherent importance that outstrips its power; its role as a major energy supplier enhances its power further. Geostrategic and material factors are only part of particularistic foreign policy power. Weaker states remain able to influence U.S. policy through various ideational means, as some liberal and constructivist IR scholars have noted in their work on small and middle powers. Much of this work has focused on the promotion and diffusion of global norms.[9] However, these leaders can also have a more direct influence on particular policy decisions. In these cases, the following processes of ideational influence are particularly significant: information exchange, cognitive framing, rhetorical framing, and policy options. First, information exchange and consultation is an important aspect of largely cooperative relationships, and has been discussed by authors studying alliance dynamics (though little in Latin America).[10] The leader of a weaker state may be seen as an expert who can offer insights into events in his or her own country or region. In certain situations, consultation can affect how policymakers understand, or cognitively frame, a problem. Finally, the leaders of weaker states might be in a position to present or advocate for policies that are being considered. As in the exchange of information, the leaders of weaker states might be seen as sources of expertise when suggesting policy solutions, though clearly self-interested recommendations could certainly undermine this. In summary, while the leaders of weaker states in asymmetrical relationships lack coercive power, they are able to exercise influence through a number of subtler channels. These three categories of strategies are not exclusive to

[8] Ruth Leacock, *Requiem for Revolution: The United States and Brazil, 1961–1969* (Kent, Ohio: Kent State University Press, 1990), p. 13.

[9] The classic work is Martha Finnemore and Kathryn Sikkink, "International Norm Dynamics and Political Change," *International Organization* 52, no. 4 (1998).

[10] See Thomas Risse-Kappen, *Cooperation among Democracies: The European Influence on U.S. Foreign Policy*. Princeton Studies in International History and Politics (Princeton, N.J.: Princeton University Press, 1995); Jeremy Pressman, *Warring Friends: Alliance Restraint in International Politics* (Ithaca, N.Y.: Cornell University Press, 2008).

weaker-state leaders. However, their comparative lack of material capabilities is likely to make weaker-state leaders more dependent on derivative, collective, and particularistic foreign policy power.

Conclusions for U.S.–Latin American Relations

What does the U.S.-focused literature on U.S.–Latin American relations miss, and how does a focus on interaction add to our understanding? As discussed in Chapter 1, the literature on U.S.–Latin American relations can be broadly divided into three camps: an "establishment" school, a "revisionist synthesis," and a more recent "internationalist" approach. The establishment school is characterized by a focus on the "security thesis" as the central explanation for U.S. policy and the argument that the United States has been, on the whole, a beneficial presence in the hemisphere. Under the security thesis, the primary concern of U.S. policymakers has been to make sure no external rival could use Latin America as a base from which to threaten the United States. U.S. and Latin American interests are not necessarily harmonious, but nor are they incompatible. In the "revisionist synthesis," which emerged as a critique of the early establishment school, "the distinguishing feature of U.S. relations with Latin America has been the prevalence of conflict and exploitation." The United States, according to this view, is an imperial presence, and its relations with its southern neighbors are heavily influenced by the need for cheap raw materials and exploitable markets.[11]

The models coincide in their focus on the actions of the United States as a sufficient explanation for hemispheric relations. Under the security thesis, Latin American territory might be important as a base for external powers, but Latin American actors are not treated as independent of the United States or its potential extra-hemispheric rival. What matters is the U.S. perception of and responses to potential extra-hemispheric threats. This interpretation coincides with the core tenets of realism, under which we should expect the United States, as an aspiring or de facto regional hegemon, to expand its influence to prevent the rise of peer competitors.[12] U.S. power is beneficial because of the stability it provides (akin to hegemonic stability theory), through the benefits of trade, or because of its example and promotion of democratic governance.

Revisionist authors also offer U.S. actions as an adequate explanation for U.S.–Latin American relations, exploring interventions as a primary example of the United States' imperial urges. The perspective has expanded to include factors such as U.S. prejudices as explanations for exploitative U.S. policies. Where establishment authors have, implicitly or explicitly, argued that the United States is different from other great powers – that is, exceptional in

---

[11] Gilderhus, "An Emerging Synthesis?," p. 431.

[12] The version par excellence of this thesis comes from John J. Mearsheimer, *The Tragedy of Great Power Politics* (New York: Norton, 2001).

a positive or benign fashion – revisionists hold up evidence of U.S. actions to demonstrate that the country has followed its own interests with little regard for professed principles. To make these claims, neither side has generally needed to offer much evidence from Latin America, as the key debate has been about U.S. policy to the region – not, in fact, about U.S.–Latin American relations.

Instead of trying to resolve this debate, the internationalist approach asks different questions and tries to answer them by using additional evidence. It is interactive in its focus and multinational in its research. First, this perspective sees asymmetry as the context for U.S.–Latin American relations, but not as determinant of those relations. Second, not only are the outcomes of events the product of an interactive process, but in many cases, the importance of that interaction extends to the definition of interests and the formulation of foreign policy. Therefore, it is necessary to understand the process by which goals are defined. Third, internationalist research must weigh both foreign and domestic factors in order to trace their influence on the policymaking process. Fourth, just as the United States can exercise influence on Latin America through its power, Latin American leaders can influence both the course of events and, at times, U.S. policy. However, the internationalist researcher must be open to means of influence beyond traditionally defined power resources. In summary, what has this approach unearthed about U.S.–Latin American relations that the U.S.-centric studies have not? To answer that question, I will now return by examining the four cases through the lens of the establishment, revisionist, and internationalist approaches.

Three Approaches to Four Cases

The first, and least studied, case is OPA. It has largely been treated, especially in the English-language literature, in connection with the Alliance for Progress. This act of subsuming a major Brazilian and regional foreign policy initiative into a U.S. program is symptomatic of how various approaches have usually dealt with Latin American actors. Both Republican and Democratic "establishment" authors, many of whom were members of the Eisenhower and Kennedy administrations, have offered brief discussions of OPA. Milton Eisenhower, for example, referred to OPA as evidence of continuity between the economic policy enacted late in his brother's administration and the Alliance, which was unfolding as he wrote *The Wine is Bitter*. This view was in part substantiated by Stephen Rabe's book on the Eisenhower administration, which noted that though Eisenhower's policies fell far short of Kubitschek's aspirations, the United States was responding to them. Kennedy administration officials have been divided to the extent they credit Kubitschek, ranging from claims that Kennedy's Alliance was a direct response to Kubitschek's call to those who say the similarities are just coincidence. Richard Goodwin's and Arthur M. Schlesinger's memoirs minimize the Latin American contribution, despite evidence that he was in close contact with Latin Americans before the Alliance proposal; on the other hand, Lincoln Gordon and Douglas Dillon have given central credit to OPA and Eisenhower policies.[13]

Scholar Mark Eric Williams points to "Latin American states and statesmen that offered a vision of hemispheric development, encouraged their northern neighbor to buy into it, and adeptly took advantage of the OAS machinery and Cold War climate to press their case" as "important precursors to the Alliance for Progress."[14] However, more typical are Abraham F. Lowenthal's and Peter H. Smith's treatments, which coincide with many Kennedy administration accounts by noting Kubitschek but giving full causal credit to the U.S. decision regarding how to respond to the Cuban Revolution.[15] Critiques of the Alliance have tended to focus more directly on parsing the motives and effects of U.S. aid programs. Levinson and de Onís looked at weaknesses in conception, bureaucracy, and implementation, with a critical eye toward the transition between Kennedy and Johnson. While establishment authors diverge on whether they credit OPA, none has made it a significant subject of study. If one were to synthesize an establishment view of OPA, it could reasonably be summed up as a footnote and perhaps a minor influence on a generally beneficial turn in U.S. policy to Latin America that would come from Kennedy's Alliance for Progress.

Among revisionists, OPA has gotten even less attention. Michael Latham examined the Alliance's roots in modernization theory, arguing that it was undermined by the Western-centric biases embedded in that theory's teleology. Latham briefly mentions Kubitschek and OPA, and notes that the late Eisenhower administration "added economic growth and the reduction of popular misery" to its anticommunist arsenal. However, contra Kubitschek, the United States retained interventionist and military measures as its central tools, thus undermining its own economic initiatives.[16] Schoultz argues: "Eager for a toe-to-toe contest with Castro and his Soviet supporters, Kennedy New Frontiersmen picked up the banner of Latin America's poor," before turning his focus to

---

[13] Richard N. Goodwin, *Remembering America: A Voice from the Sixties* (New York: Harper & Row, 1989); Lincoln Gordon, *A New Deal for Latin America: The Alliance for Progress* (Cambridge, Mass.: Harvard University Press, 1963). For a summary of this debate, see Darnton, "Asymmetry and Agenda-Setting in US-Latin American Relations," pp. 72–74; Roberto Porzecanski, "Alliance for Progress or Alizana para el Progreso: A Reassessment of the Latin American Contribution to the Alliance for Progress," M.A. thesis, Tufts University (2005). Ted Sorenson's memoir *Counselor* makes only brief mention of the Alliance for Progress and none of Kubitschek. Theodore C. Sorensen, *Counselor: A Life at the Edge of History* (New York: Harper, 2008).

[14] Mark Eric Williams, *Understanding U.S.–Latin American Relations: Theory and History* (New York: Routledge, 2012), pp. 199–201.

[15] Abraham F. Lowenthal, *Partners in Conflict: The United States and Latin America* (Baltimore, Md.: Johns Hopkins University Press, 1987), pp. 29–30; Smith, *Talons of the Eagle*, pp. 150–151.

[16] Michael E. Latham, *Modernization as Ideology: American Social Science and "Nation Building" in the Kennedy Era* (Chapel Hill, N.C.: University of North Carolina Press, 2000), p. 77.

U.S. support for counterinsurgency training throughout the hemisphere.[17] In a revisionist synthesis, OPA is scarcely present, but appears only to the extent that Latin American aspirations were rejected in favor of policies driven by the expansion of U.S. power through the hemisphere in prosecution of the Cold War.

What does an internationalist approach add to our understanding of OPA? My study is perhaps the third study of OPA that could fall under this label. Michael Weis situates OPA within U.S.–Brazilian relations in the early Cold War. Christopher Darnton recently examined the link between OPA and the Alliance in terms of agenda-setting theory.[18] All three of these studies, including mine, draw on archives from the United States and Itamaraty, and they converge in several respects that are significantly different from the establishment and revisionist accounts. In relation to U.S. policy, internationalist accounts have treated OPA as a necessary, but not sufficient cause of the changes in U.S. policy under Eisenhower and Kennedy. However, an internationalist approach also treats OPA as a Brazilian foreign policy, not just as a precursor to the Alliance. OPA grew out of domestic demands in Latin American societies, which were deeply linked with the democratic opening of the mid to late 1950s. OPA was a dual strategy oriented to foreign and domestic policies. The degree of Latin American cooperation reflected the (short-lived) democratization of the region, as leaders in similar domestic political positions found converging interests. This helped Kubitschek, Frondizi, and Lleras pressure the United States more effectively in the wake of the Nixon visit than during previous Latin American attempts.

In addition to offering a serious analysis of Latin American foreign policies in a case that has been mostly treated by establishment and revisionist authors as a footnote to U.S. initiatives, the internationalist approach argues for a different understanding of U.S.–Latin American relations in the case. It sees several levels of interaction between U.S. and Latin American policymakers. Building on Weis' and Darnton's work, I am especially attentive to the formation of preferences and priorities on both sides of the relationship. The Latin American priority of gaining development aid had a domestic genesis, while the Brazilian-led strategy of linking development and anticommunism was conditioned by the opportunities presented by the international system, U.S. policies, and the context of asymmetry. The proposal of OPA responded directly to a number of opportunities, starting with the attack on Nixon; it was then reshaped given the renewed interest generated by the Caribbean crisis and worsening U.S.–Cuban relations. During the fifteen years since the Second World War, various U.S. administrations showed little interest in Latin American development, refusing to consider proposals for a development bank and even going

---

[17] Schoultz, *Beneath the United States*, pp. 356–358.

[18] Weis, *Cold Warriors & Coups D'etat*; Darnton, "Asymmetry and Agenda-Setting in US-Latin American Relations."

to significant lengths to avoid an economically focused summit. OPA sought to reshape U.S. priorities by redefining Latin American underdevelopment in security terms. This was not entirely new, but the Brazilian effort took this idea, assembled a group of allies behind it, and made it politically salient. The internationalist approach makes clear that without Latin American prodding, the Eisenhower administration would have little reason to consider reversing its opposition to a development bank or establishing the Social Progress Trust Fund. These policies were direct responses to Latin American diplomatic initiatives. A range of establishment and revisionist scholars note that during the last two years of his administration, Eisenhower laid the groundwork for the Alliance for Progress. This groundwork came from an administration, which unlike Kennedy's, was not dominated by modernization theory thinking. The argument that the Alliance grew out of modernization theory alone also fails to note that similar theories were already prominent in Latin America, particularly in the Instituto Superior de Estudos Brasileiros, which shaped Kubitschek's thinking about economic development. An astute – albeit partially successful – push from several Latin American leaders caused Eisenhower to change policies that later became the Alliance's groundwork. Likewise, the case shows that the simple existence of the Latin American demand was not sufficient. Various leaders had vocalized the demand for a development bank during many years, but it was not until OPA that the proposal gained organized Latin American support and took advantage of opportunities to gain traction with U.S. policymakers. This indicates that Latin American foreign policy strategies are an important area of research if we are to understand U.S.–Latin American relations – and even to understand the formation of U.S. policy toward the region.

The case of the Panama Canal Treaties is of particular interest because numerous factors indicate that Panama should have had little success in getting the United States to change policy. It would be difficult to imagine a greater power differential than the U.S. – Panama relationship at that time, which stretched far beyond the difference in size. Historically, Panamanian independence in many respects depended on U.S. policy. Even during the negotiations, thousands of U.S. soldiers occupied a dozen bases, and the United States controlled the country's primary strategic and economic asset. Despite these factors, Panama crafted a remarkably independent foreign policy that turned its smallness to its rhetorical and political advantage. However, this is not the primary understanding of the Panama Canal Treaties offered in the establishment and revisionist literatures.

There is a clear partisan split in the establishment literature on the Panama Canal Treaties, which centers on Jimmy Carter's role and the connection between opposition to the treaties and the rise of the "new right" and Ronald Reagan. However, as a whole, the establishment has been concerned with parsing the meaning of the treaties for understanding the U.S. role in the world in the post-Vietnam era. A recent realist survey of U.S.–Latin American relations claims that the treaties intentionally "undermined regional solidarity" that threatened to challenge the United States – an interpretation that would likely seem bogus to Panamanians who so carefully crafted that very solidarity in support of their cause.[19] Another group of studies uses the treaties as a case of U.S. executive–Congressional relations, and the two-level game between presidentially appointed negotiators and the U.S. Congress, but these pay little attention to Panamanians.

Revisionist survey texts have paid the treaties little attention, even though the tale of the canal's construction was a central component in early revisionist work. Alan McPherson summarizes the treaty in a page, noting that Panamanians "cleverly framed their demand . . . in anticolonial terms" and that Carter paid a great cost for the treaties' passage.[20] Greg Grandin's *Empire's Workshop* mentions it only in regard to Reagan's rise. The most careful revisionist study was written by Walter LaFeber, who both examined Omar Torrijos' political context and recognizes the importance of pre-1977 interactions. However, LaFeber sees U.S. motivations as economic, believing the canal issue represented a "small, if formidable, obstacle to be cleared on the way to the ultimate goal of developing a workable economic relationship with Latin America . . . If the Canal problem was solved, Latin America could again act as the laboratory for United States policies in the developing nations." LaFeber eventually concluded that the final pact was a "triumph" that the United States forced upon Panama – a conclusion that does not seem to follow from his preceding analysis of Torrijos' situation and goals.[21] If one focuses solely on U.S. policy, with a proclivity to highlight examples of U.S. greed and aggression, the Panama Canal Treaties are an incongruous example.

The internationalist approach to the case shows that Panamanian actions are necessary to understanding how the negotiations unfolded. There is an even stronger case to be made that the Panama Canal Treaties would not have occurred if Panama had not aggressively and persistently sought the end of the Canal Zone and the transfer of control. It was Panamanian leaders who made the matter internationally salient and diplomatically costly for the United States, which led the State Department to take an accommodating position starting in 1974. Because Panama convinced other countries, including nearly all of Latin America, to vocally adopt its cause, the canal was highlighted by the Linowitz Commission and others, which primed the issue for Carter. At the same time, much groundwork had been laid during the Nixon and Ford administrations – despite the lack of personal commitment from either of those presidents. This was made clear by the Carter administration's

---

[19] Williams, *Understanding U.S.–Latin American Relations*, p. 237.

[20] Alan L. McPherson, *Intimate Ties, Bitter Struggles: The United States and Latin America since 1945* (Washington, D.C.: Potomac Books, 2006).

[21] Walter Lafeber, *The Panama Canal: The Crisis in Historical Perspective* (New York; Oxford: Oxford University Press, 1989), pp. 151–152, 158–162.

early affirmation of the Tack–Kissinger agreement on principles as a framework for continuing negotiations. Without Panamanian efforts during the five years preceding Carter's inauguration, the Panama Canal would not have been either significant or ready for Carter to select as a major early initiative. In many cases, Carter's arrival has been treated as both necessary and sufficient for the approval of the treaties. However, the internationalist approach demonstrates that Panama's foreign policy and U.S. political will were both necessary conditions for the treaties, and that Carter's arrival alone is not a sufficient explanation.

Because the establishment and revisionist literatures have marginalized the Panamanian side, they have missed theoretically relevant aspects of the case. For example, the case sheds particular light on the ways in which weaker-state leaders can use international institutions in pursuit of their goals, as well as the role weaker states can play in affecting the political agendas of larger ones. The March 1973 UNSC meetings emerge as a key moment, as do summits with democratically elected leaders. Second, there is a lack of emphasis on and understanding of Panamanian goals in the case, which leads LaFeber to treat Panama as the loser in the treaties. Panamanian negotiators never asked for an immediate handover of the canal, because they believed a transition was needed to ensure smooth continued operation of a national resource. The earliest Panama had demanded was a 1995 transfer. Panamanian leadership did want an immediate abolition of the Canal Zone, which they achieved in de jure terms immediately and gained de facto with a three-year phaseout of separate Zonian facilities. Panamanian goals remained relatively stable over a five-year period, though its strategies changed drastically in response to changing U.S. leadership, shifting international events, and internal politics.

NAFTA presents a very different case, especially regarding Latin American preferences. Whereas Panamanian leadership pursued stable preferences, the central focus of an internationalist case study of NAFTA is how Mexican leaders dramatically shifted priorities and how that change affected U.S.–Mexico relations. Establishment and revisionist accounts would tend to offer U.S. policies as the explanation for Mexico's changed position. Most case studies of the NAFTA negotiations have either come from the establishment literature or from literature on international negotiations or bargaining. An exception is Domínguez and Fernández de Castro's work, which situates NAFTA at the center of U.S.–Mexican relations. They focus primarily on the "important spillovers" that NAFTA produced in relations between the two countries through altering perceptions, deepening institutionalization, and intensifying intergovernmental contacts.[22] This study, along with careful examinations of the negotiations themselves by Cameron and Tomlin and Frederick Mayer, has done more to account for the motivations of the Salinas government, emphasizing the desire to "lock in" liberalizing economic reforms.

---

[22] Domínguez and Fernández de Castro, *The United States and Mexico.*

Though it is not a primary focus for them, revisionist authors have painted a different picture, using NAFTA as an exhibit in a larger critique of neoliberal or "Washington Consensus" policies of the late 1980s and early 1990s. Greg Grandin blames NAFTA for a host of Mexican economic and social problems, including increasing "the cost of meeting basic nutritional requirements." McPherson erroneously calls the agreement a U.S. "brainchild," ignoring the Mexican and Canadian roles in advocating first Canada–United States Free Trade Agreement (CUSFTA) and then NAFTA. He writes that after the Canada–U.S. pact, "Major import-export firms then doled out large contributions to U.S. members of Congress so that they would bring Mexico into the fold of NAFTA." He places full agency in U.S. hands.[23] Revisionist authors have paid more attention to links between the supposed effects of NAFTA – the 1994 peso crisis and the Zapatista uprising – than to its initiation and negotiation.

This case study of NAFTA supported many of the conclusions drawn by Domínguez and Fernández de Castro, Cameron and Tomlin, and Mayer. As these authors emphasize, achieving and institutionalizing liberal economic reforms was a central concern for Mexican policymakers. The effects were drastic for the U.S.–Mexican relationship, even if NAFTA spurred only incomplete reform of the Mexican economy and far less economic growth than many hoped. Going beyond these excellent works, I have explored the roots and short-term implications for bilateral relations of the Mexican decision to seek a trade agreement with the United States. I find that both domestic and international factors weighed heavily on Mexican leaders' recalculation of national interests. It was not simply a desire to lock in reforms, but a belief that the world was in the midst of a profound transformation. This in large part drove a desire to alter relations with the United States through a new Mexican foreign policy, one presaged on restraining the United States and gaining influence through interdependence instead of pressing for autonomy through opposition to a wide range of U.S. actions that could be labeled interventionist. The cases of OPA and the Panama Canal show that, through certain strategies, Latin American leaders have been able to take an initial negative response and change it. NAFTA shows how, without U.S. pressure, a Latin American government opted for a radically new approach and took the lead in redefining its relationship with the United States.

The case of Plan Colombia represents the shift in U.S.–Latin American relations in the post-Cold War era, in which drug trafficking has become a major point of both cooperation and contestation. The establishment literature has tended to be supportive of U.S. actions, though with a partisan split focused on the distribution of aid between military, human rights, and development projects. The general consensus is that U.S. policy was "driven by drugs," in

---

[23] McPherson, *Intimate Ties, Bitter Struggles*, pp. 113–114.

Russell Crandall's phrase.[24] Establishment writers, often in military or policy think tanks, have emphasized the later successes of the Colombian Army and have held up Colombia as an example of how the United States can successfully engage in state-building projects or confront drug-trafficking organizations or insurgents across the globe.[25] The assessments of Plan Colombia tend to diverge more extensively when concerned with the later period after the transitions from Colombian President Andrés Pastrana to Álvaro Uribe and from U.S. President Bill Clinton to George W. Bush. However, the key explanation of Plan Colombia centers on the U.S. response to a surge in cocaine production and exports from Colombia, with an assumption that U.S. policymakers were the near-exclusive architects of that response.

Revisionist authors have offered a very different interpretation. The most critical scholars have argued that Plan Colombia represents no less than the new face of U.S. imperialism. Plan Colombia, Germán Rodas argues, is aimed at drugs only on the surface; its true purpose was to open a military front against Venezuelan President Hugo Chávez.[26] James Petras connects it to the Central American civil wars of the 1980s, and also described Plan Colombia as a U.S. counterattack against left governments in Venezuela, Bolivia, Ecuador, and Cuba, "which can contribute to undermining the mystique surrounding the invincibility of U.S. hegemony."[27] Grace Livingstone argues that the U.S. government subverted Pastrana's original, peaceful plan and converted it into a "battle plan."[28] Villar and Cottle echo this analysis (and many of the same quotations), writing: "Clinton militarized the nation and financed the counterinsurgency with the political support of George Soros' organization, Human Rights Watch."[29] In making the claim, though, they do not account for evidence that Pastrana had been seeking large escalations in material military assistance and enhanced cooperation through training and intelligence sharing even during his preinaugural period.

To an extent that establishment authors have not recognized and revisionists have explicitly rejected, the final Plan Colombia was the product of cooperation between U.S. and Colombian leaders – not a replacement of a Colombian plan with a U.S. plan. In this cooperative process, Colombian leaders explicitly pursued their own interests, recognizing and using the U.S. focus on drugs but not

---

[24] Crandall, *Driven by Drugs: US Policy toward Colombia*, 1st edn. (2002).

[25] Marcella, *The United States and Colombia*; Jason Campbell, Michael E. O'Hanlon, and Jeremy Shapiro, *Assessing Counterinsurgency and Stabilization Missions* (Washington, D.C.: Brookings Institution, 2009); Paul Wolfowitz and Michael E. O'Hanlon, "Plan Afghanistan," *Foreign Policy*, October 28, 2011.

[26] Rodas Chaves, *El Plan Colombia*. See also, Estrada Álvarez, ed., *Plan Colombia*.

[27] James Petras, "Geopolitics of Plan Colombia," *Economic and Political Weekly* 35, no. 52/53 (2000).

[28] Livingstone, *Inside Colombia*.

[29] Oliver Villar and Drew Cottle, *Cocaine, Death Squads, and the War on Terror: U.S. Imperialism and Class Struggle in Colombia* (New York: Monthly Review Press, 2011), Chapter 6.

kowtowing to it, despite the precariousness of their own positions. Colombian priorities were primarily born out of their domestic weakness – the military was being challenged for control of Colombian territory and the economy was in dire condition. In addition, the country had been largely isolated internationally as the preceding President Ernesto Samper was consumed by drug-money scandals. Under those circumstances, Pastrana's priority was to strengthen the military and civil capabilities of the weak Colombian state as quickly as possible, which implied gaining assistance from the international community. That said, Plan Colombia does not represent the simple fulfillment of Colombian priorities. Rather, the internationalist approach shows that those priorities were conditioned by an asymmetrical international environment, clearly seen in the structure of the transnational drug market and the distribution of resources. Because of that context, Colombian foreign policy strategies were directed at obtaining resources from the United States and, to a lesser extent, Europe, based on a justification of "shared responsibility" for the consequences of drug trafficking. Many in the Clinton administration realized that attacking drug trafficking was a means to the Colombian government's goal of strengthening the state, not its primary concern. However, the Clinton and Pastrana administrations emphasized that portion in their public arguments as an instrumental tactic to boost support in the U.S. Congress for greater appropriations. The two governments acted strategically and in tandem because of the perception that their interests coincided.

The internationalist approach presents a richer, more complex understanding of U.S.–Latin American relations, in which there are many significant actors instead of one. However, the shift is more than a tradeoff between richness and parsimony because it throws into question the central theses of the establishment and revisionist authors. Revisionists who have treated Latin America as a victim of U.S. aggression must grapple with a situation in which power explains only part of the story. Caricatures of Latin American leaders as imperial lackeys do not hold up to scrutiny when those leaders shift between conflict and cooperation as they pursue their own interests. Kubitschek and Torrijos were nobody's puppets; though cooperative in tone, Lleras Camargo and Pastrana both put Colombian interests first as they dealt with the United States. Establishment authors, even those who limit themselves to explaining U.S. policy through a "bureaucratic" approach, must take Latin American actors more seriously as a possible source of influence on the U.S. policymaking process. My approach does not overturn the key establishment school claim, the security thesis; however, it does demand an exploration of how Latin Americans sought to affect U.S. perceptions of threats and shape responses to them. Above all, the demonstrated influence of Latin American leaders means that studying U.S. policy is not a sufficient proxy for understanding U.S.–Latin American relations.

This book has presented four case narratives, based on multinational research, that focus on the interactions between U.S. and Latin American leaders. It has been motivated by the central question, how do Latin American leaders try to influence U.S. policies, and can they succeed in doing so? The answers to those questions indicate the value of this focus for improving our understanding of U.S.–Latin American relations and the role of nongreat powers in IR. Understanding the interactions of great powers and weaker states, in the Western Hemisphere and beyond, requires an exploration of both sides. Assuming that the leaders of weaker states simply "do what they must" ignores how they actively shape agendas, reframe problems, promote options, and achieve influence to advance their own priorities. Research into the perspectives of multiple states can lead to richer interpretations not only of frequently studied cases but of foreign relations more broadly.

References

Robert J. Alexander, *Juscelino Kubitschek and the Development of Brazil* (Athens, Ohio: Ohio University Center for International Studies, 1991).

Stephen E. Ambrose, *Eisenhower: Soldier and President* (New York: Simon & Schuster, 1990).

Octavio Amorim Neto, *De Dutra a Lula: A Condução e os Determinantes da Política Externa Brasileira* (Rio de Janeiro, Brazil: Elsevier: Campus, 2012).

Cynthia J. Arnson, ed., *The Peace Process in Colombia and U.S. Policy* (Washington, D.C.: Woodrow Wilson International Center for Scholars, 2000).

Carlos Arriola, ed., *Documentos Básicos* (México: SECOFI, Grupo Editorial Miguel Ángel Porrua, 1994).

G. Pope Atkins, *Latin America in the International Political System* (Boulder, Colo.: Westview Press, 1989).

Mohammed Ayoob, "Inequality and Theorizing in International Relations: The Case for Subaltern Realism," *International Studies Review*, Vol. 4, No. 3 (2003), pp. 27–48.

Peter Bachrach and Morton S. Baratz, "Two Faces of Power," *American Political Science Review*, Vol. 56, No. 04 (1962), pp. 947–952.

James Addison Baker and Thomas M. DeFrank, *The Politics of Diplomacy: Revolution, War, and Peace, 1989–1992* (New York: Putnam, 1995).

Godfrey Baldacchino, "Thucydides or Kissinger? A Critical Review of Smaller State Diplomacy," in Andrew F. Cooper and Timothy M. Shaw, eds., *The Diplomacies of Small States: Between Vulnerability and Resilience* (New York: Palgrave Macmillan, 2009), pp. 21–40.

Moniz Bandeira, *Brasil, Argentina e Estados Unidos: Conflito e Integração na América do Sul: Da Tríplice Aliança ao Mercosul* (Rio de Janeiro: Civilização Brasileira, 2010).

Michael Barnett and Raymond Duvall, "Power in International Politics," *International Organization*, Vol. 59, No. 01 (2005), pp. 39–75.

Mariano Bertucci, "Scholarly Research on U.S.–Latin American Relations: Where Does the Field Stand?," *Latin American Politics and Society*, Vol. 55, No. 4 (2013), pp. 119–142.

Gustavo Biscaia da Lacerda, "Panamericanismo entre a Segurança e o Desenvolvimiento: O Operação Panamericana e a Aliança para o Progresso" (M.A., Universidade Federal do Paraná, 2004).

Sebastian E. Bitar, *US Military Bases, Quasi-Bases, and Domestic Politics* (New York: Palgrave MacMillan, 2015).

Cole Blasier, *The Hovering Giant: U.S. Responses to Revolutionary Change in Latin America.* Pitt Latin American Series (Pittsburgh, Pa.: University of Pittsburgh Press, 1976).

James G. Blight and Philip Brenner, *Sad and Luminous Days: Cuba's Struggle with the Superpowers after the Missile Crisis* (Lanham, Md.: Rowman & Littlefield Publishers, 2002).

G. Matthew Bonham, Victor M. Sergeev, and Pavel B. Parshin, "The Limited Test–Ban Agreement: Emergence of New Knowledge Structures in International Negotiation," *International Studies Quarterly*, Vol. 41, No. 2 (1997), pp. 215–240.

Sandra P. Borda, "The Internationalization of Domestic Conflicts: A Comparative Study of Colombia, El Salvador and Guatemala," (Ph.D. thesis, University of Minnesota, 2009).

Mark Bowden, *Killing Pablo: The Hunt for the World's Greatest Outlaw* (New York: Atlantic Monthly Press, 2001).

Hal Brands, *Latin America's Cold War* (Cambridge, Mass.: Harvard University Press, 2010).

Jacqueline Braveboy-Wagner, "Opportunities and Limitations of the Exercise of Foreign Policy Power by a Very Small State: The Case of Trinidad and Tobago," *Cambridge Review of International Affairs*, Vol. 23, No. 3 (2010), pp. 407–427.

Jacqueline Anne Braveboy-Wagner and Michael T. Snarr, "Assessing Current Conceptual and Empirical Approaches," in Jacqueline Anne Braveboy-Wagner, ed., *The Foreign Policies of the Global South: Rethinking Conceptual Frameworks* (Boulder, Colo.: L. Rienner, 2003), pp. 13–30.

Christopher S. Browning, "Small, Smart and Salient? Rethinking Identity in the Small States Literature," *Cambridge Review of International Affairs*, Vol. 19, No. 4 (2006), pp. 669–684.

Hedley Bull, *The Anarchical Society: A Study of Order in World Politics* (New York: Columbia University Press, 1977).

Sean W. Burges, *Brazilian Foreign Policy after the Cold War* (Gainesville, Fla.: University Press of Florida, 2009).

______ "Mistaking Brazil for a Middle Power," *Journal of Iberian and Latin American Research*, Vol. 19, No. 2 (2013).

Maxwell A. Cameron and Brian W. Tomlin, *The Making of NAFTA: How the Deal Was Done* (Ithaca, N.Y.: Cornell University Press, 2000).

Jason Campbell, Michael E. O'Hanlon, and Jeremy Shapiro, *Assessing Counterinsurgency and Stabilization Missions* (Washington, D.C.: Brookings Institution, 2009).

Diego Cardona, "La Política Exterior de la Administración Pastrana (1998–2002)," in Sandra Borda and Arlene B. Tickner, eds., *Relaciones Internacionales y Política Exterior de Colombia* (Bogotá, Colombia: Universidad de los Andes, Facultad de Ciencias Sociales, Departamento de Ciencia Política-CESO, 2011), pp. 195–225.

Jimmy Carter, *Keeping Faith: Memoirs of a President* (New York: Bantam Books, 1982).

______ *White House Diary* (New York: Farrar, Straus and Giroux, 2010).

Jaime Caycedo Turriago, "Una Guerra Social de la Globalización," in Jairo Estrada Álvarez, ed., *Plan Colombia: Ensayos Críticos* (Bogotá, Colombia: Universidad Nacional de Colombia, 2001), pp. 179–214.

Amado Luiz Cervo, "Política Exterior e Relações Internacionais do Brasil: Enfoque Paradigmático," *Revista Brasileira de Política Internacional*, Vol. 46, No. 3 (2003), pp. 5–25.

Amado Luiz Cervo and Clodoaldo Bueno, *História da Política Exterior do Brasil* (Brasília, D.F.: Editora UnB, 2011).

Phillip Chicola, reflections in *The Peace Process in Colombia and U.S. Policy*, ed. Cynthia J. Arnson, Working Papers of the Latin America Program, No. 246 (Washington, D.C.: Woodrow Wilson International Center for Scholars, 2000), pp. 32–37.

Alan Chong and Matthias Maass, "Introduction: The Foreign Policy Power of Small States," *Cambridge Review of International Affairs*, Vol. 23, No. 3 (2010), pp. 381–382.

Ozgur Cicek, "Review of a Perspective: Subaltern Realism," *The Review of International Affairs*, Vol. 3, No. 3 (2004), pp. 495–501.

Paul Coe Clark, *The United States and Somoza, 1933–1956: A Revisionist Look* (Westport, Conn.: Praeger, 1992).

Adam Clymer, *Drawing the Line at the Big Ditch: The Panama Canal Treaties and the Rise of the Right* (Lawrence, Kan.: University Press of Kansas, 2008).

Commission on United States–Latin American Relations, *The United States and Latin America, Next Steps: A Second Report* (New York: Center for Inter-American Relations, 1976).

Michael L. Conniff, *Panama and the United States: The Forced Alliance* (Athens, Ga.: University of Georgia Press, 2001).

Dean A. Cook, "U.S. Southern Command: General Charles E. Wilhelm and the Shaping of U.S. Military Engagement in Colombia, 1997–2000," in Derek S. Reveron, ed., *America's Viceroys: The Military and U.S. Foreign Policy* (New York: Palgrave Macmillan, 2004), pp. 127–162.

Licurgo Costa, *Uma Nova Política para as Américas: Doutrina Kubitschek e Opa* (São Paulo: Livraria Martins, 1960).

Martha L. Cottam, *Images and Intervention: U.S. Policies in Latin America* (Pittsburgh, Pa.: University of Pittsburgh Press, 1994).

Richard B. Craig, "Colombian Narcotics and United States–Colombian Relations," *Journal of Interamerican Studies and World Affairs*, Vol. 23, No. 3 (1981), pp. 243–270.

Russell Crandall, *Driven by Drugs: U.S. Policy toward Colombia*, 1st edn. (Boulder, Colo.: Lynne Rienner Publishers, 2002).

______ *Driven by Drugs: US Policy toward Colombia*, 2nd edn. (Boulder, Colo.: Lynne Rienner Publishers, 2008).

______ *Gunboat Democracy: U.S. Interventions in the Dominican Republic, Grenada, and Panama* (Lanham, Md.: Rowman & Littlefield Publishers, 2006).

______ *The United States and Latin America after the Cold War* (New York: Cambridge University Press, 2008).

Pepper D. Culpepper, "The Politics of Common Knowledge: Ideas and Institutional Change in Wage Bargaining," *International Organization*, Vol. 62, No. 1 (2008), pp. 1–33.

Robert A. Dahl, *Modern Political Analysis* (Englewood Cliffs, N.J.: Prentice-Hall, 1976).

—— "The Concept of Power," *Behavioral Science*, Vol. 2, No. 3 (1957), pp. 201–215.

Christopher Darnton, "Asymmetry and Agenda-Setting in US–Latin American Relations: Rethinking the Origins of the Alliance for Progress," *Journal of Cold War Studies*, Vol. 14, No. 4 (2012), pp. 55–92.

—— *Rivalry and Alliance Politics in Cold War Latin America* (Baltimore, Md.: Johns Hopkins University Press, 2014).

Rodolfo O. de la Garza and Jesús Velasco, *México y su Interacción con el Sistema Político Estadounidense* (México: CIDE, Centro de Investigación y Docencia Económicas: M.A. Porrúa Grupo Editorial, 2000).

María Mercedes de la Guardia de Corró, *Hasta la Última Gota: Gabriel Lewis Galindo* (Cali, Colombia: Cargraphics, 2009).

Alexandra Delano, *Mexico and Its Diaspora in the United States: Policies of Emigration since 1848* (New York: Cambridge University Press, 2011).

Alexandra de Mello e Silvia, "A Política Externa do JK: Operação Pan-Americana" (Rio de Janiero: Fundação Getulio Vargas, 1992).

John Dinges, *Our Man in Panama: How General Noriega Used the United States and Made Millions in Drugs and Arms* (New York: Random House, 1990).

Michael Dobbs, *One Minute to Midnight: Kennedy, Khrushchev, and Castro on the Brink of Nuclear War* (New York: Alfred A. Knopf, 2008).

Jorge I. Domínguez and Rafael Fernández de Castro, *The United States and Mexico: Between Partnership and Conflict* (New York: Routledge, 2001).

Jack Donnelly, "Sovereign Inequalities and Hierarchy in Anarchy: American Power and International Society," *European Journal of International Relations*, Vol. 12, No. 2 (2006).

Autran Dourado, *Gaiola Aberta: Tempos de JK e Schmidt* (Rio de Janeiro: Rocco, 2000).

Milton Stover Eisenhower, *The Wine Is Bitter: The United States and Latin America* (Garden City, N.Y.: Doubleday, 1963).

Todd Eisenstadt, "The Rise of the Mexico Lobby in Washington: Even Further from God and Even Closer to the United States," in Rodolfo O.De la Garza and Jesús Velasco, eds., *Bridging the Border: Transforming Mexico–U.S. Relations* (Lanham, Md.: Rowman & Littlefield, 1997), p. 89.

Rómulo Escobar Bethancourt, *Torrijos: Colonia Americana, No!* (Bogotá, Colombia: C. Valencia Editores, 1981).

Carlos Escudé, *Foreign Policy Theory in Menem's Argentina* (Gainesville, Fla.: University Press of Florida, 1997).

Jairo Estrada Álvarez, ed., *Plan Colombia: Ensayos Críticos* (Bogotá, Colombia: Universidad Nacional de Colombia, 2001).

Peter B. Evans, Harold Karan Jacobson, and Robert D. Putnam, eds., *Double-Edged Diplomacy: International Bargaining and Domestic Politics* (Berkeley, Calif.: University of California Press, 1993).

David N. Farnsworth and James W. McKenney, *U.S.–Panama Relations, 1903–1978: A Study in Linkage Politics* (Boulder, Colo.: Westview Press, 1983).

Louise L'Estrange Fawcett, "The Origins and Development of the Regional Idea in the Americas," in Louise L'Estrange Fawcett and Mónica Serrano, eds., *Regionalism and*

Governance in the Americas: Continental Drift (New York: Palgrave Macmillan, 2005).

Richard E. Feinberg, "Regionalism and Domestic Politics: US–Latin American Trade Policy in the Bush Era," *Latin American Politics and Society*, Vol. 44, No. 4 (2002), pp. 127–151.

Guillermo Fernández de Soto, *La Ilusión Posible: Un Testimonio sobre la Política Exterior Colombiana* (Bogotá, Colombia: Grupo Editorial Norma, 2004).

Martha Finnemore and Kathryn Sikkink, "International Norm Dynamics and Political Change," *International Organization*, Vol. 52, No. 4 (1998), pp. 887–917.

Max Paul Friedman, "Fracas in Caracas: Latin American Diplomatic Resistance to United States Intervention in Guatemala in 1954," *Diplomacy & Statecraft*, Vol. 21, No. 4 (2010), pp. 669–689.

_______ "Retiring the Puppets, Bringing Latin America Back In: Recent Scholarship on United States–Latin American Relations," *Diplomatic History*, Vol. 27, No. 5 (2003), pp. 621–636.

Max Paul Friedman and Tom Long, "Soft Balancing in the Americas: Latin American Opposition to U.S. Intervention, 1898–1936," *International Security*, Vol. 40, No. 1 (2015).

William L. Furlong and Margaret E. Scranton, *The Dynamics of Foreign Policymaking: The President, the Congress, and the Panama Canal Treaties* (Boulder, Colo.: Westview Press, 1984).

Eduardo Galeano, *Open Veins of Latin America: Five Centuries of the Pillage of a Continent* (New York: Monthly Review Press, 1973).

Alexander L. George and Andrew Bennett, *Case Studies and Theory Development in the Social Sciences* (Cambridge, Mass.: Massachusetts Institute of Technology Press, 2005).

Mark T. Gilderhus, "An Emerging Synthesis? U.S.–Latin American Relations since the Second World War," *Diplomatic History*, Vol. 16, No. 3 (1992), pp. 429–452.

Marcelo Giugale, O. Lafourcade, and Connie Luff, *Colombia: The Economic Foundation of Peace* (Washington, D.C.: World Bank, 2003).

Piero Gleijeses, "The View from Havana: Lessons from Cuba's African Journey, 1959–1976," in Gilbert M. Joseph and Daniela Spenser, eds., *In from the Cold: Latin America's New Encounter with the Cold War* (Durham, N.C.: Duke University Press, 2008).

Guadalupe González González, "Las Estrategias de Política Exterior de México en la Era de la Globalización," *Foro Internacional*, Vol. 41, No. 4, (2001), pp. 619–669.

Richard N. Goodwin, *Remembering America: A Voice from the Sixties* (New York: Harper & Row, 1989).

Lincoln Gordon, *A New Deal for Latin America: The Alliance for Progress* (Cambridge, Mass.: Harvard University Press, 1963).

Greg Grandin, *Empire's Workshop: Latin America, the United States, and the Rise of the New Imperialism* (New York: Metropolitan Books, 2006).

_______ *The Last Colonial Massacre: Latin America in the Cold War* (Chicago, Ill.: University of Chicago Press, 2004).

George W. Grayson, *The North American Free Trade Agreement: Regional Community and the New World Order* (Lanham, Md.: University Press of America, 1995).

Julie Greene, *The Canal Builders: Making America's Empire at the Panama Canal* (New York: Penguin Press, 2009).

Michael Grow, *U.S. Presidents and Latin American Interventions: Pursuing Regime Change in the Cold War* (Lawrence, Kan.: University Press of Kansas, 2008).

J. Gustavsson, "How Should We Study Foreign Policy Change?," *Cooperation and Conflict*, Vol. 34, No. 1 (1999), pp. 73–96.

Stefano Guzzini, "The Concept of Power: A Constructivist Analysis," *Millennium – Journal of International Studies*, Vol. 33, No. 3 (2005), pp. 495–521.

Peter Hakim, "Is Washington Losing Latin America?," *Foreign Affairs*, Vol. 85, No. 1 (2006), pp. 39–53.

Michael I. Handel, *Weak States in the International System* (London; Totowa, N.J.: F. Cass, 1981).

Jeanne A.K. Hey, "Three Building Blocks of a Theory of Latin American Foreign Policy," *Third World Quarterly*, Vol. 18, No. 4 (1997), pp. 631–657.

———, ed., *Small States in World Politics: Explaining Foreign Policy Behavior* (Boulder, Colo.: Lynne Rienner Publishers, 2003).

Stanley E. Hilton, "The United States, Brazil, and the Cold War, 1945–1960: End of the Special Relationship," *Journal of American History*, Vol. 68, No. 3 (1981), pp. 599–624.

Mônica Hirst and Andrew Hurrell, *The United States and Brazil: A Long Road of Unmet Expectations* (New York: Routledge, 2005).

J. Michael Hogan, *The Panama Canal in American Politics: Domestic Advocacy and the Evolution of Policy* (Carbondale, Ill.: Southern Illinois University Press, 1986).

J.F. Hornbeck and William H. Cooper, "Trade Promotion Authority and the Role of Congress in Trade Policy," November 4, 2010, RL33743, (Washington, D.C.: Congressional Research Service, Library of Congress, 2010). Available online: http://fpc.state.gov/documents/organization/152034.pdf.

David Patrick Houghton, "Reinvigorating the Study of Foreign Policy Decision Making: Toward a Constructivist Approach," *Foreign Policy Analysis*, Vol. 3, No. 1 (2007), pp. 24–45.

Andrew Hurrell, *On Global Order: Power, Values, and the Constitution of International Society* (Oxford; New York: Oxford University Press, 2007).

Omar Jaén Suárez, *Las Negociaciones de los Tratados Torrijos-Carter: 1970–1979* (Panamá: Autoridad del Canal de Panamá, 2005).

——— *Las Negociaciones sobre el Canal de Panamá: 1964–1970* (Bogotá, Colombia: Grupo Editorial Norma, 2002).

William J. Jorden, *Panama Odyssey* (Austin, Tex.: University of Texas Press, 1984).

Gilbert M. Joseph, Catherine LeGrand, and Ricardo Donato Salvatore, eds., *Close Encounters of Empire: Writing the Cultural History of U.S.–Latin American Relations* (London: Duke University Press, 1998).

Arie Marcelo Kacowicz, *The Impact of Norms in International Society: The Latin American Experience, 1881–2001* (Notre Dame, Ind.: University of Notre Dame Press, 2005).

Miles Kahler, *Liberalization and Foreign Policy* (New York: Columbia University Press, 1997).

Renata Keller, "A Foreign Policy for Domestic Consumption: Mexico's Lukewarm Defense of Castro, 1959–1969," *Latin American Research Review*, Vol. 47, No. 2 (2012), pp. 100–119.

Robert O. Keohane, "The Big Influence of Small Allies," *Foreign Policy*, No. 2 (1971), pp. 161–182.

Georgina Kessel, *Lo Negociado del TLC: Un Análisis Económico sobre el Impacto Sectorial del Tratado Trilateral de Libre Comercio* (México, D.F.: McGraw Hill, 1994).

Yuen Foong Khong, *Analogies at War: Korea, Munich, Dien Bien Phu, and the Vietnam Decisions of 1965* (Princeton, N.J.: Princeton University Press, 1992).

Henry Kissinger, *Years of Renewal* (New York: Simon & Schuster, 1999).

Paul Krugman, "The Uncomfortable Truth about NAFTA: It's Foreign Policy, Stupid," *Foreign Affairs*, Vol. 72, No. 5 (1993), pp. 13–19.

Juscelino Kubitschek, *Meu Caminho para Brasília* (Rio de Janeiro: Bloch Editores, 1974).

_______ *Meu Caminho para Brasilia: A Escalada Política*, Vol. 2 (Rio de Janeiro: Bloch Editores, 1976).

_______ *Meu Caminho para Brasília: Cinqüenta Anos em Cinco*, Vol. 3 (Rio de Janeiro: Bloch Editores, 1978).

Walter LaFeber, *Inevitable Revolutions: The United States in Central America* (New York: Norton, 1983).

_______ *The New Empire; an Interpretation of American Expansion, 1860–1898* (Ithaca, N.Y.: Cornell University Press, 1963).

_______ *The Panama Canal: The Crisis in Historical Perspective* (New York; Oxford: Oxford University Press, 1989).

David A. Lake, *Hierarchy in International Relations* (Ithaca, N.Y.: Cornell University Press, 2009).

Michael E. Latham, *Modernization as Ideology: American Social Science and "Nation Building" in the Kennedy Era* (Chapel Hill, N.C.: University of North Carolina Press, 2000).

Mark Atwood Lawrence, "Containing Globalism: The United States and the Developing World in the 1970s," in Niall Ferguson, ed., *The Shock of the Global: The 1970s in Perspective* (Cambridge, Mass.: Belknap Press of Harvard University Press, 2010), pp. 205–219.

Ruth Leacock, *Requiem for Revolution: The United States and Brazil, 1961–1969* (Kent, Ohio: Kent State University Press, 1990).

William M. LeoGrande, "From the Red Menace to Radical Populism: U.S. Insecurity in Latin America," *World Policy Journal*, Vol. 22, No. 4 (2005), pp. 25–35.

William M. LeoGrande and Peter Kornbluh, *Back Channel to Cuba: The Hidden History of Negotiations between Washington and Havana* (Chapel Hill, N.C.: University of North Carolina Press Books, 2014).

Jerome I. Levinson and Juan de Onís, *The Alliance That Lost Its Way: A Critical Report on the Alliance for Progress* (Chicago, Ill.: Quadrangle Books, 1970).

Jack S. Levy, "Qualitative Methods and Cross-Method Dialogue in Political Science," *Comparative Political Studies*, Vol. 40, No. 2 (2007), pp. 196–214.

James M. Lindsay, "Congress and Foreign Policy: Why the Hill Matters," *Political Science Quarterly*, Vol. 107, No. 4 (1992), pp. 607–628.

Sol M. Linowitz, *The Making of a Public Man: A Memoir* (Boston: Little, Brown, 1985).

Sol M. Linowitz and Kalman H. Silvert, *The Americas in a Changing World: A Report of the Commission on United States–Latin American Relations* (New York: Quadrangle, 1975).

Ronnie D. Lipschutz, ed., *On Security, New Directions in World Politics* (New York: Columbia University Press, 1995).

Grace Livingstone, *Inside Colombia: Drugs, Democracy and War* (New Brunswick, N.J.: Rutgers University Press, 2004).

Alberto Lleras Camargo, "The Alliance for Progress: Aims, Distortions, Obstacles," *Foreign Affairs*, Vol. 42, No. 1 (1963), pp. 25–37.

Soledad Loaeza, "La Política de Acomodo de México a la Superpotencia. Dos Episodios de Cambio de Régimen: 1944–1948 y 1989–1994," *Foro Internacional*, Vol. 50, No. 3–4 (2010), pp. 627–660.

Tom Long, "Putting the Canal on the Map: Panamanian Agenda-Setting and the 1973 Security Council Meetings," *Diplomatic History*, Vol. 38, No. 2 (2014), pp. 431–455.

Kyle Longley, *The Sparrow and the Hawk: Costa Rica and the United States during the Rise of José Figueres* (Tuscaloosa, Ala.: University of Alabama Press, 1997).

Carlos Alfredo López Guevara, "Panamá Tiene Derecho a Denunciar la Convención del Canal Ístmico de 1903 por Violaciones a la Misma por Parte de Estados Unidos," (Panamá: Centro de Impresión Educativa, 1971).

Abraham F. Lowenthal, *Partners in Conflict: The United States and Latin America* (Baltimore, Md.: Johns Hopkins University Press, 1987).

______ "United States Policy toward Latin America: 'Liberal,' 'Radical,' and 'Bureaucratic' Perspectives," *Latin American Research Review*, Vol. 8, No. 3 (1973), pp. 3–25.

Abraham F. Lowenthal, Theodore J. Piccone, and Laurence Whitehead, *The Obama Administration and the Americas: Agenda for Change* (Washington, D.C.: Brookings Institution Press, 2009).

Steven Lukes, *Power: A Radical View* (London: Macmillan, 1974).

Angus Maddison, *The World Economy* (Academic Foundation, 2007).

John Major, *Prize Possession: The United States and the Panama Canal, 1903–1979* (New York: Cambridge University Press, 1993).

Gabriel Marcella, *The United States and Colombia: The Journey from Ambiguity to Strategic Clarity* (Carlisle Barracks, Pa.: Strategic Studies Institute, U.S. Army War College, 2003).

William L. Marcy, *The Politics of Cocaine: How U.S. Foreign Policy Has Created a Thriving Drug Industry in Central and South America* (Chicago, Ill.: Lawrence Hill Books, 2010).

Ana Margheritis, "Interamerican Relations in the Early Twenty-First Century," *Latin American Politics and Society*, Vol. 52, No. 4 (2010), pp. 137–146.

Lisa L. Martin, *Democratic Commitments: Legislatures and International Cooperation* (Princeton, N.J.: Princeton University Press, 2000).

Frederick W. Mayer, *Interpreting NAFTA: The Science and Art of Political Analysis* (New York: Columbia University Press, 1998).

David G. McCullough, *The Path between the Seas: The Creation of the Panama Canal, 1870–1914* (New York: Simon & Schuster, 1977).

Alan L. McPherson, *Intimate Ties, Bitter Struggles: The United States and Latin America since 1945* (Washington, D.C.: Potomac Books, 2006).

Alan McPherson, "Courts of World Opinion: Trying the Panama Flag Riots of 1964," *Diplomatic History*, Vol. 28, No. 1 (2004), pp. 83–112.

John J. Mearsheimer, *The Tragedy of Great Power Politics* (New York: Norton, 2001).

Alex Mintz, "Applied Decision Analysis: Utilizing Poliheuristic Theory to Explain and Predict Foreign Policy and National Security Decisions," *International Studies Perspectives*, Vol. 6, No. 1 (2005), pp. 94–98.

Alex Mintz and Steven B. Redd, "Framing Effects in International Relations," *Synthese*, Vol. 135, No. 2 (2003), pp. 193–213.

George D. Moffett, *The Limits of Victory: The Ratification of the Panama Canal Treaties* (Ithaca, N.Y.: Cornell University Press, 1985).

Leandro Morgenfeld, *Vecinos en Conflicto: Argentina y los Estados Unidos en Conferencias Panamericanas* (Buenos Aires: Ediciones Continente, 2010).

Alexander J. Motyl, "Is Everything Empire? Is Empire Everything?," *Comparative Politics*, Vol. 38, No. 2 (2006), pp. 229–249.

Aaron Coy Moulton, "Building Their Own Cold War in Their Own Backyard: The Transnational, International Conflicts in the Greater Caribbean Basin, 1944–1954," *Cold War History*, Vol. 15, No. 2 (2015).

Graeme S. Mount and Mark Gauthier, *895 Days that Changed the World: The Presidency of Gerald R. Ford* (Montréal: Black Rose Books, 2006).

Gerardo L. Munck, "Tools for Qualitative Research," in Henry E. Brady and David Collier, eds., *Rethinking Social Inquiry* (Lanham, Md.: Rowman & Littlefield, 2004), pp. 105–122.

C.A. Murgueitio Manrique, "Los Gobiernos Militares de Marcos Pérez Jiménez y Gustavo Rojas Pinilla: Nacionalismo, Anticomunismo y sus Relaciones con los Estados Unidos (1953–1957)," *Historia y Espacio*, No. 25 (2014), pp. 39–97.

Manuel Antonio Noriega and Peter Eisner, *America's Prisoner: The Memoirs of Manuel Noriega* (New York: Random House, 1997).

Joseph S. Nye, *Soft Power: The Means to Success in World Politics* (New York: Public Affairs, 2004).

Thomas F. O'Brien, "Interventions, Conventional and Unconventional: Current Scholarship on Inter-American Relations," *Latin American Research Review*, Vol. 44, No. 1 (2009), pp. 257–265.

Mario Ojeda. *Alcances y Límites de la Política Exterior de México* (Mexico City: Colegio de México, 1976).

Carlos Ozores, "Omar Torrijos y sus Proyecciones en la Política Internacional," *Revista Lotería*, Vol. Agosto–Diciembre, No. 305–309 (1981).

Robert A. Pastor, *Exiting the Whirlpool: U.S. Foreign Policy toward Latin America and the Caribbean* (Boulder, Colo.: Westview Press, 2001).

______ "Review: Explaining U.S. Policy toward the Caribbean Basin: Fixed and Emerging Images," *World Politics*, Vol. 38, No. 3 (1986), pp. 483–515.

______ "The United States and Central America: Interlocking Debates," in Peter B. Evans, Harold Karan Jacobson, and Robert D. Putnam, eds., *Double-Edged Diplomacy: International Bargaining and Domestic Politics* (Berkeley, Calif.: University of California Press, 1993).

______ "The United States: Divided by a Revolutionary Vision," in Robert A. Pastor, ed., *A Century's Journey: How the Great Powers Shape the World* (New York: Basic Books, 1999), pp. 141–238.

Robert A. Pastor and Tom Long, "The Cold War and Its Aftermath in the Americas: The Search for a Synthetic Interpretation of U.S. Policy," *Latin American Research Review*, Vol. 45, No. 3 (2010), pp. 261–273.

Andrés Pastrana Arango and Camilo Gómez, *La Palabra Bajo Fuego* (Bogotá, Colombia: Planeta, 2005).

Mark Peceny and Michael Durnan, "The FARC's Best Friend: U.S. Antidrug Policies and the Deepening of Colombia's Civil War in the 1990s," *Latin American Politics and Society*, Vol. 48, No. 2 (2006), pp. 95–116.

James Petras, "Geopolitics of Plan Colombia," *Economic and Political Weekly*, Vol. 35, No. 52/53 (2000), pp. 4617–4623.

Thomas R. Pickering, "Anatomy of Plan Colombia," *The American Interest*, Vol. 5, No. 2 (2009).

Roberto Porzecanski, "Alliance for Progress or Alizana para el Progreso: A Reassessment of the Latin American Contribution to the Alliance for Progress," M.A. thesis, Tufts University (2005), p. 39.

Jeremy Pressman, *Warring Friends: Alliance Restraint in International Politics* (Ithaca, N.Y.: Cornell University Press, 2008).

Robert D. Putnam, "Diplomacy and Domestic Politics: The Logic of Two-Level Games," *International Organization*, Vol. 42, No. 03 (1988), pp. 427–460.

Stephen G. Rabe, *Eisenhower and Latin America: The Foreign Policy of Anticommunism* (Chapel Hill, N.C.: University of North Carolina Press, 1988).

――― "The Elusive Conference: United States Economic Relations with Latin America, 1945–1952," *Diplomatic History*, Vol. 2, No. 3 (1978), pp. 279–294.

――― *The Most Dangerous Area in the World: John F. Kennedy Confronts Communist Revolution in Latin America* (Chapel Hill, N.C.: University of North Carolina Press, 1999).

Stephen J. Randall, *Colombia and the United States: Hegemony and Interdependence* (Athens, Ga.: University of Georgia Press, 1992).

Alfredo Rangel Suárez, "The Military and the Peace Process in Colombia," in Cynthia J. Arnson, ed., *The Peace Process in Colombia and U.S. Policy* (Washington, D.C.: Woodrow Wilson International Center for Scholars, 2000).

Thomas Risse-Kappen, *Cooperation among Democracies: The European Influence on U.S. Foreign Policy*. Princeton Studies in International History and Politics (Princeton, N.J.: Princeton University Press, 1995).

Maryse Robert, *Negotiating NAFTA Explaining the Outcome in Culture, Textiles, Autos, and Pharmaceuticals* (Toronto: University of Toronto, 2000).

Germán Rodas Chaves, *El Plan Colombia: Análisis de una Estrategia Neoliberal* (Quito, Ecuador: Ediciones Abya-Yala, 2002).

Diana Marcela Rojas Rivera and Adolfo León Atehortúa Cruz, "Ecos del Proceso de Paz y el Plan Colombia en la Prensa Norteamericana," in Universidad Nacional Instituto de Estudios Políticos y Relaciones Internacionales, ed., *El Plan Colombia y la Internacionalización del Conflicto* (Bogotá, Colombia: Editorial Planeta Colombiana, 2001).

Roberto Russell and Juan Gabriel Tokatlian, "From Antagonistic Autonomy to Relational Autonomy: A Theoretical Reflection from the Southern Cone," *Latin American Politics and Society*, Vol. 45, No. 1 (2003), pp. 1–24.

Carlos Salinas de Gortari, *México: Un Paso Difícil a la Modernidad* (Barcelona: Plaza & Janés Editores, 2000).

Daniel Sargent, Jonathan Haslam, Max Paul Friedman, and Hal Brands, "Online Roundtable: Hal Brands' Latin America's Cold War Hal Brands, Latin America's Cold War," *Journal of American Studies*, Vol. 46, No. 01 (2012).

W.M. Schmidli, "Tracking the Cold War in Latin America," *Reviews in American History*, Vol. 40, No. 2 (2012), pp. 332–338.

Thomas Schoonover, "Max Farrand's Memorandum on the U.S. Role in the Panamanian Revolution of 1903," *Diplomatic History*, Vol. 12, No. 4 (1988), pp. 501–506.

Lars Schoultz, *Beneath the United States: A History of U.S. Policy toward Latin America* (Cambridge, Mass.: Harvard University Press, 1998).
______ *That Infernal Little Cuban Republic: The United States and the Cuban Revolution* (Chapel Hill, N.C.: University of North Carolina Press, 2009).
Nina M. Serafino, *Colombia: U.S. Assistance and Current Legislation* (Washington, D.C.: Congressional Research Service, 2001).
Maram Sheldon, "Juscelino Kubitschek and the Politics of Exuberance, 1956–1961," *Luso-Brazilian Review*, Vol. 27, No. 1 (1990), pp. 31–45.
James F. Siekmeier, *The Bolivian Revolution and the United States, 1952 to the Present* (University Park, Pa.: Pennsylvania State University Press, 2011).
David Skidmore, "Explaining State Responses to International Change: The Structural Sources of Foreign Policy Rigidity and Change," in Jerel A. Rosati, Joe. D. Hagan, and Martin W. Sampson, III, eds., *Foreign Policy Restructuring* (Columbia, S.C.: University of South Carolina Press, 1994), pp. 43–64.
Thomas E. Skidmore, *Politics in Brazil, 1930–1964: An Experiment in Democracy* (New York: Oxford University Press, 2007).
Peter H. Smith, *Talons of the Eagle: Dynamics of U.S.–Latin American Relations* (New York: Oxford University Press, 2000).
Maria Regina Soares de Lima and Mônica Hirst, "Brazil as an Intermediate State and Regional Power: Action, Choice and Responsibilities," *International Affairs* 82, no. 1 (2006), pp. 21–40.
Theodore C. Sorensen, *Counselor: A Life at the Edge of History* (New York: Harper, 2008).
Susan Strange, "The Persistent Myth of Lost Hegemony," *International Organization*, Vol. 41, No. 04 (1987), pp. 551–574.
Stephen M. Streeter, "Campaigning against Latin American Nationalism: U.S. Ambassador John Moors Cabot in Brazil, 1959–1961," *The Americas*, Vol. 51, No. 2 (1994), pp. 193–218.
Juan Antonio Tack, "La Lucha de Omar Torrijos por la Recuperación de la Integridad Nacional," *Revista Lotería*, Vol. Agosto–Diciembre, No. 305–309 (1981).
Jeffrey F. Taffet, *Foreign Aid as Foreign Policy: The Alliance for Progress in Latin America* (New York: Routledge, 2007).
Carlos Gustavo Poggio Teixeira, *Brazil, the United States, and the South American Subsystem: Regional Politics and the Absent Empire* (Lanham, Md.: Lexington Books, 2012).
David P. Thompson, "Pablo Escobar, Drug Baron: His Surrender, Imprisonment, and Escape," *Studies in Conflict & Terrorism*, Vol. 19, No. 1 (1996), pp. 55–91.
Arlene Tickner, "El Pensamiento sobre las Relaciones Internacionales en América Latina," in Sandra Borda and Arlene B. Tickner, eds., *Relaciones Internacionales y Política Exterior de Colombia* (Bogotá, Colombia: Universidad de los Andes, Facultad de Ciencias Sociales, Departamento de Ciencia Política-CESO, 2011), pp. 551–573.
______ "Intervención por Invitación: Claves de la Política Exterior Colombiana y de sus Debilidades Principales," *Colombia Internacional*, Vol. 65 (2007), pp. 90–111.
______ "Latin American IR and the Primacy of lo Práctico," *International Studies Review*, Vol. 10, No. 4 (2008), pp. 735–748.

Arlene Tickner and Carolina Cepeda, "Las Drogas Ilícitas en la Relación Colombia-Estados Unidos," in Alejandro Gaviria Uribe and Mejía Londoño, eds., *Políticas Antidroga en Colombia: Éxitos, Fracasos y Extravíos* (Bogotá, Colombia: Universidad de los Andes, 2011), pp. 205–234.

Arlene Tickner, Diego García, and Catalina Arreaza, "Actores Violentos No Estatales y Narcotráfico en Colombia," in Alejandro Gaviria Uribe and Mejía Londoño, eds., *Políticas Antidroga en Colombia: Éxitos, Fracasos y Extravíos* (Bogotá: Universidad de los Andes, 2011), pp. 413–445.

Juan Gabriel Tokatlian, "Colombia, el Plan Colombia y la Región Andina: Implosión o Concertación?," *Nueva Sociedad*, Vol. 173 (2001), pp. 126–143.

______ "The Political Economy of Colombian–U.S. Narcodiplomacy: A Case Study of Colombian Foreign Policy Decision-Making, 1978–1990," Ph.D. thesis (Johns Hopkins University, 1991).

Blanca Torres, "Estrategias y tácticas mexicanas en la conducción de sus relaciones con Estados Unidos (1945–1970)," *Foro Internacional*, Vol. 50, No. 3–4 (2010), pp. 661–688.

United Nations Economic Commission for Latin America, ed. *International Cooperation in a Latin American Development Policy* (New York: United Nations, September 1954).

Tullo Vigevani and Gabriel Cepaluni, "A Política Externa de Lula da Silva: A Estratégia da Autonomia Pela Diversificação," *Contexto Internacional*, Vol. 29, No. 2 (2007), pp. 273–335.

Oliver Villar and Drew Cottle, *Cocaine, Death Squads, and the War on Terror: U.S. Imperialism and Class Struggle in Colombia* (New York: Monthly Review Press, 2011).

Hermann von Bertrab, *Negotiating NAFTA: A Mexican Envoy's Account* (Westport, Conn.: Praeger, 1997).

Gregory Weeks, *U.S. and Latin American Relations* (New York: Pearson Longman, 2008).

______ "Recent Works on U.S.–Latin American Relations," *Latin American Research Review*, Vol. 44, No. 1 (2009), pp. 247–256.

Sidney Weintraub, *Unequal Partners: The United States and Mexico* (Pittsburgh, Pa.: University of Pittsburgh Press, 2010).

W. Michael Weis, *Cold Warriors & Coups D'etat: Brazilian–American Relations, 1945–1964* (Albuquerque, N.M.: University of New Mexico, 1993).

______ "The Twilight of Pan-Americanism: The Alliance for Progress, Neo-Colonialism, and Non-Alignment in Brazil, 1961–1964," *The International History Review*, Vol. 23, No. 2 (2001), pp. 322–344.

David A. Welch, *Painful Choices: A Theory of Foreign Policy Change* (Princeton, N.J.: Princeton University Press, 2005).

Alexander Wendt, *Social Theory of International Politics* (New York: Cambridge University Press, 1999).

Laurence Whitehead, "A Project for the Americas," in Abraham F. Lowenthal, Theodore J. Piccone, and Laurence Whitehead, eds., *The Obama Administration and the Americas: Agenda for Change* (Washington, D.C.: Brookings Institution Press, 2009), pp. 203–224.

Mark Eric Williams, *Understanding U.S.–Latin American Relations: Theory and History* (New York: Routledge, 2012).

Gilbert R. Winham, "Dispute Settlement in the NAFTA and the FTA," in Steven Globerman and Michael Walker, eds., *Assessing NAFTA: A Trinational Analysis* (Vancouver: Fraser Institute, 1993), pp. 251–270.
Paul Wolfowitz and Michael E. O'Hanlon, "Plan Afghanistan," *Foreign Policy*, October 28, 2011.

Index